Amkoullel, the Fula Boy

Amkoullel, the Fula Boy

Amadou Hampâté Bâ

TRANSLATED AND WITH AN INTRODUCTION
BY JEANNE GARANE

With a foreword by Ralph A. Austen

Duke University Press   Durham and London   2021

Translation, Foreword to the Translation, and Introduction
© 2021 Duke University Press
Text copyright © Actes Sud, 1991
All rights reserved

Production editor: Lisa Lawley
Designed by Drew Sisk
Typeset in Portrait Text and Agnes by Westchester
Publishing Services

Library of Congress Cataloging-in-Publication Data
Names: Bâ, Amadou Hampaté, author. | Garane, Jeanne,
[date] translator. | Austen, Ralph A., writer of new foreword.
Title: Amkoullel, the Fula boy / Amadou Hampâté Bâ ;
translated and with an introduction by Jeanne Garane ;
with a foreword by Ralph Austen.
Other titles: Amkoullel, l'enfant Peul. English
Description: Durham : Duke University Press, 2021. |
Includes bibliographical references and index.
Identifiers: LCCN 2020057981 (print)
LCCN 2020057982 (ebook)
ISBN 9781478013273 (hardcover)
ISBN 9781478014188 (paperback)
ISBN 9781478021490 (ebook)
Subjects: LCSH: Bâ, Amadou Hampaté—Childhood and
youth. | Fula (African people)—Biography. | Fula (African
people)—Social life and customs. | Oral tradition—Mali. |
Ethnologists—Mali—Biography. | Authors, Malian—20th
century—Biography.
Classification: LCC DT551.45.F85 B2813 2021 (print) |
LCC DT551.45.F85 (ebook) | DCC 966.23/01092 [B]—dc23
LC record available at https://lccn.loc.gov/2020057981
LC ebook record available at https://lccn.loc.gov/2020057982

Cover art: Handwritten passage by Amadou Hampâté
Bâ from *Sur les traces d'Amkoullel, l'enfant peul* (In search of
Amkoullel, the Fula boy), 1998: "I am an autodidact of the
French language, and an autodidact of the Malian bush.
I am a member of the constellation of the elders of the
twentieth century, which was a time when, in my country,
learning to read and write in French were rather more a
curse than a blessing."

CONTENTS

ix   Foreword to the Translation
      Ralph A. Austen

xv   Introduction: Between Memory and Memorial
      Jeanne Garane

AMKOULLEL, THE FULA BOY

3   Preface to the Original Edition
      Théodore Monod

7   Author's Foreword
      Amadou Hampâté Bâ

11   **CHAPTER 1: ROOTS**
      My Dual Heritage 11
      Pâté Poullo, My Maternal Grandfather 15
      The Story of My Father Hampâté, the Lamb in the Lion's Den 20

38   **CHAPTER 2: KADIDJA, MY MOTHER**
      Kadidja's Dream 39
      Kadidja and Hampâté: A Rocky Marriage 42
      Kadidja and Tidjani 45
      The Toïni Revolt 49
      Kadidja's Quest 64
      The Trial 79

83   CHAPTER 3: EXILE

Tidjani's Long March 85

Kadidja's Village 87

On the Road to Bougouni with My Mother 98

Kadidja Battles the Boss of the *Laptot* Boatmen 100

Birth of My Little Brother 105

A Father in Chains 111

An Ember That Does Not Burn 115

Death of My Early Childhood 121

Danfo Siné the *Dan* Player 124

Death of My Old Master 127

In the Shade of Great Trees 136

Freedom at Last! 137

142   CHAPTER 4: RETURN TO BANDIAGARA

A Day in the Life of a Child 145

The White Man's Excrement and the Town Made of Trash 149

I Establish My First Association 153

A Handful of Rice 156

At School with the Masters of the Word 159

Sinali's Garden 161

Boy and Girl Valentines 168

Kadidja and Tidjani in Crisis 173

Circumcision of My Brother Hammadoun 176

The Great Battle 185

194 **CHAPTER 5: AT THE WHITE MAN'S SCHOOL**
Requisitioned by Force *194*
    The Commandant and the Five-Franc Coin *202*
    Primary School *209*
    My First Encounter with Wangrin *218*
    The Death of My Big Brother *220*
    The School at Djenné: My Primary Studies Certificate *223*
    The Great Famine of 1914: A Vision of Horror *234*
    Declaration of War *241*
    Flight *251*
    On the Trail with the War Dogs *256*
    The Three Colors of France *259*
The Land-Roving Pirogue of Metal *264*
The Abysmal Lair of the Great Black Hyena *266*

270 **CHAPTER 6: IN THE MILITARY TOWN OF KATI**
My New Waaldé Association *274*

A Hasty Circumcision *278*

Return to School *281*

The Warrant Officer and the King's Son *282*

296 **CHAPTER 7: FINAL STUDIES IN BAMAKO**
My Second Primary Studies Certificate *296*

In Vain Pursuit of the Wind *299*

Boarding School in Bamako *311*

The Consequences of a Refusal:
Exile in Ouagadougou *317*

I Bid Farewell on the Riverbank *326*

329 Translator's Acknowledgments
331 Notes
345 Bibliography
351 Biographies
353 Index

FOREWORD TO THE TRANSLATION

Ralph A. Austen

It is a great honor and pleasure to be invited to write a foreword for the English translation of Amadou Hampâté Bâ's *Amkoullel, the Fula Boy*. Not only have I admired, studied, and enjoyed this work for more than twenty years, but I also spent a good part of that time in a frustrated effort to manage such a translation. Jeanne Garane has finally achieved this goal in splendid fashion through her own skills and initiatives as a translator, a scholar of Africa and its literature, and a fund raiser.

The honor of my role is enhanced by its juxtaposition with the preface to A. H. Bâ's *Amkoullel, l'enfant peul: mémoires* by Théodore Monod, a major scholar of Africa in his own time and a founder of IFAN (Institut français [now fondamental] d'Afrique noire). Unlike myself, who came to the study of A. H. Bâ after this great African intellectual had already passed away, Monod not only knew A. H. Bâ personally but also played a critical role in his professional and spiritual life.[1] His preface, unlike my foreword, thus constitutes a key element of this book.

In her own introduction to the translation, Jeanne Garane provides an excellent background account of A. H. Bâ's life and its historical context. I feel no need to repeat that task here. Instead I want to reflect upon the relationship between the "literary" products of A. H. Bâ's late years (the two volumes of his memoir and the "novel" *L'Etrange destin de Wangrin: ou, Les roueries d'un interprète africain*) and his earlier career as a researcher, cultural statesman, and advocate of an ecumenical version of Sufi Islam. I put the terms "literary" and "novel" in quotes because A. H. Bâ himself insisted that "mes seules oeuvres de 'création'" (my only creative works) were the religious poetry he composed in his own Fulfulde language.[2]

Of course, in his capacities as ethnographer, folklorist, and religious teacher, A. H. Bâ had dealt quite intensively with literary texts, especially narrative ones, but his role had always been to record, translate, and analyze them rather than to claim authorship. He never fully acknowledged the distinction between such efforts and the books others would consider to be literary works: *Wangrin*, as he and his wife and literary executor, Hélène Heckmann, insisted in the introductions to two editions of this book, was not a novel but an accurate account of a real person's life.[3] In his own foreword to *Amkoullel, l'enfant peul: mémoires* A. H. Bâ asserts that the accounts of his life and world he presents here derive not from literary imagination but rather from a capacity for "memory of an almost inordinate fidelity and accuracy" (page 7 in this volume). A. H. Bâ also wanted to supplement the personal and family narrative that makes up the core of *Amkoullel* with "a number of commentaries on certain aspects of African culture and sociology," but most of these were cut, with the author's consent, in the interest of brevity (page 6).

The role within Sudanic culture that A. H. Bâ most revered, and which he sought to continue in the modern colonial/postcolonial era, was that of "traditionalist," or "traditionist," a term he seems to have coined himself to define individuals with deep knowledge of their people's history and culture and the ability to transmit it to future generations, often via musical and narrative performance skills.[4] In *Amkoullel*, two men are cited as exemplary traditionists: the first, Koullel, a figure in the court of A. H. Bâ's stepfather and from whom the author earned his nickname (meaning "Koullel's little Amadou," or "son of Koullel") (page 63); and the second, who receives more attention than Koullel, Danfo Siné, a *doma* (man of knowledge) in the southern Mali community of Bougouni, where A. H. Bâ and his family were exiled during much of his early childhood (pages 124–27).

The writing of *Amkoullel* fits less easily into the role of traditionist than does the work of A. H. Bâ's research career. The common denominator is memory, but in the memoir this capacity is mainly (especially after the opening sections on the precolonial history of his family) directed at the author's own life and experiences rather than at the deep past. In technical terms, it is more oral history than oral tradition. Moreover, A. H. Bâ is here not the recorder, translator, and critic of texts he hears from others but instead the performer of his own story. It is well-established from the testimony of those who knew him (see Monod's preface) that A. H. Bâ was a great storyteller, and the memoir takes the form of a series of stories whose narrative content is laced with humor and drama.

It is the engaging quality of these tales that accounts for the much wider readership gained by the two volumes of his memoirs and *Wangrin* than by any of A. H. Bâ's more scholarly writings. But readers need not consider themselves to be indulging in a guilty pleasure by exercising such a choice. First, these three books hold a unique place in the repertoire of African literature since they deal in knowledgeable detail with the colonial era in its classical (pre-World War II) form. This is a subject largely neglected by African memoirists and novelists, primarily because most were born too late to have experienced it as fully as did A. H. Bâ—to say nothing of his "older brother," Wangrin. A. H. Bâ not only portrays many of the abuses of the French colonial regime, as noted by Garane, but also reveals the degree of agency Africans retained within it, both to counter and sometimes to profit from such oppression.

Around the time A. H. Bâ wrote *Amkoullel*, the concept of "tradition," upon which he had based his entire career, was coming under fire from postcolonial theorists, who claimed it existed only in an "invented" dialogue with modernity, often deployed for the political purposes by both colonial regimes and their African antagonists or successors.[5] There is no evidence that A. H. Bâ used his concept of tradition for political purposes, but his many claims about the fixity and esoteric meanings of the texts and rituals he studied provide an easy target for such "deconstruction."

Yet *Amkoullel*, in its various accounts of everyday life in the urban settings of colonial Mali, provides its own, not always self-conscious, insight into the transformation of historical African culture into "tradition." The setting in which A. H. Bâ learns from both Koullel and Danfo Siné is the *cour* (courtyard, but also court) of his stepfather, Tidjani Thiam, a private urban space to which he has been relegated after having been deposed from his chiefdom. The performances that inspire the young Amadou are now cut off from any real politics and constitute a mélange of local cultures (A. H. Bâ's own Fula, the majority Mande of Mali—the identity of both Koullel and Danfo Siné—and Islam). While these ethnicities and/or belief systems were never entirely separate in the precolonial past, they are now brought together in ways that allow A. H. Bâ to represent them collectively as "tradition" and bring his vision out into the world via the colonial language of French.

In his analysis of oral literature in the Sudanic region, A. H. Bâ, influenced by his collaboration with the Griaule School of French anthropology, put special emphasis upon the theme of initiation, labeling several of the texts he collected and published *contes* or *récits initiatiques*. *Amkoullel* also includes discussion of initiation, although less in terms of symbolic representation than by descriptions of the circumcision rituals that formally induct boys of the Sudanic region into manhood. However, the subject of the specific ceremony described here at some length (pages 177–85) is not Amadou himself, but rather his older brother, Hammadoun, and his age mates. In order to respect the hierarchy of age within the family, Amadou was supposed to be circumcised two years later. But by that time he had been forcibly enrolled in a European-style school, whose schedule would not allow him the time to go out into the local *brousse* (uncultivated countryside), where most of this ritual takes place. A further two years afterward, Amadou, embarrassed by the prospect of being treated as a subservient child by his own age peers, arranges "a hasty [*à la sauvette*] circumcision" for himself in a French medical clinic (pages 278–80).[6]

This effort to preserve and yet transform historical practices may also explain the relationship—or lack of one—between initiation and the youth associations A. H. Bâ organizes in his hometown, Bandiagara, and his second site of exile, the southern Mali town of Kati. In his description of orthodox circumcisions, A. H. Bâ notes that the boys who go through such a ritual together form a lifelong bond of egalitarian comradeship (thus the refusal of family elders to let Amadou be circumcised together with his older brother, Hammadoun). Having ultimately been circumcised on his own, A. H. Bâ never became a member of such a fraternity. However, shortly after his family returned to Bandiagara, Amadou, at about the age of eight, formed his first *waaldé*, or youth association. A. H. Bâ's accounts of such groups, pursued at far greater length than initiation (pages 153–56, 168–73, 185–93, and 274–76) provide some of the most engaging passages in his entire memoir. These accounts are also the best indicators of how both remembered local culture and new colonial-era practices can be blended into "tradition."[7]

As reported by A. H. Bâ, the waaldé functions something like a combination of a street gang and a training institution. Most of the time its members are concerned with games, pranks, and a good deal of low-level theft from the vegetable and fruit gardens of the city. They do, however, have a formal organization with offices that echo a precolonial Sudanic polity, including chiefs, Islamic judges, griots (here less bards than diplomatic intermediaries) and a *moutassibi* (public prosecutor or snoop).[8] The proto-adolescent inclinations and the precocious formality of the waaldé come together in their stylized relations with other Bandiagara youth associations: intense but chaste courtships of parallel female associations, and violent but never fatal battles with rival male groups. The waaldé are multiethnic and cross lines of caste and slavery but, like Bandiagara itself, seem to be dominated by Fula and Toucouleur of noble descent. The age divisions of these associations seem to parallel those of circumcision fraternities (Amadou's older brother headed his own waaldé), but there appears to have been very little connection between the waaldé and any initiation rituals.

The still preadolescent Amadou left Bandiagara for a French colonial school in 1912, but after graduating three years later, moved to the southern Mali town of Kati, where his mother and stepfather had settled after quarreling with their Bandiagara household. In Kati, the dominant Bambara (that is, non-Muslim Mande) population initiated their children into a series of power societies of the very type that A. H. Bâ would later study together with his French anthropological colleagues. During his previous stay (from about age two to eight) at Bougouni, in this same region, Amadou had himself been initiated by Danfo Siné into the lowest level of local ritual associations; but he had been forbidden by the piously Muslim Tidjani Thiam from participating in their ceremonies.[9]

Early in his second southern sojourn, A. H. Bâ was violently attacked for entering the sacred space of a more senior Bambara power society. He decided to counter this force with the same kind of "secular" youth association he had so happily led in Bandiagara. Given the great ethnic heterogeneity of Kati, a military post now in the midst of training African recruits for World War I, he had no difficulty in organizing such a group and even avenging himself upon the Bambara youths—not with a waaldé but with a *ton*, a Mande term that primarily references initiation fraternities. It was also in this context that the now fully adolescent Amadou had himself circumcised.

For those interested in the genesis of A. H. Bâ's career as a researcher, his engagement with tradition can be seen as emerging from these early encounters with not only the lessons of "traditionists" but also the tensions of being properly initiated into what was now a colonized and multicultural African world. But *Amkoullel* should be rewarding—as well as entertaining—for anyone seeking to encounter that world on its own terms, which is to say through the vividly remembered early life of someone who personally experienced its many travails and treasures.

INTRODUCTION

Between Memory and Memorial

Jeanne Garane

> My rightful place is among the ranks of the elder sons of the century.
> —Amadou Hampâté Bâ

Autobiography is often defined as the narration of an individual life told in intimate detail, while memoir is characterized as the narration of a life lived in its historical context. *Amkoullel, the Fula Boy*, and its sequel, *Oui, Mon Commandant: mémoires II* are both autobiography and memoir, for they intertwine pre-colonial and colonial history with the narration of Amadou Hampâté Bâ's personal trajectory.[1] The events recounted in *Amkoullel, the Fula Boy* take place within a time frame that dates from about 1860, with the story of A. H. Bâ's ancestors, and 1922, when he leaves his family and is sent to Ouagadougou to begin serving in the French colonial administration. *Oui, Mon Commandant!* covers the years between 1922, when A. H. Bâ began his career as a colonial civil servant, and the late 1930s and early 1940s, at the outbreak of World War II, when A. H. Bâ was about forty years old and began working for the IFAN (Institut français d'Afrique noire, renamed the Institut fondamental d'Afrique noire following independence in 1960).[2] A third volume, which promised to cover A. H. Bâ's later years, has never been published.

Amkoullel, the Fula Boy tells the poignant story of a childhood and adolescence that began in the former capital of the Toucouleur Empire, in Bandiagara,

Mali, during a period of tremendous upheaval. By 1900, the year of A. H. Bâ's birth, the colony of French Sudan had been in existence for just twenty years. Founded following the defeat of the Toucouleurs in 1889 by soldiers under the command of Colonel Louis Archinard, French Sudan became part of a larger federation of colonies known as French West Africa, or Afrique Occidentale Française (AOF) in 1895.[3]

The impact of these historic events came to weigh heavily on A. H. Bâ. It is partly for this reason that, rather than beginning his life story with the scene of his own birth, *Amkoullel* begins with Bâ's "prehistory," that is, with the story of his noble paternal and maternal lines, and their intimate connections to the Fula empire of Massina (1818–1862) and to the Toucouleur conquerors who destroyed it. Given that his mother and father were Fula and his stepfather was Toucouleur, Bâ begins his narrative with an overview of the history of these two related but warring groups. As he explains in chapter 1:

> According to African tradition, an individual cannot be separate from his lineage, for he is merely an extension of those who continue to live on through him. . . . Therefore, it would be unthinkable for the old African that I am, born at the dawn of the twentieth century in the city of Bandiagara, Mali, to begin the story of my personal life without first evoking my two paternal and maternal lineages. . . . Both of them are Fula, and both were intimately involved, although they were in opposing camps, in the sometimes tragic historic events that marked my country throughout the nineteenth century. The entire history of my family is in fact tied to the history of Massina (a region in Mali located in the inner Niger River bend), and to the wars that tore it apart. These wars pitted the Fula of the Fula Empire of Massina against the Toucouleur army of El Hadj Omar, the great conqueror and religious leader who came from the West and whose empire, once it had vanquished and absorbed the Fula empire of Massina in 1862, extended from eastern Guinea all the way to Timbuktu.
>
> Each of my two lineages is directly or indirectly related to one or the other of these two opposing parties. (pages 11–12)

For Amadou Hampâté Bâ, this "dual historical and emotional heritage" (page 12), along with the profound social upheavals wrought by the advent of French colonialism, were such that the fickleness of fate would become a particularly prominent theme in his work. He remarks, "Every time I had started down a nice, straight path in my life, fate seemed to enjoy flicking its finger, sending me reeling in a completely different direction than the one I should have taken, and causing me to alternate between periods of good luck and misfortune" (page 194). A. H. Bâ later enumerates these misfortunes and their reversals: the male members of his father Hampâté's family were massacred by the Toucouleurs at the fall of the Fula empire of Massina, and his father was one of the sole survivors. He was immediately forced to go into hiding and began to work as a butcher's assistant (an occupation considered beneath his station by the Fula nobility to which he belonged). After his father's death, when A. H. Bâ was three years old, he was adopted by Tidjani Thiam. This Toucouleur chief of the coveted province of Louta had married A. H. Bâ's mother, Kadidja, and A. H. Bâ then became his heir apparent, in line for the chiefdom. But Tidjani Thiam was deposed by the French, imprisoned, and sent into exile. As A. H. Bâ puts it in reference to the unpredictability of fate, "Flick! We are all sent into exile and I become the son of a convict" (page 194). The situation again changes and the family returns home to Bandiagara from exile. Just as things seemed to have returned to normal, writes A. H. Bâ, "Flick! I am brutally snatched away from the traditional activities that would surely have led me to enter the time-honored career of *marabout* and teacher. Instead, I'm forced to attend 'the White Man's school,' which the Muslim populace of the time regarded as the most direct route to hell" (page 195).

Indeed, in chapter 5, A. H. Bâ recounts in vivid detail how he was "requisitioned" by the colonial administration and forced to attend French primary school. Later, A. H. Bâ would complete his studies at the Bamako Professional School. In the final chapter of *Amkoullel*, A. H. Bâ provides a brief history of the school, explaining:

> It had originally been created in 1854 by Faidherbe in Kayes, Mali, which at the time was the headquarters of the Upper Senegal and Middle Niger colony. Very officially called the School for Hostages, its ranks were filled by forcefully requisitioning the sons of chiefs and other dignitaries from recently conquered regions, with the aim of ensuring their submission. However, when they could, some of these chiefs sent captives in place of their sons, a decision that they perhaps came to regret later on. In 1908, when Governor Clozel transferred the colony's headquarters from Kayes to Bamako, the school was reopened in that city and given the more discreet but nevertheless explicit name, School for Sons of Chiefs. With the development of the administration and the increased need for native subaltern personnel, it then became the Bamako Professional School. Later, it was renamed Upper Primary School, then Terrasson de Fougères School, before becoming known today as the Lycée Askia Mohammed.[4] (pages 311-12)

While the School for Hostages was intended to transform A. H. Bâ and his schoolmates into (more or less reluctant) products of the French *mission civilisatrice* (civilizing mission), in *Amkoullel* A. H. Bâ shows how he decided to use his French education to his advantage and "learn the language of the commandant in order to be able to speak to him directly, without having to go through an interpreter" (page 206).[5] This is certainly one of the reasons why he later decided to write in French, although he also wrote poetry in his first language, Fulfulde, the language spoken by the Fula people.[6]

The French title of A. H. Bâ's memoir is *Amkoullel, l'enfant peul: mémoires*. *Peul* is the French translation of the Wolof word, *pël*, which refers to the "Fula, Fulani, or Fulbe" people of the Sahel region of West Africa. As A. H. Bâ explains in chapter 4, "Amkoullel" was the nickname given to him by "the great storyteller, historian, and traditionalist Koullel, who had become so attached to me in my childhood that I had been given the nickname Amkoullel (meaning 'Koullel's little Amadou,' or 'son of Koullel')" (page 63). The French title, *Amkoullel, l'enfant peul*, echoes the title of the 1953 autobiography by Guinean writer Camara Laye, *L'Enfant noir*, translated by James Kirkup in 1954 as *The Dark Child: The Autobiography of an African Boy*.[7] But where Camara Laye's title echoed European designators of Africans by skin color alone, A. H. Bâ's title specifically refers to his culture and ethnic identity.

While often lighthearted and humorous in its reconstruction of A. H. Bâ's boyhood escapades (for example, the tale of the time when Amkoullel and his friends went to see whether the excrement of the white colonizers really was black), the text also documents the cruelties and injustices meted out by French colonial administrators and those Africans who worked with them, for the impact of such acts on A. H. Bâ's family was immediate.[8] Thus, even as it works to preserve a written record of A. H. Bâ's culture and traditions that were threatened by colonialism and postcolonial modernity, the work serves as a kind of historical memorial lest these injustices be forgotten or covered up. As Benaouda Lebdai explains in *Autobiography as a Writing Strategy in Postcolonial Literature*, postcolonial autobiographies and memoirs provide readers with a unique lens through which to access the past while allowing us to understand how individuals negotiated their life trajectories under oppressive situations. Such writing offers both "a path of resistance and a liberating experience . . . while participating in the rehabilitation of autobiographical texts as literary."[9]

It could be said that *Amkoullel, the Fula Boy* and its sequel, *Oui, Mon Commandant!*, embody the culmination of A. H. Bâ's lifelong efforts to inscribe oral traditions (defined as a sociocultural-historical knowledge archive held in living memory) from the West African Sahel, for they are at once the literary inscription of his personal memorial archive, a record of his training as a practicing specialist in the preservation and recitation of Sahelian oral traditions, and a first-hand account of life under the French colonial regime.

As we learn in reading *Amkoullel*, Amadou Hampâté Bâ was immersed in the oral tradition from an early age. As he explains in chapter 5, "Someone once asked me when I had begun to collect oral traditions. I replied that I had begun in my early youth and never stopped. I had had the luck to be born and to grow up in an environment that was a permanent academy of everything concerning African history and traditions" (page 127). In his foreword to *Amkoullel, l'enfant peul: mémoires* A. H. Bâ also remarks on the prodigious accuracy and fidelity of his memory, explaining that "from childhood, we were trained to observe, to watch, and to listen, so that every event was inscribed in our memory as if it were in virgin wax.... I do not need to *remember*; rather, I see it all on a sort of interior screen, and all I have to do is describe what I see. In order to describe a scene, I only have to relive it" (page 7).

However, although A. H. Bâ asserts that "people of my generation, and more generally, people who come from an oral tradition and did not rely on writing, possess memories of an almost inordinate fidelity and accuracy" (page 7), not everyone was in a position to collect and perpetuate oral traditions as was A. H. Bâ.

In *Amkoullel*, A. H. Bâ explains how his talent for storytelling came to be enlisted in the colonial production of knowledge about Africa. He was twelve years old when the interpreter Wangrin enlisted him in the collection and translation of traditional tales for

> Mr. François-Victor Equilbecq, a senior civil servant from the Office of Native Affairs who was passing through Bandiagara and who was touring the entire country in order to collect the greatest possible number of tales from the French Sudan. When Mr. Equilbecq arrived in Bandiagara in June 1912, the district commandant summoned Chief Alfa Maki Tall and asked him to send the newcomer all of the men, women, and children who knew any tales. I was among the children who were chosen. (page 219)

Even as the French colonial mission civilisatrice sought to impose French culture and language upon its colonial subjects by means of its colonial schools and imported administrative structures, it was also dedicated to creating a kind of inventory of the cultures and peoples that it was colonizing that became known as "Africanism," the production of European knowledge "about" Africa. In being asked to contribute tales to Mr. Equilbecq, A. H. Bâ had been drawn into the process.

In chapters 4 and 5, A. H. Bâ recounts how as a young boy he witnessed the overwhelming power of colonial authority on his stepfather Tidjani Thiam, whom the French had deposed from his position as chief of Louta province in punishment for his use of force in putting down a rebellion that resulted from a plot that had led Tidjani to believe he had been ordered to do so by the French administration.[10] *Amkoullel* vividly recreates scenes in which Tidjani walks in shackles and carries out forced labor. He portrays Tidjani's imprisonment in solitary confinement in minute detail along with his mother's valiant efforts to get her husband released. In one scene, when the little Amkoullel sees Tidjani in chains, he grabs a hatchet and runs toward his father "in order to try to break the chains and irons," crying, "when I grow up I will avenge my father" (page 112).

A. H. Bâ's dedication to preserving Sahelian oral traditions thus goes hand in hand with this personal vow of vengeance to such an extent that many of the figures who inhabit *Amkoullel* are heroically portrayed, as though they themselves had stepped from the annals of an oral epic. For instance, A. H. Bâ describes his stepfather Tidjani Thiam as a fearless "Titan" who possesses superior strength, and as an excellent marksman and horseman who exhibits noble probity when faced with the dishonesty of his enemies and the cruelties of the colonial administrators. Tidjani is a fitting match for the narrator's mother, Kadidja, described as an exceptional "woman of iron" who is known as "Queen of the Milk" in her women's association, harbors a fierce warrior soul, and never backs down when faced with adversity. Indeed, she is vividly portrayed as a formidable fighter in chapter 4, when she defends herself and other women against the unwanted advances of a maniacal and corrupt boatman, and in chapter 5, when she mobilizes an army of women to help her find her husband and then later disguises herself in men's clothing in order to make secret visits to her husband's jail cell—all under the nose of the colonial commandant.

It was after these events that A. H. Bâ, alias Amkoullel, was "requisitioned" to attend the School for Hostages. Once he had received his Primary School Certificate, or Certificat d'études primaires, he was again coerced into becoming a reluctant participant in the colonial machine, for he was forcibly enlisted into the ranks of colonial auxiliaries and assigned to become a colonial clerk and occasional interpreter in the very system that had upended the lives of everyone around him.[11]

Because he had followed his mother's wishes and did not complete his secondary studies at the Ecole normale de Gorée in Senegal, the colonial administration decided that he would be punished and sent to work in the new colony of Haute-Volta (Upper Volta; now Burkina Faso). A. H. Bâ was assigned the title *écrivain temporaire à titre essentiellement précaire et révocable* (temporary secretary classified as essentially revocable and subject to repeal), "for there was truly nothing lower that could be found in ranks of the administrative hierarchy" (page 319). He was thus sent out on a journey of one thousand kilometers from Bamako, Mali, to Ouagadougou in Haute-Volta. He explains that "at a time when simply failing to salute the commandant or the flag was cause for administrative internment, it was out of the question for a 'French subject' to disobey an order emanating from even the lowliest bearer of a parcel of colonial authority, and here was an order from the Governor himself. If I had refused, I would have been automatically sent to prison for noncompliance, without any other justification or trial" (page 319).

In order to reach Ouagadougou, A. H. Bâ walked, traveled by train, by water, and on horseback, under surveillance by a district guard whom he eventually befriended. As he was waiting in Koulikoro for a pirogue that would carry him to Mopti, Bâ attended a storytelling session and

> for the first time, I took down in writing everything that I had heard, either word for word when it was possible, or in a general overview. I had brought a stock of large ledger books along with me. One of them became my first "journal." In Koulikoro, and for the entire rest of my trip, I would write about the principal events of each day, and especially anything that I saw or heard that was of interest and that had to do with our oral traditions. Once I had gotten into the habit of doing this, I never stopped, and I have continued to do this for the rest of my life. (page 325)

The irony of using the colonizer's ledger books for the recording of oral traditions under threat from colonialism should not be lost on the reader.

Saving Libraries from Burning

A. H. Bâ began to gain international recognition for his work after he joined the IFAN in Dakar, Senegal, in 1942, upon the recommendation of its founder and director, Théodore Monod. Indeed, the friendship and patronage of Monod played an essential role in Amadou Hampâté Bâ's career. For instance, it was Monod who first presented A. H. Bâ's 1943 translation of the Fula initiation tale *Kaïdara* at the first international conference of West African specialists, the Conférence internationale des africanistes de l'ouest.[12] It was Monod who first drew attention to the teachings of Bâ's spiritual mentor Tierno Bokar in a 1950 essay in the journal *Présence Africaine*. It was Monod who wrote the preface to *L'Empire peul du Macina*. And in naming A. H. Bâ to the IFAN in Dakar, he had effectively removed Bâ from a difficult situation in Mali, where colonial officials viewed his adherence to Hamallist Muslim beliefs with suspicion.[13] It was Théodore Monod who wrote the preface that precedes *Amkoullel*, included in this volume.[14]

By the early 1960s, A. H. Bâ had already presented his translations into French of a number of traditional Fula and Bambara tales, and these were later published in collaboration with well-known European researchers and ethnographers. *Kaïdara: récit initiatique peul* was published in collaboration with Lilyan Kesteloot, and *Koumen: texte initiatique des pasteurs peul* with Germaine Dieterlen. He had published his lengthy oral history of the Fula empire of Massina, *L'Empire peul du Macina*, in 1954, and the portrait and philosophy of his spiritual teacher, *Tierno Bokar: le sage de Bandiagara*, in 1957.[15] In 1974, A. H. Bâ won the Grand prix littéraire d'Afrique noire for *L'Etrange destin de Wangrin: ou, Les roueries d'un interprète africain* and was awarded the prize a second time in 1991 for *Amkoullel, l'enfant peul: mémoires*.

Following his UNESCO address to the Africa Commission in 1960, where he was representing Mali, Amadou Hampâté Bâ became known to many as the man who proclaimed, "En Afrique, quand un vieillard meurt, c'est une bibliothèque qui brûle" (In Africa, when an elder dies, a library burns), in reference to the fact that the transmission of oral traditions was increasingly under threat. As Abiola Irele puts it, A. H. Bâ's "burning library" statement expresses a tragic "sense of calamity at the prospect of the disappearance of the values of [the oral] legacy in our present situation of intense social and cultural change."[16] Today, A. H. Bâ's "burning library" aphorism has become so well-known as to have become a kind of cliché.[17] However, it is important to place the statement in historical context and to read it as an impassioned trace of decolonial resistance. In the words of Nadia Yada Kisukidi, such resistance participates in the oppositional practices of subjects who are confronted with multiple forms of loss and erasure and "l'oblitération de leurs souffrances" (the obliteration of their suffering).[18]

In chapter 6 of *Amkoullel*, "In the Military Town of Kati," A. H. Bâ attributes the onset of the "burning libraries" phenomenon to the massive enlistment of West African youths in World War I. As A. H. Bâ explains:

> Although this is not a well-known fact, one major effect of the war of 1914 was that it precipitated the first great *rupture in the oral transmission of traditional knowledge*, not only within the initiation societies, but also in the trade brotherhoods and corporations of craftsmen, whose workshops had

once served as veritable centers of traditional instruction. The hemorrhage of young people sent to the front—from which many would never return—the intensive recruitment of forced laborers on behalf of the war effort, and the mass exodus of people to the Gold Coast deprived the old masters of their all-important successor groups. In a more or less distinct manner, depending on the region, this caused the first great eclipse in the oral transmission of a vast cultural heritage. Over the decades that followed, this process would gradually become more acute under the effects of new social factors. (page 294)

In this context, one can understand A. H. Bâ's work to document aspects of Sahelian forms of knowledge as a preservationist struggle in the advent of what Kisukidi names the "undecolonisable," that is, "ce qui a disparu sous les coups d'une violence coloniale totale et vers quoi il est impossible de faire retour" (that which has disappeared beneath the blows of total colonial violence and to which it is impossible to return).[19]

Nevertheless, as Kisukidi further demonstrates, the "undecolonisable" also constitutes "la limite de tout projet de décolonisation épistémique dès lors qu'il s'effectue sur le site institutionnel de l'université et demeure solidaire des normes de connaissance qui y sont mises en oeuvre" (the limit of any project of epistemological decolonization when it is undertaken at the institutional site of the university and colludes with the norms of knowledge that are in process there).[20] Kisukidi asserts that the recognition of such limits should not lead to despair but to the recognition and acknowledgment of constraints placed on forms of knowledge within institutional settings.

It would be an understatement to say that A. H. Bâ and his work have often been entangled within such institutional constraints, given that much of his work first appeared under the aegis of colonial authority. Moreover, it would be disingenuous not to acknowledge that the present translation of *Amkoullel* into English, complete with the present introduction, the original preface by Théodore Monod, and the new foreword by Ralph A. Austen, also potentially places this work within a new set of constraints. Indeed, as Richard Watts compellingly demonstrates in *Packaging Post/coloniality*, postcolonial works have long been framed by paratextual elements such as the present introduction, which are intended to "insert the text within a particular cultural context."[21] Moreover, the act of translating, publishing, and promoting a work such as *Amkoullel* to new audiences similarly introduces the text to new interpretive readerships. As Lydie Moudileno aptly writes in "Qu'est-ce qu'un auteur postcolonial?," "la traduction participe de l'expansion des savoirs sur l'Afrique qui caractérise notre contemporain global" (translation participates in the expansion of knowledge about Africa which characterizes our contemporary global era).[22] For this reason, as Moudileno and her coparticipants in the 2016 collection *Ecrire l'Afrique-monde* point out, it is important to interrogate "la manière dont nous . . . recevons en tant que critiques, professeurs, et commentateurs des productions culturelles de l'Afrique" (the manner in which we . . . as critics, professors and commentators receive African cultural products).[23] To this end, it is useful both to retrace the initial trajectory of *Amkoullel*'s publication history and to reflect upon the ways in which this translation enlarges A. H. Bâ's readership.

Publication of A. H. Bâ's Memoirs, Postcolonial Memory, and the Cosmopolitan Present

The time that elapsed between the events that unfold in A. H. Bâ's memoirs and their date of publication is quite great. A. H. Bâ passed away in May 1991, at the age of ninety-one, and *Amkoullel, l'enfant peul: mémoires* was published in September of that year. *Oui Mon Commandant!* was published posthumously in 1994. Given the political climate in France in the 1990s and official attempts either to forget or to whitewash the colonial past, their publication was rather timely. As Nicolas Bancel and Pascal Blanchard write in their 2008 essay:

> Colonial history has been the object of a process of repression that has also maintained the myth of the French civilizing mission. The function of this myth was to avoid opening "a painful page from our past" the contemporaneous consequences of which were judged as potentially dangerous particularly given the presence on French territory . . . of . . . "descendants" of immigrants from the former colonies. Until the beginning of the 1990s, the marginalization of colonial history was the response to the double injunction to forget a historic traumatism that upset the [self] representation of the country, and to forestall any upsurge in colonial confrontations.[24]

The publication of A. H. Bâ's memoirs has certainly played a role in helping to counteract the erasure of the colonial past while continuing to contribute to present discussions surrounding the construction of that past.[25] Given that A. H. Bâ's work continues to circulate in an ever-widening readership, it is worth mentioning that his work is also integral to postcolonial circuits of literary authorship. Indeed, contemporary writers such as Ahmadou Kourouma, Alain Mabanckou, Tierno Monénembo, Yambo Ouologuem, and Abdourahman A. Waberi have engaged with A. H. Bâ's work in various ways.[26]

In his 2011 book *Postcolonial Francophone Autobiographies from Africa to the Antilles*, critic Edgard Sankara interrogates the reasons behind A. H. Bâ's popularity and even what he calls his "canonization" in France, as *Amkoullel* has now been incorporated into the French secondary school curriculum. Sankara suggests that A. H. Bâ's memoirs, along with his own religious ecumenism, have been received as an appealing counterdiscourse to contemporary perceptions in France of Islam as a form of political and religious extremism.[27] Another explanation for the initial appeal of *Amkoullel* in France, according to Sankara, is the "dialogicity" of the text and the ways in which it addresses non-African readers by explaining certain cultural practices both in the text and through the use of explanatory footnotes. Although Sankara sometimes reads this "dialogicity" as a sign that *Amkoullel* was primarily written for a French audience, I would instead argue that A. H. Bâ, who began working as a translator at the age of twelve and who continued to practice translation throughout his life, employs a translational, cosmopolitan aesthetic which strategically amplifies the potential for his writing to appeal to multiple and diverse readerships. As Paul Bandia demonstrates in *Translation as Reparation*, this translational aesthetic is employed by many African European-language writers as a transnational and transcultural mode of expression. Souleymane Bachir Diagne calls this African translational aesthetic "penser de langue à langue" (thinking from language to language) and recognizes the decentering power of translation as holding ethical value.[28]

I would add that Bâ's translational aesthetic is also "trans-temporal," for although the events narrated in *Amkoullel* occur in the late nineteenth and early twentieth centuries, they continue to resonate with contemporary readers precisely because, as Sankara also points out, the narrator is also an excellent storyteller and constantly interpolates his audience. This interpolation allows readers to be placed in a trans-temporal and coeval imaginary dialogue with the narrator and his text. As Kwame Anthony Appiah sees it, this sort of cosmopolitan conversation crosses "boundaries of identity—whether national, religious, or something else," and can be generated through imaginative engagement with literary and other works of art that speak "from some place other than your own."[29] Appiah writes, "Cosmopolitans suppose that all cultures have enough overlap in their vocabulary of values to begin a conversation" (57). But this conversation can also transcend "talking" to enable a metaphorical "engagement with the experience and ideas of others" (85). Indeed, this invitation to converse that *Amkoullel* extends to its readers constitutes a prime example of what Achille Mbembe calls "Afropolitanism," a cultural, historical, and aesthetic sensibility exhibited in a way of inhabiting the world that recognizes the "imbrication" of different worlds and a "capacité de reconnaître sa face dans le visage de l'étranger et de valoriser les traces du lointain dans le proche, de domestiquer l'in-familier, de travailler avec ce qui a tout l'air de contraires" (an ability to recognize one's face in that of the stranger, and to value the traces of what is distant in what is nearby, to tame the unfamiliar, and to work with what at first seem to be complete opposites).[30] It is precisely because A. H. Bâ's memoirs carry these "Afropolitan" traces that they have been variously cast by a diverse audience of readers as colonial bildungsroman, oral epic, historical documentary, and ethnographic fiction.

Translating *Amkoullel* into English: Why Now?

I first became engaged in studying the work of Amadou Hampâté Bâ while reading *L'Etrange destin de Wangrin: ou, Les rouseries d'un interprète africain*. I decided to further research the prominent role that indigenous African interpreters (and thus the act and fact of translation) played in the French conquest and administration of colonial French West Africa. I visited the French colonial archives in Aix-en-Provence in 2012 and then went to Senegal in 2013 to research the topic at the IFAN, where Amadou Hampâté Bâ himself had also worked. In both Aix-en-Provence and Dakar, I found that the author who had most consistently documented the role and importance of indigenous African interpreters was A. H. Bâ. I also discovered that his writing on this topic in *L'Etrange destin de Wangrin*, *Amkoullel, l'enfant peul: mémoires*, and *Oui, Mon Commandant!* is often cited by scholars of West Africa who read French but seems to be unknown among members of the Anglophone community of researchers, particularly in the field of Translation Studies.[31] I came to believe that this was because the memoirs have never before been translated into English.

Given the global impact and importance of Amadou Hampâté Bâ's work, it is indeed astonishing that there exist only three translations of his writings into English: *The Fortunes of Wangrin* and *A Spirit of Tolerance: The Inspiring Life of Tierno Bokar*, and an out-of-print translation by Daniel Whitman of the Fula initiation tale *Kaïdara*. It is therefore high time for an English-language translation of Amadou Hampâté Bâ's memoirs. Why have they only now been translated into English some thirty years after they were first published in French? Why me?

One response to the first question is supplied by Taylor Eggan in an August 13, 2017, online essay entitled, "The Strange Fate of Amadou Hampâté Bâ in the Anglophone World." He writes that the dearth of English-language translations of A. H. Bâ's works may be due to the fact that they are "difficult to categorize by genre."³² It is true that, as was the case throughout his life, neither A. H. Bâ nor his works always fit into neat generic categories. As Christiane Ndiaye notes:

> Among the volumes bearing his signature are historical narratives that read like traditional tales [*L'Empire peul du Macina*], hagiographies and narrative epics that read like novels [*Vie et enseignement de Tierno Bokar*], a biography that many readers took for an autobiographical novel [*L'Etrange destin de Wangrin*], and so on. All of these writings are delicately situated between orality and writing, between lived reality (history) and fiction, between the individual and the collective, and between languages. That this prolific production should end with an autobiography, the most ambiguous genre of them all, should not surprise us.³³

A second response to the question surrounding the belated translation into English of A. H. Bâ's memoirs could be that potential publishers may simply have found the sheer length of the work daunting. In its current French 2012 edition, the *Memoirs* total 865 pages on onion skin paper. But I was so scandalized to discover that one of the largest and most powerful language communities on the planet, speakers and readers of English, did not have access to A. H. Bâ's memoirs unless they were able to read them in French or in one of the other languages into which they have already been translated that I felt called to undertake this translation without first obtaining any guarantee that they would later find a publisher. This required taking a leap of faith that also involved a fair amount of sheer determination. It is for this reason that this translation and the research that led to it were entirely supported by a series of grants from the University of South Carolina and from the Camargo Foundation, for which I am extremely grateful.³⁴

Some readers may find it strange to conceive of writing a translation as a "calling." And yet this idea is present in Walter Benjamin's landmark essay on translation, "The Task of the Translator," first published in 1923. Benjamin asserts that a great work choses its translator, rather than the inverse. Indeed Benjamin asserts:

> A translation issues from its original—not so much from its life as from its afterlife. For a translation comes later than the original, and since the important works of world literature never find their chosen translators at the time of their origin, their translation marks their stage of continued life. The idea of life and afterlife in works of art should be considered with an entirely unmetaphorical objectivity.³⁵

Thus, a translation extends the life of a text by granting it a new life in another language. This is exactly what Amadou Hampâté Bâ himself was doing as he collected and translated the traditional "oral" knowledge of his region, translated it, wrote it down in French, and eventually published it.

To extend the "life" of *Amkoullel* by translating it into English is my project here. An English-language translation published in 2021 amplifies the power of A. H. Bâ's memoirs to both bear witness to the past and to reinsert his work into an ongoing dialogue with contemporary readers, writers, and scholars who share an Afropolitan aesthetic.

Amadou Hampâté Bâ knew very well that he would continue to live through his work, and that his work would live after he had passed away. He once declared, "Combien de fois des jeunes gens m'ont dit: 'Monsieur Hampâté Bâ, vous êtes dépassé.' Je leur ai répondu: 'Mais c'est vous qui n'êtes pas arrivés.'" (How many times have young people said to me: 'Mister Hampâté Bâ, your time has passed.' I reply, 'You are the ones who haven't arrived yet.')[36]

For a man who was so invested in preserving knowledge of the past, Amadou Hampâté Bâ was very preoccupied with the future, and in 1984, he wrote an open letter addressed to those same youth of Africa and the world "who hadn't arrived yet." Even here, A. H. Bâ emphasizes the role of "fate" in the current configuration of global culture. "Young people of Africa and the world," he wrote,

> fate has determined that at this end of the twentieth century, at the dawn of a new era, you shall be as a bridge that connects two worlds; the world of the past, where old civilizations aspire only to bequeath to you their treasures before they disappear, and the world of the future, full of uncertainties and difficulties, it is true, but also rich with new adventures and fascinating experiences. It is up to you to take up the challenge and to ensure that a mutilating rupture does not occur, but instead the serene continuity and fertilization of one age by the other.[37]

A. H. Bâ further encourages the youth to open themselves to the outside in order to "give and to receive," and insists on the importance both of enriching and preserving their mother tongues and of perfecting their knowledge of French ("that language inherited from colonization") in order to maintain and foster intercultural communication. In a film entitled *Amadou Hampâté Bâ, le sage du fleuve Niger* (Amadou Hampâté Bâ, sage of the Niger River) he asserts, "Nobody is at home anymore. We are all citizens of the world. . . . We have a birth place, we must all be citizens of everywhere. . . . That is why it would rather be a good idea for us to be in understanding, listening to one another in order to try to discover what we have in common so that we can build our future happiness."[38]

He believed that in order for cross-cultural dialog to take place, it was necessary to be able to listen to one another. But he also insisted that non-Africans would need to set aside preconceived notions about Africa "in order to become pupils who know absolutely nothing."[39] For A. H. Bâ, it was the collected (and as yet little known) traditional knowledge of Africa that could help teach the future citizens of the world. To emphasize this point, he was fond of repeating the following admonition transmitted from the wise initiates of the African "bush" to those who would seek to discover their knowledge:

> If you want me to teach you, you must stop being you, to be me. Forget yourself in order to be me. Otherwise, if you keep being you, although we are face to face, we will be . . . as distant from one another as the sky is from earth. This means that you must not take what I am going to tell you and compare it to what you already know . . . you must empty yourself of what you know in order to learn. That is when you are told that you must know that you do not know. *Anda a Anda.* The Fula expression says, "*Sa andi a anda a andat.*" If you know that you do not know, you will know. "*Sa anda a anda a andata.*" If you do not know that you do not know, you will not know.[40]

In undertaking to translate *Amkoullel*, I tried to adhere to these injunctions. "Stop being you, to be me. Forget yourself in order to be me." As the translator Sika Fakambi put it in an extension of A. H. Bâ's widely recited tale, "A l'école du caméléon," to translate is to engage in "le parler caméléon," or "chameleon speech"—to use a kind of spoken or written word where the speaker or translator adapts her language to the situation in which she finds herself.[41]

In order to render the flavor of A. H. Bâ's French-language writing into English, I chose to recreate the somewhat formal and even heroic language register that A. H. Bâ uses in both narration and dialogue. One example of this is visible in the section devoted to A. H. Bâ's maternal grandfather, in the scene where he informs El Hadj Omar that he has renounced everything in order to join him:

> Neither have I come to join you with the intent of acquiring knowledge because in this world you can teach me nothing that I do not already know. I am a *Silatigui*, a Fula initiate. I know the visible and the invisible. I have what we call "an ear for the bush." I understand the language of the birds, I can read the prints of small animals on the ground, as well as the patches of light that the sun projects through the leaves; I know how to interpret the murmurs of the four great winds and the four lesser winds as well as

the movement of clouds through space, because for me, everything leaves a sign and speaks a language. (page 16)

However, in places where A. H. Bâ relates dialogue spoken in the jargon known as *le français des tirailleurs*, locally known as *forofifon naspa* (a kind of lingua franca mixing French and West African languages developed by the French military and indigenous infantrymen during the French colonial period, I use the implantation of certain recognizable French, or approximated French (and English), words in the translated text. In the example below from chapter 5, where Amkoullel's stepfather, Tidjani Thiam, is working in a forced labor camp under the supervision of a cruel guard, the narrator contrasts dialogue that was spoken "correctly," if forcefully, in the Bambara language, with that of the "incorrect" jargon found at the end of the passage:

> This surly guard, who had nicknamed himself *gonfin yirijougou feere* (black chimpanzee flower of a venomous tree) never stood up unless he got the urge to whip the first prisoner within arm's reach when he felt like it and without any particular reason. . . . "You had better pray to your ancestors that my 'little brother' (his whip) that you see tucked under my arm here does not become dislodged, otherwise he'll come and plow into your criminal backs like a *daba* cuts through the weeds in the fields. The Commandant is up there on top of the hill, where he is perched like the great eagle of the skies, but down here in the valley, I am like the hippopotamus that rips up the rice fields. Here, I am the one in command, and not the Commandant." Then he would add in his "infantryman's French" (called French *forofifon naspa*): "Get to work! *Travadjé, travadjé!* (Work, work!). Otherwise, you pigs, I'll pigwhip you good!" (page 124)

Scenes such as these occur repeatedly in *Amkoullel*. In recording past injustices, even as it vividly recreates A. H. Bâ's childhood and adolescence, the text also provides readers with a lens through which to view events that some would rather forget.

The Legacy of A. H. Bâ

Although Amadou Hampâté Bâ passed away in 1991 (in Abidjan, Ivory Coast, where he had served as Mali's ambassador), he lives on in the hearts and minds of many. He is present on the internet and on social media. The Fondation Amadou Hampâté Bâ, located in Abidjan, Ivory Coast, and directed by his daughter, Roukiatou Hampâté Bâ, is on Facebook, and many of the interviews and addresses that he gave over the years are posted on YouTube.[42] His writings are read aloud in French and in translation.[43] The African Studies Centre at Leiden University in the Netherlands has posted an extensive web dossier on A. H. Bâ.[44] Following the English-language translation of his *Vie et enseignment de Tierno Bokar: Le sage de Bandiagara* (translated by Fatima Jane Casewit as *A Spirit of Tolerance: The Inspiring Life of Tierno Bokar*), this portrait of A. H. Bâ's influential Sufi Muslim spiritual teacher who favored interfaith cooperation and understanding was adapted to the stage and directed by Peter Brook in a performance at Columbia University in 2005.[45] He is present in the theatrical French-language sketches of Fula actor and comedian Saïdou Abatcha (also available on YouTube), and his life was the subject of a recent play by Bernard Magnier, the editor at Actes Sud responsible for republishing A. H. Bâ's *Memoirs* in 2012. The play was performed in France in March 2018 with Le Tarmac Theater, and it was quite appropriately entitled *Le Fabuleux destin d'Amadou Hampâté Bâ* (The fabulous destiny of Amadou Hampâté Bâ). A. H. Bâ's well-known novel, *L'Etrange destin de Wangrin: ou, Les roueries d'un interprète africain*, has been translated into English, Italian, German, and Japanese and is the subject of numerous essays and books. Even before they were republished in 2012 by Actes Sud, *Amkoullel, l'enfant peul: mémoires* and *Oui, Mon Commandant: mémoires II* had already been translated into Dutch, German, Italian, Japanese, Korean, Spanish, and Portuguese.

All told, A. H. Bâ published fifteen books and a great number of articles, poems, and stories in French and Fulfulde, and many more works still remain unpublished. His contributions are global in scope. The *MLA International Bibliography* lists fifty articles and books dedicated to various aspects of his work. A World Cat search under the heading "Amadou Hampâté Bâ" lists 234 works in 820 publications in 11 languages and 5,347 library holdings.[46] A. H. Bâ's work has been studied by ethnologists, historians, literary scholars, religious studies experts, and translators. Somewhat like the chameleon in "A l'école du caméléon," in which A. H. Bâ exhorted listeners to learn from "that very great professor, the chameleon" for its ability to change itself and adapt to the place in which it happened to be, A. H. Bâ was and is many things to many people: a teller of traditional tales, an African sage, an orator, an initiate, a spiritual leader, a philosopher, a historian, an ethnographer, an autobiographer, a biographer, a poet, a translator, an interpreter, a novelist, a colonial clerk, an ambassador, a father, a husband, a son. As Austen and Soares remark, "given Hampâté Bâ's many facets . . . it has not been easy to characterize him or pin him down."[47] According to A. H. Bâ, such a transformative and chameleon-like ability "n'est pas de l'hypocrisie; c'est d'abord de la tolérance, et puis le savoir-vivre" (is not hypocrisy; rather, first it is tolerance and then savoir-vivre). While his ability to adapt to diverse situations was necessary for surviving the numerous reversals of fortune that marked Amadou Hampâté Bâ's life, this "penser-caméléon" is directly related to what Achille Mbembe identifies in "L'Afrique qui vient" (Africa in view) as the transformative power of "une sorte d'intelligence rusée" (a wily intelligence) where "ce que l'on est et ce que l'on devient est le résultat de notre capacité à exploiter les potentiels de situation" (what one is and what one becomes is the result of our capacity to exploit situational potentials).[48]

Amkoullel, the Fula Boy

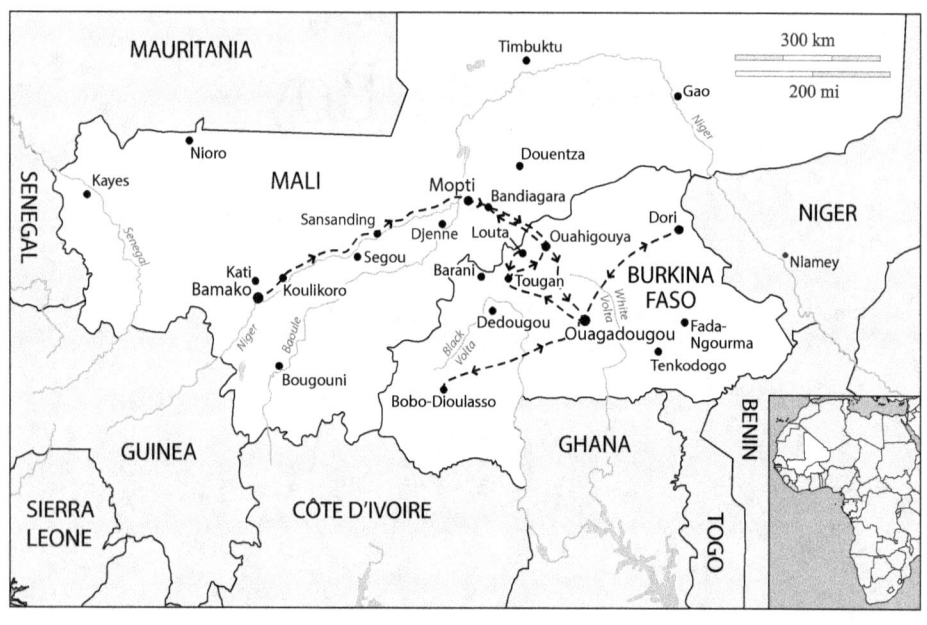

PREFACE TO THE ORIGINAL EDITION

Théodore Monod

I was of course very moved to learn that Amkoullel had requested that the preface to this volume be written by his old friend, whom he called his "Quiet River."[1] In fact, it was around 1941 or 1942 that we met, and it was then that our deep friendship—which united us in several ways—was born. First, we had in common our joint participation in researching the West African past. Perhaps even more importantly, we shared the conviction that our religious beliefs obviously converged, rather than dividing us. Following apparently different paths, both of us were climbing the same mountain to that summit above the clouds where the supernatural light that must enlighten every man awaits. The teachings of Tierno Bokar contributed greatly to opening Amkoullel's heart and mind to all aspects of true spiritual life. Thus he always welcomed spirituality with joy and gratitude whenever it appeared.

One day, we had made a pilgrimage to Bandiagara, to the house and grave of Tierno Bokar. We had wished (he and I) to introduce his friends to one of the most beautiful texts of religious literature, known as the "Hymn to Love," inserted by the Apostle Paul into one of his letters.

We went together to the Bandiagara mosque where my companion translated the following well-known passage, which concludes as follows, into Fulfulde: "So faith, hope, love abide, these three; but the greatest of these is love."

Those who were listening found the text very beautiful and questioned me about its origin. Without going into too much detail, I took the liberty of accepting the response that Amkoullel gave them: "The author is a Sufi from the Banou Israel people."

This tale demonstrates the open-mindedness of my friend.

I must also add, by the way, that in his daily life, rather than isolating himself on the lofty summits of thought or religion, Amkoullel was also in many ways a man like any other man. He knew how to laugh, had a ready sense of humor that could lead to gentle mockery, and possessed a particular talent for telling stories, and—by extension—for telling traditional tales. A number of his writings are in fact stories, whether they are symbolic texts or, more simply, light-hearted tales, as, for example, the tale with the somewhat surprising title, "The Calamitous Coccyx."

The form known as "Youthful Memories" is part of a well-known but perilous literary genre, because it is the place of encounter between the greatest successes and most powerful thoughts and the most meager banalities. The good intentions of the memoirist will never replace genius, and not everyone will have the luxury of being able to evoke, as did Chateaubriand, his childhood at Combourg.

In telling us the story of his youth and, in fact, of his first twenty years, Amadou Hampâté Bâ introduces us into a world that will be particularly informative for today's reader. It is the world of the West African savanna, with its peaceful immensities, its bush scorched by the sun or battered by the tempests of the rainy season, with its sandstone plateaus and the immense Niger River that remains the central artery of the entire region.

Nevertheless, although the narrative is centered in the small city of Bandiagara, other places are mentioned in succession, such as Mopti, Sansanding, Segou, Bougouni, Koulikoro, Kati, and so on. While at the beginning of the twentieth century, Bandiagara would witness the implantation and occupation by the French military as a conquered land, the country remained passionately attached to the grand memories of its history and, of course, to the two principal episodes in that history: the rise of the Fula Empire of Cheikou Amadou in Massina, and the conquest of that country by the Toucouleurs under El Hadj Omar. Passions were still running high when, in his childhood, the author would find himself submerged in the eddies of a past about which he himself would later become the historian.

The kingdom of Bandiagara (1864–1893) was, of course, Muslim. This fairly strict Islam governed matters of faith as well as social matters. For example, boys were obligated to learn the Koran by heart, although some of them would never understand its full meaning because they did not know Arabic.

The clarity of detail in a narrative that reproduces even the oldest of past conversations is astounding. It is clear that the author is relying on his own personal memories as well as on information gathered from outside sources. The present work contains an extremely rich spoken history archive that bears witness to a veritable civilization based in oral tradition, one capable of conserving often ancient narratives told in surprising detail.

Fula children grow up adhering to a double allegiance: that of a veritable honor code, and of complete respect for the mother's wishes. A Fula child who has been raised on stories of the lofty acts of his ancestors must regulate his conduct according to a strict moral code. Therefore, there are some things that a well-born Fula will refuse to do.

After honor, here is the second part of the diptych: the mother. A Fula can disobey his father, but never his mother. The rule is absolute. Amadou Hampâté Bâ would undergo this experience when Kadidja forbade him to leave for Gorée Island, the training ground of the best African employees in the colonial administration. Bâ's mother was, in fact, of exceptional caliber, and this noble, gracious, and strong Kadidja reappears in one hundred pages of the narrative.

As he was leaving his mother in Koulikoro to occupy his first position in the colonial administration, Amkoullel watched Kadidja as she left the riverbank without looking back. "The wind was billowing through the hems of her *boubou* and lifting her delicate head veil. She looked like a damselfly preparing for flight."

After the honor and respect due to the mother, a third element of Fula society lies in the practice of generosity. Amkoullel's stories contain a great number of instances where a giver (who has the means to do so) returns a favor by way of a gift (whether large or small) of livestock, clothing, various objects, and, at times, cash. This ubiquitous practice of gift-giving is part of Fula custom.

Twenty years in the life of a young Fula amounts to a host of stories, anecdotes, and descriptions of the greatest variety. One discovers with interest, for example, the function of youth groups that can include up to fifty young boys who belong, by the way, to all social classes, whether nobles or *rimaïbé* captives.

Amadou Hampâté Bâ's sense of humor is always discernable and the picturesque is never lacking. Take, for example, the most unusual tale of the boys' expedition whose goal it was to discover whether, as rumor had it, the excrement of the White-Whites was, in fact, black.

Scenes of horror are equally represented in this volume, for instance, as on the occasion of a severe famine, a tragedy that was scored into the author's memory.

As a devout Muslim, he would always seek to discover justification in his faith for the caprices of Fate. In 1947, he wished to see his friend Ben Daoud once again. This was a person whom he had known as rich and honored, the son of King Mademba of Sansanding. He found him living in poverty, stripped of all his possessions, destitute, and on the brink of starvation. Nevertheless, in the face of the cruelty of Fate, his friend had retained a perfect serenity and moral courage, which evoked the author's utmost admiration. He wrote, "Ben Daoud Mademba Sy, whom I first met in 1919 during my summer vacation and then met again in 1947, remains for me one of the men who has most deeply touched my life."

It would be unjust not to mention the author's style here. It is of a remarkable quality throughout and is frequently enriched by the most picturesque of images and comparisons. We clearly sense here the qualities of an author who has expert knowledge of the rules and requirements of telling stories and tales. Amadou Hampâté Bâ remains a marvelous storyteller. There is no doubt that this work will serve, in the happiest of ways, the memory of our friend who has passed on.

May the many who will come to know him through this message sent from beyond the grave feel morally enriched and fortified as they become acquainted with he who was at once a sage, a learned man, and a spiritual being, and who will remain for many the best witness of this line from scripture: "For the spirit of God blows where it wills . . ." (John 3:8).

A Note from the French Publisher, Actes Sud

Amadou Hampâté Bâ's original manuscript contained a number of commentaries on certain aspects of African culture and sociology. Because of the length of the work, it was decided, with the author's permission, to showcase the narrative and to delete a good many of these commentaries. The reader will find these in the author's more specialized works.

AUTHOR'S FOREWORD

Amadou Hampâté Bâ

On African Memory

A number of friends who have read this manuscript were surprised that the memory of a man over eighty years of age could reproduce so many things in such minute detail.[1] This is explained by the fact that people of my generation and, more generally, people who come from an oral tradition and who did not rely on writing possess memories of a rather inordinate fidelity and accuracy. From childhood, we were trained to observe, to watch, and to listen, so that every event was inscribed in our memory as if it were in virgin wax. Everything was there: the setting, the characters, the words, even the most minute details in clothing. For example, when I describe the uniform worn by the first circle commandant that I had ever seen in close proximity during my childhood, I do not need to *remember*; rather, I see it all on a sort of interior screen, and all I have to do is describe what I see. In order to describe a scene, I only have to relive it. And if a tale was told to me by someone else, it is not only the content of the narrative that my memory has recorded, but the entire scene: the bearing of the narrator, his clothing, his gestures, his mimicry, and the ambient noises, such as the sounds of the kora that Djeli Maadi was playing while Wangrin was telling me the story of his life and that I can still hear to this day.

When an event is reconstructed, the entire film recording runs from beginning to end. That is why it is very difficult for an African of my generation to "summarize." We tell the entire tale, or we do not tell it at all. We never tire of hearing the same story again and again. For us, repetition is not a flaw.

On Chronology

Because chronological order was not the first concern of African narrators, whether they were traditional storytellers or family members, I have not always been able to provide the exact date (within a year or two) of the events that are recounted, except when known outside events allowed me to place them. In African stories, where the past is relived as a present experience, outside of time, as it were, there is at times a kind of disorder that upsets Western minds but in which we feel perfectly at home. We reside there, at ease, like fish in a sea, where water molecules mingle and form a living whole.

Zone of Reference

In speaking of "African Tradition," one should never generalize. There is no *single* African tradition, there is no *single* Africa, there is no *single* African, there is no *single* African tradition that is the same in every region and for every ethnic group. Of course, there are a good number of shared elements: the recognition of the presence of the sacred in all things, of the relationship between the visible and the invisible worlds, of the relationship between the living and the dead, in the shared sense of community, in the religious respect for the mother, and so on. But there are also a number of differences: in deities, in sacred symbols, in religious interdicts. The social customs that stem from these practices vary between regions, ethnic groups, and, sometimes, between villages.

The traditions that I discuss in this narrative are generally those of the African savanna, which stretches from east to west, south of the Sahara, and, in particular, those of the Fula, Toucouleur, and Bambara communities of the region that was once known as Bafour, in Mali, where I grew up.

Dreams and Predictions

Another thing that sometimes bothers Westerners when they read African stories is the frequent intervention of premonitory dreams, predictions, and other phenomena of this kind. But these sorts of events, which for us are part of daily life, are intricately woven into African life and do not surprise us in the least. In times past, it was not rare to see a man arrive on foot from a distant village with the sole purpose of making an announcement or of giving instructions that he had received in his dreams. Once he had done this, he would quite naturally take his leave, like a postman who had simply come bearing a letter to its addressee. Not to mention these types of phenomena in the course of telling a story would have been dishonest of me, because they were, and undoubtedly still are, part of our lived realities.

On the Transcription of African Words

In order to facilitate the reading of African words, rather than applying rules set by linguists, we have preferred to favor phonetic transcriptions. For example, *ou* replaces *u*, or *è* replaces *e*. We have equally favored a French naming system for ethnic groups. In the case of certain proper names, differences in spelling regarding the names of certain persons are to be explained by the fact that in everyday usage, these names, which are derived from Arabic, have undergone a number of phonetic transformations. For example, the honorary title of Cheikh (where the *kh* corresponds to the Spanish pronunciation of the letter "j") is transcribed as Cheik, Cheikou, Chékou, and even Sékou, when used as a proper name. The same rule applies to the name of the Prophet Mohammad, which can become Mohammed, or even Mamadou, and for Ahmed, which becomes Ahmadou, as the case may be.

1

Roots

My Dual Heritage

According to African tradition, an individual cannot be separate from his lineage, for he is merely an extension of those who continue to live on through him. This is why, when one wishes to honor someone, that person is greeted by calling out his clan name, for instance, "Bâ! Bâ!," or "Diallo! Diallo!," or "Cissé, Cissé!," rather than his personal name (in Europe this is known as one's first or given name), for it is not just one isolated individual who is being greeted but, through him, his entire ancestral line.

Therefore, it would be unthinkable for the old African that I am, born at the dawn of the twentieth century in the city of Bandiagara, Mali, to begin the story of my personal life without first evoking my two paternal and maternal lineages, if only to place them in context. Both of them are Fula, and both were intimately involved, although they were in opposing camps, in the sometimes tragic historical events that marked my country throughout the nineteenth century. The entire history of my family is in fact tied to the history of Massina (a region in Mali located in the inner Niger River bend), and to the wars that tore it apart. These wars pitted the Fula of the Fula Empire of Massina against the Toucouleur army of El Hadj Omar, the great conqueror and religious leader who came from the west and whose empire, once it had vanquished and absorbed the Fula Empire of Massina in 1862, extended from eastern Guinea all the way to Timbuktu.

Each of my two lineages is directly or indirectly related to one or the other of these two opposing parties. I thus received at birth a dual historical and emotional heritage, and many of the events in my life have been touched by this fact.

"Not so fast!" will undoubtedly be the reaction from non-African readers with little exposure to the great names of our history. "Before you go any further, just who are the Fulas and the Toucouleurs?"

I will begin with my Fula ancestors. If the question is easily asked, it is not easily answered, because these nomadic people who have driven their herds across the entire African savanna south of the Sahara, from the shores of the Atlantic Ocean to those of the Indian Ocean, as it has done for millennia (the rock art depicting cattle in the Tassili n'Ajjer caves discovered by Henri Lhote bear witness to this), constitute a veritable enigma of history.[1] No one has yet been able to pierce the mystery of their origins. Fula legends and oral traditions almost all refer to an ancient Eastern origin. But according to different versions, this origin is sometimes described as Arab, Yemeni, or Palestinian, is sometimes Jewish, and is sometimes thought to be even more distant, with its roots located in India. Our traditions speak of several great migratory currents out of the East during very ancient times. Some of these, which traversed Africa from east to west, are said to have arrived in the Fouta Tooro region of Senegal, a region from which they would much later set off once again toward the East, in new migratory waves, during a time period closer to ours.

Intrigued perhaps by the physical appearance of the Fulas, by their relatively light skin color (which can be darker depending on the degree of intermixing), by their long, straight noses, and their often rather thin lips, European scientists and researchers have tried, each according to his or her discipline (history, linguistics, anthropology, ethnology), to find a solution to the mystery of Fula origins. Each has followed his or her own hypothesis, sometimes investing as much energy in defending it as in refuting those of others, but nobody has provided a clear response. They most often agree to assign the Fula a more or less "oriental" origin, with a rather varied degree of intermixing between a non-Negro Semitic, or Hamitic element, and the Blacks of Sudan without providing further details. For modern African historians, the Fula are of purely African descent.

Whatever the case may be, and this is the profound originality of the Fula, over time and space, and throughout their migrations, their intermixing, the contributions from outside elements, and the inevitable adaptations they have made to their surrounding environments, they have been able to retain their identity and preserve their language. They have retained their cultural heritage and, even with their conversion to Islam, have maintained their own initiatory and religious traditions, each of which is connected to their deep conviction regarding their identity and their nobility. While they may not know where they came from, they know who they are. "The Fula knows himself," as the Bambara say.

With poetic wit, my old friend Sado Diarra, chief of the village of Yérémadio, near Bamako, used to express Bambara thinking vis-à-vis the Fula in the following way: "The Fula are a surprising mixture. A white river in lands where black waters flow, a black river in lands where white waters flow, they are an enigmatic people that capricious whirlwinds have carried from the rising sun and scattered almost everywhere from east to west."

Buffeted by thousands of historical events that are more or less known, the Fula were effectively scattered like will-o'-the-wisps over all the grassy regions of the African savanna south of the Sahara. "Everywhere present, but nowhere at home," constantly seeking new watering holes and rich pasture, by day they would drive their great humped cattle with horns shaped like lyres or crescent moons, and by night they would give themselves over to improvised poetic jousting matches. Sometimes oppressed, dispersed in diasporas or settled by force in restricted areas, sometimes turned conquerors and organized into kingdoms, following their conversion to Islam, they would go on to found great empires: among them, the Sokoto Empire (in the region of Nigeria), founded in the seventeenth century by Ousmane Dan Fodio, and the Fula Empire of Massina (in the region of Mali), founded at the beginning of the nineteenth century by Cheikou Amadou, in the heart of the fertile inner bend of the Niger River.

Attracted by its vast, grassy prairies, successive waves of Fula herdsmen, originating especially from the Senegalese Fouta Tooro and Ferlo regions, had settled in Massina centuries before the founding of this last empire. My distant paternal ancestors arrived there around the fifteenth century. They settled on the right bank of the Bani River (an affluent of the Niger) between Djenné and Mopti, in a land that was called Fakala, meaning, "for all," because the Fula cohabitated there with the various ethnic groups of the region: Bamabaras, Markas, Bozos, Somonos, Dogons, and so on.

In 1818, when Cheikou Amadou founded the *dina* (or Islamic state) in the country which historians have called the "Theocratic Fula Empire of Massina" (whose history I have recounted elsewhere), the population of the entire Niger Bend was already in majority Fula.[2] My paternal ancestors, the Bâs and the Hamsalahs, who occupied the role of chiefs in the Fakala region, pledged a vow of allegiance to Cheikou Amadou. They also continued on as pastoralists, since no Fula worth his salt, even if he is no longer nomadic, could conceive of living without having a herd to care for, not so much for economic reasons but out of an ancestral and almost sacred love for the animals, his brothers, since they have been his constant companions since the dawn of time. According to an old adage, "a Fula without a herd is like a prince without a crown."

The community of the dîna, modeled after the very first Muslim community of Medina, prospered for twenty-eight years under the enlightened guidance of Cheikou Amadou. Cheikou Amadou had succeeded in freeing the Fula from the domination of local sovereigns by organizing and more or less sedentarizing them within the reaches of a powerful, independent state and, what was no small feat, by regulating the dates and trajectories of the seasonal migration of the herds in concert with local farming communities. After his death in 1845, and the death of his son Amadou Cheikou in 1853, the situation of the community deteriorated under the reign of his grandson Amadou Amadou, who died in 1862 during the events that accompanied the taking of the capital Hamdallaye by the Toucouleur armies of El Hadj Omar. The Fula Empire of Massina, where my paternal lineage had flourished, had seen its day.[3]

Now they step onto history's stage: those "Toucouleurs" whose name, by its very sound, never fails to surprise the uninitiated reader. A brief explanation is in order. This name, which has nothing to do with any notion whatsoever of color, is derived from the Arabic or Berber word *Tekrour*, which at one time referred to the entire Fouta Tooro region of Senegal. The Arabic-speaking Moors called the inhabitants of this land *Tekarir* (the singular form is *Tekrouri*). According to Maurice Delafosse, this name, deformed through its pronunciation in Wolof as *Tokoror* or *Tokolor* became, in its final French deformation, *Toucouleur*.

Over the course of a distant and obscure historical process, the inhabitants of this land, although of different ethnic backgrounds (probably primarily Fula once this group had arrived en masse in the Fouta Tooro region, although there were also Serer, Wolof, Soninké, etc.), all became speakers of Pulaar, which then became for them a factor of linguistic and even of cultural unity.[4] The Toucouleur people are therefore not an ethnic group in the true sense of the word, but rather an assemblage of ethnic groups bound by the use of the same language, who, over time, became more or less mixed through intermarriage. The Toucouleurs themselves have their own designation: *Halpulaar*, those who speak *Pulaar*; they are also called *Foutanké*, those who are from Fouta.

Regarding pure Fula traditions, notably the religious and initiatory traditions, these have been carried on solely by the Fula pastoralists who live deep in the bush, that is, far removed from any cities or villages.

The two peoples who, in the year of 1862 fought each other in Massina on the outskirts of Hamdallaye, thus had a good many things in common: their religion, their language, sometimes their ethnicity, and even their original homeland, since the ancestors of the Fulas of Massina had also come from the Fouta Tooro centuries before. The "Fulas of Massina" and the "Toucouleurs" of El Hadj Omar nevertheless comprised two distinct political entities. Because they will be present throughout this entire narrative, I will retain these two designators in order to maintain clarity for the reader. They themselves would later use the designators "old Futa" (*Foutakindi*) to name the Fulas of Massina who had been in the country for centuries, and "new Futa" (*Foutakeiri*) to name the Toucouleurs who had arrived in the country with El Hadj Omar.

Pâté Poullo, My Maternal Grandfather

Among the victorious Toucouleur army that penetrated Hamdallaye, there was a Fula from Fouta Tooro who had once given up everything in order to follow El Hadj Omar. His name was Pâté Poullo of the Diallo clan, and he was my future maternal grandfather. I would later hear his oft-recounted tale.

Pâté Poullo was a Fula herdsman from deep in the bush of Dienguel in Senegal and a *silatigui*, or grand master of pastoral initiation and a kind of priest of this religion, and therefore a spiritual leader of the entire tribe.[5] Like all silatigui, he was gifted with uncommon abilities: he was a seer, soothsayer, and healer; he was a talented judge of character and could interpret the mute sign language of the bush. Although young, he enjoyed an eminent position in society. But one day, while on a journey, he chanced to see and hear El Hadj Omar, the grand master of the Islamic Tidjaniya brotherhood, who was on a tour of the Fouta Tooro.[6]

As soon as he arrived home, Pâté Poullo summoned his brothers, close relations, and tribal representatives and announced his intention to renounce everything in order to follow El Hadj Omar. "But first," he told them, "I wish to ask your permission. If you consent, I will compensate you for my departure by leaving my entire herd to you. I will leave empty handed, with nothing but the hair on my head and the clothes on my back. As for my silatigui's staff, before my departure, I will ritually bequeath it to the one most qualified to inherit it."

His relatives were greatly surprised, but in the end they all gave him this blessing: "Follow your path and go in peace and only in peace!" And this is how my grandfather renounced his wealth, herds, and power, and, armed only with his herdsman's staff, set out to join El Hadj Omar.

Upon finding him again in a city whose name I have forgotten, he introduced himself: "Cheikh Omar, I have heeded your call and I have come to join you. My name is Pâté Poullo Diallo and I am a 'Red Fula,' a Fula herdsman from deep in the bush. In order to free myself from my obligations, I have left my entire herd to my brothers. I was as rich as a Fula can be rich. It is therefore not with the goal of acquiring wealth that I have come to join you, but solely to answer God's call, because a Fula would not leave his herd to search for any other thing.

"Neither have I come to join you with the intent of acquiring knowledge because in this world you can teach me nothing that I do not already know. I am a silatigui, a Fula initiate. I know the visible and the invisible. I have what we call 'an ear for the bush.' I understand the language of the birds, I can read the prints of small animals on the ground, as well as the patches of light that the sun projects through the leaves; I know how to interpret the murmurs of the four great winds and the four lesser winds, as well as the movement of clouds through space, because for me, everything leaves a sign and speaks a language. This knowledge that is inside of me, I cannot renounce it, but perhaps it could be of use to you? As you travel with your companions, I could be 'responsible' for the bush and guide you through its perils.

"This is to tell you that I have not come to join you for worldly things. I beg you to receive me into Islam, and I will follow you wherever you go, but on one condition: on the day that God allows your cause to triumph, and when you have power and great riches at your disposal, I request that you never name me to any commanding posts, neither as a military chief, nor as a provincial chief, nor as a village chief, nor even as a district chief. Because a Fula who has abandoned his herds can never be given anything to equal their worth.

"If I have chosen to follow you, it is solely so that you may guide me toward knowledge of the One God."

Greatly moved, El Hadj Omar accepted my grandfather's conditions and called for the conversion ceremony to proceed. And in fact, for the rest of his life, my grandfather accepted neither honors nor duties of command. A purely spiritual alliance was formed between the two men and soon developed into a deep friendship. As an expression of trust, El Hadj Omar placed Pâté Poullo in charge of watching over and caring for the small herd that he had personally inherited from his Fula mother, a herd that followed him everywhere and from which he would draw, along with the fruit of the Koranic lessons that he never stopped giving, food and sustenance for his own family.

From that day forward, enlisted under the banner of El Hadj Omar, Pâté Poullo followed him throughout his campaign toward the East. And that is how, one day in 1862, as conquerors, they penetrated Hamdallaye, the capital of the Fula Empire of Massina founded forty-four years earlier by Cheikou Amadou. El Hadj Omar would remain there for two years. During his final nine months there, all his enemies (Fulas, Kountas from Timbuktu, and others) formed a coalition to lay him siege. Their armies, encamped along the sturdy perimeter wall that he had had built for the protection of the city, let nothing through. The blockade was unrelenting, the famine atrocious. The Toucouleurs were at times reduced to the utmost dire straits.

It was during these dramatic times that, thanks to a few of drops of milk, Pâté Poullo formed a bond of friendship with a nephew of El Hadj Omar named Tidjani Tall (son of Amadou Seydou Tall, the older brother of El Hadj Omar). No one yet suspected that he would later become the new sovereign of the Toucouleur kingdom of Massina, that he would found the city of Bandiagara, where I was born, and that he would play an extremely important role in the history of my family, both on the paternal and maternal sides, thereby indirectly influencing my own destiny.

One day during the siege, a milk cow that had escaped the notice of the enemy soldiers had managed to approach one of the gates in the perimeter wall. Immediately, she was allowed into the city where, quite naturally, she was entrusted to the good care of Pâté Poullo. Every night, he left the city undetected in search of forage for the cow. Every morning, after he had milked the good cow, he would carry a great calabash brimming with milk to El Hadj Omar, who would share the precious liquid among his family members, himself, and Pâté Poullo. But on each of these occasions, my grandfather carried an extra portion of milk, which he had hidden in a small goatskin, to Tidjani, in thanks for his strange abilities; he had read Tidjani's destiny in the features of his face. "Here is the rest of your father El Hadj Omar's milk," he would tell him.[7] "Drink it for you will be his heir." And Tidjani would drink. This is how a solid bond was formed between them, founded on affection and gratitude, and which ever after never flagged.

In 1864, when the situation became unbearable, El Hadj Omar decided to send his nephew Tidjani outside the walls to gather reinforcements. He advised Tidjani to go to Doukombo in Dogon country and to seek out his friend, the distinguished Ellé Kossodio, in order to ask for his help in recruiting an army to rescue them. He handed him a great amount of gold in order to facilitate the task, and he appointed three Toucouleur soldiers to accompany him. Then he called my grandfather: "Pâté Poullo, go with Tidjani. You will be of more use to him than I. You once promised to 'take responsibilty' for the bush on my behalf. Today, my wish is that you 'take responsibility' for Tidjani. Go with him and be his guide, his light. Make sure that the way is clear of danger, and then return and tell him what he must do."

El Hadj Omar then took Tidjani's hands, placed them in Pâté Poullo's hands and told him: "Consider Pâté Poullo as your father, just as you do me. He will be your companion and your eyes and ears in the bush. Everything that he tells you to do, you must accept. If he tells you to camp, you must camp. If he tells you to break camp, you will break camp. As long as you are in the bush, follow his advice strictly. But as soon as you reach the city, the initiative will again be yours, as the city is not his domain. I entrust you each to the other, and both of you to Allah, who never betrays."

Favored by a deep, black night and guided by Pâté Poullo, the small group was able to slip out of Hamdallaye and cross enemy lines without being detected. They soon arrived without mishap in Doukombo, at the residence of Ellé Kossodio. Ellé Kossodio began by taking Tidjani to see the great Dogon hunter Dommo, who lived seven kilometers away in the heart of a great basin-shaped plain in a place called Bannya'ara, "the great basin," for elephants would go there to drink. It is in this place that Tidjani would later found the capital of his realm, which the Toucouleurs would come to call Bannyagara and which was one day transcribed into an official register by a French official as Bandiagara, and the name remained.

It was on this occasion, I believe, that an incident took place in which my grandfather was involved and which played an important role in Tidjani's future choice of this place.

As was his habit, Pâté Poullo went out to explore the surrounding bush. When he returned, he found Tidjani resting in the shade of a great balanza tree thick with foliage, while nearby there was a small balanza tree whose thin leaves allowed most of the sunlight to pass through. Compelled by inspiration, Pâté Poullo exclaimed, "What, Tidjani! Your father El Hadj Omar is in the shade (a prisoner, unable to act) and you too are sitting in the shade? Who is going to step into the sunlight for you two? Rise and go sit on the rock lying at the foot of the small balanza tree that you see there. This is not the time for you to sit in the shade, but in the sun." (In Fulfulde, "to sit in the shade" means that one has finished working and may rest; to "be in the sun" means to be at work.)

Tidjani, who always followed Pâté Poullo's advice to the letter whenever the mysteries of the bush were involved, rose and gathered up his saddle and bridle. The Toucouleurs who were accompanying them took offense: "Really

Tidjani? Pâté Poullo treats you like his child! Get up, sit here, sit there!" Without saying a word, Tidjani went and sat down on the rock. Pâté Poullo, who had watched the entire scene declared, "Tidjani, son of Amadou Seydou Tall! You who have accepted to go sit on this rock, I have something to tell you. I give you my word as a Fula from Dienguel, that one day, right here on this spot, you will found a capital city that will be the talk of the entire Niger Bend and from which nothing save your natural death will dislodge you. On that day, I will ask you to give me the land on which this rock sits so that I may be able to build my compound and raise my lodgings."

Four years later, Tidjani would establish and develop on that very spot the capital of his kingdom, where he alone would reign for twenty years until his death. The rock on which he had sat, famous in Bandiagara, is still in the courtyard of the compound that I inherited from my mother, who herself had inherited it from her father, Pâté Poullo.

My grandfather later explained that if Tidjani had remained in the shade of the great balanza tree on that day, and if he had still been there when it came time to perform the Asr prayer (that moment in the afternoon when the sun begins its decline), he never would have become a ruler, nor would he have founded a kingdom in that place. Of course, this is not very logical in the Cartesian sense of the word, but for us elders, particularly for "men of knowledge" (silatigui for the Fulas, *doma* for the Bambaras), logic rested on another vision of the world in which humanity was connected in a subtle and vibrant way to all the surrounding environment. For them, the configuration of things at certain key moments of existence took on a precise meaning that they were able to interpret. *Listen*, it was said in Old Africa, *everything speaks, everything has a voice, everything seeks to communicate its knowledge to us.*

Aided by Ellé Kossodio and his companions, Tidjani succeeded in raising an army of 100,000 men in the region. In the meantime, he learned that Hamdallye had been completely destroyed by fire and that at the urging of his men, El Hadj Omar had ventured out and had cleared a route for himself all the way to Déguembéré, in Dogon country. With his sons and last remaining companions, he had taken refuge in a cave on a mountainside and had been surrounded by Fula and Kounta armies from Timbuktu.

Tidjani pressed onward as quickly as possible in order to extricate his uncle, but when he arrived at Déguembéré, it was too late. Just a few hours earlier, El Hadj Omar had met his demise. For reasons that remain obscure, a powder keg had exploded inside the cave, and he had perished with his companions in the explosion.

Mad with grief and rage, Tidjani led his men in an attack on the Fula and Kounta armies and pushed them back a considerable distance. As he pursued the fugitives, he waged a ferocious crackdown on the land. Following the great battle known as Sebara, where the Fulas of Fakala were vanquished, he gave the order to execute males of all ages who belonged to the important families of the Fula Empire, essentially the families related to Cheikou Amadou, the founder of the empire, and the Bâ and Hamsalah families. At Sofara, in my paternal family alone, forty people were executed on the same day. All of them were my grandfathers, my great-uncles, or my paternal uncles. Only two young boys escaped: Hampâté Bâ, who would become my father, and who happened to be far from the country at the time, and a young cousin whose fate I do not know.

After settling in different cities in the region, Tidjani finally decided to place the capital of his realm in Bandiagara, since the site was well protected. From there, he was able to carry out a series of victorious maneuvers against his enemies. He became the master of the land, although he still had to make war against the pockets of Fula resistance that were scattered throughout the country, and that were supported by the Kountas of Timbuktu. Pâté Poullo, who was in charge of the royal flock, was still at his side. Let us leave him for a moment in order to join the young boy who had miraculously escaped the massacre and who was to become my father.

The Story of My Father Hampâté, the Lamb in the Lion's Den

I have no memory of my father, because unfortunately I lost him at a moment when I had spent only three years in this turbulent world where, like a shard from a broken calabash carried away on the river, I would later float at the whim of the political and religious events that were unleashed by the colonial presence.

One day, when I was about four or five years old, I was playing near Niélé Dembélé, that wonderful woman who had been my "servant-mother" since my birth and who had spent her entire life in the company of my father, when suddenly I turned and asked her, "Niélé, what was my father like?"[8]

Taken aback, she was speechless for a moment. Then she cried, "Your father! A good master!" And to my utter amazement, she broke into tears, drew me to her and pressed me tightly to her breast.

"Have I said something bad?" I asked. "Must we not talk about my father?"

"No, no, you haven't said anything bad," replied Niélé. "It's just that you have moved me by reviving in my mind the memory of the man who saved my life when I was a child by snatching me away from the grip of a cruel and capricious mistress who beat me constantly and barely fed me. Hampâté was not just your father, for by his bounty and his affection, he was also mine.

"You wish to know what he was like? Well, he was of medium build, and well proportioned, and not a sack of meat with puffed out cheeks. He was as quiet as a cavern in the wild bush, and almost never spoke except to say what had to be said. His fine Fula lips lightly revealed his white teeth in a half smile that constantly illuminated his face. But beware! If he fixed his gaze on someone, his male lion's eyes could make that person piss in terror!

"Because you have questioned me today about your father, it is because the time has come for you to know his story."

I sat down next to her, and it was then that for the first time, and from beginning to end, she told the incredible story of Hampâté. His is a story that was told and retold in our family as well as in a good number of households in Bandiagara, for it was as if it had come from a novel. I had already heard bits and pieces of it, but this time, the story was told to me alone, as if to an adult. Of course, I did not retain all of it on that day, but I was to hear it again a good many times over. This is how I am able to insert a number of details, notably historical ones, into Niélé's narrative, details that were likely not present at first.

Niélé began by recounting the circumstances by which, in a single morning in Sofara, I had lost "forty grandfathers," and how Hampâté, who was then only a young boy about twelve years old, had miraculously escaped. He was already an orphan, for he had lost both his father and his mother. On that sad day he also lost all those who would naturally have supported him: the uncles who had replaced his parents, and all his cousins.

Following the executions, the leading Fulas of Fakala were given permission to bury their dead. As they proceeded to identify them, they noticed that the body of young Hampâté was not among the Sofara victims. After making a number of discreet inquiries throughout the country, they learned that the boy was in Kounari, where he was in imminent danger of being discovered, since Tidjani's armies and governors were everywhere.

As soon as their torments began to recede a bit, they held a council. It was of the utmost imperative to save young Hampâté, the lone male survivor of a decimated family, and to find a way to protect him from the fate that threatened him. The Hamsalah family tree could in no way be allowed to die. Had not the venerated founder of the Fula Empire of Massina, Cheikou Amadou, himself once said, "The Hamsalah of Fakala are 'human gold.' If such a thing were possible, I would sow them like plants in order to always have them among us."

On the advice of two Fulas who had rallied behind King Tidjani in Bandiagara, the notables decided to hide Hampâté in the very capital where the king himself resided. He would be sought everywhere, they thought, save in the shadow of the monarch who had condemned his entire family. Who would dream that a lamb would come to take refuge in a lion's den? Hassane Bocoum, a Diawando from Fakala, was given the task of traveling to Kounari to collect Hampâté and take him in secret to Bandiagara to live with a trusted landowner.[9] It so happened that during his sojourn in Kounari, Hampâté had formed a fast friendship with a young Fula boy his own age, Balewel Diko, a descendant of the famous Gueladio, the former *peredio* king of Kounari.[10] This young boy had become so attached to Hampâté that he categorically refused to be separated from him, come what may. He asked his father for permission to join the expedition that was to take Hampâté away. Since our two families were connected, his father accepted.

In Bandiagara at that time there lived an old butcher whose name was Allamodio. He belonged to the *rimaïbe* (sing. *dîmadjo*) class, that is, the class of "house captives," servants tied to a particular family from generation to generation.[11] Given his status as a former dîmadjo of the Hamsalahs, he was entirely devoted to the family. Well, this old butcher, who had taken refuge in Bandiagara, had entered into the good graces of King Tidjani to such an extent that Tidjani had liberated him and had charged him with supplying meat to all the Toucouleurs. My grandfather, Pâté Poullo, who had become the manager of Tidjani's herds, had been instructed to each day place at Allamodio's disposition as many animals as were necessary to serve the needs of the inhabitants. In fact, during the entire length of Tidjani's reign, no single Toucouleur, no single Fula who had rallied to Tidjani's side, nor any member of the royal entourage had to pay anything whatsoever for subsistence. The state supplied their meat and food, and copious meals were offered daily to the poor at no charge.

The organ meats of the animals became the property of Allamodio, who made a good profit from selling them, but he used the money only to help the underprivileged. His generosity was so proverbial that he had earned the nickname of "Allamodio," a word that, in Fulfulde, literally means "God Is Good." Never before had a man so deserved his moniker! His home had become the refuge of those in need, whether they were war orphans or victims of fate who, upon arriving in Bandiagara, knew not where to go nor how to get by. Well nigh thirty young boys and twenty or so indigent adults were living in this way in his vast compound.

King Tidjani, who held him in high esteem, had declared his residence to be sacrosanct. One day, some jealous courtesans had come to tell him, "Tidjani, your head butcher is hosting anyone who asks him for shelter and is doing so without any oversight." Tidjani had replied, "If a man who is my enemy enters Allamodio's residence, even if he does not become my friend, he ceases to be my enemy." Nobody was thus better suited than Allamodio to take in and to hide in his own home the descendant of the Hamsalahs of Fakala, a family to which he had remained viscerally attached. Hassane Boucoum had entrusted Hampâté to him "in the name of all Fakala," strongly advising him never to reveal the child's true identity, for to do so would have been the surest way to send him to the cemetery. Hampâté and his little comrade, Balewel Diko, were given the same instructions for discretion and prudence.

The two friends thus settled in with Allamodio, who taught them the trade of butcher's assistant. For the sons of important families, this trade was somewhat scorned and not considered very suitable, but Hampâté and Balewel were able to overcome their prejudice. Out of gratitude for their benefactor, who had personally taken a great risk in lodging them without revealing their presence, they ardently set to work, fueled by the sole desire of assisting to the best of their abilities their new "father" who was no longer a young man.

Hampâté—unlike me!—could spend an entire day without speaking. "Hello," Goodbye," "Yes," "No," "Don't do that," "Pardon," "Thank you," constituted the essential content of his speech. His serious conduct and his discretion, along with the courage and fidelity of Balewel, touched the old butcher. Soon Allamodio gave them his complete trust and grew to depend on them. He affectionately called them "my hands and my feet."

One fine day, he made Hampâté his treasurer. He gave him the keys to his storehouse and cowries and charged him with making payments and deposits for him in town.[12]

Years went by. Hampâté and Balewel were living peacefully in the most complete anonymity, apparently forgotten by the royal power. Nothing seemed to indicate at that time that one day things could ever be any different.

During this time, Bandiagara had not stopped growing. It had become the renowned and flourishing capital of the Toucouleur kingdom of Massina, masterfully led by Tidjani (son of) Amadou Seydou Tall (whom we will henceforth call Tidjani Tall, to simplify things), while the western part of the old Toucouleur

Empire of El Hadj Omar remained under the authority of El Hadj Omar's eldest son, Amadou Cheikou, sultan of Segou and commander of the faithful.

Over the years, Tidjani Tall's anger and resentment toward those who were responsible for the death of his uncle El Hadj Omar had subsided. Moreover, a good number of Fakala Fulas had rallied behind him. A Fula named Tierno Haymoutou Bâ, who was El Hadj Omar's personal friend and head of his army, now held the position of supreme general of the armies and leader of the council of elders. In particular, he was in charge of the Fulas who had rallied to the cause and who were serving under his command in Tidjani's troops. A great protector of the Fula refugees from Massina and Fakala, Tierno Haymoutou Bâ was able to intervene with the king, and his presence in Bandiagara no doubt persuaded a number of people to join Tidjani's side.

Thanks perhaps to this fortunate influence, and thanks also to the advice of a number of other *marabouts* in his entourage, Tidjani Tall understood that terror does not seat authority on a solid foundation, and that the best means of ensuring peace in the country lay instead in forgiveness and respect for the lives of others, their possessions, and their customs.[13]

Being a highly intelligent man and an astute head of state, he decided to implement a policy of reparation and reconciliation between the Fulas of Massina and the Toucouleurs living in his state. In order to avoid descending into perpetual conflict, he set out to create a veritable fusion between the two communities throughout the kingdom by way of marriage. He enacted a law whereby every Fula woman who had lost her husband in the war would have to marry a Toucouleur, while every Toucouleur woman who had lost her husband in the war would have to marry a Fula from Massina—except, of course, in such cases where, according to the Koran, kinship ties would have forbidden it. He also decreed that no prisoner of war of noble birth, that is, who was free, would be placed in captivity.[14] These laws had such a positive effect on the people, and in Africa the population is always quick to assign nicknames, that they christened Tidjani *Hela hemmba*, "breaker-bonesetter," in other words, "He who breaks something and then repairs it."

A few months after the enactment of this law, during one of his expeditions against remaining pockets of Fula resistance, Tidjani's army took the city of Tenengou and returned with prisoners. Among them was a very distinguished Fula lady from Massina, Anta N'Diobdi Sow, great-granddaughter of the Hamsalahs and a member of the Sammodi family, founder of the city of Diafarabé. She was Hampâté's maternal aunt. Because her husband had been killed during the fighting, in accordance with the new law, she was promised her freedom on the condition that she would agree to marry a Toucouleur.

Anta N'Diobdi was not only of noble lineage; she was also extremely beautiful and possessed a strong personality. Marriage proposals flooded in. She had a number of suitors from among the military leaders, provincial leaders, important marabouts and other influential personages in Tidjani's entourage. Each time, Anta N'Diobdi disdainfully replied, "I will never marry a man whose hands have been blackened and fouled by gunpowder, and who, moreover, is a coward. Only a coward would agree to fight using a gun. To hide behind a tree and to kill from a distance is not really to do battle! Real bravery means eye to eye combat with a spear or a sword, chest to chest! I will only ever accept as my husband a man who has never used a gun. In fact, in Fula women's initiation rites, I am 'Queen of the Milk' and gunpowder and milk do not go well together. The powder would sully my milk."

The rejected candidates considered themselves duly insulted and complained bitterly to Tidjani. This sparked Tidjani's curiosity along with a desire to see this intractable woman with his own eyes and to hear with his own ears the words that had been attributed to her. He sent for her.

"From what I understand," he told her, "you do not wish to marry any of my brave companions because they have supposedly been sullied by gunpowder? Don't you know that, while anyone can take in powdered millet and use it for food, only the brave can take black gunpowder into their nostrils in order to be covered in glory?"

Anta N'Diobdi smiled and lowered her head demurely.

"We are slowly coming to an agreement, are we not, my sister?"

"Venerable King, never have we been so opposed as on this particular point. It goes without saying that you can impose your point of view and even your will on me, but you will never convince me that a man who fights with a gun is as brave as one who attacks his enemy with sword and spear."

This was very bold on her part, since the Toucouleurs who belonged to Tidjani's entourage all fought with guns. Although he had understood this Fula woman's disdainful allusion perfectly, Tidjani did not become angry. He found an excuse for her in the suffering that the loss of her husband and the humiliation of her family members must have caused her.

"Because you abhor those who snort black gunpowder," he told her, smiling, "I also have 'Red Ear' Fulas like you, bred and raised on milk and butter, who would never fight alongside me unless it was with a knife.[15] Among them is someone that I particularly cherish: he is a great silatigui from Dienguel in Senegal who once gave up his herds, his power, and all his wealth in order to follow El Hadj Omar on the one condition that he would help him achieve union with God. He is like a father to me. He is from the Diallo clan and is named Pâté Poullo. My sister, agree to meet him and he will pay you a visit. If you could find him attractive, I would be delighted."

As Fula modesty demanded, Anta N'Diobdi kept her eyes lowered and returned home without responding. A few days later, she received a visit from Pâté Poullo. He was a light-skinned man, tall, solid and well built, who had never fought using any other weapons than spear and saber. She found him to be suitable. "At least," she said to herself, "there is no chance that this one will sully my milk with gunpowder!" It went without saying that the Milk Queen would esteem the Fula silatigui. Their wedding ceremony was performed. From their union six children would be born, and among them was my mother, Kadidja.

During this period, thanks to the protection afforded by Tierno Haymoutou Bâ, a good many Fulas from Fakala had ended up in Bandiagara. Most of them were regular visitors to Anta N'Diobdi's house. Anta N'Diobdi, who had formerly resided in Tenengou, knew nothing of the rescue of Hampâté and thought that he had been killed along with all his family members. One day a griote from Fakala who had taken refuge in Bandiagara came to pay a visit.[16] In the course of their conversation, the griote declared, "Your nephew Hampâté is in Bandiagara."

"Hampâté? That is not possible. He is dead."

"No, he is alive. If you do not believe me, talk to Mamadou Tané, the confidant of all the refugees from Fakala."

Anta N'Diobdi sent for Mamdou Tané. "Is what they are telling me true?" she asked him.

"Yes. Hampâté is very much alive." And he told her of the circumstances by which the child had escaped the massacre and how he had been taken to Bandiagara. "We had been ordered," he added, "to hide him with Allamodio and to ensure that he was living in the most complete anonymity. And until now, this is what we have done."

Overwhelmed at hearing this news, Anta N'Diobdi immediately sent someone to look for her nephew. When she saw him cross her threshold, she cried for joy. She wanted to know everything about how he had been living. Hampâté told her his story.

Anta N'Diobdi gave thanks to God for having allowed at least one male member of her family to survive, and then quite naturally asked her nephew to come and live with her. To her astonishment, the young man refused. "Mother," he said, "I am sorry, but I must stay with Allamodio. This old butcher has become my father and my place is with him. I cannot abandon him." Although it was against her wishes, Anta N'Diobdi could do nothing but allow him to leave.

The immense joy that she had felt was suddenly marred by something that she could not bear and that gradually began to eat away at her, for her nephew, the only surviving descendant of the Hamsalahs, was living at the lower rank of a poor butcher's assistant and doing so in complete anonymity. That night, she did not say a word to her husband about the encounter, but from that day forward, the sadness that overcame her was so strong that she could no longer eat or drink. She stopped laughing and spent her nights moaning and crying, softly singing sad songs about her family's misfortunes.

Pâté Poullo soon noticed this change and began to worry. At first he thought that it would pass, but after weeks went by, he decided to break his silence. "Anta," he said, "you have changed. You are no longer the same. You seem to regret our union. And yet, I belong to a lineage that is as pure as yours. The king honors me with his trust and friendship. I am not an insignificant person in Bandiagara. As for my material wealth, I am well-off. You have one thousand head of cattle at your disposal, and I manage twenty thousand head of the royal herd. Indeed, my entire fortune is in your hands. Do what you want with it. Be happy, make me happy, and spare me from hearing my rivals crow disparagingly, 'We knew all along that Anta N'Diobdi would never be happy with Pâté Poullo!' And if by misfortune my tenderness and my wealth are incapable of making you happy and that at whatever cost you must withdraw the hand that you have so generously given me, then say so. I may be able to survive that shame and misfortune. Even if my heart is desperate, it will be with a smiling mouth that I will say, 'Ask me for a divorce if you wish,' and if you do ask me, I will allow you to leave. But never, never, ever, will my mouth open itself on its own accord to say 'I divorce you.'[17] And yet, know that if you must leave one day, that day will mark my entrance into a darkness beyond death and the beginning of an endless night."

Receiving no response, Pâté Poullo arose, seized his spear, and left the house as though in a dream. Anta N'Diobdi remained slumped and motionless. When Pâté Poullo returned very late that evening, he found that his wife was still lying where he had left her upon leaving. He approached and took her head gently into his hands and pressed it to his chest. Her face was swollen and she had been crying. Overwhelmed, Pâté Poullo said, "Anta, even if I were not your husband, in my capacity as *bi dîmo*, a noble and well-born Fula, I have the right to your trust and I must help you and support you in your pain. I beg you, speak to me!"

Anta N'Diobdi, who had let down her long Fula hair, finally raised her head. She pushed back the tendrils that were hiding half of her face, and in a weak voice unburdened her heart.

"Yes, it is true," she said, "that I am carrying a painful weight, but it is not because of you! Under no circumstances should you think that I am unhappy with you, quite the contrary! Our meeting was a fortunate one. But what has been gnawing at me for a month, what makes my nights sleepless, my days unbearable, my food bland, and my drink insipid, is an affair that concerns my family's honor, an affair as delicate as it is grave."

"What can this affair be, Anta?"

"You know that my family from the Fakala belongs to one of the Massina families whose male descendants, young and old, were condemned to death by King Tidjani Tall, and that forty members of my family were executed on one single day in Sofara."

"Yes, alas, I know!" cried Pâté Poullo. "Unfortunately, the laws of war are more akin to the reflexes of ferocious beasts than to the actions of normal human beings."

"It so happened that two boys were noticed to be missing from among the bodies of the men of my family. Well, I have just discovered, in this very neighborhood, right here in Bandiagara, one of the surviving boys. He is my very own nephew Hampâté, the son of my deceased sister. He is in hiding with Allamodio, the king's chief butcher, and lives in complete anonymity. Nobody knows who he is. What sends me into despair is to see a descendant of the Hamsalahs, the hope of my country and my family, living without a name in the degrading proximity of a butcher's shop. For almost a month now, I have been struggling to become accustomed to the idea, but to no avail. I have hesitated to speak to you about this, because I did not want a misunderstanding or a subject of disagreement to develop between you and King Tidjani. But because you insist on knowing about the cause of my sadness, I will tell you everything. In truth, I can no longer bear this situation. So here is what I have decided. Whatever happens, I am asking you to take my nephew Hampâté to King Tidjani and to reveal his true identity, so that everyone can know who he is. You will beg the king, on your behalf, or on my own, as you see fit, to safeguard the life of my nephew. If he refuses, you will ask him to have Hampâté executed immediately so that his soul may join without delay those of his fathers who have preceded him into the other world, where he will perhaps be no worse off than here."

Pâté Poullo stared at his wife. His face seemed to stiffen, and he began to sweat profusely. "Do you realize what you are exposing your nephew to?" he asked.

"Yes, I know. I have purposefully chosen death for him rather than anonymity, which is another way to die. I would rather see him dead and buried under his real name, than to see him live with no identity. And I would also like you to tell Tidjani this: 'If he has my nephew executed, I would understand his act, and I would not even condemn it.' It is the law of war. If I myself, by a reversal of fortune, were to become his conqueror, I would not hesitate to cut his throat. But I ask him the favor of saving the body of my nephew from the 'drag of degradation' reserved for the condemned so that I may bury him honorably."[18]

Pâté Poullo did everything in his power to curb his wife's resolve and to dissuade her from such a dangerous undertaking, but in vain. He summoned Hampâté to his house and informed him of the decision taken by his aunt and asked for his opinion of the situation.

Hampâté, who was only seventeen or eighteen years old at the time, responded, "My mother, Anta N'Diobdi, my only remaining parent, has every right over me, including the right to life or death, and it would be out of the question for me to refuse the fate that she has chosen for me. I owe her respect and obedience. Here in Bandiagara, it is she who attends to my family's honor. If she feels that I must die in order to save that honor, then let me die!"

"By Cheikh El Hadj Omar's prayer beads!" cried Pâté Poullo, "If Tidjani knew the true mettle of his enemies, he would be a thousand times more on the alert than he is now!"

"We are not the personal enemies of Tidjani Tall," interrupted Anta N'Diobdi, "but we will defend our land and our honor. An enemy can be vanquished physically and sent into slavery, but no one will succeed in taming his soul and his mind to the point of impeding his capacity for thought."

Faced with such determination, Pâté Poullo had no other choice but to take Hampâté to see the king and to implore his clemency. He chose a Friday on which to do so, as it was the Islamic holy day and the day on which Tidjani was accustomed to performing numerous good works and according pardons. The following Friday, after attending the great communal Friday prayer at the mosque, Pâté Poullo and Hampâté, followed by Balewel, who had decided to share every aspect of Hampâté's fate, headed toward the palace. Pâté Poullo was among the very restricted number of notables who could enter the royal palace at any hour of the day or night. He had only to pronounce the current password to the guards. Thanks to this open sesame, the three companions crossed unhindered through three well-guarded vestibules, and then went to wait at the foot of the stairway that led to the private apartments of the king on the floor above.

A bit later, Tidjani returned from the mosque where he had lingered. As soon as he saw Pâté Poullo, his face broke into a large smile. "Ah, here is my father Pâté! May this Friday be a day of good fortune for us all!"

"May God hear you, O Tidjani, son of Amadou, son of Seydou Tall!" replied Pâté Poullo.

Tidjani glanced inquisitively at Hampâté and Balewel. "What brings you to me, father Pâté?" he inquired. "I will wager that you have come to present these handsome young men to me." And he began to walk toward the stairway.

"Yes, I have come to present them and to plead for the cause of one of them, the one named Hampâté. His companion is called Balewel Diko, and he has decided to share Hampâté's fate, come what may."

Tidjani began to climb the stairs, drawing Pâté Poullo, whose hand he was holding, along with him. "What fault has this young man committed?" he asked.

"I will tell you once we have reached the audience chamber," replied Pâté Poullo. And he signaled to the young men to wait for him below.

When they reached the great hall, Tidjani went out for a moment in order to remove some of his clothing. He returned shortly, wearing a simple *tourti* (ample under boubou) and wide pants, and then comfortably settled in. To receive a visitor in this guise was to demonstrate his trust and the extent of his familiarity with Pâté Poullo.

"Well," he said, "what crime has your protégé committed?"

"It is a crime that is not his fault. His crime is to have been born into the Bâ family of the Hamsalahs of Fakala. Because of this he falls under the death sentence that was decreed against all the male members of his family. Now he has become my nephew by marriage, because I married his aunt Anta N'Diobdi."

"Ah! He is the nephew of that Fula woman whose beauty and courage I so admired!"

"Yes, and it is she who has forced me to come here and present him to you, regardless of the consequences."

Pâté Poullo then faithfully recounted to the king everything that his wife had said. "I have thus come here, *Fama* [King], to ask you to spare the life of Hampâté who, from now on, is my child to the same extent as my firstborn son."

Tidjani remained silent for a good long while and then said, "Father Pâté! This is the second time that I have run up against Anta N'Diobdi, this male soul lodged in a woman's body. You will tell her that I myself am going to adopt her as my aunt, first because she is your wife, and also because she is one of those who have a sense of honor and a religious respect for it. As for Hampâté, I will think of him as a temptation that God has placed on my path to see how far my vengeance could carry me. If the hundreds of enemies executed in Sofara, Fatoma, and Konna have not avenged the death of my father El Hadj Omar, the additional death of this young man will certainly not avenge it! My dear Pâté, rest assured. I accept your request, and I am publicly sparing Hampâté's life. However," he added, smiling, "let me tell you something. Ten days after his arrival in Bandiagara, I had already been informed of his presence. I would be a very sorry excuse for a leader if I did not know what was happening in my kingdom or, what's more, in my own city. I did not want to bother Hampâté since I had considered that God himself had placed him in my care. It did indeed seem unconscionable to hide the condemned within the very confines of he who had pronounced the sentence.

"Now that Hampâté, who was my uninvited guest, has become my cousin—since he is your nephew—I am going to make a donation: I give him the amount necessary to pay a dowry and marry a woman, a spacious compound, a horse and bridle, a gun, seven spears, a halberd, a sword, a piece of blue guinea cloth sixty cubits in length, a piece of white cretonne cloth, a starched Haussa turban, a pair of embroidered boots, two pairs of Djenné slippers, and ten milk cows. Finally, I would like him to join my army in the ranks of the Fula troops commanded by Tierno Haymoutou Bâ. Then he will no longer be an anonymous butcher's assistant."

Pâté Poullo was as happy as a Fula whose cow has just given birth to a female calf! Unable to throw his arms around the king's neck, he bowed deeply before him in thanks.

The king pulled him up. "Please, Pâté, there will be no such gestures between us!"

Hampâté and Balewel, who had remained at the bottom of the stairs, were invited to ascend. Pâté Poullo informed Hampâté of the pardon that had been accorded by the king and the rich gifts that had been bestowed upon him. Then he informed him of the king's wish that he join his army under the command of Tierno Haymoutou Bâ. With downcast eyes, Hampâté remained silent for a moment, and then he said, "I thank God and King Tidjani Amadou Seydou Tall for having accorded me my life. I am very honored by the king's generous gesture, and I thank him from the bottom of my heart. But concerning my enlistment, may I be permitted to tell him that there are three things that I will never allow myself to do. First, to take up arms against the people of my country, that is, against the Fulas of Massina; second, to take up arms against King Tidjani himself, who, rather than cutting my throat, has opened his arms magnanimously and has showered me with gifts; third, to abandon the old butcher Allamodio, who has been a real father to me. I have vowed to stay by his side in order to serve him until my death or until he dies."

Following these words, there was an oppressive silence that seemed endless. Pâté Poullo feared the worst. But far from being angry, King Tidjani exclaimed,

"Wallahi! By God! Noble blood speaks! Loyal young man, you deserve the respect and admiration of everyone, including the king." And extending his hand to Hampâté and Balewel, he told them, "Go out and live in Bandiagara as free Muslims, with all the rights due to the Toucouleur citizens of our city!"

The king did not leave Balewel empty handed. He gave him a horse, a gun, a halberd, seven spears, and three costly garments.

In the company of the two young men, Pâté Poullo returned home. Radiant and proud as a conqueror returning from battle, he gave his wife the good news. Anta N'Diobdi's joy was immense. But when her husband informed her of the three things that Hampâté had told the king that he would never do, she almost stopped breathing! The idea that her nephew would continue to work as a butcher's assistant with Allamodio was stifling. She took a moment to regain her composure, but finally she gave it some thought and said, "And yet, it is more shameful to be ungrateful than to be a butcher's assistant."

She turned to Hampâté. "Go," she said, "return to Allamodio, and serve him, I accept. My soul will cry about it every day out of chagrin, but my reason will dry the tears that family pride will make me shed. When it is honor that makes a sacrifice acceptable, then the sacrifice becomes sublime. You have chosen to live in opaque obscurity although a grand and radiant sun is offering to shed its rays upon you. May the Lord take note of your conduct and give you sons who will glorify your name!"

(Here ends Niélé's narrative. What follows has been reconstructed from stories handed down in the family by the main actors or witnesses to this story, in particular Balewel Diko.)

Still seconded by his faithful companion, Hampâté thus continued to live with the old butcher Allamodio. Shortly after his reinstatement, he founded the first association (*waaldé* in Fulfulde) of young Fula men from Massina in Bandiagara. Subsequently, thanks to the encouragement of the king, who had looked favorably upon this initiative, his waaldé was expanded to include boys of diverse backgrounds. Indeed, much later, this association would play an important role in Fula and Toucouleur politics in Bandiagara, since it favored the good relations envisioned by the king between the Toucouleurs and Fulas of Massina.

Years passed. Allamodio, who had become quite old, depended more and more on the two young men in order to carry on his business. Hampâté was no longer just in charge of the finances. He was also a buyer throughout the countryside, for Allamodio and for himself, of animals whose meat was resold for their common benefit.

As soon as the Fulas of Fakala, who were mostly herders, learned that the heir to the Hamsalah was out of danger, in order to help him, they began to send him their animals to be slaughtered. Over the years, Hampâté became a trusted intermediary between the herders of a particular region in the Niger Bend, on the one hand, and the livestock merchants in Bandiagara, on the other. From his various activities, he drew a comfortable revenue, generally using it to purchase unfortunate captives, especially children, in view of freeing them or improving their lot. He acted both out of natural generosity and out of religious duty, in accordance with the command and the example of the Prophet Mohammed himself.

Over the course of his life, Hampâté purchased fifteen captives. He freed six of them, while the remaining nine refused to leave him. He treated them rather more like his adopted children than as his servants. Among them, there were two he had saved from cruel masters and whom he particularly cherished: Beydari and Niélé Dembélé. Niélé Dembélé, a Mianka from the San region in Mali, would later become, for my older brother, Hammadoun, and myself, the most attentive and tender of "servant-mothers," while Beydari, my father's trusted confidant, would be named by my father as he lay on his deathbed, as his only heir and leader of the entire family!

Beydari had been captured at the age of about eleven or twelve at the taking of Bousse (locality in the district of Tougan in today's Burkina Faso). Since slavery had not yet been abolished in the French colonies, the child had been given as a gift to an indigenous noncommissioned officer in the French army, who took him to Bandiagara and sold him to a griot of the Talls named Amfarba. Amfarba had assigned him to work at his wives' household chores.

To say the least, the poor boy had not ended up in a charitable environment. From the first call to prayer at dawn until late at night, sometimes even until midnight, he worked without pause, carrying out tasks that were beyond his physical capacity. He fed himself on leftovers and from what he could scrape from the bottoms of cooking pots. After two years of this life of famine and fatigue, walking about half naked and sleeping on the ground (and during the dry season, the nights are very cold in this region), the poor fellow had nothing but skin on his bones. After walking through stagnant water, he had caught the "Guinea worm," a parasite whose larvae accumulate in the lower parts of the legs where they wait further contact with water in order to escape. His feet and ankles were swollen beyond measure. In spite of his condition, one of Amfarba's wives sent him one morning to the market one kilometer away, under a leaden sun. His legs were so swollen and painful that the boy could not take twenty steps without searching for some rare patch of shade where he could cool his bare feet, burned by the overheated earth. Seeing that he had not returned on time, Amfarba's wife went to complain to her husband. She accused the boy of being nothing but a lazy, disobedient child who was no doubt entertaining himself along the way. Anger overtook Amfarba. Seizing his whip of hippopotamus hide, he rushed out to find the boy, whom he soon met. With a full basket on his head, Beydari was walking slowly, dripping with sweat and crying out at every step.

"You are a sluggard, lazy, and disobedient!" shouted Amfarba. "This will help you stretch your legs!" And he began to whip the poor boy with all his might. As he tried to run, the swellings in the boy's legs burst open before the larvae were ready to come out. In spite of the blood that began to trickle from the child's feet, Amfarba continued to beat him.

It was then that Hampâté, who was returning from the mosque, providentially appeared from around a bend in the road. The boy ran to him, crying, "Oh Papa, save me, save me! He is going to kill me! He is going to kill me!"

And he threw himself into Hampâté's arms, just at the moment when Amfarba was going to strike a blow that would certainly have knocked him unconscious.

Hampâté caught Amfarba's hand in midair. "You brute!" he exclaimed indignantly. "Have a heart! Would you treat your own son or relative in this manner? This child suffers as you suffer. He is a human being and has a mother and father somewhere is this world."

Enraged, Amfarba replied, "In that case, if you care so much about him, buy him!"

Hampâté took him at his word. "Fine! Name your price!"

"One hundred thousand cowries," replied Amfarba.

Hampâté removed a carnelian ring from his finger and handed it to Amfarba. "Take this ring to Ousmane Djennonké and tell him that I said to give you one hundred thousand cowries. He will ensure that the ring is returned to me."

Then he picked up the basket containing the provisions that the child had bought and handed it to Amfarba. "Carry this to your wife," he said. "This boy is no longer your captive!"

Hampâté took the boy home. As soon as they arrived, he baptized him "Beydari," a name that means "increase" or "benefit" as in "benediction." Then he cured him. When the child was healed, he gave him suitable clothes to wear. Beydari was expecting to be ordered to carry out certain tasks, but to his great surprise, my father simply told him, "Go out and play with other boys your age."

In truth, Beydari did not always heed this recommendation because he liked to stay by my father's side. He followed him everywhere and never went to play with his friends until my father's work was done. It was during that time that he made friends with a boy of the royal family, young prince Koreïchi Tall, and that he joined his young people's association. Here is one example of the gestures that illustrate my father's approach. Before buying new clothes for Beydari, as was the custom on the eve of important Muslim feasts, he would first inquire what the young prince would be wearing. Once informed, he would buy the same for Beydari.

Seeing that Hampâté treated Beydari like a son, old Allamodio decided to consider him as his grandson. And this is how Beydari learned the butcher's trade, which he practiced his entire life.[19]

Meanwhile, King Tidjani had passed away. His power, which had come into being in 1864, had been maintained in all of Massina until his death in 1888. As we know, he had carried out massive executions at the beginning of his reign. He had uprooted entire villages and groups of people and had installed an entire local administration, but he had continued to be at war with pockets of resistance. Yet in the long run, things had become relatively calm, and finally, this man who had been baptized "breaker-bonesetter" became perhaps one of the most effective leaders to have reigned in the Niger Bend. Just as he had been implacable in his conquest, thanks to his keen understanding of local politics, he showed that he could be an enlightened leader in his kingdom. There is a saying that is still current in Massina that goes, "When Tidjani arrived, the people cried, 'Wororoy en boni Tidjani wari!' (Oh! We're in for it now, Tidjani is here!) But at his funeral, the same people shed tears as they proclaimed, 'Wororoy en boni Tidjani mayi!' (We're in for it now, Tidjani is dead!)."

Hampâté was no longer a young man when he married his first wife, one of his cousins, named Baya. Their union remained sterile. This was an unfortunate situation, since all Fakala and Pemaye were counting on Hampâté's children to regenerate the Hamsalah tree. Prominent Fakala Fulas who had taken refuge in Bandiagara took it upon themselves to consult marabouts, soothsayers, and fortune tellers of every ilk in order to know whether their hopes would be fulfilled. The oracles were unanimous. Baya would never carry Hampâté's fruit, as their respective procreative "spirits" were deemed incompatible. These unhappy predictions had an influence on Baya's mood. She became bitter and almost unbearable. She could no longer tolerate having anyone in her presence. She could barely tolerate her own shadow. Finally, she went too far.

One evening when Hampâté was away, Balewel Diko, his longtime friend, arrived at Baya's house accompanied by a few friends belonging to their association. He asked to dine. Baya could not refuse since it was the custom of the association members to dine each night at the home of one of its members. The wives of the members were accustomed to this, and in any case, in large African families there was always enough food prepared so as to accommodate last-minute guests or visiting strangers. Baya had the dinner brought out but kept muttering, "Ah! How unfortunate I am to be the wife of a vagabond who forgets to return home at dinnertime! I am neither a slave nor a lowborn woman to be treated this way by an inconsiderate husband. Really, I have had enough of this Hampâté!" And either intentionally or by an involuntary reflex, she uttered an oath targeting Hampâté's deceased mother. At a time when an insult to a person's mother constituted the most serious of offenses and was settled at spear- or knifepoint, this was indeed singularly inappropriate, and all the more shocking because it had been uttered in the presence of her husband's friends. In truth the affront was unpardonable.

Balewel, for whom Hampâté and himself were one and the same, and who considered Hampâté to be his alter ego, exclaimed indignantly, "What Baya! Do you dare to insult Hampâté's mother in my presence? I would rather have heard your mouth insult my own mother rather than Hampâté's. Don't even think about doing it again!"

"And what if I did," retorted Baya, "would the heavens fall from the sky to the earth? Would the mountains vomit the contents of their fiery bellies?"

"It will be none of those things," replied Balewel, "except for the death of your marriage to us."

"With whom, 'us'?" said Baya incredulously.

"With us, Hampâté and Balewel."

Baya withdrew the insult with a snicker. Outraged, Balewel shouted, "Leave this house! I divorce you!" With these words, all Hampâté's friends rose as if they were a single man. They left the house without finishing their meal, an extremely serious gesture in Africa, where to not consume a woman's food is a sign of rejection and rupture. This clearly meant, "All Hampâté's friends have divorced you."

Baya entered into an indescribable fury. She rushed into her room and rapidly gathered all her clothes and household utensils into large bundles, which she then had taken to the vestibule that sheltered the entrance to the house. She spread out a mat and sat down, waiting for the return of her husband. Upon returning home, Hampâté, who knew nothing about the incident, found his wife sitting erect under the vestibule next to her baggage, apparently waiting for no one knew what. As we have seen, Hampâté was neither demonstrative nor loquacious. Without straying from his usual composure (his friends said that he was as calm and quiet as peanut oil), he began by greeting his wife, and then asked, "What are all these packages? What is going on?"

"What is going on is that your little friend and god Balewel Diko has divorced me in your name and on your account. Therefore, I have packed my things and I am waiting to hear whether you confirm that decision."

"If my little friend and god Balewel Diko has divorced you," Hampâté calmly replied, "then consider yourself divorced." And without one more word, he stepped into the house.

In dismay, Baya broke into tears. She requested that her baggage be transported to her parents' house, which was done that very night by Hampâté's servants. The next day, when the news spread throughout the city, nobody faulted Balewel or Hampâté. Modern minds will probably find this difficult to understand. How could it be acceptable for a man to make the decision to "divorce" his friend's wife and have the friend accept it as a fait accompli without further discussion? The answer lies in the fact that in the old days, a true friend was not someone "else," he was oneself, and his word was our word. True friendship counted more than kinship, except in matters of succession. This is why tradition recommended that one have many friends, but not too many "real" friends. Moreover, relatives had the same privileges. A brother, father, or mother could "divorce" a man in his absence, and in general the man in question would oblige. It cannot be said that this was a custom, since this did not happen frequently. If it did occur, it was accepted, since such a decision was not taken lightly. If the reverse were true, the community, family, or village could oppose the decision.

2

Kadidja, My Mother

If I had followed the rules of African decorum, this work would have opened with the story of my mother. This would be so even if I were merely following the Malian adage that proclaims, "Everything that we are, and everything that we have, we owe but once to our father, and twice to our mother." We say that a man is nothing but a distracted sower of seeds, whereas a mother is considered to be the divine workshop in which the creator has a direct and unmediated hand in the formation and development of a new life. This is why, in Africa, mothers are respected and elevated almost to the level of divinity. May my mother forgive me for not having begun this narrative with her tale in spite of everything that I owe her. But chronological order has its laws. At least she will play an essential role from here to the very last page of this work.

Hampâté had suffered so much with his first wife that he could not bring himself to remarry in spite of the pressures to do so that were brought to bear by his entourage. In fact, in those days, African society had no respect whatsoever for celibacy, for it was thought to be evidence of immaturity or selfishness. Bachelors had no "right" to speak in gatherings of elders; this privilege could only be "lent" to them. They were not given any positions of authority, not even that of neighborhood headman.

A number of matches were proposed, but Hampâté refused them all. Time was passing. Thus, Anta N'Diobdi finally suggested that he marry her own daughter, Kadidja. He agreed, but because his cousin had not yet reached marrying age, they had to wait a while.

Hampâté's greatest concern was to have children. A marabout in Bandiagara named Wourma Abdou, who was famous for his divinatory gifts, told him one day, "I do not see many children in your destiny, but I see that you will have many grandsons and great grandsons. Here is my advice: first adopt a young captive. This adoption will open the door to paternity for you."

It was at that time that Hampâté took in Niapandogoro, a young female captive who was nursing a two-month-old baby. He adopted the baby and named her Baya. From that day forward, Niapandogoro's only task was to nurse her baby and to watch over her. As for the baby, Hampâté took care of her himself. He bathed her, took her for walks, took her to the market, and had her sleep with him at night in the manner of African mothers. He was both her father and her mother.

Later, the infant would be named Nassouni, and we will meet her many times more in the course of this story, because even after she married, she never left my mother, Kadidja, nor my own wife, Baya. Nassouni was with my family when she died in 1983 in Bamako.

Kadidja's Dream

It was around this time that young Kadidja had a dream that would mark her deeply because of the predictions that issued from it and that came true, one after another, throughout her life. In this dream, she saw the Holy Prophet enter the courtyard of her family's home. He told her to go and get her brothers and sisters and to come and share with him a large meal that her mother had prepared. They all took their seats around the dish and ate until there was nothing left. Then, keeping Kadidja's brothers and sisters by his side, the Prophet raised his eyes to look at Kadidja and ordered her to leave. When she awoke the next morning, she was overwhelmed by a feeling of self-disgust and fell into a dark and silent mood. Her father did not think much of it, but her mother began to worry. "What is wrong, my dear Kadidja?"

Kadidja told her about her dream, and then added sadly, "If God's Prophet has kept my brothers and sisters at his side and has sent me out all alone, it must be because he found me unworthy of staying with him. I will be cursed for the rest of my life as a coarse and unlucky person who does not deserve the company of God's Envoy." And she burst into tears, sobbing in her mother's arms.

Distraught by her daughter's anguish, Kadidja's mother did not take the dream lightly. "Take heart," she said, "your uncle Eliyassa Hafiz Diaba is a great marabout who knows the science of the interpretation of dreams. He is supposed to come to see me today, after the Friday prayer at the mosque. He will be able to discover the true meaning of your dream."

When the uncle arrived, Anta N'Diobdi told him about her daughter's dream. He questioned Kadidja concerning everything that she had done during the day and the evening in order to determine that nothing that she had done had influenced her dream. He then ordered her to go and purchase some raw cotton, clean it, and spin it herself, and then go and sell her skeins at the market. With the profits from the sale, she was to then go and purchase a beautiful new mat and put the rest of the money aside.

When everything was ready, the uncle returned. He dipped a reed pen into a special kind of ink and covered the mat with letters, symbols, and verses from the Koran, arranged in a specific order. He then advised Kadidja to eat a very light evening meal and to take a ritually prepared bath before going to sleep on the mat in the very same house where, in her dream, she had eaten her meal with the Prophet and her brothers and sisters.

Kadidja did everything that her uncle had told her to do. The next day, her uncle took the mat, carefully examined what was left of the symbols that he had drawn, and then had it washed in order to erase all remaining traces of ink.

"Go immediately and give this to a poor person," he told Kadidja. "Give away all the remaining money, and then come back. I will wait for you here."

Upon her return he made the following predictions, which were based on different parts of her dream as well as on the marks that he had observed on the mat. "My niece Kadidja will outlive all her relatives. She will inherit from all her brothers and sisters, because she will be the last to die at the end of a very long life. None of her brothers or sisters will have children. She will marry twice. From her first marriage, she will have three children. It will be difficult for them to live, but if one survives, that will suffice. He will be an important source of support for her. Her second marriage will ruin her. She will give six children to her second husband, but these children will be rather more of a burden for her. Kadidja will encounter great difficulty throughout her life. But she will triumph over all her enemies, male or female, and she will overcome all the painful events that will occur over the course of her life."

With the passage of time this surprisingly detailed prediction came to pass in even the tiniest detail.

As Kadidja grew up, adored by her parents, she truly was "daddy's little girl." Not only was her father, Pâté Poullo, the intendant of the royal herd, but in addition, in remembrance of the "Hamdallaye drop of milk," he had received a permanent gift of one thousand head of cattle from King Tidjani, which were always replaceable in case of loss for whatever reason. It thus goes without saying that the family lived comfortably.

Pâté Poullo had given Kadidja an almost masculine education, but without removing any of her femininity. Beautiful, joyful, full of life, willful, and even, it must be said, a bit stubborn, she promised to be an assertive woman who would be difficult to resist.

She had created and was the leader of a waaldé for young women that included all the most noble and beautiful girls of her age in Bandiagara. It was at this time that she was given her first nickname, *Djandji*, "joyfully provisioned." Later, she would be called *Poullo*, "Fula woman," in the sense of "noble woman," which became *Flamousso* with the Bambaras. Because of her uncommon force of character, she would also come to be called *Debbo tiiom timba*, "woman in pants." Her first son, Hammadoun, would call her *Dadda* (which must have been a deformation of Kadia, diminutive of Kadidja), a name that continued to be used by members of the family and that would come to be used by all the children of Bandiagara.

By age twelve, she had already received marriage proposals from almost all the important Toucouleur families of Bandiagara. Her mother had refused at least twelve formal offers. All the important men in the kingdom who had once wanted to marry Anta N'Diobdi now wished to win Kadidja's hand for their sons. When they learned that Anta N'Diobdi had decided to give her daughter to her nephew Hampâté, that Fula from Fakala who continued to live with a butcher, they took it very badly. For them, not only was Hampâté a stranger, he was also an enemy. They violently opposed this proposed marriage and sought to prevent it by any means possible.

None of this helped to bring peace to poor Hampâté, who became the target of jealous suitors who never missed an opportunity to provoke him. But Hampâté was not a wisp of straw that could be broken between a thumb and an index finger, and backing him up were the forty members of his association, who were ready to die on his behalf and who would give a good thrashing to anyone who dared to utter a malicious word about him.

Neither was Anta N'Diobdi a woman who was easily swayed. Fortified by her husband's trust, along with support from the king's favorite wife, she persisted through thick and thin. Finally, when Kadidja had reached an acceptable age, the wedding took place.

Kadidja and Hampâté: A Rocky Marriage

Furious, the prominent members of the kingdom who had been spurned swore to do everything in their power to ensure that the union between Kadidja and Hampâté remained childless and unhappy. Although such activities were forbidden by the Koran, they mobilized marabouts, tiers of knots, throwers of hexes, and sorcerers of every ilk in their quest to smite the marriage and render it childless. In spite of this coalition, Kadidja gave birth to three children: a girl named Gabdo and two boys: my older brother, Hammadoun, and yours truly. However, truth be told, Gabdo lived only for six months, and my brother Hammadoun, a boy who had received his fair share of every gift of the mind, heart, and body, met a tragic death at about fifteen years of age. Finally, as Uncle Eliyassa had proclaimed, I was to be the sole survivor of the union between Kadidja and Hampâté.

If we believe the notation inscribed on my legal documents, I was born in Bandiagara "around 1901." But after doing some cross-checking, I am now rather inclined to think that my birth date is between December 1899 and January or February 1900 (because it took place at the height of the cold season)—more likely at the beginning of 1900, because apparently I was born during the year in which Aguibou Tall traveled to France, a trip that took place in 1900. Thus, there is every indication that I am rightfully placed among the ranks of the "elder sons of the century."

At the time of my birth, my grandmother Anta N'Diobdi happened to be in Taykiri (a locale close to Mopti and at a distance of about seventy-six kilometers from Bandiagara), where she had followed her herds in search of new pasture. As soon as Kadidja had reached the end of the forty-day period during which a new mother must not leave her house, she wished to join her mother in order to present the baby to her, as custom requires, and to rest a bit by her mother's side.

I was still too little to be carried on my mother's back, as African women do. So my mother procured a large calabash, lined it with linens and soft, warm cloth, and laid me inside as though it were a cradle. My servant-mother, Niélé, placed the calabash on her head and we set out. This is how, at the count of just around forty-one days of being present in this world, I began to travel. And since then, I have never stopped, except when fatigue and old age finally forced me to sit still, around the year 1982.

During our journey, the temperature dropped to such a degree that I apparently almost died. Kadidja remained with her mother for about two or three months, and then she brought me back to Bandiagara.

The birth of three children and the death of little Gabdo had not appeased the hatred felt by the enemies of the Hampâté-Kadidja couple. In fact, these events even seemed to have added fuel to the fire. The "war of the spells" continued. Every day, knotted cords or malicious talismans were found in the house, put there by people, we knew not how, who had been able to get in. They were everywhere: in the courtyard, in the bedroom, in the bathrooms, in the kitchen, and even in the cistern, where sometimes frogs were found to have been attached. Very often in the morning, Pâté Poullo came to tell Kadidja, "Be careful, there is something here today." And that was always the case.

As time went by, was it that the spells took their effect, or did the heavy atmosphere of animosity weigh on the marriage? Or quite simply was it the result of a great difference in age and temperament, Kadidja being young, vivacious, and playful, and enjoying an animated social life, and Hampâté, who almost never spoke, being much older and more serious? In any case, one fine day, Kadidja was gripped by a kind of repugnance toward her husband. She could no longer tolerate him. She fled the conjugal household as though it were ridden with plague and repeatedly returned to her parents. Curiously, however, as soon as she was at a distance from Hampâté, she spoke only of him and of his qualities. But as soon as she returned home to him and entered his presence, she felt a violent need to run away from him.

Each time, sick at heart, her father and mother took her back to Hampâté. They were set on keeping their word to him, and they also did not wish to lose face or become the laughingstock of those to whom they had refused their daughter's hand. But Kadidja had only one idea in mind: to leave Hampâté, no matter what the consequences for herself or for the reputation of her family.

After her parents took her back to Hampâté, she was so despondent and so unhappy that little by little she lost her appetite and the will to live. She who had been so joyful and affable became irritable and morose. Everything irritated her. It was then that Hampâté, concerned for Kadidja's very life, decided to give her back her freedom.

He convened a family council. When everyone was present, he declared to his in-laws, "I know, as do you, that Kadidja does not hate me at all, but rather, she has fallen under the influence of a powerful spell that neither you nor Eliyassa Hafiz Diaba, nor I myself can succeed in undoing. If you continue to wish to impose my presence upon Kadidja, I fear that she will fall gravely ill, or even commit an irreparable act. So, I prefer to see her alive and happy in someone else's house than ill and unhappy under my own roof. Please allow me then, without any rancor, to restore her freedom in order to safeguard our family ties, which must remain solid and intact, come what may."

This is how, out of affection for Kadidja, Hampâté divorced her amicably, all the while remaining attached by indissoluble ties, because not only was she his cousin, the daughter of his only close relative from Bandiagara; she had also given him his two boys, who were the joy of his life.

This separation, which became effective upon our return to Bandiagara, coincided with a period of deep mourning for Kadidja, for she then lost both her father and her older brother, Amadou Pâté.

As he often did, Pâté Poullo had gone out with his herds into the bush to the east of Bandiagara. He could not stay for long in Bandiagara without regularly returning to his world, the natural world where, for him, everything was alive, everything spoke and had meaning. It was there that he passed away, taking his secrets and most of his traditional knowledge with him. Nevertheless, he had taught a certain amount of it to my mother, since she was also, as was her mother, Anta N'Diobdi, "Queen of the Milk."

My father Hampâté died just short of three years after his separation from Kadidja. Since she had remarried in the meantime, he had insisted that I stay with him. I was therefore about three years old when he died, and my brother, Hammadoun, was about five.

As I have already said, on his deathbed, my father named as the only heir of all his possessions and head of the family not one of his children—we were in any case too young—but Beydari. Never was trust placed in better hands! For us, Beydari was, on every occasion, a devoted tutor, an affectionate older brother, and a scrupulous manager of the family's wealth. In addition to my brother and myself, the family included Beydari and the eight other "captives" (rimaïbé) whom we had inherited and who had never wished to leave us. Among them was Abidi Hampâté (they all shared my father's name), our dear Niélé, and young Nassouni, whom my father had raised as his own daughter.

Beydari and his companions had been given the task of raising us, educating us, and defending us, and that they did, as God is my witness! Hammadoun and I were most certainly the happiest "young masters" in all Bandiagara. The faithful friend Balewel Diko did not leave us either. It is largely thanks to his stories, added to those of Niélé and Beydari and then to those of my mother, that I was able to reconstruct this entire narrative.

As soon as I was old enough to understand her, Niélé never tired of telling me about my father, and tears filled her eyes when she spoke of the great generosity that he kept hidden behind his outward taciturnity. His house, she said, was always open to anyone. He was a good listener and never contradicted people, but his piercing gaze sometimes troubled his interlocutors, so much so that some of them preferred to speak with him through an intermediary, as custom allowed. Happily, his smile would attenuate the troubling effects of his gaze. He could become terribly angry, but only in serious cases, for example, in the face of flagrant injustices committed by the powerful against the weak. Throughout his life, he gave money away more than he lent it, because he did not like to ask for the repayment of a debt. He had charged his "captives"—it would be more accurate to call them his children—with teaching us piety, probity, generosity toward the poor and infirm, and respect for the elderly. As for our religious education, he had insisted that it be placed in the hands of Tierno Bokar, a close family friend about whom I will say more later.

That was my father Hampâté, who should have died but who instead lived, who refused the honors offered by a king in order to continue in the service of an old butcher, and who preferred to give a beloved woman her freedom rather than see her live unhappily by his side. May God welcome you into his mercy, Hampâté, my father, and may the weight of the earth be light upon you!

Kadidja and Tidjani

My mother had scarcely recovered her freedom before all the formerly defeated suitors—most of them were Toucouleurs of the Tall clan, that is, the clan of El Hadj Omar and his son Aguibou Tall, who was King of Bandiagara at the time—returned again to ask for her hand. It was then that Tidjani Amadou Ali Thiam, who had not been among the first group of rejected suitors, solicited Kadidja's hand and was chosen by her.

The Thiams constitute another Toucouleur clan, and they are the traditional rivals of the Tall clan, which did not make things any easier. Tidjani Amadou Ali Thiam was, as his name implies, the son of Amadou Ali Thiam, who was at the time the chief of Louta, the largest and richest province of the Toucouleur kingdom (located in today's Burkina Faso). That meant that he was a prince and the presumed heir to a chief's "turban." It was not for this reason that Kadidja chose him. She did so because she already knew him quite well. Tidjani (whom I will call Tidjani Thiam for the sake of simplicity) was in fact the inseparable friend of Bokar Pâté, Kadidja's older brother, and of Tierno Bokar Tall, a young man from a family of marabouts who was entirely devoted to religious life and who would later become my spiritual teacher.

When Tierno Bokar, who was himself a great-nephew of El Hadj Omar (in Africa we would say that he was his "grandson") had arrived in Bandiagara with his mother in 1891, in flight from the advancing French army, he had been "adopted" (in the African sense of the word) by Tidjani Thiam's father, who considered him as his own son. It was at this time that a close friendship between Tierno Bokar, the young Tidjani Thiam, and Kadidja's brother, Bokari Pâté, was born. The friendship was so close knit that in all Bandiagara, they were known only as the "inseparable three."

Tierno Bokar had struck up a friendship with my mother, Kadidja, whom he called "little sister," and indeed throughout her life my mother fulfilled the role of little sister for this holy man. But this little sister role was somewhat unusual. Because she was always frank and direct, she took the liberty of speaking freely to him in a way that no one else in Bandiagara would have dreamed of doing. She asked him the most pointed and direct questions—something rarely done in Africa—and she did this at the urging of Tierno Bokar himself.

I was born, so to speak, into his hands. He came to see my parents almost every day. As soon as he arrived, he called for me. When he prayed, he placed me on his lap. When he took a nap, he laid me against his chest. And when he walked in the courtyard, he set me on his shoulders, to my great delight, and sang religious poems to me, in particular, the religious poem composed by El Hadj Omar entitled "The Barque of the Blessed." My mother later told me that he loved to entertain me and make me laugh. With others, I was apparently a somewhat distant child, for those who held me in their arms could not get me to look at them. But when Tierno picked me up, I would gaze at his face and burst into laughter.

As the close friend of my uncle Bokar Pâté, of my mother, and also of my father Hampâté, he was, according to African tradition, their brother, and hence my uncle. But he would become much more than that throughout my life. He would be my spiritual father, the one who would mold my mind and my soul and the one to whom I owe everything that I am today.[1]

In choosing Tidjani Thiam to be her second husband, my mother thus knew whom she was dealing with and did not go outside the circle of friends who were dear to her. For his part, Tidjani Thiam liked Kadidja very much and admired her qualities. It was this reciprocal love that helped them achieve a successful marriage and keep it intact through thick and thin, despite the succession of tragic events that they would have to face.

Kadidja's decision had scarcely become public before a firestorm of protest burst forth. Rejected for the second time, the Talls were furious at having been passed over in favor of a Thiam, since for generations these two important Toucouleur families had been in more or less constant rivalry when they were not downright hostile toward one another. No matter what the position of a Tall, a Thiam had no regard for him. If one of them did something, the other would do the same or try to surpass him. On the battlefield, never would a Tall or a Thiam try to flee if a member of the rival clan were present. For members of both clans, to die a thousand deaths was preferable to losing face before their rivals. Very serious incidents that pitted the Thiams against King Aguibou Tall concerning the chiefdom of Louta stretched this clan rivalry to the breaking point. In this climate, Kadidja's choice was felt to be a veritable provocation.

It was during this time that Tidjani's father, who had been chief of the province of Louta for just two years, died suddenly. Being the older son of Amadou Ali Thiam, Tidjani thus inherited the turban of Louta—although not without some difficulty, caused by King Aguibou Tall—and left Bandiagara for his new residence, accompanied by a brilliant entourage and his two wives: his cousin and first wife, Kadiatou Bokari Moussa, granddaughter of the king of Konna and the daughter of a military leader; and Diaraw Aguibou, daughter of King Aguibou Tall. Since the wedding with Kadidja had not yet taken place, Kadidja remained in Bandiagara.

Unfortunately, by virtue of an all-too-common attitude in Africa, which holds that no death nor any illness is ever considered to be "natural," but is instead thought to be caused by someone, there was a public outcry against my mother. Tidjani's wives, along with most of the members of his family (particularly the female ones), attributed the sudden death of Amadou Ali Thiam to the ill fortune brought on by Kadidja. "What!" they exclaimed to anyone who would listen, "Tidjani has barely asked for the hand of Kadidja Pâté, and already his father has died! What will happen to the family when Kadidja Pâté joins us?"

Tidjani, who loved my mother deeply, turned a deaf ear. From his location in Louta, he continued to make arrangements with the two families in order to finalize the marriage. The process took more than a year. When the wedding was finally celebrated, Tidjani was still in Louta, while my mother was in Bandiagara. But this was not a drawback, since, according to custom, the couple was not obligated to be present at the ceremony. It sufficed that ritual presents, such as the dowry and kola nuts, be exchanged in the presence of prominent witnesses and religious figures and that these prominent men recite the appropriate verses of the Koran for the marriage to be, as we say, "knotted" or "tied up." In fact, it was this custom that sometimes made it possible for some parents to "knot" a wedding even in the absence of their child.

As soon as the ceremony had concluded, Tidjani's first act was to officially adopt me, since his wives had not given him any sons. In the administrative documents containing his official information, he named me as his "first son," and therefore his eventual successor. This deed was one for which his family never forgave him and was generally condemned by all Toucouleurs, whether

Talls or Thiams. They could not understand how one of their own could have chosen a Fula and, even worse, a descendant of the Bâs and Hamsalahs of Fakala to succeed him. As for his wives, they declared war to the death on my mother, who, according to them, was behind my intrusion into the prerogatives that were supposed to be reserved for the Toucouleur conquerors alone.

My father Hampâté (this occurred shortly before his death) had reacted quite badly upon learning that Tidjani Thiam had officially adopted me while he himself was still alive. As his natural rights allowed, he would not permit me to be taken to Louta. Despite my father's opposition and the hostility of the Toucouleurs, my name remained in Tidjani Thiam's documents, since for the French colonial authorities, the will of a provincial chief (and therefore a "canton chief," in their eyes) was law. Although I remained under the tutelage of my paternal family alone, officially, I was still Tidjani Thiam's "first son" and thus the heir apparent to the turban of Louta.

Meanwhile, my grandmother Anta N'Diobdi, who had returned to Taykiri near Mopti, fell gravely ill and died. Accompanied by her two brothers, Bokari Pâté and Hammadoun Pâté, my mother traveled to Taykiri to take care of problems relating to the estate. Niélé accompanied her in order to care for me. For the second time in my existence, I completed the trajectory Bandiagara–Taykiri, but this time I was not perched atop Niélé's head in a great calabash but rather was tied to her back in a more conventional fashion.

Kadidja found that all her mother's affairs were in order, because her mother had had time to formulate her will in consultation with an eminent marabout who lived in that town. My mother would later report its terms as follows: "I want my children to know that I personally have divided the wealth that I leave behind, so that they do not argue and do not part ways over the inheritance. I ask that my sons gather around their sister, Kadidja, and that they serve as a shelter to her in times of trouble. My little captive Batoma has neither father nor mother beyond me. In losing me, she loses everything. My soul and my spirit will curse anyone from my family who makes Batoma suffer. From henceforth, she will carry my family name, Sow, and I will not sleep happily or peacefully in my grave if anyone makes her suffer. I leave ten thousand five-franc coins to my daughter, Kadidja, so that she may be able to settle in comfortably with her husband while impressing her cowives who are both princesses."

In addition to this fortune, my mother inherited a herd of two hundred thirty-eight head of livestock, out of the seven hundred head left by her mother, in addition to a case full of gold and silver jewelry. Rich was she as a result and thus found herself free from all material worry, while emotionally she was overwhelmed by a succession of unfortunate events that struck her with the regularity of a ticking clock. She had just divorced her husband, a man who was also her cousin, and whom she liked, but whose presence she could paradoxically no longer stand; she had lost her father and then her older brother, Amadou Pâté; Tidjani Thiam had scarcely asked for her hand, instantly turning all his relatives into her enemies, before he lost his own father; and the wedding had barely taken place before she lost her own mother, Anta N'Diobdi.

That was a lot for one woman to bear. But the worst was yet to come.

The Toïni Revolt

While my mother was preparing to join her husband in Louta, a revolt broke out in Toïni, a city in the province that fell under the authority of Tidjani Thiam. The consequences of this revolt would be so dramatic for Tidjani that they would cause him to be deported and put into prison, while my mother and I would spend years in hardship and exile far from Bandiagara. "You were three years old," my mother would tell me, "when I became Tidjani Thiam's third wife. I was preparing to join my husband, when one morning, at around ten o'clock, like a carrier pigeon bearing bad news, a messenger gave King Aguibou Tall a letter from Tidjani that was intended for the district commandant, informing him that a riot had broken out in Toïni in Louta province."

Before proceeding further, a brief historical note is necessary in order to explain the chain of events that would lead to the extremely severe sentence that was handed down to Tidjani Thiam. In fact, Tidjani Thiam was the indirect victim of acts that were tied to events that had taken place well before his birth and that were linked to the ancestral animosity between the Tall and Thiam clans, to the point that it was said of them, "They can live neither together nor apart without fighting."

Following El Hadj Omar's death in 1864, when his nephew Tidjani Tall established the Toucouleur kingdom of Massina, he assigned the leadership of the country, with a few exceptions, to the three principal Toucouleur families: the Talls, the Thiams, and the Ouanes. The leadership of Louta province fell to Ousmane Oumarou Thiam, uncle of Tidjani Thiam.

King Tidjani Tall died during the year 1888. In 1893, French troops under the command of Colonel Archinard seized Bandiagara, which for two years had been under the rule of Amadou Cheikou, elder son of El Hadj Omar, who had come to take refuge in the city following the capture of Segou by the French. Amadou Cheikou would later engage in a series of desperate battles in the region, but he was outmatched in men and in arms and was gradually forced to withdraw to the region of Sokoto (in the north of today's Burkina Faso), where he died around the year 1897. Of the vast empire founded by El Hadj Omar, only the eastern Toucouleur kingdom of Massina founded by Tidjani Tall remained, and it no longer had a leader.

A shrewd political strategist, Colonel Archinard did not want to immediately eliminate Toucouleur power, whose administrative structures and hierarchies could, at least for a time, be useful to him. He put into place a clever compromise by proposing that the government of the French Republic "name" as king of Bandiagara another of El Hadj Omar's sons. This was Aguibou Tall, former king of Dinguiraye (Fouta Djallon), who had rallied to Archinard's cause sometime earlier and had arrived in Bandiagara at his side. This proposal was accepted by Paris, and this is how Aguibou Tall became king of Bandiagara—by virtue of a decree issued by the president of the French Republic, which had itself cut the throat of its last king!

Aguibou Tall was much criticized for rallying to the French, but if truth be told, it is thanks to him that a good number of human lives were saved during a period when, in any case, there was no longer any hope for the Toucouleurs against the superior French army. Thanks to Aguibou Tall, a good number of Toucouleurs who had been taken prisoner at the capture of Segou, Nioro, Djenné, Bandiagara, and Douentza were liberated. Family leaders who wished to return to Fouta Tooro in Senegal, or Fouta Djallon in Guinea, were repatriated under military protection. There is no doubt that without the mediation of Aguibou Tall, the Toucouleurs would have faced a much more painful destiny.

Eminently intelligent and cultivated, the new king possessed undeniable qualities, but unfortunately, he was filled with a tenacious rancor toward the Thiams, whom he had never forgiven for destroying a small mosque, in faraway Fouta Tooro, that El Hadj Omar's grandfather had built in the courtyard of his home. He thus took a rather dim view of the spectacle in which the forever insolent and rather sarcastic Thiams were enthroned at the head of the richest province in the land, and he seized the first possible pretext to try to cut them down.

A rather disrespectful poem concerning Aguibou Tall had been circulated at some point, and he attributed its authorship to his nephew Ousmane Oumarou Thiam, head of Louta province, who had been put into power by King Tidjani Tall himself. Ousmane was the son of one of Aguibou's sisters. Out of respect for his maternal uncle, and in order to bow to the wishes of his mother who had perhaps hoped for a pardon, Ousmane did nothing to defend or protect himself. Alas, he was executed following a shameful public lashing. The Thiams reacted so strongly to this that it was feared they would rebel. King Aguibou Tall was able to avoid this worst case scenario only by naming another Thiam to head the Louta province, Amadou Ali Thiam, cousin of Ousmane and father of Tidjani, Kadidja's future husband. All this occurred around the year 1900.

Amadou Ali Thiam was not a man who could be impressed by a Tall, king or not, and the speech he gave during his investiture ceremony had done nothing to appease matters. A short time after that, an unfortunate horse race, in which two of Amadou Ali Thiam's coursers insolently defeated the king's favorite horse, only served to poison the atmosphere. A storm was brewing, but it never had time to manifest. Amadou Ali Thiam passed away only two years after his investiture.

Tidjani Thiam, the eldest son of the defunct chief, inherited the turban of Louta. However, he still needed to be officially named by the king during the traditional investiture ceremony. Aguibou Tall delayed the ceremony for such a long time that some even thought that he wanted to take over the chiefdom himself. Finally, pushed into action by the French authorities, who feared that there would be an uprising, he resigned himself to naming Tidjani Thiam as head of the province. As a peace offering and as a sign of honor, he even gave Tidjani Thiam the hand of one of his daughters in marriage, Princess Diaraw Aguibou Tall (Diaraw meaning daughter of Aguibou of the Tall clan). Such gestures were frequent in those days, and a refusal would have constituted an unforgiveable offense. Even as these events were unfolding, the process leading to the finalization of Tidjani's marriage to my mother were under way.

Tidjani Thiam moved to Louta accompanied by a particularly brilliant court. As his principal coadjutor he had his young brother Badara (Amadou Ali) Thiam, the most popular young man of the realm, whose praises were sung far and wide by his griotes. Tidjani's other brothers also followed him, in case their assistance would be needed. Almost all his comrades from his waaldé age group association also joined him in Louta, where he showered them with gifts. His longtime friends Tierno Bokar and Bokari Pâté also accompanied him, but as they were called back to Bandiagara by their obligations, they did not stay long.

Unfortunately in Louta, Tidjani did not have a good adviser who could call for moderation in times of trouble or who could suggest that he take a diplomatic approach. He had only a marabout named Tierno Kounta Cissé whom Amadou Ali Thiam had named *cadi* (judge). But he was not very well educated and did not know much beyond the Koranic texts. His influence on Tidjani during times of trouble was not always for the best, and in fact, he would later share in the misfortunes and exile of his protégé.

Tidjani Thiam's own education left him ill-prepared to assume such a delicate function as that of provincial chief, as it required mediating between the local populations, the king, and the colonial authorities. According to the customs of Toucouleur seigneurs, his father, Amadou Ali Thiam, had raised him with an iron hand, forcing him to live and work among the captives, stable boys, and peasants so that he would thoroughly understand the lives of his future subjects and also be prepared for any future hardship. "I am making you live like this today," he would say, "in anticipation of what tomorrow may bring." The fact remains that Tidjani had barely spent any time with any seigneurs or courtiers, and he was much more familiar with fieldwork and horse care—he was an exceptional horseman—than he was with the ceremonial and *savoir vivre* of princely courts.

Like any good peasant, he was unworldly and rather hard-headed. He attached religious, if not superstitious, value to his word. In his view, to lie or to contradict himself was not only a sign of cowardliness, which was beneath him, but a grave sin against divine law.

It is thus an understatement to say that he was little prepared to face the political ruses of his enemies! On top of that, he was not good with money. He considered it as vulgar dross and squandered it carelessly. These various character traits would, when the time came, cause him great difficulty.

On one fine day in 1902, Aguibou Tall, who had been named king by the good graces of the French Republic, was purely and simply deposed by a new decree from the president of this very same Republic. France had deemed that the time had come to take on the direct administration of the country through its own representative, a colonial administrator named as district commandant by the governor of the territory, who was then in residence in Kayes, Mali.

Aguibou Tall no longer held the title of king, but he remained the traditional chief of the Toucouleurs, who continued to call him fama (king), and official instructions were given to handle him with kid gloves. The district commandant had been given orders to consult with him and to take his opinions into account concerning the country's general political issues. Politically speaking, the French Republic had cut the fama's throat, but it had not dared, as it had done to its own last king, to cut off his head. It preferred to allow him to die a slow death.

As soon as King Aguibou Tall was deposed, those of his court who had been present only because they had been drawn there by the gifts and honors they had received took their leave. A number of them went to Tidjani Thiam's court in Louta. It was then that the griots and the somewhat brazen captives began once again to recite the poem that had led to Ousmane Oumarou Thiam's death sentence. This unfortunate conjuncture cruelly fanned the flames of the fama's bitterness and added fuel to the fire of the Tall-Thiam feud. The consequences of this would fall heavily on the shoulders of Tidjani Thiam. The Toïni revolt would serve as the detonator.

Every year, it was the duty of the provincial leaders (who had subsequently become canton leaders following the administrative reform and the deposing of the king) to collect, on behalf of the colonial administration, taxes levied on the populations. The job went with the position. This tax was known as a "capitation," or head tax, because it was calculated according to the number of "heads" that were in each family. This was indeed a most unjust form of taxation, because a family, whether it was rich or poor, was taxed according to the number of its members alone. Indeed, this tax was known as "the price of one's soul." He who was unable to pay it could not live in peace. Either he was sentenced and imprisoned, or, in order to procure the necessary sum, he was forced to sell or pawn his belongings if he had any, or even his own children, a practice which, alas, became commonplace at the time.

Toward the end of the year 1902 (or during the year 1903), just as the marriage between Tidjani and Kadidja had finally been "tied together" by the two families and as my mother was preparing to join her husband, a serious incident arose in the province of Louta. Not all the taxes had come in. The shortfall had occurred in a region populated by the Samo people, who, it must be said, had just undergone a very difficult year of farming. They refused to pay the tax and openly rebelled. Tidjani Thiam informed the Bandiagara district commandant, who at that time was Commandant Charles de la Bretèche. The commandant sent him a troop of fifteen native *tirailleur* infantrymen, who had been ordered to collect the taxes by any means whatsoever, for the governor of the territory had absolutely demanded it.

Tidjani immediately went out on campaign, followed by the fifteen native tirailleurs, his marabout and adviser Tierno Kounta Cissé, a number of friends and courtiers, and his brother and coadjutor Badara Thiam, who was also constantly accompanied by his own retinue of friends and griots.

The large Samo town of Toïni, which had already stood up to the administration's authority, was the prototype of a fractious village. Tidjani Thiam entered the town and settled in, firmly intending to leave only once the last franc of the tax was paid. At the time, the material upkeep of tax collectors (food and lodging) was the responsibility of a town's inhabitants. It was a very heavy burden. In order to avoid it, the villagers conferred and decided to hide their livestock so that they would not have to provide meat to the little troop of Toucouleurs. Only a single animal remained in the village, a very handsome white billy goat who sported the beard of a patriarch and whose neck was adorned with a number of necklaces made from the teeth of wild animals and other hunting trophies. This was the "house billy goat"—or rather the animal mascot—of Tombo Tougouri the Fierce, a young hero whose exploits in hunting as well as in battle were praised, retold, and sung about in all the surrounding villages.

An unhappy fate had it that upon seeing this superb, plump billy goat pass by his front door, Badara Thiam had it killed in order to feed his friends. When Tombo Tougouri returned from the hunt, blowing on his trumpet to announce his return, he was surprised to find that his beloved billy goat had not come running to meet him. He looked everywhere for him. The villagers did not dare to tell him what had happened. Finally, one of them mustered the courage to reveal his goat's ignominious end. Tombo Tougouri did not say a word. He went and picked up his bow and his quiver, which held three arrows with poisoned points, placed his ritual cap trimmed with lion's skin upon his head, donned his battle tunic decorated with hunting trophies, and still without saying a word, marched straight into the Toucouleur encampment. The Toucouleurs were seated with Badara Thiam under a vestibule in a courtyard and were listening to music. Tombo Tougouri approached, glanced around the courtyard, and spied the head of his goat tossed carelessly into a corner. He burst in upon them, furious. "Who gave the order to kill my goat?"

"I, Badara Thiam, did. What do you have to say about it?"

"I have to say that you had better stand up because your mother has given birth to a corpse.[2] You will not live longer than my goat, and your soul will accompany his."

And the young man rapidly loaded his bow with three arrows and took position to shoot. Seeing that he was in danger, Badara rushed toward his horse who was standing nearby, untied him, and bridled him. But before he had time to jump into the saddle, Tombo Tougouri called out, "Badara Thiam, if you are not afraid, turn and face me!"

The dominant flaw of the Toucouleurs and the Fulas is a sometimes quite illogical temerity. Hence, instead of taking cover, Badara Thiam turned and ran toward Tombo Tougouri with no other weapon in hand than the reins to his bridle. He had not advanced more than a few steps before Tombo Tougouri fired his three arrows: the first struck his chest, the second his belly, and the third his groin. At the force of the blows, Badara stumbled, but he still had the strength and the courage to break the shafts of the arrows, and with the barbs planted in his flesh, he jumped onto the back of his horse, a famous courser named Nimsaali.

Meanwhile, Tombo Tougouri had been able to hit eight others, three of whom died moments later. But he did not have time to take cover either. Charging him on horseback, Badara commanded the horse to rear up, sending Tombo Tugouri reeling so that he landed a few meters away. Immediately, the Samo archer was overpowered and tied up like a bundle of wood. As for Badara, exhausted by this prodigious show of strength, he tumbled from his horse and expired almost immediately.

The calamity had occurred in a low-lying area of the village. Dismayed by the inevitable consequences that would soon follow, the Toucouleurs withdrew to higher ground, where Tidjani Thiam and his companions were staying. They gave him an accounting of events and announced the death of four people, among them his brother Badara Thiam. At this moment, the Samo war cries were echoing all around them, announcing an immanent attack. Upon hearing Tombo Tougouri singing their war song at the top of his voice, the Samos arose in unison as if they were one man, and, in order to free him, charged on the district where Tidjani and his men were staying.

The sergeant in command of the infantry was ready to stop the Samo avalanche with a salvo, but Tidjani opposed him. He gave the order to let them advance. He climbed to the rooftop terrace so that all the Samos could see him, as they were familiar with his marksmanship. Never had one of his bullets missed its mark, and they knew it. He started shooting in order to stop them from getting within an arrow's reach. If he hadn't done so, it would not have taken them more than six hours to wipe out the entire Toucouleur camp. Then he called for a retreat to Louta, where his fortified palace would offer certain shelter as they waited for events to unfold.

Between Toïni and Louta was a distance of about ten or twelve kilometers. Tidjani Thiam and six of his armed captives took charge of covering the retreat.[3] The Samos did not dare to approach too closely, but they continued to shoot arrows at the convoy anyway. Tidjani succeeded in incapacitating all those who came too close, wounding about twenty people. He did not wish to cause a massacre while waiting to receive further instructions.

Upon reaching Louta, he and his troops took refuge inside his palace and ordered the doors to be closed. There were enough provisions on site to last a very long time. The Samos of Toïni were able to cause an uprising in the entire region except for two districts in Louta. In addition, groups of Fulas around the country who had remained faithful to Tidjani helped him to the best of their abilities.

Tidjani immediately wrote a detailed report of the events and sent a messenger to deliver it to King Aguibou Tall in Bandiagara, with the request to rush it on to the district commandant for a decision. The report was written in Arabic, but in those days, every district commandant had an interpreter of Arabic on hand. Tidjani thus naïvely placed his fate in the king's hands. However, due to administrative reform, Tidjani's status as canton chief meant that he was answerable only to the district commandant. If he had sent his message directly to the commandant, there would have been no repercussions. But it did not even occur to Tidjani to do this, and nobody who was close to him advised him to do so.

It took the messenger two and a half days to reach Bandiagara. "Like a carrier pigeon bringing bad news," to repeat my mother's expression, he reached the town before the noon hour on the third day. He went immediately to Aguibou Tall to deliver the message and emphasized the urgency with which it was to be transmitted to the district commandant. "Every moment lost is one step closer to death for Tidjani Thiam and those who are with him."

And yet, the king did not transmit the report. It was only at about four o'clock in the afternoon, as he was going to the mosque for the afternoon prayer, that he announced publicly that Tidjani Thiam and his men had been attacked by Samo rebels and that there were four deaths, Badara Thiam among them. The mosque immediately emptied out. The death of Badara, who had been beloved in Bandiagara, provoked great sorrow in everyone. Cries and lamentations soon erupted in almost every compound in the city. Alerted by the clamor, Commandant Charles de la Bretèche sent someone to Aguibou Tall's residence to inquire about the cause of the outcry. Meanwhile, the captain and military commander of the region sounded the alarm and mobilized a company in preparation for possible trouble. Uprisings were still very much feared at that time, since Bandiagara mountain had not yet been entirely subdued and the Toucouleurs were known for their warrior traditions.

King Aguibou Tall went in the company of several dignitaries to the residential palace and finally gave Tidjani Thiam's report to the district commandant. It was almost five o'clock in the afternoon. The commandant chastised him sharply for having waited so long to transmit the news. He had only heard indirectly of the siege of Louta by Samo rebels, a grave event. Aguibou Tall got angry. He pointed out, correctly by the way, that since he had been deposed from his functions, he was not at all obliged to communicate anything whatsoever to the district authorities concerning political events in the region.

Commandant de la Bretèche, who knew Tidjani and even felt a kind of fondness for him, understood the extent of his great political inexperience, since nothing had obligated him to go through Aguibou Tall. But he also knew that the former king was to be handled with care. The instructions from the governor were categorical on this point.

He asked Aguibou Tall to prepare the fifty Toucouleur *goumier* infantrymen that were stationed in the city for war. And with the consent of the garrison's captain-commandant, he promised to send two sections of tirailleurs and a squad of district guards as reinforcements, along with all the ammunition they would need. He gave the order to send these men to Louta to protect Tidjani and to tell him not to take any further action and to wait for the army to arrive on the scene. The army would be carrying instructions from the governor that Commandant de la Bretèche would solicit by telegraph. It goes without saying that the content of this kind of conversation, which would have taken place in the presence of one or more indigenous interpreters, did not remain secret for long.

It was late in the evening when Aguibou Tall and the district commandant parted company, each with his own ulterior motive in mind. The next day, as King Aguibou Tall had ordered, the war drums began to beat and the cylindrical metal bell was rung in alarm. Bandiagara awoke and entered a state of war. The Toucouleurs were quite up in arms over what had happened. For them, Badara's little finger was more valuable than fifty Samos!

In spite of the recommendation by Charles de la Bretèche that the expedition make haste, it did not leave Bandiagara until rather late in the afternoon. The king had placed his second oldest son, Tidjani Aguibou Tall (Tidjani, son of Aguibou Tall) in charge of leading it. Before his departure, he had given him a verbal message, to be passed on to Tidjani Thiam, that ostensibly contained the commandant's instructions. Tidjani Aguibou Tall left Bandiagara at the head of his men. They advanced rapidly, and the convoy arrived in Louta in two days' time. Their arrival spread panic among the Samos, who fled Louta and took shelter in several fortified villages around the region, firmly intent on putting up a fierce defense.

As soon as he arrived, the son of Aguibou Tall took Tidjani Thiam aside and gave him his father's message, in these approximate words, as Tidjani later reported them to the commandant, and then after that, to my mother and to his friends and family: "Tidjani Thiam, my father, Aguibou, has asked me to tell you that he has obtained from the commandant that you be sent tirailleurs, guards, goumiers, weapons, and ammunition. He has done his duty. Now you must do yours and avenge Badara and his companions so that never again will a Samo dare to touch a hair on any Toucouleur head and, even less, make any attempt on their lives."

Not a word was said about the district commandant's instructions to wait. These instructions would not be known until later! Encouraged by the verbal message transmitted by the son of Aguibou Tall himself, Tidjani Thiam believed that he had the authority to punish without delay his brother's killers and to put down the rebellion. Leaving aside the tirailleurs and district guards, who were part of the colonial army, he sent only the Toucouleur goumiers to pursue the fugitives across the entire Gondougou region. The large villages tried to resist, but the enraged goumiers won the day. The repression was terrible. The principal villages were ransacked and there were many deaths. The survivors were captured and brought to Louta in chains.

While this drama was unfolding in the province, Commandant Charles de la Bretèche was making his way toward Louta, accompanied by King Aguibou Tall and their entourage. En route, Aguibou asked the commandant, through the interpreter Bâbilen Touré, what the governor's instructions were.

"I received the order," replied the commandant, "to hold talks with the Samos in order to try to bring them to see reason, and to use force against them only as a last resort, in the event they are unwilling to listen."

The king smiled. "If I know the Thiams, their insubordination, and their spirit," he said, "Tidjani Thiam will not wait for such a protocol. As soon as he has the goumiers on hand, all of them Toucouleurs like himself, he will avenge his brother and his companions and will cut the Samos down, or I don't know the Thiams!"

"How dare he go against the instructions that I told you to give him!" exclaimed Charles de la Bretèche.

"Mon Commandant, the Thiams have never taken the Talls seriously enough to obey their orders," replied Aguibou.

Charles de la Bretèche privately told the interpreter Bâbilen Touré of his concerns (thanks to him, my family would later learn the content of these conversations). "I hope," he told him, "that Tidjani has not rushed headlong into the trap that I suspect the old king has laid for him!"

When the convoy arrived in Domoni, about ten kilometers from Louta, the commandant decided to spend the night there. If they left the next morning, they would arrive in Louta at around lunchtime.

Did Aguibou suspect that Charles de la Bretèche was not at all convinced that Tidjani Thiam would undertake such repressive action of his own accord? Did he worry that his own son, to whom he had given the verbal message, may have let the cat out of the bag through his own probity? For whatever reason, after dinner, he sent a rider on a fast horse to Louta to ask his son to come and speak to him. The young man arrived at Domoni toward midnight. The father and son met. Nobody knows what the father said to the son, but the resulting chain of events can give us an idea. The young man left in the middle of the night and arrived in Louta before daybreak. He shut himself inside his room and did not come out until the arrival of Commandant de la Bretèche and his escort. Nevertheless, his nocturnal expedition and meeting with his father had not gone unnoticed in Domoni, as it was later discovered.

After leaving Domoni, the commandant got wind of what had happened in the province, but it was only upon arriving in Louta, where he found almost one thousand men and women tied with their hands behind their backs and unceremoniously thrown out in the sun in the main square, that he obtained definitive confirmation of what he, until then, had refused to believe. Before even dismounting from his horse, he ordered the immediate release of the prisoners and ordered that they be given food and medical treatment. "Who ordered this terrible punishment?" he cried angrily. Without waiting for a reply, he turned to his interpreter. "Bâbilen! Go find Tidjani Thiam and tell him to come with you to see me immediately. We must speak in private." And he went up to the first floor of the palace.

When the commandant was face-to-face with Tidjani, he shouted unceremoniously, "Who gave you the order to put down the rebels before my arrival?"

As he awaited the translation of this question, Tidjani felt himself turning to stone. "Mon Commandant," he replied, "my father Aguibou told his son to tell me that he had obtained from you tirailleurs, guards, goumiers, and ammunition so that I could repulse and punish the Samos who killed my companions. I was not told to wait for your arrival."

The commandant nodded his head, and then turned to the interpreter. "Tell Tidjani Thiam that he has just been stupidly had by a man who has never forgiven his adversary. Tell him that I never gave him the order to shoot, and that, quite to the contrary, I gave the order to wait for my arrival and to do nothing. Now he will have to state publicly and in the presence of the king himself what he has just told me, otherwise he is lost, socially and politically."

Tidjani, who believed in the notion of *n'dimaakou* (the strict observation of the duties of nobility, of justice, and of morality that were de rigueur for the Fulas as well as for the Toucouleurs), was sure that he could count on the testimony of the king's son. He reassured the commandant. "Do not worry. Tidjani Aguibou Tall is an extremely noble spirit. He will confirm the message. His nobility would not allow him to lie in public."

Tidjani still did not know that Aguibou's son had spoken secretly with his father during the night in Domoni, and that he had returned before dawn, in all likelihood having received firm instructions. Indeed, if he had publicly revealed the exact content of the king's oral message, the king could have been held responsible, or equally responsible, for what had taken place.

The commandant, the interpreter, and Tidjani Thiam all went back down to the palace courtyard where talks were being held. A temporary office had been set up under a large tent. The commandant settled in with King Aguibou, while Tidjani Thiam, his cadi Tierno Kounta Cissé, the interpreter Bâbilen Touré, and several prominent men from the Fula and Samo communities also took their places under the tent.

The commandant took the floor. "Interpreter! Ask Tidjani Thiam, Chief of Louta province, who gave him the order to subdue the insurgents, since the orders that I had sent him by way of Aguibou Tall—who, fortunately, is present here—were to wait for my arrival before attempting to take any action."

"Mon Commandant," replied Tidjani Thiam, "my namesake, Tidjani Aguibou Tall, who is present here, transmitted a verbal message from our father, King Aguibou, which said, 'As for me, I have been able to obtain from the district commandant tirailleurs, guards, goumiers, weapons, and ammunition. I am sending it all to you under the command of your cousin and namesake, Tidjani Aguibou Tall. I have done my duty. It is now up to you to do yours and to avenge Badara and his companions so that never again will a Samo dare to touch a hair on any Toucouleur head and, even less, make any attempt on their lives.' I thought," added Tidjani Thiam, "that I had a free hand. That is why I drove back and put down all the attackers."

The commandant turned to King Aguibou and asked him if what Tidjani Thiam had just asserted was true.

"Never did I give my son such a message!" cried the king. "Tidjani Thiam is falsifying the truth. I will not tolerate his attempt to involve me in problems that are his alone."

The commandant summoned the king's son and questioned him.

"Mon Commandant," replied the young man, "my father instructed me to tell my namesake that he had obtained from you combatants, weapons, and ammunition to eventually be used to restore order in the land, but that he should wait for your arrival in Louta before taking any action."

Upon hearing these words, Tidjani was transfixed with surprise and indignation. Recovering his wits, he advanced toward the young man, and with a disdainful sneer he said, "I understand that you wish to save your father's head, but never again will you dare to look me in the eye! In that case, since neither you nor your father wish to assume responsibility for your actions, once again, the Thiam that I am will redeem the death of the Talls that you are and prove that a Thiam may die, but that he never breaks his word."

Incensed, King Aguibou tried to intervene, but the commandant, who wished to deter any irreparable damage, calmed him down.

Turning to the interpreter Bâbilen Touré, Tidjani Thiam then pronounced the words that were to seal his fate. "Interpreter, tell the commandant not to seek beyond myself the person responsible for the crackdown on the Samos. I acted of my own accord. I had to avenge my brother and my men who were killed, I was given that opportunity, and I took it. This is my sole and final declaration."

The district commandant now understood what had really happened, but because Tidjani Thiam refused to defend himself, he could do nothing. He was forced to order his arrest as well as that of his cadi and adviser Tierno Kounta Cissé. He also had Tombo Tougouri, the perpetrator of several murders and injuries, arrested along with several prominent Toucouleurs and Samos.

All Tidjani Thiam's wealth (about three thousand head of cattle, goats, and sheep; two hundred horses, among which were the two renowned coursers, Nimsaali and Kowel-Birgui, who had won the famous race that defeated Aguibou Tall's horse; sixty servants; several kilograms of gold and silver; and about five million cowries) was confiscated. The palace was evacuated and handed over to the guard of a chief brigadier and a group of district guards.

The commandant organized the convoy that was to return to Bandiagara, where a ruling would be made regarding the affair. Tidjani was allowed to ride his favorite horse, Kowel-Birgui. His two wives, as well as his servants and courtiers, were part of the convoy.

As they were making their way, it is not known what unfortunate idea suddenly gripped Tidjani, who was riding in proximity to the commandant. As though possessed by sudden insanity, Tidjani abruptly rammed the commandant with his horse. The violence of the blow sent the commandant and his horse tumbling to the ground. Luckily, since he was a good cavalry officer and used to falls, he was able to remove his feet from the stirrups in time to avoid having his horse land on top of him. He had been thrown a good distance but arose uninjured. His only reaction was to cry out, "Poor Tidjani! Poor Tidjani! He wants me to kill him at all costs!" From that day onward, for the rest of his life, Tidjani would never stop saying, "Poor Tidjani!" which developed into a sort of verbal tic.

Not only did the commandant refuse to place him in handcuffs, but he allowed him to get back on Kowel-Birgui and rode next to him for the rest of the journey.

As soon as they arrived in Bandiagara, Tidjani Thiam, his cadi Tierno Kounta Cissé, and all the other defendants were incarcerated. Tidjani Thiam was placed in an unknown location, shrouded in the utmost secrecy.

The gossips once again began to attack my mother, whom they considered to be the cause of all the ills that had befallen Tidjani and his family. "Tidjani only got what he deserved!" exclaimed the Toucouleur Tall and Thiam women above all. They had never been able to get over the fact that Tidjani had married a Fula woman, even if she was the daughter of Pâté Poullo, and that on top of that, he had adopted me and named me as his successor. "How could anyone go and marry a devil woman who is nursing a demon and expect to obtain happiness?"

The "demon" was yours truly. Hadn't my birth closely followed the divorce of my parents? Nobody had forgotten that Tidjani had lost his father shortly after he had asked for Kadidja's hand, and that Kadidja's own mother had passed away a few days after the finalization of their marriage. Tidjani's arrest had the effect of bringing to a boil the heated indignation of the women.

My mother was greatly affected by this, but she was not—as has already been made clear—a woman who could be easily beaten down. Made of tempered steel, she was able to confront any danger and overcome any obstacle. She was afraid of nothing. She never failed to take up a challenge, no matter where it came from, and when she undertook something, she followed it through to the very end, no matter what the cost. Very pious and well educated in religious matters—she knew a good part of the Koran by heart—she was, on the contrary, not at all superstitious and never hesitated to stand up to marabouts, charlatans, or other casters of spells. Without being aggressive by nature, once she was provoked, she never avoided a fight or an accusation. "God has clad me in iron," she would later say, "so that I can defend my friends and relatives." And God knows that, like a mother lioness, she would fight to defend them, come what may!

Days passed and nobody knew what had happened to Tidjani Thiam. Nobody knew whether he was even still alive. He seemed to have been swallowed up by the night. According to some, the Whites had thrown him down a well, while for others, they had shot him on the very night of his arrival in Bandiagara.

Still others held that Tidjani had been placed in a cage, as though he were a wild animal, and deported. Everyone concurred when it was said that he would never be seen again. His gravesite would remain unknown, and nobody would be able to go there and pray for the peace of his soul.

Tidjani's grieving wives did not know whether they were widows or not. Tidjani's own mother, old Yaye Diawarra, a former amazon warrior in the troops of the first king of Bandiagara, Tidjani Tall, cried so much that her tears ran dry. Her two beloved sons, Tidjani and Badara, the only hope that had kept her alive, had been cruelly snatched from her, one of them pierced by three arrows in Toïni, the other carried off by the Whites and seemingly lost somewhere between earth and sky.

Diaraw Aguibou no longer dared to look her cowives in the face in light of the conduct of her father, the king, and her half-brother, Tidjani Aguibou Tall. And yet, nobody in the family, neither the women nor the servants, and still less the children, made her feel that her relatives were the cause of the terrible misfortune that had befallen them all. Everyone tried to spare her feelings. Diaraw did not suffer any less horribly for it, all the more so because her father had made no gesture whatsoever to console her or to lessen her burden in spite of the cruel situation in which the family found itself, since all Tidjani's wealth had been confiscated.

One day, the great storyteller, historian, and traditionalist Koullel, who had become so attached to me in my childhood that I had been given the nickname Amkoullel (meaning "Koullel's little Amadou," or "son of Koullel"), came to the house. He caught Diaraw singing an improvised lullaby in verse to her little boy, who was a few months old, as women did in those days, and in which she expressed all her sorrow.

> Sleep my child, sleep, so that I can keep watch
> And wait for your father whom your grandfather arrested.
> Am I a widow? Are you an orphan?
> No soothsayer can tell us.
> I asked the sun.
> The stars remain mute.
> The moon was not more eloquent.
> The shadows told me,
> "We have swallowed your husband. Woman, cry!"
> The dawn of presence is far away,
> The beloved is absent.
> Thiam, where are you? I, Tall, am asking you.

Koullel repeated this lullaby to the other members of the family, who were so immersed in sorrow that food and drink had become tasteless. Everyone immediately learned it by heart, including the elderly and austere Yaye Diawarra, who no longer did anything but count her prayer beads from morning until night. The touching little song was no longer just for putting to sleep the little prince who had had his rights taken away before he even knew that he had any. It became a balm that Tidjani's relatives poured over each other's hearts. Like smoke rising from a burning mass, the little song drifted out of the house and floated down the streets of their neighborhood. Bystanders got ahold of it, minstrel griots adopted it, and they put it to music and spread it across the country. Inspired by Diaraw's lullaby, the great griote and singer Aïssata Boubou herself composed elegies in memory of Badara Thiam, the hero of Toïni.

King Aguibou understood that the honor of the Thiams had grown as a result of a tragedy that should have physically and spiritually annihilated them. He threatened Aïssata Boubou with a public whipping if she did not stop singing poems in honor of Badara. But this threat only served to heighten the griote's poetic ardor. In response, she composed a wonderful new poetic song where she declared to the king,

> Whether whipped until there is blood
> Or placed in chains and put in prison,
> That will not silence me.
> Father, forgive me,
> But nothing will reduce me to silence!

Kadidja's Quest

Tidjani's fate continued to be shrouded in mystery. The absolute secrecy surrounding him was as impenetrable as the wall that, it is said, surrounds our world and separates us from the afterlife. There was no news.

Despite her courage and the strength that she gained from her prayers, Tidjani's mother, Yaye Diawarra, was at wits' end. She called for Kadidja, who had become her favorite daughter-in-law. "My daughter Kadidja," she said, "I cannot go on! In my head I feel the 'crazy worm' that drives animals mad. Anxiety troubles my brain. When I think of my son Tidjani, I feel a kind of vertigo and the leaves on the trees turn yellow or red before my eyes. If I don't find out what has happened to my son, I feel that I will go insane. I would rather die by my own hand than lose my mind and become a burden to you all, which would only add to everything that you have already endured since my son's arrest.

"Kadidja, here is why I have asked you here. I have complete faith in you. In case I lose my mind before I die, I would like you to be the only person in the entire family to take care of me. I will give the formal order to our most faithful captives Sambourou and Yabara."

And she burst into tears.

As an amazon, Yaye Diawarra had taken part in dozens of battles and had stepped over corpses under a hail of bullets in order to go feed and care for the wounded, all without fear or tears. Now this exceptional woman was suddenly moaning and crying, her head pressed against her daughter-in-law's chest! Kadidja was shaken. In the manner of an African mother consoling her baby, she dried her mother-in-law's hot tears with her lips and tongue. This spontaneous act calmed the old woman. "Oh, Kadidja," she said, "you have just proven to me what my instincts had already told me concerning the greatness of your soul and the purity of your love for my son Tidjani, for nothing but love for her son could inspire a woman to drink his mother's tears."

Kadidja began to cry as well, from pity but also from the joy she felt at finally being understood. "O mother Yaye," she said, "promise me that you will fight the 'crazy worm' that is making you wish for death! Promise me that you will live so that you may continue to pray for your son and to bless us. I ask you this. Give me thirty-three days. With God's help, I promise that I will obtain information about my husband. And if I must climb to the heavens to do it, I will obtain the ladder of the prophets in order to do so!"

Because she was a good judge of character, Yaye Diawarra took her at her word. "My daughter," she told her, "I know that you could catch even the stars if you set your mind to it. But be careful, the Whites do not trifle with what they have forbidden. They make their lackeys drink potions made from such powerful magic that when our people enroll in their service, they cease to be themselves! They forget family ties, friendship, and dignity and only ever have one idea in mind: to remain faithful to the Whites and to serve them at all costs. They repeat the refrain, 'I'm doing my job! I'm doing my job! I don't know anyone!'"

"Thank you for this advice, Mother. I will be careful, but the Whites do not scare me. My father, Pâté Poullo, was a great Fula silatigui, gifted with great knowledge and power. At my birth he bathed me to protect me against magical potions and the evil eye.[4] Therefore do not fear for me."

In order to organize her course of action more effectively and get out from under the weighty and untrusting presence of her cowives, Kadidja left her husband's household and returned to her father's compound in the Deendé Bôdi district. She immediately called a family council, composed on one hand of her brothers, Bokari Pâté and Hammadoun Pâté, and on the other, of my father's three principal former servants who represented my paternal family: Beydari Hampâté, Abidi Hampâté, and Niélé. Turning to face her brothers, Kadidja began to speak. "From now on," she said, "there is no longer a place for me anywhere unless it is near you. In my husband's household, outside of my mother-in-law, everyone casts sideways glances at me. Nobody dares to accuse me to my face, but they whisper behind my back, saying, 'She is the newest wife, she must be cursed, the one bringing the bad luck, the cause of the misfortune that weighs upon us.' And they cannot forgive the fact that Tidjani Thiam officially named my son to be his principal heir."

Bokari Pâté, childhood friend of Tidjani and Tierno Bokar, replied, "Kadidja, your cowives hold your 'star' responsible for the loss of the Louta turban.[5] The best way for us to respond is to obtain a turban for Tidjani Thiam that nobody can take from him. How? By putting our wealth and ourselves at his disposal in order to help him."

"To help Tidjani," said Kadidja, "we will have to find him and set him free."

"With the fortune that we have inherited from our father," cried Bokari Pâté, "we can triumph over every obstacle, thank God!"

Next it was Beydari's turn to speak. "As you know, at his death my father and master, Hampâté, left me his entire fortune. Even though I am a captive, it is I who am his heir instead of my two young masters, Hammadoun and Amadou. I am their guardian and protector, and I am ready to give up my life for them. Because Tidjani Thiam adopted Amadou as his older son and successor, his misfortune also automatically becomes that of his adoptive son, and therefore Hammadoun's and mine. Therefore, in the name of my young masters, I am placing the entire fortune that I inherited at Kadidja's disposal, so that she may have the means to wash away the insults of her cowives and undertake any action that she deems necessary in order to locate her husband."

Kadidja had never doubted her brothers' support, as they had already demonstrated their generosity when they were dividing the estate of Anta N'Diobdi. Nevertheless, like Beydari, they demonstrated a confidence and nobility of attitude that touched her deeply. This further strengthened her determination. She now had a considerable fortune at her fingertips, and thus had every means for action. To follow the adage, "When Poverty says, 'State your needs so that I can deprive you in misery,' Fortune whispers in its master's ear, 'State your desires. I will satisfy them immediately.'"

Kadidja had promised her mother-in-law that she would have news about her son within thirty-three days.[6] To make such a promise to the mother of one's husband was akin to making a vow to a divinity. Kadidja thus found herself doubly committed. First because of the number of days she had chosen, and second because of the venerable character of the woman to whom she had made her promise. She decided to set out immediately on her campaign, albeit not without taking several traditional precautions in order to protect herself from malignant forces, whatever their origin. As the Fulas say, "Before you put a scorpion in your mouth, you had better prepare your tongue."

In Bandiagara there lived a famous and respected old woman marabout. Born in Hamdallaye (capital of the Fula Empire of Massina) during the time of the venerable Cheikou Amadou, she had been dubbed Dewel Asi, or "the little woman who dug deeply" (implying that she had dug deeply into mystical knowledge). She taught the traditional Islamic disciplines—the Koran, of course, but also the *hadiths* (the words and actions of the Prophet), Arabic grammar, logic, and jurisprudence in accordance with the four great Islamic schools of law in addition to Sufi spiritual traditions—and she did all this while also weaving very beautiful straw mats that were artfully decorated with symbolic designs. Until 1910 or 1911, the date of her death, her Koranic school was one of the most thriving in Bandiagara. This saintly woman was also a close relation of Gabdo Hammadi Ali, one of Kadidja's maternal aunts. My mother paid Dewel Asi a visit.

"I have come to see you," Kadidja said, "so that you will bless me and guide me. For I have indeed decided to raise Sonngo, the great sacred mountain of the Dogons, with a wisp of straw. I am aware of my folly, but nothing is impossible when God is on one's side. I have come to ask you to put God on my side."

"Raise Sonngo with a wisp of straw? What an image! What is your Sonngo, and what is your wisp of straw?"

"My Sonngo is to raise the veil of mystery that shrouds my husband Tidjani Thiam's fate. And my wisp of straw is myself."

Dewel Asi sunk into a long meditation. When she came out of it, she said, "A woman who wishes to save her husband or her child is worthy of aid. Concerning myself, I have neither strength nor power, I am nothing but a wisp of straw like you, but because you wish it, I will pray to God to consent to be on your side. As for you, it will be necessary to first carry out a propitiatory sacrifice. For this, you must go and clothe seven poor people, seven widows, and seven orphans from head to foot, and you must free a captive. Then come back and see me in three days or in seven days, when you have done all this."

Before withdrawing, Kadidja offered the holy woman a large gold ring that she had brought with her to thank her for her kindness. Dewel Asi refused to take it.

"Keep this jewel," she said, "put it in a sachet, and always keep it with you. Later, there will come a day when you will be in great need. You will discover that there will be nothing left of all the jewelry that you inherited from your mother, except for this gold ring. On that day, think of me, give thanks to God, and use it on my behalf in order to get out of a difficult situation."

Strangely, fifteen years later, a fire would destroy our entire house in Bamako, and all that my mother had left to her name was this single gold ring.

Upon returning home, Kadidja told the family about her encounter with Dewel Asi. She immediately proceeded to sell the number of livestock necessary to be able to clothe twenty-one people from head to foot, and had a tailor and a shoemaker carry out this task. Finally, in agreement with her brothers and with the person in question, she liberated Barkérou Pâté, one of her family's captives, but not before giving him generous gifts according to the recommendations of the Prophet. She gave him two complete suits of clothing and a sum of money that was significant for the time, in addition to two thousand cowries and two milk cows, which would allow him to constitute his own herd.

Since she accomplished all this within seven days, Kadidja went back to see Dewel Asi. The holy woman, who had abandoned all her other occupations, had spent the week fasting (according to Muslim rites, every day, from sunup to sundown) and praying for Kadidja. On a piece of paper she drew a kind of talisman made up of Koranic verses and the names of God in Arabic and then handed it to Kadidja. "Have this paper covered in silk cloth," she told her, "and then enclose it in stitched lambskin. This work must be done by a shoemaker who is known for his moral purity. Before setting to work, he must perform the ritual ablutions in order to be in the required state of physical and religious cleanliness. The sachet must take the form of a triangle. You must wear it across your chest."

Kadidja entrusted this task to the most virtuous shoemaker of Bandiagara, a woman so pious and venerated that she was no longer called by her own proper name but by the reverential name of Inna Mamma Tamé, "Mother of Mamadou Tamé."

Armed with her talisman and filled with the certainty that the prayers of the holy woman had drawn God's mercy down upon her, Kadidja was ready to begin her investigation. She was still the leader of the largest women's association in Bandiagara, the very same one that she had founded in her youth. This association included among its members a very beautiful young dîmadjo (that is, belonging to the class of "house captives" or family servants) named Koorka Bâbilâli, who had married a chief brigadier of the district guards, who was himself a dîmadjo from Kounari. Kadidja asked Koorka to come to her house.

"Sister," she said, "I am no longer dead or alive. I eat, I walk, I go to bed, but only out of sheer habit. Everything is dark for me, as if I were inside a dark dust tornado on a stormy day. Ever since my husband, *Naaba* (king), was arrested by the Whites, no being, not even a fly or an ant, or even the slightest whiff of air has come to give me even a trace of news about him.[7] Koorka, we have been friends since childhood, we belong to the same age association. You are now the wife of the chief brigadier. If my husband is alive and in prison somewhere, your husband has every means of knowing that, and you yourself can find out where. There are certain moments when a husband's mouth is close to his wife's ear, moments when a woman regains the upper hand and when the toughest man becomes more tender and unconsciously tells his secrets to his companion."

"Kadidja!" Koorka replied. "We grew up together, we have been friends since our most tender years, and your parents adopted me as if I were their dimadjo and born into their household. Do not worry, you can count on me as well as on all the women in our waaldé association who are married to guards. There are a good dozen of them who live in the guard camp. One of us will surely find out something."

Koorka Bâbilâli returned immediately to the guard camp where she called a meeting with her friends Morobara Bo and Maartou Nawna. "Isn't it true that at one time or another, all of us have been indebted to Kadidja Pâté?" she said.

"Certainly, Koorka! That is the absolute truth!" replied the women.

"Do you know the adage that says, 'What is the use of a friendship between a man and a monkey unless it is so that the monkey can help the man dislodge his stick on the day when that stick gets stuck in the highest branches?'"

"Yes, Koorka, how true!" they replied.

"Well, my friends, you know that Naaba, our generous Naaba was arrested by the Whites and put who knows where. But we are the wives of three men of rank, chiefs of the district guards. It cannot be possible that our husbands do not share in the commandant's secrets. Between the district commandant and the district guards, there is an affinity of name that favors trust. It is the commandant who commands, but it is the guards who arrest and watch the prisoners. Sisters, Kadidja is counting on us in order to discover the truth. If necessary, each of us must pester our husbands at an opportune time. We must find out whether Naaba is dead or alive. If he is alive, try to find out where he is being kept, and if he is dead, where he is buried."

Next, Koorka summoned her friend Kenyouma, whose husband was the commandant's own bodyguard. "Kenyouma," she said, "we are both childhood friends of Kadidja Pâté. As the leader of our waaldé she has always been honorable and generous and has always responded to our appeals. Today she is the one who needs our help in order to find out where her husband is. Let us be like the palace mice, secret agents who can go anywhere and listen without being seen."

"We need to get our friends Moro Pennda and Kadiatou Komseer involved," replied Kenyouma. "They both speak French and they've entered 'colonial marriages' with White men.[8] Well, you know that Whites don't keep secrets from each other, and they also confide more easily in their wives than Blacks do."

And so it was done. The net was cast. All they had to do was wait for it to fill with information so that they could haul it in for Kadidja, who would sift through it herself.

Kadiatou "Komseer" was married to the *commissaire*—which explains her moniker. Her husband, who often questioned her in order to collect information through cross-referencing, found the naïveté of the young woman's responses entertaining. He was far from suspecting that this beautiful and candid creature was about to pry the truth out of him with a good bit more cunning than he possessed himself.

The very next day, after this little feminine plot was hatched, while the commissaire and his wife were at the breakfast table, Kadiatou Komseer let out a scream and collapsed on the bed. As though under the effects of great pain, she rolled and moaned. The commissaire, who loved her madly, came and bent over her. He was in a panic. "What's wrong?"

"Oh!" cried the young woman, wringing her hands. "An evil spirit has taken over my body! It has completely taken over my body. He will kill me unless he is driven out of me."

The commissaire immediately called for the African medical assistant Kalando Beydari, who was in charge of the dispensary. Kalando was a healer "in the manner of the Whites," which was like saying that he had no understanding whatsoever of the maladies that evil spirits can sometimes inject into the sons of Adam. Kadidja was delirious for several days. She claimed that she was being pursued by the ghost of Tidjani Thiam, whose throat had been cut by the Whites and whose body had been packed into a box that they had thrown over one of the cliffs and into the void. Kalando Beydari was clearly out of his depth. He advised them to find a native healer. The commissaire's cook, in cahoots with Kadiatou, declared that he would take care of it. He called for Mannawel, a dîmadjo from Tidjani's family who had grown up in Kadidja's house and who, it must be said, had never been a healer in any shape or form. After prescribing baths and the burning of certain plants for Kadiatou, he recommended that the commissaire speak to her only in extremely gentle tones, especially during her fits, in order to calm her down and reassure her.

Near midnight, a haggard Kadiatou sat up in her bed. "Ohh!" she moaned. "Commissaire! Tidjani's ghost is here, saying that his cadaver is demanding a grave."

"Calm down, Kadiatou, calm down!" said the commissaire in his softest voice. Tidjani Thiam is not dead, he is in prison. In a couple of months, he will appear before a tribunal and he will not be killed, you'll see! White people don't like to kill. Come now, don't worry, it was just a bad dream!"

Pretending to be reassured by her husband's words, Kadiatou lay back on the bed, in all aspects looking like someone who had just been freed from beneath a heavy weight. The next morning, so as not to raise any suspicions, she remained in bed until Mannawel arrived. Ceremoniously, he administered her medications while she gave him a malicious look.

Finally, Kadiatou rose and took her breakfast, to the great satisfaction of her husband. Extremely relieved to see that his wife was feeling better, he called his dog and went to carry out his duties. He was whistling softly, as the Whites do when they are happy.

As soon as he had crossed the threshold, Kadiatou turned to Mannawel. "Quick, go and tell Koorka Bâlilâli that Naaba is alive. He's locked up in prison while waiting to appear before a tribunal."

Mannawel hurried over to Koorka Bâlilâli's and then both of them went to see Kadidja in order to give her the good news, which they had obtained through the consummate dexterity of Kadiatou Komseer. But they still had to discover the prison in which Tidjani was locked up, because there were two: a civilian prison and a military prison.

Meanwhile, the commissaire had arrived at the headquarters of Commandant Charles de la Bretèche in order to give him his usual daily report. The commandant asked him about his young companion.

"She has been extremely ill, but she is getting better," replied the commissaire. "Can you imagine? She has endless nightmares where she thinks that she is being chased by the ghost of Tidjani Thiam, whose cadaver, she says, is calling for a grave!"

"Truly," replied the commandant laughingly, "this Tidjani Thiam and his brother Badara, indeed like all the Thiams, have an extraordinary influence in this country. I would not wish to be in the shoes of the commandant who would have to announce Tidjani's death, if he happened to die in prison."

"What is going to happen to him?"

"I am awaiting the order to send him before the criminal tribunal. Personally, I will do everything in my power to save him, even though he almost killed me on the road. But he is not a bad sort. In this affair, he is more to be pitied than blamed. Tidjani Thiam has unfortunately run up against a man, Aguibou Tall, who is like the pointed peak of a tall mountain. Anyone who runs into him either loses his life or lots of feathers."

Fate had it that this conversation was clearly overheard by Garba Tieman, the commandant's bodyguard and husband of Kenyouma, Kadidja's other friend. For the past two weeks, the unfortunate Garba could no longer cough or sneeze in his home before his wife would make a scene. "Cough and sneeze, that is all you know how to do!" she would chide. "But when it is a matter of finding out where your commandant has put Tidjani Thiam, well, then, none of your organs work! I married the wrong man. I'm thinking that maybe I should get a divorce and go find a man who doesn't automatically obey the Whites just because they gave him a red fez and blue leggings!"

At noon, Garba Tieman headed home. He was quite happy that he had overheard the conversation between the two Whites, and walked along playing his one-stringed instrument the *jourou kelen* and singing at the top of his voice the air known as *djonngoloni*, a warrior song composed in honor of a Bambara military fortress that had long resisted the attacks of the Sultan of Segou, Amadou Cheikou, the eldest son of El Hadj Omar. When he arrived at his house, as custom required, his wife presented him with cool water to wet his throat, and warm water to wash the sweat from his body. After washing up, Garba Tieman took his meal. In order to favor good digestion, he stretched out in his hammock made from baobab fibers and, with a satisfied air, he began to sway in it and burped loudly, which is not at all considered rude in Africa.

Kenyouma approached him. "Something tells me that today you met Konyouman, the legendary magician of good fortune."

"Yes, I met Konyouman, and this divine guide allowed me to discover..." and he stopped.

"Allowed you to discover what?"

"To discover something that it is dangerous to talk about, but that nonetheless cannot be kept quiet."

"Say it! It's about Naaba, isn't it?"

Garba leaned out of his hammock. He cast a long glance around the courtyard in order to ensure that nobody except his wife would be able to hear his words. Reassured, he slowly nodded his head down and up, a signal that in Africa means, "yes-yes." Kenyouma became more affectionate. "I never doubted that you were a worthy stud," she said, "but a stud that sometimes needs to be spurred into rearing up."

"Tidjani Thiam is alive!" Garba finally blurted out, no longer able to contain himself. "My ears heard it from the mouth of the commandant himself, and it is therefore a certitude. He is in prison, and he will soon be judged publicly. The commandant said that he would support him."

As soon as her husband had left the house, Kenyouma rushed to Koorka Bâbilâli in order to pass on the information. Koorka in turn tackled her husband and manipulated him so completely that before long, she had been able to learn that Tidjani, after having spent the first ten days of his detention in military prison, had then been transferred to civil prison, as a security precaution, and put into one of the deepest cells in the second courtyard. In fact, it was feared that, as rumor had it, the Toucouleurs, and especially the Thiams, would attempt a rescue.

Twenty days had passed since Kadidja had begun searching for her husband. She had spent the price of several dozen bulls on gifts and sacrifices, but it wasn't a useless expenditure. She was now absolutely certain that her husband was alive, and she knew where he was—at the very end of a second interior courtyard in the civilian prison where the most formidable prisoners were kept.

Kadidja purchased a complete suit of men's clothing: loose pants, boots, an under boubou, an outer boubou, a turban, and a sword. Clothed in these garments, she was unrecognizable. In the middle of the night she made her way to the White neighborhood, accompanied by the faithful Beydari, who followed along behind her at a safe distance in order to protect her from any possible danger. It was past midnight. Only a few sounds pierced the silence at disparate moments: the cries of a baby awakened by hunger, the hooting of a barn owl—known as a sorcerer-bird, hungry for the blood of newborn babies—and the barking of a few dogs, intended to chase away thieves and evil spirits.

In those days, it truly was suicide to venture like this into the White Man's neighborhood at an hour at which the sentinels had the right to shoot on sight anything that moved in a manner out of the ordinary. But with God's help, the eyes and the ears of the guards and the dogs were miraculously made blind and deaf. Kadidja and Beydari crossed the White neighborhood along the main artery that led directly into the guard camp. Next to the camp loomed the civilian prison, just across from a large tamarind tree. By day and by night the prison guards had acquired the habit of resting beneath its branches as they waited their turn for duty. When they had arrived at a distance of about twenty meters from the tree, Kadidja said to Beydari, "Go under the tamarind tree. Carefully awaken the man who is sleeping on the large *tara* (wood and hide bed). That should be the chief brigadier. Tell him that Kadidja Pâté asks him to come and speak to her behind the prison wall where she is waiting."

Although Beyadari approached on tiptoe, he was not able to reach the chief brigadier without waking him. Quick and well-trained, the officer jumped on him and grabbed him with both hands. But Beydari, who was six feet tall and weighed two hundred-twenty pounds, was not a novice fighter. While explaining "I am not here to hurt you," he easily loosened the arms that were holding him and continued, "I am Beydari Hampâté. My mistress, Kadidja Pâté, whom I have accompanied here, requests that you go speak to her behind the prison wall."

The chief brigadier enjoyed a solid reputation for his ferocity. But he was a Toucouleur and his wife also belonged to Kadidja's waaldé association. He loosened his hold on Beydari. Alerted by the noise, the other guards had awakened. The chief brigadier ordered them to remain calm and to await his return, and then he fell in behind Beydari. In spite of his orders, a guard followed him at a distance, his arm in firing position.

When Bouraïma Soumaré reached the other side of the wall, he suddenly found himself facing a man armed with a sword. Thinking that Beydari had drawn him into an ambush, he tried to turn around and call for backup, but he froze at the sound of a woman's voice. In Fula, the voice began to sing the words of a song that had been composed in his honor by the famous Aïssata Boubou. He recognized the voice of Kadidja Pâté. He was so moved by this that this man known for his cruelty and intransigence was instantly transformed into a tender and compassionate poet. In those days, Fula-Toucouleur gallantry required that when a woman addressed a man in poetic verse he must immediately reply. Bouraïma Soumaré promptly responded,

> Djandji, sister of Amadou Pâté,[9]
> Djandji, what troubles you today,
> That in darkness deep
> You try to enter a house of doom
> Guarded night and day by dogs vicious and black?
> Djandji, what troubles you, tell me!

Kadidja knew that the ferocious beast had been changed into *koumbareewel*, the trumpeter hornbill that gracefully dances and sings. "I have risked my life," she said, "and the life of my faithful Beydari to come and see you and to ask you, for the sake of compassion, to let me see my husband. I know that he is alive and that he is locked up in one of the cells in the second courtyard."

"Kadidja, what you are asking me to do is like asking me to go and shoot at the commandant's testicles!"

"Bouraïma Soumaré," said Kadidja firmly, "if I myself were to go on this very night and shoot at the commandant's testicles, and if I were to come back alive, then would you let me see my husband?"

Such determination troubled the chief brigadier. Without giving him time to catch his breath, Kadidja continued, "I know that my husband is behind this wall. I swear to you Bouraïma, that if I cannot look him in the eyes on this very night, tomorrow morning I will not see the rising sun's yellow disc."

"And what will you do if I refuse to take you to your husband?"

"I will commit an act of madness that will cost me my life. Aïssata Boubou will have a new theme to improvise on that she can add to her repertoire. She will be able to sing about my death just as they sing of the death of Aminata Bîdane, the heroïne of Sâ."

Bouraïma Soumaré, who knew Kadidja Pâté and had no doubt that she was capable of committing such an unfortunate act on a whim, considered the dishonor that would foul his name if she ended up dying by her own hand because of him. This merciless guard who had never had to exercise his ferocity on his Toucouleur relatives, and even less on his fellow inhabitants of Bandiagara, was now facing his first case of conscience. Suddenly he was again a Muslim Toucouleur, that is, a man who was ready to save a relative even if it cost him his own life. He remembered a saying (hadith) from the Prophet, recited by Cheikou Amadou and El Hadj Omar under the appropriate circumstances, in which the Prophet recommended to each of the faithful not to leave this world without, at least once in life, having broken the law (sharia) in the name of compassion. Bouraïma felt his heart melt.

"Oh, Kadidja," he said, "I know the risk that I am taking if one of my guards betrays me out of meanness. But too bad! I do not wish to be less courageous than a woman. Come. I will take you to see your husband. And if Charles de la Bretèche finds out about it, let him make the ceiling of the sky crash to the floor of the earth!"

"Do not worry," said Kadidja, "the dome of the sky will stay where it is, the commandant will never find out, and your guards will keep quiet. Just give me their names."

Bouraïma gave Kadidja the names of the ten men who were on duty with him. He went to get the prison keys and then addressed his men. "Kadidja Pâté has come to ask us, in the name of God and in solidarity with the people of Bandiagara, to allow her to communicate with her husband for a few moments. I have accepted her request because we have no choice. Either we will have to arrest this woman, which I do not wish to do, or we will have to allow her to see her husband. All of us are from Bandiagara, and it would be unthinkable for us to arrest Kadidja Pâté. If we did that, neither we nor our wives would count for even the weight of a fly in the opinions of our fellow citizens. We would be pointed at or looked down upon as despicable sellouts to the Whites."

"Chief Brigadier," cried the guards, "we stand behind you! What you do, we will have also done!"

Bouraïma and Kadidja approached the prison entrance. Bouraïma opened the main door, which led to a courtyard. They crossed it in silence. Then he opened another door that led to a second courtyard. He stepped inside, followed by Kadidja, and headed toward a third heavy door that stood opposite the second door. It opened onto a corridor that led to the cell, whose door was as thick as the phalanx on a finger. Bouraïma opened it. The cell was as dark and narrow as a tomb, and they could see nothing. Bouraïma called out, "Tidjani Thiam! Tidjani Thiam!"

"Who is calling me? What do you want from me?" said Tidjani's weakened voice.

"It is I, Bouraïma Soumaré, chief brigadier. Come out, I have some information for you."

Kadidja stood to the side. After a few minutes, which to her seemed interminable, Tidjani's bent silhouette appeared. Filthy and covered with sweat, he was wearing nothing more than a pair of pants whose legs had been rolled to his thighs because of the stifling heat that prevailed inside the dungeon. The ceiling was so low that Tidjani was unable to stand completely upright. He could only sit, squat, or lie down. A small opening, placed at the end of a conduit, allowed a bit of air to circulate, but no light could penetrate it. He was allowed out for thirty minutes a day, but only after ten o'clock at night, so he never got to see the restorative light of day.

"Someone from your family wishes to speak to you," said Bouraïma Soumaré.

"That could only be Kadidja," exclaimed Tidjani.

"Yes, Naaba!" cried Kadidja. And stepping from the corner where she had been waiting, she threw herself into her husband's weakened arms. "How did you know it was me?"

"Oh, Poullo![10] Deep in this dungeon, I have been telling myself, 'If ever anyone manages to come and see me in this tomb, it will be Kadidja.' My intuition did not mislead me, thank God!"

"Naaba," said Kadidja, "your mother is dying from worry. Every day she cries enough tears with which to fill a calabash. What runs from her nose is no longer a viscous liquid but bright red blood. For her, you have died under horrible circumstances and this idea haunts her to such an extent that she is thinking of ending her life. I asked her to keep living and to give me thirty-three days to find out what had happened to you. Thank God, I have found you. You are weak but you are alive. Now you must say something and give me a sign that your mother will recognize in order to convince her that you really are still in this world and that the message truly does come from you."

"When you see my mother," replied Tidjani, "say this to her: 'Mother, I saw Tidjani.' And then contrary to custom, you will look her straight in the eyes. She will do the same. Then you will take her right hand, and as you unfold each finger beginning with the index, you will say this. 'One, Tidjani sends his regards. Two, he is alive. Three, he is not ill. Four, he praises God and thanks Him.' She will know that this comes from me. Then you will take my ring, which I now give you, and contrary to Fula custom, you will place it on her middle finger. Finally, with a smile, you will pronounce this sentence, which is part of Bandiagara's motto: *Biiribaara bantineeje* (Puffy clouds float over the giant silk-cotton trees)."

When the time had come for them to separate, Kadidja said to her husband, "Now that I know the way to your cave, no wild animal can stop me from coming here. I will come back often, God willing!"

She thanked Bouraïma Soumaré, and then joined Beydari, who was waiting for her under the tamarind tree. They returned without incident to the Deendé Bôdi neighborhood just before the first light of dawn. The voice of the muezzin rose, calling the faithful to the first prayer of the day, puncturing the silence that still encased the sleeping city at that hour.

Never had the muezzin's words been more resonant in their true meaning for Kadidja than on that particular morning. "Allâhou akbar! Allâhou akbar!" (God is greatest! God is greatest!)[11] For Kadidja, yes, God really was greatest. During that entire night, she had sincerely felt as though she had been supported by a force that, for her, had facilitated everything and opened all doors. But she had also understood that this power and grandeur escaped any description and all definition. It had been like a complete and sovereign presence that had enveloped and carried everything.

She felt no need to recover her strength. Rested without having slept, relaxed without having rested, she waited impatiently for the first rays of the rising sun. She wanted to take advantage of this particularly happy and peaceful moment to go and pour the most soothing of balms onto her mother-in-law's heart.

When the beneficent star finally rose above the horizon, spreading light and life over the world, Kadidja proceeded toward her husband's compound. Old Yaye Diawarra was in the courtyard under the veranda made from millet stalks that sheltered the front of her house. Draped in white and seated on a sheepskin, her face was turned toward the east, in the direction of Mecca, and she was counting her prayers with her beads. The first chickens to awaken were pecking around the mortars, looking for grains of millet that had fallen into the dirt. Kadidja's arrival upset the birds. The big rooster and boss of the farmyard sounded the alarm by crowing and flapping his wings. All of his little flock rushed to their perches in the chicken coop and alighted there while waiting to find out what the nature of the danger was. This uproar among the chickens drew Yaye Diawarra from her meditations. As she turned her head to see what the fuss was about, she spied Kadidja, dressed all in white, standing in front of the entrance to her vestibule. The emotion that she felt was so overpowering that she could not move. But she was able to overcome her paralysis, and pronounced the ritual words of welcome. "*Bissmillahi*, Kadidja![12] In the name of God, welcome! Did you spend a peaceful night? Come and sit next to me, my daughter."

"Good morning, Mother. Yes, God willing, I spent a peaceful night. And I have come to give you news of my attempts to find out where the Whites have hidden your son, my husband."

The old woman hung her head. "Whatever the news that you have brought may be, know, O Kadidja, that I will never forget your devotion and your love for my son and for me. When I saw you walk out of this house once you had made the decision to do everything in your power to find him, your male courage made me take heart. I recovered the strength that I once had in battle, which allowed me to confront the greatest dangers with a nonchalance that came to me from I know not what sky. This is just to tell you that I now stand ready to accept the fate that God has chosen for my son and for me." Then she fell silent.

"Mother," said Kadidja, "I saw Tidjani."

Yaye Diawarra raised her head crowned with hair as thick and white as combed cotton. Kadidja took the opportunity to look her straight in the eyes. Then she took her right hand and unfolded each of her fingers while repeating the formula that Tidjani had given her. "One, Tidjani sends his regards. Two, he is alive. Three, he is not ill. Four, praise God and thank Him."

Yaye, whose hands were trembling, was nevertheless able to hold her tongue since she had noticed that Kadidja had not finished. Kadidja had begun to untie a knot that had been fashioned in the hem of her ample boubou. From it, she took Tidjani's ring, slid it onto the old woman's middle finger, and then pronounced these words: "Biiribaara bantineeje." With a cry, Yaye threw herself into her daughter-in-law's arms. And then she began to cry for joy, just as one month earlier she had cried from sorrow.

After a few moments, the two women prudently got ahold of themselves, for it was important that the other members of the family remain completely unaware of this news for fear that their extreme joy would betray Kadidja and those who had helped her.

With a happy heart, Kadidja returned home. She took her breakfast with an appetite that surprised Batoma, the former "captive daughter" of Anta

N'Diobdi who was now living with her. In the days that followed, Kadidja made sure to discreetly give gold jewelry, costly balls of amber, and chunks of coral to the wives of the guards who had been on duty with Bouraïma Soumaré. She also succeeded in turning in her favor the fifty district guards who were stationed in the Bandiagara police squadron. From that point on, the prison doors were open every night, from the nightly clarion call at nine o'clock to the muezzin's call to prayer at dawn.

Kadidja not only visited her husband every night, she also took Tidjani's official griot guitarist Ali Dièli with her. It goes without saying that the guards had taken it upon themselves to transfer Tidjani to a larger and more comfortable—or as comfortable as could be expected in prison—cell. Tidjani did not return to his tomb-cell except in cases of a visit from the district commandant or his assistant, or the colonial civil servant who ran the prison.

The Trial

One morning in the streets of Bandiagara, Dièli Bâba, the public crier, began to beat the small drum that he carried under his armpit. As he beat his drum, he shouted in Fula, Bambara, and Dogon, "Hear ye, hear ye, inhabitants of Bandiagara! Men, women, children, nobles, people of caste, and captives! The commandant greets you through my mouth. I am only an announcer, a public crier. It must therefore be noted that it is my job to proclaim. Hear ye, people of Bandiagara! Let no one hold this against me, but the commandant has given me the task of announcing to you that in seven days, not including today, a hearing before the Grand Tribunal will be held in the Great Hall of Palavers to judge Tidjani Thiam, the cadi Tierno Kounta Cissé, the Samo Tombo Tougouri, and others also inculpated, whose names are not worth mentioning, so I will not mention them.

"The commandant has told me to tell you that the hearing will be public. Everyone is allowed to attend. Nevertheless, the commandant warns those who might be tempted to use the occasion to free Tidjani Thiam by force. To them, the commandant announces, still through my mouth, that one hundred tirailleurs and three 'White-White' officers will be ready to receive them with gunfire from guns that are not loaded through the mouth of their barrels but through their butts. These are shameless guns that fart powder and vomit bullets of red copper, and they never miss their mark. Regards, good listeners!"

This announcement, repeated in all the districts for three days, brought a considerable crowd of people from neighboring areas into Bandiagara.

Kadidja Pâté and Tidjani Thiam's two brothers multiplied their visits to marabouts and dignitaries in Bandiagara. On his side, King Aguibou Tall declared to the commandant that he was opposed to having his son, Tidjani Aguibou Tall, called to the tribunal as a witness for the prosecution. Charles de la Bretèche, who had received formal instructions from the governor enjoining him to handle the former king with kid gloves and even to turn a blind eye to certain acts that could be legally reprehensible, consequently found himself stripped of the crucial argument that would have allowed him to assign responsibilities in the Louta affair. In fact, the king sent his son very far away from Bandiagara, placing the commandant before a fait accompli. On the day of the hearing, his son was neither in Bandiagara nor in the surrounding area, and therefore could not testify.

The day of the trial finally arrived. Following colonial usage, the tribunal, in its capacity as a tribunal of Second Instance, was presided over by the commandant himself, while the First Instance tribunal was presided over by the commandant's assistant. He was assisted by several native judicial assessors, all from Bandiagara, and his interpreter Bâbilen Touré, who loudly repeated all the words that were spoken on both sides.

Tidjani Thiam and his fellow detainees appeared before the court in chains. Tidjani Thiam was called to approach the bench.

In accordance with standard usage, the commandant, in his role as president of the tribunal, asked Tidjani, through an interpreter, "What is your surname, given name, profession, and domicile?"

Abdallah, a friend of Tidjani's who was watching the proceedings, could not contain his indignation. He exclaimed loudly in Fula, "It is truly surprising to see how God, who has given so much to the White people in the area of science for the fabrication of machines and other material objects, has otherwise affected their minds with a certain imbecility! Isn't it a proof of idiocy on the part of the commandant to ask Tidjani Thiam for his surname, given name, profession, and domicile? Who does not know the son of Amadou Ali Thiam in this country?"

Offended by the question, Tidjani in turn cried, "Has the commandant forgotten who I am to such an extent that he does not even remember my name and my title? Well, I am Tidjani, son of Amadou Ali Thiam, chief of Louta province, arrested for having avenged his brother and his men who were assassinated in Toïni while they were collecting taxes on behalf of France."

Without appearing to attach any importance to Tidjani's statement, which had been translated by the interpreter, the commandant continued, unperturbed. "Accused! Raise your right hand and swear to tell the truth, all of the truth, and nothing but the truth!"

Now that was too much. As though struck by a barb, Tidjani stood up and shook his chains in fury. He tried to raise his hand in order to point his index finger at the commandant in order to underscore what he had to say. But unable to do so, he leaned across the bench and cried out in a voice that trembled with indignation. "How can you think that I would not tell the truth, seeing that I have not even opened my mouth in order to expose the facts? The truth, I do not exercise it for the pleasure of any man, be he king or *toubab* (European).[13] I exercise it because Allah, through the mouth of his envoy Mohammed, has commanded always to tell the truth. But because it has been insinuated that I might not tell it, and because I have been asked to swear in order to be sure that I will not lie, I refuse to swear. And from now on, from my mouth neither the truth nor a lie will be heard by anyone. Do with me as you wish. I will not speak."

So saying, he sat down and became as still as a thick ball of shea butter. To the end of his trial, he never opened his mouth and refused to answer any questions. His brother Abdoul Thiam asked the tribunal for permission to respond in his older brother's place.

The trial lasted for two weeks. The absence of King Aguibou Tall's son intrigued everyone, especially the tirailleurs, the district guards, and above all the Toucouleur goumiers of Bandiagara, whom the young man had led all the way to Louta and who had been able to carry out their repressive acts before the arrival of the commandant without him even trying to stop them, as he normally should have done if there had been instructions to the contrary. Unfortunately, the absence of this essential witness, added to the public admissions that Tidjani had made in Louta and his refusal to defend himself, took from commandant Charles de la Bretèche all means of coming to the aid of his protegé by shedding further light on the events. All that remained were the events that were examined without nuance. At least he was able to save Tidjani's life by referring only to "exactions" and "abduction of persons."

Tidjani Thiam and Tierno Kounta Cissé were each condemned to three years in prison, one year of which would be in solitary confinement (that is, without visitors and without any time outdoors), as well as banishment for a period of time that was kept secret. We would not find this out until much later, along with the political reasons behind it.

Accused of murder, Tombo Tougouri was condemned to a very long prison sentence.

All of Tidjani's wealth that had been confiscated—riches, animals, and livestock—were sold at auction. The only thing left was the compound in

Bandiagara that he had inherited from his parents and where his mother, his wives, and those close to him continued to live.

King Aguibou Tall bought all Tidjani's livestock and was preparing also to buy the entire lot of horses, in hopes of acquiring with the herd the famous coursers Nimsaali and Kowel-Birgui that he had coveted for so long. Commandant Charles de la Bretèche, who understood Toucouleur psychology very well, knew that the king would do anything in order to obtain the two stallions who, by their victory, had enflamed the Tall-Thiam conflict. He knew that if he succeeded, he would congratulate himself on having had the last word in the affair, thus provoking a violent reaction from the Thiams. Intent on defusing a new conflict, without telling the king, the commandant ordered the purchase of the two horses by the captain of the Spahis. Then he quietly had them sent to Koulikoro, where the squadron was stationed.

When the herd was brought to auction, King Aguibou saw that the two coursers were missing. Unable to contain himself, he asked the commandant where they were. The commandant replied that they had been sent to Koulikoro, to the captain of the Spahis. Aguibou's only response was to recite this proverb: "A drum beats louder than a guitar." In other words, "Might always makes right."

3

Exile

One morning, the commandant called Tidjani into his office. "Because of the rumors that are circulating throughout the country," he told him, "in order to avoid the risk of any disturbances, the administration finds itself in the position of having to remove you from Bandiagara immediately. You will be transferred to Bougouni."

There was an additional motive behind this transfer. Tidjani and Tierno Kounta Cissé had been condemned to spend their first year in complete isolation. The prison in Bougouni was the only one equipped to receive prisoners sentenced to solitary confinement. It was known as the Haut-Sénégal-and-Niger penal colony. This is why they were being sent there, and it was undoubtedly also done in order to distance them from a region mostly populated by Fulas and Toucouleurs.

Tidjani replied, "Since I've left Louta and I no longer live in my home in Bandiagara, I don't care anymore where they send me."

Kadidja, who had been informed of her husband's upcoming transfer, sought out the interpreter Bâbilen Touré. She asked him to intervene on her behalf so that the commandant would allow her to accompany her husband. What couldn't a colonial interpreter do in those days, as long as the supplicant was able to buttress the request with "the nocturnal item," a gift given quietly under cover of night, far from prying eyes! But Kadidja was wealthy enough to be able to buy off those whose support she needed, and she never shrank from paying the price. Bâbilen advised her to request an audience with the commandant and to arrive at his office with her head and face appropriately composed for the occasion.

Charles de la Bretèche had already heard about this extraordinary Fula woman well before the revolt in Louta had broken out. He was therefore amenable to receiving her. In addition, it must be said that Bâbilen had also, as we say, "used his good mouth" on Kadidja's behalf.

Through the mediation of the interpreter, Kadidja asked the commandant for permission to accompany her husband to Bougouni. "If he happened to die along the way," she explained, "a member of his family must be present in order to administer the traditional religious rites. Otherwise, his soul will never cease lamenting and roaming in this world below, where it could even become nefarious to the living."

The commandant looked at Kadidja in commiseration. He reflected for a moment, chewing pensively on the end of his pencil, and then he told her, "I do not have the authority to allow anyone to accompany Tidjani Thiam, since as you know, he was sentenced to solitary confinement, as was his cadi, Tierno Kounta Cissé. No visits, and no accompaniments are therefore permitted. Indeed, if the facts of the indictment had been adhered to, both of them should have been condemned to death or to solitary confinement in perpetuity. But in the verdict, I took into account certain circumstances that I uncovered and that even led me to forget that Tidjani, in a sort of fit of despair, almost killed me out on the road—as though he had wanted to prevent me from helping him. I therefore cannot give you permission to accompany him. On the other hand, I cannot prevent anyone from traveling from Bandiagara to Bougouni. The road is open. All that is necessary is to request the required pass."

Kadidja did not need to hear the message more than once. She thanked the commandant for his kindness and then asked him to please issue her and her servant Batoma Sow a pass to travel to Bougouni. The commandant had the document delivered to her right away, with the note, "Traveling with her servant Batoma Sow."

Kadidja returned home armed with this precious piece of paper, which was a veritable talisman capable of eliminating many an obstacle. She quietly proceeded to sell over forty head of livestock and then bought everything that they would need for a very long journey. Bougouni was in fact over seven hundred kilometers distant from Bandiagara, to the south, right in the middle of Bambara country.

She tried to take me with her, but Beydari, the head of my paternal family, was firmly opposed to the idea because of my age and the precarious nature of the journey.

Tidjani's Long March

The administration took great care to shroud Tidjani's departure and that of his unfortunate companions in secrecy. They continued to fear some kind of desperate move from the Thiams, who could not bear to see their friend burdened with a defamatory punishment in place of the true culprits. But what action could remain secret when the chiefs of the guards who were in charge of organizing the departure had as wives the sly foxes that you've already met? One day, Koorka Bâbilâli walked in on her husband as he was giving final instructions to Chief Brigadier Bouraïma Soumaré concerning the journey. The brigadier was to assume command of the convoy until Segou, the city where there would be a changing of the guard. Koorka immediately told my mother. That very evening, she asked Bouraïma Soumaré if she could become an unofficial member of the convoy. Bouraïma accepted but told her to meet them in a place located about thirty kilometers from Bandiagara.

When the day arrived, at the first crowing of the cock, while the entire city was still asleep, the inmates were removed from their prison cells. Tidjani and Tierno Kounta were joined together by the same chain. As for Tombo Tougouri, his hands were tied behind his back. A strong rope was placed around his neck and tied to the pommel on the saddle of one of the guards on horseback. A few Samo prisoners followed behind. The convoy set off as silently as possible on the road toward Segou.

At the appointed place, my mother, accompanied by Batoma, joined the convoy, following at a short distance behind. With her she had three pack oxen that she had loaded with things to eat and other provisions she planned to replenish along the way.

The men trudged along at a rate of about twenty-five kilometers a day on their best days, as they were at the mercy of intemperate weather and wild animals, which in those days were abundant between Bandiagara and Segou.[1] At times they took advantage of the old trails that had been cleared by El Hadj Omar's army or by Colonel Archinard's army as he was pursuing El Hadj Omar's eldest son, Amadou Cheikou, across the country.

After skirting Djenné, the convoy headed toward the large Bambara town of Saro, where on that day the large weekly market was being held. Bouraïma Soumaré decided to stop there in order to replenish supplies for his men.

Tidjani Thiam and Tierno Kounta, who had given their word that they would not try to escape, had been untied at Djenné. This had allowed Tidjani, who had the gift of uncommon strength and who had been used to performing hard work since childhood, to clear the route with large swipes of his machete, much to the satisfaction of the guards and his fellow travelers. As for Tombo Tougouri, he had refused to promise that he would not try to escape. His hands therefore remained tied behind his back.

When they reached the market, Bouraïma Soumaré and the guards dispersed among the stalls seeking to restock their provisions and renew their supplies of kola nuts, tobacco, and other sundries. They had left Tombo Tougouri seated in the shade of a kapok tree in the company of a single guard who, under the double effects of heat and fatigue, soon fell asleep. Before long, the guard's head was lolling on his chest.

A young Samo woman had come to the market to sell her wares. As she was passing the kapok tree, she spied the sleeping guard and Tombo Tougouri, whom she identified as a Samo hunter by his ritual scars. She approached him. They exchanged a knowing look. She had undoubtedly understood that the prisoner wished to have his hands freed, since she disappeared and returned almost immediately armed with a knife. Slipping behind Tombo Tougouri, she deftly cut the ropes that had encircled his hands, leaving only a single strand that the prisoner easily untied. Tierno Kounta, who was nearby, had observed the woman and had understood what was happening. He alerted Tidjani. "Pretend you didn't see anything," Tidjani advised. "We will say nothing for the time being. Let us wait."

Upon their return, the guards noticed nothing. Bouraïma Soumaré decided that the little group would spend the night there and that they would leave the next morning at dawn. At nightfall, after a groom had hand-fed him his meal mouthful by mouthful, Tombo Tougouri stretched out and closed his eyes. District guard Tiessaraman Coulibaly leaned his loaded gun against a low wall (when they were out on a mission, their weapons were always loaded), and like all his cohort, he lay down on the ground and immediately fell into a deep slumber.

Late into the night, Tombo Tougouri carefully threw off the ropes. Then, sliding slowly on his back in such a way that he would not be taken by surprise in an unusual position, he inched toward the guard's gun. Tidjani, who was not sleeping, was watching. When Tombo Tougouri had almost reached the loaded gun, he leaped up to seize it. But a violent kick in the flank stopped him in mid-motion. Before he could recover his wits, Tidjani had grabbed the weapon and pointed it at him. Tombo Tougouri was writhing in pain on the ground. "Make one move and I'll turn you into a corpse," said Tidjani. The Samo knew very well that the person whose brother he had killed on account of a goat was capable of sending him into the nether world without a second thought. His entire body began to shake, but it was only his nerves that had betrayed him. The events that followed prove that his heart felt no fear.

Bouraïma Soumaré and his companions were jolted awake. They had no difficulty overpowering Tombo Tougouri, although he had recovered all his strength. He was like an enraged boar who had been cornered by a pack of dogs. Bouraïma Soumaré asked him what he had intended to do with the gun. With a snicker he replied, "First, kill Tidjani Thiam and his cadi, and second eliminate everyone among you who would have tried to stop me." There is no doubt that without Tidjani's intervention, carnage would have ensued.

Bouraïma Soumaré understood that he was dealing with a diehard whose body was shaking much more out of anger than from fear. In order to avoid any further incidents, he put him in iron chains, which slowed the convoy even more.

When they arrived at Segou, the chief brigadier told the authorities of Tombo Tougouri's attempt and emphasized Tidjani Thiam's courage.

Tombo Tougouri was detained in Segou, where he served a lengthy and extremely arduous sentence. But he was to survive and finally returned to his village of Toïni. When I stopped there in 1932, he was still living there. The other Samo prisoners also remained in Segou.

Because the population of the country was majority Bambara, the authorities decided that Tidjani Thiam and Tierno Kounta Cissé were no longer dangerous and that they could risk taking them to Bamako by way of the river. They embarked on a prison pirogue under an escort of three guards. Kadidja and Batoma, who up to that point had followed the convoy at a distance, embarked in a separate pirogue.

At Koulikoro, the last stop on the river before Bamako, the prisoners left the river and were taken by railroad to Bamako, where they were handed over to the commandant. Guarded by a new escort, they set out once again and walked the 160 kilometers that still separated them from Bougouni, the final destination of their long and challenging journey.

Kadidja's Village

In Bougouni, the orders concerning the sentence to solitary confinement that had been sent along preceding the arrival of the two prisoners were taken extremely seriously by the commandant in power at that time. A narrow cell, bristling with spikes and built into a kind of deep, dank, and dark cave had been prepared for the two unfortunate men. They were lowered into it as soon as they arrived. The trunk of a young mahogany tree had been attached to the side walls and made to span the cell from end to end. Tidjani and Tierno Kounta were placed at either end of the trunk. Their feet were shackled in iron rings attached to very short chains which were then nailed to the wood of the tree.

It was in this squalid and insalubrious black hole, where neither human being nor light of day were ever seen, that Tidjani and Tierno Kounta were going to live, as if inside a pigsty. Their food was lowered down by means of a bucket attached to the end of a long rope, and another bucket was used to flush out the premises.

Kadidja had requested an audience with the district commandant, but he had not consented to receive her. She was fortunate to find a close Fula relative in the city, Galo Bâ. Originally from Fouta Tooro in Senegal, he had followed the French column that pursued Samory and had ended up settling in Bougouni where he started a family. Kadidja also found a distant cousin of Tidjani's named Mamadou Thiam, who was the manager of a small commercial trading post.

One of these two relatives, I am no longer sure which, put her in contact with the Bougouni canton chief. This was Tiemokodian, the greatest traditional Bambara chief in the land. Touched by my mother's misfortunes, he welcomed her into his own home. Within a few months, she had won over Tiemokodian's wives and children, and then Tiemokodian himself. She would braid the hair of the chief's wives into artistic styles "in the Fula manner," and taught them new recipes. This is how she entered into a close familiar relationship with the greatest chief in the land and became acquainted with the prominent citizens of Bougouni. At the beginning of her stay, she did not speak a single word of Bambara and had to use an interpreter, who was most often Galo Bâ. But because she had a talent for learning languages, as did almost all Africans in those days, she quickly learned the basics of the local language, and it was not long before she had learned to speak it fluently.

Despite numerous attempts, Kadidja had not been able to communicate with her husband. The orders were brutal. The district commandant exercised a constant and unrelenting surveillance. The least that can be said is that the commandant—whose name will not be mentioned here out of respect for his family—was rather strange.

His greatest joy was to visit the prison, the munitions depot, and the treasury several times a day and even during the night. This was facilitated by the fact that he could only fall asleep between three o'clock and six o'clock in the afternoon. No treatment had been able to return his capacity for sleep, a faculty that he had lost following an illness in Indochina. In addition, he was afflicted with a strange nervous tic. At regular and frequent intervals, his mouth would open and close, as though he were biting on air. And each time that the contraction of his mouth muscles allowed it, he would cry out as though demented. He quickly earned the nickname "Coumandan Dajenje Kloti," which meant "Commandant-twisted mouth-bursts-out-yelling." A few months later, he was laid low by a pernicious fever and was evacuated to France.

Luckily for my family, he was replaced by Commandant de Courcelles, a man who possessed great humane qualities. It was not long before he was nicknamed *Denkelen-bourou*, "Trumpet for an only son," because every day between two o'clock in the afternoon and eight o'clock in the evening, he would play a wind instrument called a cornet.[2] His servant Ousmane Ouaga Traoré told everyone that this instrument was made from solid gold and that it had been specially cast for the commandant by goldsmiths in France at the request of his parents, who were fabulously rich nobles. Unable to prevent their son from going off to the colonies, they had given him this souvenir gift so that he could play airs reserved for the upper nobility of France. He could thus "play the flute" any time that his heart could no longer contain its nostalgia. "My boss's instrument," he would declare to anyone who would listen, "cost the equivalent of five hundred handsome milk cows plus fifty purebred Sahel stallions!" This was his way of burnishing the reputation of his boss and, by association, his own.

The commandant's largesse—he was very generous—contributed much to making these words ring true.

The commandant's residence was built atop one of the hills that rise to the east of Bougouni. This hill was called *coumandan-koulou*, "commandant's hill." The entire valley that spread out below that hill belonged to the great Bambara chief Tiemokodian, or rather, it fell under his traditional jurisdiction as "master of the earth," a ritual position that allowed him to make sacrifices to the earth spirits so that human beings could use the land without inflicting damage. This is where he kept his own fields of millet, corn, and yams.

Shortly before the arrival of Commandant de Courcelles in Bougouni, Kadidja had asked chief Tiemokodian to kindly cede her a plot of land at the foot of the hill in order to build some huts for housing and to grow food. Tiemokodian told my mother that Mother Earth belonged to God and the ancestors and that it was too sacred to be possessed by anyone. Thus, no property could be ceded to her. Nevertheless, no master of the earth could refuse the use of it to anyone who wished to cultivate an undeveloped parcel. All that was required was the "payment to custom" of ten kola nuts, one tobacco pouch filled with tobacco that could either be chewed or smoked, seven lengths of white cotton cloth, a young cockerel, and a piece of rock salt. Kadidja paid the custom. This gave her the right to ask for the piece of land that suited her and, following the ritual ceremony celebrated by Tiemokodian, to use it not as a piece of "property" but as a kind of usufruct.

She chose a two-hectare plot that was at a distance of about two kilometers from the city, at an intersection where one road led west toward Guinea, one led to the northwest toward Bamako, and to the south, one led toward Ivory Coast.[3] The road leading to Bamako was, in fact, being widened.

Kadidja had an idea in mind. The caravans of Dioula merchants who made the roundtrip trajectory between the salt-producing lands to the northeast and the lands where kola nuts were grown to the south (in Ivory Coast) all traveled this road.[4] Therefore, she planned to build on this plot not only a cluster of dwellings for the family, but also a welcome station where the traveling Dioulas would find food and lodging. She had discussed this with Tiemokodian, who had then submitted the project idea to Commandant-twisted-mouth-bursts-out-yelling. He had given his permission. Kadidja began by having two large wells dug on the parcel: one for the family and one for the travelers. Next, she had the encampment proper built. It included several thatched huts and a very large shelter that measured twenty meters by five.[5] In this way, the Dioulas would no longer have to leave the road in order to replenish their provisions, rest up, or sleep in Bougouni center. The people of Bougouni, who were always quick to give names to all things, baptized the place *foulamousso-bougou*, "the village of the Fula woman," and later, Kadidiabougou, "Kadidja's village."

My mother had asked a Dioula woman from Bougouni to show Batoma how to make the boiled millet cakes that the Dioulas were partial to, especially for breakfast in the morning. Batoma became such an expert at it that she even began to sell them in neighboring markets.

In addition, all the wives of the district guards came to get their hair braided by my mother, who ended up becoming their confidante and their trusted adviser.

When the Commandant de Courcelles arrived in Bougouni, he found the encampment operating at full capacity, bustling with activity. He learned, not without some surprise, that the locale had been founded by a woman who was an outsider to the region, a Fula who, on top of that, was the wife of a detainee. Wishing to learn more, he asked to see the complete dossier of the prisoner Tidjani Thiam and read it closely. He concluded that the truth about what had happened in Louta had been far from established during the investigation and that the verdict did not help to clarify things any further. Intrigued, he ordered that Tidjani and Tierno Kounta be brought to his office. He was presented with two exhausted men with weakened limbs, half blind and squinting in the light of day, their skin covered in dirty scabs and running sores, and smelling of the latrines. Tierno Kounta, who was much older than Tidjani and more frail in his physical makeup, could no longer stand. They each had beards that had been growing for several months.

Commandant de Courcelles immediately ordered that the prisoners be removed from what was called the *kaso-kolon* (prison-well) and that they be transferred to a normal cell. Then he ordered the native assistant physician to care for them until they recovered their strength. With the complicity of the guards, Kadidja regularly sent them provisions.

The commandant, nobody knows why, became engrossed in "the Tidjani Thiam affair." Had he gotten his information from one of his servants, a Toucouleur of the Ly clan who had ties to the Thiam clan by marriage and to whom Kadidja had told the entire story? Whatever the case may have been, legal expert that he was, he combed through the dossier. He found gaps and even a technical error in the verdict that had condemned Tidjani and Tierno Kounta. He sent a report to the authorities. I do not know how he went about it, but in the end the verdict was revised by a higher authority in Kayes, the location of the Haut-Sénégal-Niger headquarters. The sentence to solitary confinement was modified to become a sentence to a common-law prison. The forced residence in Bougouni for a period of time that had been kept secret was retained, but in this case it was a matter more political than juridical, as we would discover later.

Once they had finally returned to the light of day in their new prison cells, Tidjani and Tierno Kounta were given permission to receive visits from their friends and relatives. Despite the medical treatments and the good food, it took them several months to recover from their ordeal. As soon as they recovered their strength, they were constrained to labor at the tasks that all common-law prisoners were required to perform. The hardest jobs in those days were related to the building of a road through the forest that led from the river's edge all the way to the Bamako highway. The track that the Dioula merchants coming from Bamako were in the habit of taking, in order to join Bougouni without a detour, was being widened.

Once he had recovered his strength, Tidjani Thiam turned out to be an exceptional trailblazer and cutter of big trees. He was tireless! Happy to be out in the fresh air again, he swung his ax with his powerful arms, all the while singing great poems in Arabic, particularly the famous *Bourda* by Cheikh Mohammed el-Bushiri and *Safinatu Saada* by El Hadj Omar, which had been composed in honor of the Prophet.

Tidjani was reaping the fruits of the severe education that his father had put him through in his youth and that had given him his extraordinary strength and endurance. All the African princes who had been incarcerated in Bougouni during the colonial period died there except for my father Tidjani. Even Tierno Kounta was not to survive for long. Every time he struck a tree trunk with his ax, Tidjani would say, "Thank you father! I thought that you didn't love me. I didn't know that you were preparing me for this!" And he would cut down the tree in record time!

In order to follow the progress of the construction project, Commandant de Courcelles did not need to go to the site. All he had to do was to walk down to the first brow of the hill and train the big eyes of his powerful binoculars on the site. He seemed to take pleasure in seeing Tidjani, a Toucouleur prince and former chief of a large province, accept working harder than a captive and, it seemed, with real joy. Ultimately, Courcelles noticed that it was practically Tidjani who was leading the work and not the chief of the district guards, who spent most of his time sitting in the shade of a tree, sipping his millet beer.

This surly guard, who had nicknamed himself *Gonfin yirijougou feere* (Black chimpanzee flower of a venomous tree) never stood up unless he got the urge to whip the first prisoner within arm's reach when he felt like it and without any particular reason. "My tongue and my hand are itching," he liked to say, "for prisoners are made to be insulted and whipped." And every time he said this, he would run headlong into the group of prisoners, whipping them ever harder, to the front of him, to the left, and to the right, spewing lewd insults all the while. When he tired of the beatings, he would place his hands on his hips, the whip gripped tightly under his arm, burp loudly from time to time to emphasize his situation as a man who had eaten his fill, and shout at the prisoners in Bambara. "You had better pray to your ancestors that my 'little brother' (his whip) that you see tucked under my arm here does not become dislodged, otherwise he'll come and plow into your criminal backs like a *daba* cuts through the weeds in the fields. The commandant is up there on top of the hill, where he is perched like the great eagle of the skies, but down here in the valley, I am like the hippopotamus that rips up the rice fields. Here, I am the one in command, and not the commandant." Then he would add in his "infantryman's French" (called French *forofifon naspa*): "Get to work! *Travadjé, travadjé!* (Work, work!). Otherwise, you pigs, I'll pigwhip you good!"

Unbeknownst to Gonfin, the Commandant de Courcelles had continued his discreet surveillance. After several months of work, the road, fifteen kilometers in length, was almost finished.[6] All that was left was to build a small bridge. Gonfin suddenly decided to have some large packing crates brought in, each of which had been used to transport twelve bottles of alcohol packed in woven straw sleeves. He distributed the crates to the prisoners and ordered them to go and fill them with dirt and to carry them back to the bridge. "I order you," he barked, "to finish backfilling near the bridge and to reinforce that roadway today, this very day, before the sun goes down." He loaded his gun with five bullets and leaned it up against a tree. "Oh, Comrade Hot-Shot," he said to his gun, "you rest right here up against this tree until some poor, misguided prisoner forces me to use you against him." Then he turned to the prisoners. "Get to work!" he cried, "make those pickaxes, shovels, and spades sing a gravedigger's song, and get those twelve crates filled with dirt. Travadjé, travadjé! Otherwise, you pigs, I'll pigwhip you good!"

There were about a dozen prisoners. Tidjani was on the pickax and shovel detail, while Tierno Kounta had been assigned to the group that was moving the crates. The prisoners were carrying them on their heads. Well, each of these crates packed with dirt weighed no less than thirty to thirty-five kilos.[7] After a few trips, Tierno Kounta was so exhausted that he collapsed, and the crate that he was carrying almost crushed his skull. Gonfin jumped up, brandishing his whip. "You shrunken ape! Get up, pick up that crate and make it quick, or you'll find out how rough Gonfin's hands really are."

Tidjani came running, shovel in hand, intent on stopping Gonfin from hitting the old man. "Gonfin," he said, "that crate is too heavy for a man over sixty. Let him catch his breath." Gonfin closed his teeth and clenched his fists. Eyes bulging, he bent toward Tidjani, who was waiting calmly for him, shovel in hand. "Up until now you could boast that you still haven't ever been baptized by the fire of my whip. Well that's over. Take this! Here's your first lick!" And he raised his whip. Just when he was about to lay it across Tidjani, Tidjani blocked the blow with the handle of his shovel. He promptly seized the whip, snatching it from Gonfin's hands. Mad with rage, Gonfin rushed toward his gun, but Tidjani threw the shovel between his legs. Gonfin tripped and fell flat on his face a few meters from the weapon. Before Gonfin knew it, Tidjani had grabbed the gun and straddled him, planting the end of it on Gonfin's forehead. "Get up! Put both hands on your head or I'll blow your brains out with your own gun. You know I'm the man who will do it, too."

In a panic, the prisoners began to shout. From atop his observation post, Commandant de Courcelles had not missed a thing. He immediately sent five guards down to reinstate order. He commanded Brigadier Toumani Kamara to wrest the gun from Tidjani's hands and to wait until he, the commandant, had arrived on the scene.

The guards came running as fast as they could. When they had reached the scene, they easily calmed the prisoners. But when Toumani Kamara asked Tidjani for the gun, he refused, saying, "I'm not going to give this gun to anyone but the commandant himself."

Someone had run to tell Kadidja that her husband had rebelled after grabbing the gun and ammunition of the head guard. Without even taking the time to cover her head or to put on her shoes, she rushed out of the house. Barefoot, hair flying, she ran until she reached the construction site, arriving at almost the same time as the commandant. She ran to her husband. Shaking and wild-eyed, he cried, "Get back! Get back Kadidja! Get away! I'm going to end this life of hell and shame!"

She threw herself upon him. "Naaba! Naaba! Have you made me come all the way here just to escape by dying and going away like a coward, leaving me behind and in trouble, alone and at the mercy of everyone? If you have decided to die, shoot me first so that I don't become a miserable widow after you die." As she was speaking she was holding Tidjani tight so that he couldn't move.

The Commandant de Courcelles walked up. "Come now, poor Tidjani. Give me that gun. Don't worry. I saw everything."

Courcelles was unaware that he had just used an expression that had never stopped ringing in Tidjani's ears since the moment that Charles de la Bretèche had said it on the road from Louta. It was as though he had pronounced a magical formula. The fury dissipated and like a wild animal who had just been tamed, Tidjani walked toward him. He instinctively stood at attention, his right hand raised to his temple, as he had seen the guards, infantrymen, and Spahis do. Then he handed him the weapon and ammunition and said in French, "Pardon, ma coumandan!"

Kadidja threw herself at Courcelles's feet, repeating in turn, "Pardon, pardon, ma coumandan!" in French and placing both hands on her temples in an awkward imitation of a military salute. The commandant smiled. He drew her up and then instructed Brigadier Toumani Kamara to take everyone to his official residence. There he ordered that Tidjani be taken back to prison and that Tierno Kounta be hospitalized, as he was visibly in a very bad state. Then he spoke privately with Gonfin. After Gonfin had left his office, the commandant summoned Kadidja. "Go back to your encampment," he told her, "and fear not. No harm will come to your husband."

Upon exiting the office, Kadidja found herself face-to-face with Gonfin, who was still standing at attention, motionless in front of the door. Their eyes met. After that, Kadidja never forgot the expression on Gonfin's face. This dull brute, who called his whip "little brother" or "traveling companion," seemed rooted in place. As far as he was concerned, he had traveled to a village called "Reversal of Fortune" on "Adversity Street." What had taken place between him and the commandant? No one ever knew. The fact remains that for eight entire days, nobody saw Gonfin walking in the streets as was his habit, stumbling, dead drunk, yelling like some demented person walking on hot coals. On the ninth day, Fambougouri Diaguité, one of the commandant's grooms, came running to see Kadidja. "Sugar my tongue so that it gives you good news!" he said. This was how a bearer of good tidings would ask for a gift. Kadidja gave him ten centimes, which at the time could be exchanged for twenty-four cowries. That was enough to pay for a good number of sweets, and was even enough to pay for an entire day's supply of food for a small family.

Fambougouri carefully wrapped his little red copper coin in a piece of cloth, placed it in the pocket of his boubou, and then looked at Kadidja and finally gave her the news. "This morning," he said, "as I was waiting for the solar disc to rise in order to honor it, I saw with my own eyes, yes, my very own eyes, Brigadier Toumani Kamara leading Gonfin out of the prison. Gonfin's wife had led a donkey packed with belongings up to the door. Brigadier Toumani handed a large envelope to Gonfin. Gonfin placed it among his belongings. Then, with his wife and his donkey, he started down the road to Bamako. I followed them with my eyes until they were swallowed by the horizon. They are gone now, flown like dead leaves before the winds that announce the coming of rain. I have the feeling that the commandant either fired or transferred Gonfin. How right Koro Zan was when he pronounced the adage, "Bits of wood from a well's rotting frame always end up falling into the water!" (In other words, sooner or later the consequences of a bad act always return to haunt the perpetrator.) It was Gonfin who called himself 'the flower of a venomous tree.' Well then, let him go and carry his fruit to a place where God himself will not take pity on him. *Amine!* (Amen)."

Like the true Fula woman that she was, Kadidja was able to keep her joy in check. Without showing any emotion, she gave Fambougouri another tencentime coin and served him a full calabash of fine millet couscous drenched in fresh milk and sweetened with sugar. From that day forward, Fambougouri counted among the most reliable informants who regularly visited her house.

But let's get back to Tidjani. In addition to having learned to wield shovels, pickaxes, hatchets, and hoes in his youth, he was also—as he demonstrated in Toïni—a marvelous sharpshooter and an expert horseman. But what the European reader will perhaps find most unusual to discover is that Tidjani, knew how to sew and embroider in the manner of the mixed-blood Arabs of Timbuktu. In the West African countries that lie south of the Sahara (an area that was once known as Bafour), the Toucouleur and Fula nobles did not have the right to exercise the trades associated with the artisan castes (ironworking, weaving, leather working, wood working, and so on), but they were allowed to embroider and sell their work.[8] Tierno Bokar himself was a remarkably talented embroiderer. I myself would later learn this art and would occasionally hand embroider magnificent boubous that would be quite expensive today!

It just so happened that the Commandant de Courcelles possessed a handsome coverlet made of a special white cloth. It was a family heirloom that he treasured as though it were a holy relic. One day, a pest of some sort, perhaps it was a mouse, chewed out the middle of the coverlet in the shape of a fairly large circle. As the commandant was lamenting over it, not knowing how to patch this disgraceful and inopportune hole, his servant Ousmane Ouaga suggested that he show the coverlet to Tidjani and ask him for advice.

Tidjani examined the piece, then asked the commandant to have three small skeins of silk sent to Bougouini: one white, one red, and one blue. One month later, Tidjani was in possession of three bobbins wound with silk in these three colors, along with all the tools necessary for a tailor-embroiderer. He rounded out the hole with scissors to give it a more uniform shape, then he filled it in using a series of fine loops. When he had finished, he encircled the work with a circular braid decorated with the colors of the French flag. This artistic embroidery work accented the beauty of the coverlet in a most unexpected way, to the great satisfaction of the commandant.

More and more intrigued by the personality of this strange prisoner, the commandant undoubtedly wished to get to know him better, for he ordered Brigadier Toumani Kamara to place a "mole" in his cell. The result of this act is unknown, but in any case, the benevolent attitude of Commandant de Courcelles toward Tidjani never flagged after that.

In the meantime, the road that led from Bougouni-center to the commandant's official residence had been completed. Tidjani was assigned the job of planting a number of young kapok saplings on both sides of this beautiful road. So doing, he was carrying out the work of a titan, for he had personally torn each and every one of them from the bush himself. Fifty-six years later, these same kapok trees planted by Tidjani Thiam while he was a prisoner would have to be cut down because of their age. This was done by order of my cousin

Ousmane Cissé, who, following the arrival of independence in Mali, would be named commandant of Bougouni district. Such are the ironies of history!

Soon Tidjani and Tierno Kounta had completed over a year of their respective sentences. Aside from the incident with Gonfin, they had not been the subjects of any unfavorable reports, whether from the prison warden or from the guards. The commandant gave the order to allow them to labor at less demanding tasks. Tierno Kounta was chosen to operate the *panka* (ventilation panel) in the office of the district treasurer. Tidjani was given the job of gardener at the official residence.

Over time, the Commandant de Courcelles befriended him. Kadidja was able to come and go as she pleased at the prison. During the day, Tidjani was allowed to walk around town as he wished, but with chains on his legs and accompanied by a guard. If he had wanted to do so, he probably could have slept at home, but he never took advantage of this possibility. He never came to Kadidiabougou (Kadidja's village) until after he had finished his daily tasks. As soon as it was nine o'clock, he returned to prison.

It was at that time that the governor, William Ponty, founder of the famous normal school that bears his name and that is located on Gorée Island in Senegal, happened to pass through Bougouni on one of his rounds. The butler and the cook who accompanied him everywhere just happened both to be Toucouleurs, and on top of that, they belonged to the Tidjaniya brotherhood, as did Tidjani Thiam and all the members of our family. These two servants, who never left the governor's side, attended to his well-being, oversaw the quality of his food, and ultimately served as a direct source of information. Kadidja entered into contact with them. She explained the entire Louta affair and then sent them one thousand kola nuts, milk, and a good millet couscous with lamb sauce. The two men explained Tidjani Thiam's case and that of his elderly companion to Governor Ponty. They even requested that the remainder of their sentences be forgiven.

Ponty was quite well acquainted with King Aguibou Tall. It is said that Ponty harbored a tenacious rancor toward him because Aguibou, during the time that Aguibou was serving as the first adviser to Colonel Archinard (before becoming "king" of Bandiagara), apparently had no consideration for William Ponty, who at the time had been nothing but the insignificant private secretary of the French conqueror.

Ponty asked the Commandant de Courcelles for his assessment of the conduct and mindset of Tidjani Thiam and his companion. Because Courcelles's report was very favorable, Ponty ordered him to prepare a dossier in favor of the two detainees, requesting a pardon for the remainder of their sentences, and to be issued on the next fourteenth of July, Bastille Day.

As the dossier was making its way through the long and torturous road of the administrative hierarchy, Kadidja learned of the death of her older brother Bokari Pâté, the childhood friend of Tidjani and Tierno Bokar. Although she was several months pregnant, she decided to travel to Bandiagara immediately. Since her business had been successful, she had saved up a comfortable sum, which allowed her to purchase large quantities of rich cloth and various other items. She loaded all of it on to pack oxen, added provisions of food, then, taking advantage of the fact that there was a caravan heading toward Bamako, she struck out, accompanied by her faithful Batoma.

Kadidja made her entrance into Bandiagara not like the wife of an inmate, but rather as a rich merchant returning from her travels and loaded with rare riches. She doled out many lengths of cloth and a good number of trinkets to her relatives, friends, and prominent members of the city.

After paying her last respects to her brother's memory, she settled the estate. It was all the easier because neither of her two elder brothers had left any children behind, just as her Uncle Eliyassa had once predicted. All that was left of her family now was her younger brother, Hammadoun, and her younger sister, Sirandou, both of them leaders of important associations in Bandiagara.

Kadidja sold about fifty head of cattle in order to cover the costs of the return trip. She began by sending her cowife Diaraw Aguibou, daughter of Aguibou Tall, to Bougouni in the first convoy. Kadiatou Bokari Moussa, Tidjani's first wife, was not among them. In fact, before leaving for his faraway exile, Tidjani had offered to divorce his wives and give them their freedom. Only his cousin Kadiatou Bokari Moussa had accepted this offer and had chosen to begin a new life.

In addition to Diaraw Aguibou, the first convoy also included three of Tidjani's brothers: Abdoul Thiam, Bokari Thiam, and Débé Thiam, as well as Gabdo Gouro, wife of Tierno Kounta, who had joined them in order to reunite with her husband.

On the Road to Bougouni with My Mother

This time, my mother was determined to take me with her to Bougouni, come what may. She called for a council meeting of the Hampâté Bâ family, which essentially included Beydari and my father's former captives, and expressed her wishes. Once again, Beydari was firmly opposed to the idea. "Our master and father, Hampâté, specifically entrusted his two boys, Hammadoun and Amadou, to us, and left us his entire fortune. We consent to allow you to spend this fortune in any way you see fit, but we cannot allow Amadou to leave. We value our little masters as we do our own lives, and even more so. It is out of the question for us to allow them to join a family other than that of their father." It must be said that Beydari and his companions did not like the Thiams at all, especially since Tidjani Thiam had officially adopted me while Hampâté was still alive.

Kadidja stood her ground. She went to plead her case before the cadi Amadou Khalil, invoking my young age (I was about five years old) and the very long separation that would ensue. It was this last argument that prevailed. Basing his decision on both Islamic law and African custom, both of which state that a child must remain with its mother at least until the age of seven, in the end, the cadi decided in my mother's favor and authorized her to take me with her to Bougouni, where her living situation was now more favorable.

Forced to submit, Beydari then decided that young Nassouni (who had been adopted and raised by my father under her prior name of Baya) would accompany us in order to take exclusive care of me. Niélé was now too old to undertake this long voyage. She had her own family and, truth be told, she did not at all like the idea of leaving the Hampâté family compound where she had always lived.

My older brother, Hammadoun, who had reached the age of seven, stayed in Bandiagara where he was, in fact, brilliantly pursuing his Koranic studies under the guidance of Tierno Bokar. My mother entrusted him into the special care of Beydari and Niélé.

Kadidja spent about two months in Bandiagara among her friends and family. During this time, a young Fula girl named Koudi Ali, originally from Bankassi and a distant cousin of my mother, was given away by her parents in marriage to Tierno Kounta. My mother accepted to take her with her to Bougouni. Because of my mother's advanced pregnancy, everyone advised her to forgo her trip and to wait to deliver her baby in Bandiagara. She would have none of it. "My husband needs me," she replied. "God will deliver me when and where he wishes to, but my place is in Bougouni with my husband."

Finally, everything was ready for her departure. One morning in 1905, at first cock's crow, the little convoy set out, preceded by several pack oxen loaded with baggage. Besides my mother and me, the convoy included Koudi Ali, future wife of Tierno Kounta, Batoma, and young Nassouni. Beydari and Abidi insisted on accompanying us to Mopti, a city located at the confluence of the

Niger and the Bani Rivers, at about seventy-six kilometers from Bandiagara.[9] We were to take the boat bound for Koulikoro, a city near Bamako. For the entire way, each of them took turns carrying me on their shoulders.

I barely have any precise memories of this first period of my life. My memory's mechanism would not really awaken until an event that occurred during the trip that I will recount later on. For the moment, I was unaware of the real implications of everything that was happening. I did not realize that, for a long time and perhaps even forever, I was leaving my father's home, and all those who had surrounded me with their affection, where I had been coddled like a little king.

Of course, I was happy to be with my mother again, but above all else, I greatly enjoyed traveling atop the shoulders of Beydari and Abidi as I was discovering a new world that was unfolding before me.

In Mopti, my mother stayed with her childhood friend Tiébéssé, as she usually did when Anta N'Diobdi brought her herd to Taykiri every year. Kadidja's primary concern was to reserve our spots on a barge. Then she went to purchase a great quantity of items that she knew were unavailable in Bamako and Bougouni and for which she hoped to obtain two or three times the price.

We left very early in the morning. Beydari and a number of relatives had come to accompany us to the river's edge at Simon quay. For the first time in my life, I stood before a vast expanse of water. In those days, there was such an abundance of it at the confluence of the two rivers that the other side was barely visible.[10] I also discovered the solid, locally built pirogues and the great barges made of wood or of iron that seemed enormous to me.

I have no memory of boarding the boat. Since I was attached to Nassouni's back, I think that I must have fallen asleep before noticing anything whatsoever. When I awoke, the sun was already high in the sky. We were sailing along the right bank of the Niger. The left bank was hardly visible, since it was almost a kilometer and a half away.[11] We sailed past long pirogues loaded to the brim. They cut through the water, propelled by the vigorous strokes of the Bozo punters, whose ample movements, of uncommon grace, kept time with the rhythm of their songs.

Kadidja Battles the Boss of the *Laptot* Boatmen

Our flotilla was composed of three large barges, flat-bottomed boats with no decks that, in addition to transporting passengers, also handled the transport of merchandise and local products on the Niger River between Koulikoro (near Bamako) and Mopti for the Deves-et-Chaumet Company. Each vessel was manned with ten punters and boatmen, who in those days were called *laptots*.[12]

We were navigating against the current, which made our progress very slow. For about a week we traveled with no problem. Our laptots avoided stopping in the ports of large cities such as Sansanding, Segou, or Nyamina. They undoubtedly had a good number of things on board that needed to be kept hidden, and they feared being discovered by the authorities.

At a few days' distance from Koulikoro, the last stop on the river before Bamako, a sharp quarrel broke out between my mother and the head laptot of one of the three barges, who also happened to be in charge of the entire convoy. The other laptots fearfully called him "boss." He had literally lost his mind over the beautiful Koudi Ali and Nassouni, who were then in the flower of their youth. He had harassed both of them, one after the other. In the end, he had even attacked Nassouni, but luckily for her, she had been able to defend herself. When my mother found out about the incident, she complained indignantly to the laptot who was in charge of our own barge, but since he was in mortal fear of his "boss," who was known to be a nefarious fornicator, he kept silent and did not dare to intervene. Since Kadidja was not in the habit of letting things go, when the chief laptot's barge was next to ours, she took advantage of the moment to hop aboard the other vessel and ordered the libidinous "boss" to cease his insalubrious attacks.

"Is that so?" he snickered. "Well listen here. If you want to finish this trip without any trouble you'd better give me one of your young girls. If you don't, I'll make you suffer like hell, and nobody here will defend you!"

"If you are in the habit of attacking the women who travel on your barges," my mother retorted, "I'm warning you that my girls will not be among that number. You'd better calm down, or you'll pay the price!"

Incensed at seeing a woman stand her ground in front of his laptots, the "boss" insulted my mother with an obscenity. Entirely unruffled, my mother threw the insults right back at him. Paying no mind to my mother's advanced pregnancy, the enraged head laptot slapped her hard. She stumbled and would certainly have fallen into the water if a young laptot hadn't caught her in time by her boubou. Recovering her balance, she grabbed an earthenware cook pot that happened to be within reach and hurled it at the chest of the chief laptot with all her might. Before he had been able to recover from his surprise, she managed to get back on to our own barge.

Incensed, the chief laptot grabbed an extremely long punt pole and struck my mother on the head with a violent blow, the force of which was fortunately softened by the thickness of her hair. Immediately my mother took up our terracotta cook pot and struck it on the ground. She grabbed a large and very sharp shard and flung it as hard as she could at the chief laptot. The projectile hit him squarely on his right side and left a deep cut. Blood began to flow. "You're half panther, half lion!" he roared. "You'll pay a lot more for this than you ever planned!" And he bent down to pick up his punt pole. This time my mother was ready for him. She quickly grabbed a machete that was lying nearby, which had probably been used for cleaning fish. The chief laptot, who had not noticed my mother's quick move, raised his long pole in order to strike a second blow, but just when the pole was about to hit her on the head, she stepped to one side and with a large swipe of the machete, chopped it clean off. The chief laptot stood in a daze, staring down at the stub of the pole that was left in his hand. Before he could recover, my mother launched another shard straight at his chest. Then she broke the clay cook oven on the spot where she and the other women had been cooking our food, and piled the broken pieces in front of her. Every time her adversary tried to hit her with a different pole, she and the young girls pelted him with large, extremely sharp shards. In spite of this, he was able to strike and wound her several times.

The battle lasted for quite some time. Nevertheless, not one laptot on any of the barges did anything whatsoever to defend my mother or to try to calm her assailant. As a result of all this turmoil, our two barges were rocking violently in the water and had drifted a good distance from one another. In a mad fury, the chief laptot began to bellow to his punt men as though completely unhinged. "Come alongside that woman's barge! I'm going to kill her!"

He was about to leap onto our barge, and nobody knows how things would have turned out, when, as providence would have it, a laptot cried, "The commandant's barge!" This made them all freeze in their tracks. Indeed, at about a kilometer's distance before us, the outline of a large barge flying the French flag was coming into view. It was heading straight toward us, propelled by a large number of laptots. It was the commandant of Koulikoro district, who was out taking a census.

The chief laptot gave the order to change direction so as to avoid ramming the commandant's barge. But he hadn't counted on Kadidja's audacity and ingenuity. She instructed the three young women Koudi Ali, Batoma, and Nassouni to start screaming for help as though they were about to lose their lives. Until that point, I had remained at the back of the barge where my mother had put me to keep me safe, but I ran up to her, fascinated by the approaching large boat with its flag flapping in the wind. Instinctively, I added my little voice to those of the women. Kadidja tied a white veil to the end of a punt pole and began waving it as she shouted, "Help! They are trying to kill us!" All the laptots began to worry. They begged Kadidja to be quiet. As for the chief laptot, he tried in vain to lower Kadidja's pole with its denunciatory white veil.

The large barge was drawing closer. Visible at the bow was the tall silhouette of the commandant attired in his handsome uniform, his binoculars in hand. He seemed to have been watching the scene for some time. He ordered our three barges to approach the riverbank. The chief laptot did not know what to do with himself. Having entirely lost his ardor and his arrogance, his cruelty choked back, he had nothing remaining but his trembling extremities. "Shake hard, shake harder than the leaves of a palm tree in the wind!" cried Kadidja. "You will never again beat on another man's wife, and especially not on a woman who is carrying one child in her arms and another in her belly!"

As soon as the official barge had come alongside our own, the commandant leaped onto the deck of our boat, followed by four district guards armed with muskets. He saw Kadidja covered with bloody wounds, her boubou torn and her braids undone. The deck of the barge was littered with pottery shards and various objects that had been shaken loose by the violent shocks of the two boats striking one another. "Everyone on the bank!" cried the guards in Bambara, undoubtedly interpreting the orders of the commandant. We all got off the boat. I can still see myself, pressed up against my mother's boubou as she held onto my arm while I watched the entire scene wide-eyed, especially the commandant, whose appearance at the front of the boat had seemed almost miraculous to me.

Through his interpreter, the commandant began to ask questions. My mother, who still had tears in her eyes, nevertheless responded in a calm and collected voice, exposing the facts in detail. When she mentioned Koudi Ali and Nassouni, all eyes turned to these two young girls, who were standing with their eyes modestly lowered. They were both young maidens who were extremely beautiful and very appealing. Only a saint could have resisted the feelings of desire that they inspired. The commandant asked who they were. "Koudi Ali here is my cousin," replied my mother. "And this is Nassouni Hampâté, my servant-daughter, as is Batoma Sow, who is also with me." She took out the pass that had been issued to her in Bandiagara and handed it to the commandant.

Next the commandant questioned the laptots. They all confirmed Kadidja's story and blamed their boss, whom they hated because of his brutality and bad character.

"There are thirty men here!" exclaimed the commandant. "Why is it that not one of you tried to defend these women and this child from this vile brute that you call your 'boss' and that from now on I will call my prisoner?"

"We are at his mercy!" replied the laptots. "He fires people at will. The Whites at the Deves-et-Chaumet Company trust him completely. They do whatever he asks them to do. As far as they are concerned, he is never wrong. He has us whipped on the slightest whim. He is physically stronger than we are and has anyone who complains put into prison. But the way that he has treated this woman has made us rebel to the point that secretly, we had decided to gang together in order to beat him and denounce his actions as soon as we got to Koulikoro."

"You bunch of cowards!" cried the commandant. "So you were going to wait until it was too late to take action. Know that French law severely punishes those who refuse to help a person who is in danger. All thirty of you will spend a month in prison in Koulikoro, and you will be placed on leave from your jobs for three months. As for your fearsome 'boss,' I will question him further. From now on, his life depends on whether this pregnant woman who has been beaten black and blue will live."

The interrogation did not take long. The man was a brute. He had proven that without a doubt. It is not known how, but as soon as his limbs ceased trembling he responded calmly to the commandant's questions without trying to exonerate himself. He acknowledged all the harm that he had caused and then uttered a surprising statement that would certainly have been of interest to medical researchers. "I don't drink, I don't smoke, I never steal, but alas my great illness is women. When I see one that attracts me, I am capable of killing whoever gets between me and her. My fury can last for up to three days. Like a hurricane, I overturn everything in my path until I sleep with that woman, or until I vomit or have a nosebleed." Then he began to whimper, "I'm sick, I'm sick!"

Everyone exclaimed, "Allahou Akbar!" (God is greatest!), as Muslims are wont to do when they are overtaken by events. As for me, I began to sing over and over a litany composed of the last words of the chief laptot. "I'm sick! I'm sick!" to the point where my mother, who had heard enough, had to slap me a couple of times to get me to be quiet.

The commandant wrote something on a piece of paper. He folded it, poured a bit of red wax on it, stamped it with a seal, and then handed it to my mother, telling her through the interpreter, "When you arrive in Bougouni, go to give this paper to the district commandant." He turned to Koudi Ali. "If your cousin is unable, for any reason whatsoever, to do what I have just asked, you will do it instead."

"I will," replied Koudi Ali.

The commandant attached an iron chain around the wrist of the chief laptot and moved him onto his own barge. He named Bounâfou as the head laptot for the rest of the trip and handed him another piece of paper to give to the director of the Deves-et-Chaumet Company.

This is how my mother's turbulent adventure came to an end. It had cost us an entire day, along with a forced day-long fast, as well as all our terracotta cooking utensils! I would forever after hear many a time the story of these events that occurred on this memorable day because they would become known as "The Battle between Kadidja and the Chief Laptot." It became one of the favorite tales of our family's female storytellers!

The boat finally arrived in Koulikoro. It was going no farther. After that, we had to take the train to Bamako, which was about fifty kilometers away. Of this first train trip, I have no memory whatsoever, and neither do I have any recollection of Bamako. We arrived after sundown, and at dawn the next day we struck out on the road that leads to Bougouni. We only had about 160 kilometers left to go.[13]

Birth of My Little Brother

My mother was getting more and more tired. When we arrived in the large Bambara village of Donngorna, she wanted to rest a bit. Since we had no friends or relatives to stay with, she went and introduced herself to the village chief. He granted us hospitality and housed us in his large vestibule, which served as a guest room for visitors passing through.

My mother would have preferred to give birth at her home in Bougouni, but as the saying goes, "The wishes of men cannot change God's plan." We had barely settled in when she was overcome with violent contractions. Face contorted, biting her lower lip, she began to moan and writhe as she pressed repeatedly on her belly. Great drops of sweat had broken out and were streaming down her face. Then, because she could not stand still, she began to pace back and forth in the courtyard, clutching at her back with both hands. I ran to help her, completely distraught. I hugged her legs with both arms. "Dadda! Dadda! What's wrong? What's the matter?"

Gently, she pushed me toward Koudi Ali, who held me back. I asked Koudi what was wrong with my mother. Who had made her ill? What had made her stomach swell so?

"Your mother is not ill," she replied. "In her stomach there is a little brother or sister that she is going to give you soon."

"Why is she clutching at her back like that?"

Before she could respond, I saw my mother collapse to her knees. This image of my mother on her knees will forever be etched in my memory. Koudi pulled me away. In utter terror, I fought back like a chicken that was about to have its throat cut. But she held me tight.

Alerted that my mother was in labor, the village chief had sent an old woman to help her. The old woman brought with her an earthenware jar filled with very hot water. As was the tradition, she had added the bark from certain trees and a ball of shea butter. She stirred the mixture and gave it to Kadidja to drink. Then she began to massage my mother's back. I wanted to stay and see what was going to happen to my mother. Out of the question! Koudi handed me over to Nassouni, who took me to the house of the village chief's wife. She gave me a handful of boiled peanuts to calm me down.

"You are going to have a little brother or a little sister," she said with a smile. "You must wait here."

I could hear Koudi repeating as if it were a litany, "Youssoufi! Youssoufi!" Automatically, I also began to cry, "Youssoufi! Youssoufi!" I would later learn that Youssoufi (the prophet Joseph) was the patron saint of women in labor and that invoking his name was said to facilitate the labor of childbirth.

My mother did not suffer long. Was it the effect of the decoction, or by virtue of the massages, or by the grace of Youssoufi, or all three together? The fact remains that my mother delivered her baby in less than one hour. Suddenly, I could hear the cries of a newborn. Koudi called out, "Amkoullel! Come here! You have a little brother!"

I ran toward my mother. Her suffering had ended. She was smiling. Her large belly had mysteriously disappeared. Koudi was holding up a large, light-skinned baby boy endowed with a high forehead and an abundant head of hair. The baby, who was apparently furious, had twisted up his little face and would not stop crying. Koudi calmed him with a soft voice, calling him by the lovely traditional name that is given to all newborns before they receive their true names. "Oh blessed Woussou-Woussou! You are welcome among us! Bring us long life, health, and wealth. Don't cry, don't cry, Woussou-Woussou! You are at home, with your family, and only your family!"

She turned toward me. "Amkoullel, here is your little brother that your mother made just for you. He is yours."

"Why is he crying? Isn't he happy? Is he afraid?"

Before I could get an answer, I noticed that my little brother was still connected to his placenta. "Koudi!" I cried, "why does my little brother have that bag with him? What is he going to put inside of it?"

I do not recall Koudi's response, because at that very moment, I saw the old woman return with a knife and a calabash full of water. She was also carrying a pouch containing the traditional gifts used to wash and rub the baby. With a single stroke of the knife, she sliced the cord that had attached my brother to his strange bag, and then she offered her gifts to my mother: soap, rock salt, honey, shea butter, and butter made from cow's milk. My mother prepared to wash the baby and to massage his little body in the way that African mothers do.

Even today I still remember perfectly, down to the smallest detail, the entire film that was this event. It was as though I had emerged from a sleep that until that moment had shrouded my mind and that had prevented me from clearly discerning things. It was on that day, beginning with the birth of my little brother, that I clearly became conscious of my own existence and of that of the world that surrounded me. My memory was switched on at that moment, and since then it has never stopped working.

The village chief dispatched the oldest member of the community to visit my mother. He was accompanied by the "master of the knife" of the secret Komo society of Donngorna. As I would later learn, the Komo is an ancient Bambara religious society open only to adults, whose deity, represented by a sacred mask, is also known as Komo. As for the master of the knife, he is the master of sacrifices and often the master initiator of this society.

The master of the knife examined the newborn carefully. He palpated the bones of his head, beginning with the back of his neck and ending with the forehead. He looked at his fingers, the palms of his hands, his toes, and the soles of his tiny feet. Then he withdrew without saying a word.

The elder, clothed in a yellow tunic sewn from cotton strips, was leaning on a great, leather-wrapped stick. An oxtail adorned with small bells of yellow copper was suspended from his left arm. He called for a calabash filled with clear water. He took it in his right hand and walked to the threshold of the vestibule where my mother was. There, he squatted down and addressed the newborn, with these words: "Oh Njî Donngorna! (Envoy of Donngorna!) You have come to us on behalf of He who has sent you. Welcome! Bring us joyous news. Here is your water. Accept it in exchange for our well-being and longevity."

He extended the calabash of water to my mother. "Pour a few drops into your son's mouth," he told her. When she had done this he added, "We do not know what your father will call you. For us, he is Njî Donngorna, the envoy from heaven to the inhabitants of Donngorna."

Before leaving the house, the old man warned the women: "Dine early this evening and immediately close yourselves inside your homes. The Komo god of Donngorna will make an exceptional appearance in order to come and greet his foreign guest, Nji Donngorna. But the women, the children, and all those who are not Komo initiates do not have permission to see him. If they did, they would risk death. The Komo would kill them without mercy. Therefore, be sure to stay inside."

Following his departure, every family wished to offer something to little Nji Donngorna. This one gave a chicken in welcome, that one gave a ball of shea butter wrapped in damp leaves in order to keep it from melting. Others gave a measure of ground babobab leaves, or tamarind, tomatoes, millet, maize, and so on. Donngorna was a large village with six or seven hundred inhabitants. One can therefore imagine the number of gifts that were offered to little Nji Donngorna.

Later, the public crier swept through the village streets, calling out a warning to dine early because the god Komo would be making an appearance in honor of the Donngorna newborn. A young Fula herdsman who had not left us once during our stay had translated everything into Fulfulde for us.

"What is the Komo?" I asked my mother.

"This god is not child's play!" was her only reply. I had to leave it at that.

As sundown approached, pestles reverberated softly as they were dropped into their wooden mortars for the night. From every direction, cattle, goats, and sheep could be seen returning from the pastures. The sounds of bleating and lowing blended with the barking of dogs chasing after recalcitrant goats. Dust-covered men and boys returned to the village astride spirited donkeys whose heads swung softly to and fro with the rhythm of their walk, as if such efforts would lighten their loads. They all brayed insistently as they drew closer to home, in friendly announcement of their return from the fields. Roosters crowed intermittently in the distance in salute to the mortal remains of the sun as it died in the west.

In one fell swoop, darkness shaded the hills surrounding Donngorna that the last rays of the sun had fleetingly covered with gold. Stripped of their finery, they were nothing now but formless monsters crammed together in undulating torment.

After a hasty meal, our host brought his chickens and goats inside. My mother closed herself inside the vestibule with us children and servants. A few moments later, we could hear the sound of a horn in the distance. It was the trumpet of the god Komo echoing from behind one of the hills. In the silence of night, the echo amplified until it seemed to come from everywhere at once.

A large drum soon joined in with its throaty notes, and a bullroarer added a terrifying throb. Lights were extinguished everywhere in the compound. Everyone crouched in the darkness. Playing dead was imperative, or the god Komo would certainly kill those who were not among his own.

Lying on her side on a mat, my mother nursed the newborn who suckled greedily with his eyes fixed on her face, completely unconcerned about the tumult occurring outdoors. I pressed against her and clung to her back.

Over the sound of the instruments, there rose the beautiful voice of the Komo. Backed by a choir, he sang in Bambara, a language that I unfortunately did not understand at the time. The voices drew nearer. The din of the drums and trumpets made of horn riled the village dogs. From all corners they began to bark in protest, some in long and lugubrious tones, others in short yaps as though preparing to bite. But certainly the dogs must have known that the Komo was not joking, because as soon as the god arrived at the center of the village, they fell silent, as if by magic. It was as though they had been buried deep at the bottom of the millet granaries.

The Komo swept through the village streets shouting the phrase that announced his presence. "Han-han-han-han-han-haaan! n'fani'mba!"[14] The rhythmic, husky sound, expressed by a deep, throaty "h," seemed to emanate from his very entrails. Throughout the entire ceremony the singer for the god and wearer of the sacred mask intoned this litany that etched itself so deeply in my memory that I can hear it still.

When the Komo entered the household courtyard, it seemed to me that the earth would break open. Luckily, my mother, who had sat up, laid me across her legs and bent over me in order to protect me with her body. The Komo must have been very heavy, for the earth shook beneath each of its steps. He remained in the courtyard for a period of time that to me seemed eternal. His chants endlessly repeated the name that the village elder had given to my little brother: Njî Donngorna. He proclaimed, as we learned later, that my little brother was the bearer of good fortune for the entire country that lay between the two rivers of the Niger and the Bani, a three days' walk from every direction.

Finally the god moved off, taking his fracas with him. Everyone relaxed and took a deep breath as though they had just come through a violent tornado.

We could not leave the village until a week had passed, due to an interdict that prevented all babies who were less than seven days old from crossing the sacred Donngorna River, a river that we had to cross in order to reach Bougouni. A Dioula chief and customer of my mother's happened to be returning from

Bamako, leading a caravan of donkeys laden with salt that he was taking to Bougouni. My mother asked him to give good tidings in our regard to Tidjani and other relatives of ours in the city, but she specifically asked him not to announce the birth of my little brother. She wanted to surprise her husband herself.

I was very happy to finally have a little brother. Until that point, it was I who was the "little brother" of my older brother, Hammadoun, who by virtue of tradition had every right over me, and I had been quite irritated at not having one of my own. I therefore stopped feeling frustrated.

In the end, we remained in Donngorna for ten days.[15] I took advantage of this happy time to go play with Bamoussa, the son of the village chief, a boy who must have been about a year older than I. He went completely naked, and carried across his body a bag made from strips of cotton in which he carried everything that he happened to pick up: field mice that had been caught in his traps, grasshoppers, lizards, wild fruits, and more. This changed the life that I had been living as a little Fula boy accustomed to playing among calves, kids, and lambs, and who sucked milk directly from the teats of goats and sheep.

I found my friend Bamoussa's activities to be great fun, even if they were a bit disgusting. For that reason, I chose to eat just the fruit, and left the mice, lizards, and grasshoppers to him. He would grill them over fires made from small bits of wood and wisps of straw that I helped him to gather. He owned a tiny hoe that he used for digging, a small knife, and a hatchet. In order to start a fire, he had an African lighter made of two parts: a piece of flint and a stone striker. With a supply of tinder concocted from the collected fluff of kapok trees, he could produce a fire at will. The bush was his favorite restaurant. He often ate his lunch there. Some people will be surprised to learn that a child so young (he must have been about six years old) would be capable of doing so much. The reason is that African children were extremely precocious, for their games usually involved imitating the work of adults whom they helped at a very early age. Bamoussa was no exception.

On the tenth day, I saw that three oxen were being loaded up. We were leaving. I didn't want to leave Donngorna, where Bamoussa had just shown me how to ride his father's docile little donkey. I would really have liked to enjoy all these new delights further. But I had to choose. Either I could stay in Donngorna, or I could go with my mother and my little brother, whose arrival had made me so happy and proud.

I didn't want to leave Bamoussa empty-handed. So, without asking my mother's permission, I gave him my best boubou made of bazin fabric. Bamoussa and his parents could not believe their eyes. An embroidered boubou made of fine *toubab* cotton! Never had a child of Donngorna received such a sumptuous gift. In their eyes, I could only be the son of a great king and not the son of a prisoner.

In turn, Bamoussa, also without asking his parents' permission, gave me the most precious object that a little Bambara boy of that time could possess: his *flè*, or small wooden two-holed flute, which was both a musical instrument and a means of calling for help, which every little boy carried suspended from around his neck.

He removed his flè, and put it around my neck with a kind of childish solemnity that our respective parents found touching. It was the best example of the ties that bound us. He did not speak Fulfulde, and I did not speak Bambara. We could only communicate through gestures like deaf mutes, but this had not at all compromised the warmth of our little friendship.

My mother called for our departure. My little brother was placed in a washing calabash lined with soft cloths and carried on Batoma's head as Niélé had once carried me just after my birth.

How pleasant a surprise it was for my mother when a delegation of Donngorna's prominent citizens appeared with three donkeys loaded with food and supplies, along with two young men to drive them and a young girl to help Batoma carry the calabash that held my little brother!

From that moment forward, and for as long as we lived in Bougouni, they never failed to send three donkeys loaded with provisions for their "good-luck messenger" every year following the harvest.

The convoy set off. All Donngorna had come out to hail its little messenger and accompany him to the sacred river.

Bamoussa walked next to me until we reached the river. Then I was lifted onto one of the oxen. I could not keep from crying. Nor could Bamoussa.

A Father in Chains

After walking for a day and a half, we finally arrived at Kadidiabougou, "Kadidja's village." The entire household came out to celebrate. A good bath and a rest were welcome, especially for my mother. As was his habit, Tidjani was not expected home until evening, after his day of work. We had all gathered in the courtyard to wait for him. I had never before seen him, but I knew that despite opposition from his entire family, he had chosen me as his first-born son and had even named me as his successor. He therefore must have loved me very much. I was happy to see my new father and I was waiting impatiently for him.

He finally appeared at the entrance to the courtyard, accompanied by a district guard. His legs were in chains. Upon seeing his wife standing with his newest son in her arms and me at her side, he stood stock still. Then, awkwardly, his steps impeded by the chains that held his legs, he began to walk toward us. This sight was a terrible shock. I turned to my mother. "Dadda, who put Naaba's legs in irons?"

"The toubabs from France," she replied. Instantly my heart filled with anger toward the evil toubabs. There was a hatchet lying on the ground a few steps away. I rushed to seize it and ran toward my father in order to try to break the chains and irons that encircled his ankles. The guard that had accompanied him gently removed the hatchet from my hands. He had tears in his eyes, as did Tidjani.

"When I grow up I will avenge my father!" I cried.

Aside from this little incident, the family felt only joy that night. All our friends and relatives in Bougouni came to greet my mother and to wish my little brother a long and happy life.

As soon as they were alone, my mother gave Tidjani the letter from the commandant of Koulikoro that was to be transmitted to the commandant of Bougouni. When she explained to my father how and why this paper had come to end up in his hands, he wept like a baby and bit down on the base segment of his index finger. "Oh Poullo! Poullo!" he exclaimed. "An elephant's dung can only be collected in its absence!" (In other words, there are some events than can only occur when the person it most concerns is not present.)

Kadidja hastened to soothe him. "When God avenges a man, the man has no right to keep anything in his heart. What have you been wishing for since I left, except to see me again in good health? Well, here I am, back home again with your two sons. One of them has a name, Amadou, and the other will soon be named by you, the one whom the people of Donngorna have already baptized 'Njî Donngorna.' Instead, let us thank God for his protection. And tomorrow morning, when you hand this piece of paper to the commandant, make sure to tell him that the blows that I received from the laptot did not harm me. I was delivered from the situation without harm and my child arrived safely. He is doing well. Consequently, I withdraw my complaint and ask that my aggressor be set free."

My father, who had calmed down, took the piece of paper and returned to prison, accompanied by his guard.

Koudi Ali was taken to the home of Mamadou Thiam, Tidjani's cousin, where she would stay until the day of her wedding to Tierno Kounta.

The next morning, Tidjani went to the office of the Commandant de Courcelles in order to give him the piece of paper. Before he could say a word, the commandant, aided by his interpreter, spoke to him. "Ah, here you are Tidjani! Come closer! I have some very bad news for you!" But at the same time a large smile lit up his face. As was his habit, Tidjani listened to these words without any reaction.

"As for me," he said, "I have come to tell Mon Commandant that my wife, who was pregnant when she left here, has returned in good health. She has given me a beautiful boy. Her labor and delivery went smoothly, although it was feared that her life and the life of her child were in danger as a consequence of the blows dealt her by an enraged laptot during her journey. The commandant of Koulikoro, who witnessed the scene, arrested the attacker. He is keeping him in prison as he waits to see what the consequences will be of the blows that my wife received. Mon Commandant, here is the letter that he wrote for you. I attest that my wife and child are doing well and that my wife wishes to withdraw the charges that the commandant of Koulikoro has filed on her behalf."

The commandant read the letter. "The necessary steps will be taken," he said. Then, from his comfortable armchair, he addressed my father again with a strange smile on his face. "I am sorry that I do not own an astrolabe with which to plot the sun's position as did the Ancient Arabs. But whatever its position, I can tell you that this is a special day for you. Your wife has given you a son, and I have just received in this morning's mail a letter announcing that the time remaining on your prison sentence has been removed. From this day on, you and Tierno Kounta Cissé are free! However, until further notice, you are not to travel anywhere outside of Bougouni. You are no longer prisoners, but you are still under house arrest inside Bougouni district." My father remained unperturbed. "Come now, Tidjani!" said the commandant with surprise, "tell me why neither good news nor bad news, nor ill treatment have any effect on you."

"Mon Commandant, there is no news more serious than that which destiny assigned me on the day of my birth, when it told me, 'You have entered into an existence from which you will not leave this world alive, whatever you do,' and no human power will ever be able to lodge me more snugly on this earth than the moment when I will be in my own grave. This is why no bad news can ever really upset me. I was taught to see death's arrival with the same calm feeling that I have when I see night fall as daylight declines. Every morning when I awaken, I feel as though I have received a reprieve from a death sentence. However, Mon Commandant, I am not a pessimist in spite of it all, and I would not be surprised if one day I once again became the great chief that I once was. Life is a drama that must be lived in serenity."

At this point in his life, Tidjani had learned to tame both joy and anger. He met equally the good and the evil that he had to confront. He attributed both to God and accepted the bitter and the sweet that life offered. This philosophy that he had acquired in Bandiagara at the feet of his master, Tierno Amadou Tapsîrou Bâ (who was also the teacher of Tierno Bokar), had undoubtedly given him the strength to resist without allowing himself to be laid low by the terrible ordeals that marked his existence, each of which could have unhinged the most stable of minds.

Freed from prison, my father and Tierno Kounta returned together that very day to Kadidiabougou with all their possessions, which were limited to very few items. My father's first act was to set a date for both my little brother's naming ceremony and the wedding of Tierno Kounta and Koudi Ali. The dual occasion was celebrated with the participation of all the native officials of Bougouni. Everyone brought a gift. Moustapha Dembélé, "the teaching monitor," with whom my father, in spite of his age, was learning to read and write French, presided over the two ceremonies. Tiemokodian, the great Bambara chief of Bougouni, sent a delegation composed of the most prominent members of his entourage, along with a profusion of gifts. My mother had a number of dishes prepared, along with a sumptuous lamb couscous that was savored by everyone.

As for my little brother, my father gave him the name Cheik Mohammed el Ghaali, the name of the master teacher with whom El Hadj Omar had spent several years in Medina in Arabia and who had invested him with the position of General Caliph of the Tijaniyaah of Black Africa.

News of Tidjani Thiam's liberation spread throughout Massina. Most of his friends and his age-group companions from Bandiagara took advantage of the occasion to leave that city and join him in Bougouni. The first to arrive was his old friend Koullel, accompanied by Tidjani Daw and Abdallah Kolâdo, both equally fine connoisseurs of traditional knowledge, as well as many others who all came to settle in Kadidiabougou. My mother, who had already brought her cowife Diaraw Aguibou, Tidjani's three brothers, and Tierno Kounta's first wife, Gabdo Gouro, this time brought the famous guitarist Ali Diêli Kouyaté, Tidjani's personal griot, and Tidjani's closest servants, Sambourou, Kolâdo, Bolâli, and Salmana, along with a favorite servant who always served him his meals, the gentle Yabara. Tidjani's brothers stayed with us for a while, but then Tidjani sent them back to Bandiagara to watch over the rest of his relatives.

In this way the family found itself partially reunited in Bougouni. It was not long before a veritable miniature court was established around my father. Yes, it was smaller and less brilliant than the one in Louta, but everyone said that thanks to my mother, it was better organized, better fed, and more agreeable. Every evening, the courtyard filled with Fulas, Toucouleurs, and Bambaras who came to listen to Ali Diêli sing or to hear Koullel, the master of Fula "elevated speech," tell tales. Everyone had to be fed, but thank God my mother knew how to make money. Her restaurant and encampment were very successful, and her various commercial activities prospered. Hadn't Kadidja and her brothers sworn long ago that, thanks to them, Tidjani would recover the court that he had lost in Louta?

More than twenty people took their three daily meals at the house. My mother's hospitality was such that the people of Bougouni had a saying, "At Tidjani Thiam's, meals stretch into the street," which was a way of saying that the house was always full of people. Never before had my mother been so deserving of her nickname, *Debbo diom timba*, "Woman who wears pants"!

Tidjani had once again taken up the traditional art of tailor-embroiderer. At the same time, thanks to his Islamic and Arabic background, he more or less served as a marabout for the people of Bougouni. Islam was not widely practiced in the region, so there were not many qualified Muslims. There were still fewer men with extensive religious knowledge. For this reason, Muslim Dioulas would come every day to ask my father for prayers and advice, and he soon became a respected religious guide.

An Ember That Does Not Burn

Sometime after our return to Bougouni, the Commandant de Courcelles, who was taking a census, stopped at our house. I had heard that the White-Whites—as the Europeans were called in contrast to the White-Blacks, or Europeanized Africans—were the "sons of fire" and that their light skin color was caused by the presence inside them of a burning ember. Were they not called "skins on fire"? The Africans had given them this nickname because they had observed that the Europeans would turn bright red when they were angry. I was personally convinced that they were on fire. Needled by my own curiosity, I asked Nassouni to conceal me in the folds of her large boubou. Everyone was filing past the commandant as he entered their names in a large registry. When it was Nassouni's turn, as I was quite well hidden behind her, I very carefully extended my right hand to the side. As lightly as I possibly could, I placed the tip of my index finger on the commandant's left hand, which was lying on the edge of the table. Contrary to my expectations, it did not burn a bit. I was quite disappointed. From that moment on, the White Man was "an ember that did not burn." In truth, I had been quite hidden behind Nassouni's boubou. I had not seen much of the commandant at all. I had barely even glimpsed his hand. Our true meeting would take place soon after.

My little brother, Mohammed el Ghaali (pronounced Raali) was thriving. I loved to watch after him, tickle his cheeks, his plump little arms, his round little belly, and to hear him burst into peals of laughter. Sometimes I would take him outside the house to play. One day, as we were playing by the side of the road, I suddenly saw a White Man appear before us, clothed in an extraordinary suit of clothes, and accompanied by two Black acolytes: a district guard and an interpreter. The Whites, as everyone knows, are powerful sorcerers who emit malevolent forces and it is not a good idea to spend much time in their company. But at that particular moment, it was impossible to escape; we were trapped. I grabbed my little brother and placed him between my legs so as to protect him from the "evil eye" that was emanating from the White-White and from his White-Black companions, who could only be his accomplices, just as the owl, it is said, accompanies the sorcerer everywhere he goes. My voice choking with sobs, I called out at the top of my lungs to my mother, to Allah, and to the Prophet Mohammed.

The White-White spoke to his companions in a mysterious language, and each time he stopped speaking, the White-Blacks would invariably and without fail repeat, "Oui, ma coumandan! Oui, ma coumandan!" These words were immediately engraved in my mind. This could only be a *moolorgol*, an incantation used expressly for exorcizing the evil emanating from the White-White. Automatically, I too began to repeat it, in order to distance my little brother and me from the calamity that was threatening us. I was convinced that we had fallen into the devil's trap and that the mysterious incantation would protect us. Alas, rather than sending the White-White away, it drew him to us like a magnet to iron! My brother, completely unaware of the danger, smiled and innocently held out his two little arms to the White-White, at times tapping the ground with his hands in a gesture of joyous impatience. Completely charmed, the White-White leaned over and stroked his head, his cheeks, and his chin. The gesture, clearly more paternal than diabolical, reassured me. I got hold of myself. Immediately, my innate curiosity got the better of me and I began to examine the White-White in detail.

His garments were remarkably white, but instead of hanging loosely around his body and allowing the air to circulate freely, as African clothing did, they clung tightly to the White Man's form and seemed to serve as a protective shell.

Immediately, an old legend that I had heard and which dated back to the earliest arrivals of the Whites by way of the sea entered my mind. The Whites, it was said back then, were the "sons of water," aquatic beings who lived in great cities at the bottom of the sea. Their allies were the rebel djinns (genies) that the Prophet Salomon had once thrown into the ocean depths, having banished them from the earth forever. These genies crafted marvelous objects for them in their workshops. From time to time, these "sons of water" would venture from their aquatic realm to place their marvelous objects on the shore and would gather the offerings left there by the populace, before immediately disappearing again.[16]

"This suit proves without a doubt that the White-Whites are 'sons of the water,'" I said to myself. "They are a species of giant crayfish in human form, and like every self-respecting crayfish, they must have a shell, however thin it may be." Reassured by this line of reasoning, I examined all the details of the White-White's thin shell, the image of which is engraved upon my memory as though it had been captured on a roll of photographic film. It was composed of three parts: one for its head, one for its torso, and one for its limbs. The head shell was shaped like a squash cut in half lengthwise. It was painted with a white substance reminiscent of the compound that African women make by pounding animal bones and that they use to powder their fingers in order to make their spindles turn more efficiently. The White-White's head ensconced in its shell made me think of the head of *Koumba joubbel*, the hammerhead stork, a wading bird of tropical Africa, although *Koumba joubbel*'s head was more elegantly set and its carriage more lofty. A nasty idea crept impishly to mind, one that I would in fact regret a bit later when I had gotten to know the White-Whites better. Right then and there, I wished that a nasty gecko, that lizard considered by tradition to be unclean to the point that it was nicknamed *geddel Allah* (enemy of God), would wriggle under his head shell and burrow into his long locks of hair. The very idea of it made me want to laugh.

By contrast, the shell covering the torso was artfully arranged. It was composed of two arms, with two vertical lips that met in the middle of the body, and four pockets, two above and two below. The shell's left lip was pierced with five parallel slits resembling small, half-closed eyelids. Upon the right lip were set five large golden buttons that the White-White had drawn through the five small slits. It had two more golden buttons on its shoulders and one on each pocket.

But the shell covering the lower extremities was by far the most strange: it reached down the length of each leg to the ankles, encasing them tightly. As for the feet, they were hidden inside closed black shoes that shone like polished ebony. It was obvious that these shoes had nothing whatsoever in common with those worn by Blacks, the normal inhabitants of dry land.

On his face, the White-White wore a mustache, whose coarse hairs evoked the cropped mane of a colt. His beard, of medium length, was neatly combed.

As I was observing him, the White-White leaned toward me in order to take my little brother into his arms. His body exuded a vapor to which my sense of smell was not accustomed. Although this odor was, strictly speaking, not a stench, it caught in my throat, and I was on the verge of vomiting. I was convinced that the White-White had just cast a spell on me by means of a magical incense that he had secreted from his body. Taking advantage of the fact that he was busy with my little brother, I took to my heels and ran toward the house calling to my mother for help. "Dadda! Dadda! The White-White took Mohammed el Ghaali and then he blew the smoke of his magical incense on me! I tried to eject it through my mouth, but I couldn't and the White-White blocked my throat with a spell! Dadda, hurry! Hurry and save my little brother and quick give me a bath to heal me so that I don't die!"

While I was scrambling to get my mother, the White-White, carrying my little brother in his arms, was close behind me, followed by his two White-Black assistants.

Alerted by my cries, my mother came quickly, but despite her reassuring presence, I did not have the courage to stop myself. I ran all the way into her house and hid behind the little bed that stood at the very back of the room. There, I accidentally disturbed a nesting mother hen. Furious, and no doubt motivated by maternal instinct, she attacked me and let loose a volley of pecks. I do not know how, but I found myself back in the courtyard, my body decorated with down. The deposits from my adversary had no doubt been intended to force me not to forget our encounter. I was quite ashamed at having been beaten and chased from my mother's house by a hen. Surely the White-White must have cast a powerful spell for such a disgrace to befall me, and it had happened inside my mother's own house, where I had come to escape from his spells!

Suddenly, I saw my mother enter the courtyard carrying my little brother in her arms, followed by the White-White and his acolytes. This did not surprise me. My mother, I knew, was afraid of nothing, and she was quite capable of taming even the European devils. For the White-White and his companions to be following her in this manner, as docile as fatted pet sheep, she must surely have neutralized their maleficent powers!

After arriving in the middle of the courtyard, the White-White turned toward me. He asked me, through his interpreter, why I had run away without stopping to wonder what would happen to my little brother. Completely taken aback, I was at a total loss for words. Quite vexed, I bit my lip and hung my head. The White-White then said that he had not known that Tidjani Thiam had such handsome boys. He informed us that his name was de Courcelles, and that in France he belonged to a very old clan of chiefs, and that his ancestors, during a certain period he called "the Revolution" had been stripped of their chiefdom, just as Tidjani had been. Some members of his family had even been executed and others sent to prison following the confiscation of their property. It goes without saying that for this reason, he completely understood Tidjani and felt drawn to him!

As the White-White was speaking, I gradually calmed down. I even began to feel a surge of empathy rise in my heart. He no longer frightened me, and I sincerely regretted having wished that a vile gecko would burrow into his scalp and nibble on his hair. I was tempted to beg his forgiveness for having had such an evil thought, but the fear of being severely punished by my mother held me back. In fact, she never ceased to admonish us: "Fight if you must, but never harbor ill thoughts toward anyone. Allah does not wish it, and the rules of action governing Fula nobility (n'dimaakou) condemn it."

Following a short conversation with my mother, the commandant spoke to me once again. "Your little brother is my Great Friend," he said. "But you, you are just my friend because you ran away from me. A real nobleman may die, but he never runs away."

Just as I had seen it done by the guard when he spoke to the White-White, I saluted him awkwardly, and said, "Oui, ma coumandan!" And in Fulfulde I added, "I am of noble descent by my father and by my mother. I will never again run away from a White-White, even if his name is not de Courcelles. Please, I beg you, make me a Great Friend for I cannot be smaller than my little brother. Otherwise Binta Diafara will no longer want me to be her husband." (My mother's friend Binta Diafara was the daughter of the most valiant Diafara Aïssata, famous for his courage and temerity. I had told her that I wished to marry her. To console me, she had promised to wait for me until I grew up. I considered myself to be her knight-protector.)

After hearing the interpreter's translation, de Courcelles burst into laughter. He stroked my head, and immediately elevated me to the rank of Great Friend, in parity with my little brother.

Except for a few minor details, those are the circumstances surrounding my first encounter with a White-White belonging to a race of men that, until then, I did not like in the least, out of rancor for what they had done to my father Tidjani. After he had gone, I asked my mother, "Dadda, isn't the Commandant de Courcelles a toubab?"

"Yes," she replied, "but he is a good toubab."

This response troubled me. I had decided to hate all toubabs, but how could I hate the commandant who was so nice, and who, I had heard, had done everything in his power to liberate my father? For the very first time, I was learning that the realities of this world are never entirely good nor entirely bad, and that one must know how to put things into perspective and refrain from passing preconceived judgments.

De Courcelles loved horses and he loved hunting. As for my father, he was not only an excellent horseman, he was also one of the best shots in Bougouni—which, incidentally, was a region known for its traditional huntsmen—and a skilled tracker of wild animals and big game. Two outings together were enough to convince the commandant that my father was the companion that he needed.

Commandant de Courcelles harbored a sincere fondness for us that was uncalculating and without ulterior motives. We were therefore obligated to return the sentiment and, through him, to cherish the country to which he was so deeply devoted. We no longer recoiled from discussing France or the French in our household. We stopped cursing them. While speaking of France one day, my father said to us, "The kingdom of France has two heads: one of them is very good, and one of them is very bad." At the time, I had not understood what he meant. It was only later, through experience and a better understanding of beings and things, that I learned to differentiate between the people of France and the behavior of some of its representatives when they were beyond its borders, in the colonies in particular. Was this what he had meant?

I began to tire of spending the entire day at home with my little brother as my only playmate. Of course, we got along like couscous and milk and he happily shared with me all the treats that the commandant brought him every Sunday morning, but he was very small, and I was longing for the company of children my own age. One day, my mother took me to town to visit our cousins Galo Bâ and Mamadou Thiam. The former had two boys my age, Mamadou and Issiaka, and the later had a little girl named Kadjalli. For me, they were the perfect playmates. From that time on, every morning after breakfast, I left the house to join them. A young Bambara boy named Sirman Koné soon joined our little group.

I believe it was at this time that my friends and I became affiliated with Tiebleni, the Bambara initiation society for children. Given that we were living in a Bambara milieu, this affiliation was indispensable. Otherwise it would have been impossible for us to associate with our Bougouni friends, all of whom belonged to these societies. And we would have been obligated to remain enclosed in our houses each time the sacred Komo mask left its retreat to parade through the streets on feast days and during ceremonies.[17] For us little Muslims, this affiliation was purely a formality. We were taught the secrets of the rituals, the signs of recognition, a few tales, but not much more. There was also (apparently since the days of the Mandé Empire, founded in the thirteenth century by Soundiata Keita), a purely formal affiliation with the Komo for Muslim adults living in Bambara country so that they would not be cut off from the community in which they lived. They were excused from sacrificing to the fetishes, did not consume the sacrificed food, did not drink alcohol, and did not attend any ceremonies, but at least they were not obligated to cloister themselves when the Komo appeared. These neighborly relationships of mutual acceptance rested on an ancient practice of religious tolerance in traditional animist Africa, which accepted all forms of magical-religious practice and which, because of this, knew nothing of wars of religion.

Tidjani was a fervent and devout Muslim who even inspired a good number of conversions in Bougouni and elsewhere, but this did not keep him from being extremely tolerant. For him, my affiliation to the Bambara children's associations was an additional occasion to educate me. From that time on, I learned to accept people as they were, whether African or European, all while remaining true to myself. This respect and this willingness to listen to the other, whoever he may be, wherever he may be from, while also remaining rooted in my own faith and identity, would later be one of the major lessons that I would learn from Tierno Bokar.

Death of My Early Childhood

When I had reached the age of seven, my father called for me one evening after dinner. He said to me, "Tonight will be the night of the death of your early childhood. Until now, being a child has allowed you complete freedom. Childhood bestowed rights without imposing any duties, not even the duty of serving and loving God. Beginning tonight, you will enter into your late childhood. You will have to perform certain duties, including attending Koranic school. You will learn to read and memorize by heart the texts of the sacred Koran, also called the Mother of all books."

I could not sleep that night. I was haunted by those mysterious words, "death of my early childhood." What did that mean? When people die, a hole is dug and they are buried in the earth like seeds. Was my father going to bury my "early childhood"? I knew that the millet, corn, and peanuts that were planted in the earth reappeared in the form of new shoots, but I had never seen nor heard of anyone who, like a seed, had germinated and grown up out of a grave. What would happen to my early childhood? Would it germinate into something new? I finally fell asleep with my head full of unsolvable questions. I dreamed the first dream that I would always vividly remember. I saw myself in a cemetery where the torsos of men were growing up from every grave.

My mother woke me early the next morning. She gave me a bath. I wanted to tell her about my dream while she was washing me, but for some unknown reason, I hesitated to do so. In the end, I said nothing. After my bath, she dressed me in a white boubou and then went to get two small calabashes. One was filled with goat's milk, the other with steamed balls made of millet flour.

My father came and took me by the hand and led me through "Kadidiabougou" to Tierno Kounta's house. My mother followed us, carrying the two calabashes. At the entrance, my father uttered the Muslim greeting, "As-salaam aleikoum!" (Peace be upon you.) Tierno Kounta, who had recognized Tidjani's voice, came out and responded, "Wa aleikoum essalaam! (And peace also unto you!) Bissimillahi! Bissimillahi!" (In the name of God, welcome!)

While Tierno Kounta and my father were exchanging the other customary lengthy greeting litanies, at the entrance to the house Koudi Ali spread an embroidered mat depicting the history of Massina, upon which she placed a handsome sheepskin. With a signal from Tierno Kounta, my father took his seat. He had me sit next to him, and my mother sat on my other side.

"Tierno Kounta," said my father, "our arrival at your house at such an early hour is not untoward."

"May it be so! It is with both hands open that I receive your visit!"

"Our son Amadou has reached his seventh year. We have brought him to you so that you may teach him the Koran as Muslim law dictates."

My mother held out the two calabashes. "Here is the food required by tradition: goat's milk and balls of millet."

Tierno Kounta took the two calabashes, placed them next to his prayer rug, and then went into his house. When he came out, he was holding in his right hand a small wooden tablet, and in his left hand a bowl filled with fine sand in which he had firmly planted a small gourd containing black ink (made from charred wood and gum arabic), and several reeds that had been carved into pens. He placed these objects on the ground, and then, turning to the east, he opened his palms and recited Al-Fatiha, the first surah of the Koran known as the "opener," which is a foundational ritual text in Islam. Into a small calabash he poured a bit of ink and some goat's milk, dipped a reed pen into this mixture, and then wrote a long Koranic text on the tablet. Next, he rinsed the tablet with milk, and carefully collected the milk and ink mixture. He then dipped the three millet balls into the mixture and gave them to me to eat. Then he had me drink three swallows of the mixture. It tasted much better than I had expected.

Following this little ceremony, Tierno Kounta had me pronounce the *shahada*, or Islamic profession of faith: "Achhadou an la ilaha ill'Allah[18] (I bear witness that there is no god but God) oua Mohammad rassoul-Allah" (and that Mohammed is the messenger of God). This is how he received my conversion to Islam, a conversion that would be my decision to renew on my own volition once I had reached adulthood. He once again took up the tablet and wrote seven letters of the Koranic alphabet upon it. Next, he had me sit on my heels in the traditional Muslim position, where the weight of the body is essentially placed on the left foot. He had me hold the tablet so that the top would rest on my left forearm and the bottom on my right thigh. With my right index finger, I had to point at each of the seven letters that he had traced in large characters. I was ritually prepared to receive the teachings of the sacred book.

With religious reverence, Tierno Kounta himself traced each of the seven letters with his right index finger, pronouncing each time the name that the Fulas had given them. These seven letters were those that compose the Islamic formula, *Bismillah* (in the name of God), that is found before each surah of the Koran and that Muslims utter before any action or important undertaking in their life.

Seven times Tierno Kounta repeated the lesson, and seven times I parroted him before he sent my parents away. I then had to sit in a corner of the courtyard and repeat the lesson four hundred and eight times as I traced the letters with my finger. It took me about two hours. When I had finished, Tierno Kounta told me to go and place my tablet against the inner wall of his house and go home. The next day was a Thursday, traditionally a school holiday. Therefore, I was not to return before Friday. I carefully put my tablet away and dashed home to my parents, all the while humming a neat little rhyme that gently mocked my teacher. It was a tune that all little Muslim Fulas learn well before they ever attend Koranic school.

Although I was elated to be set free, the ceremony of that first lesson had nevertheless left a big impression on me. Once home, I was so proud of what I had learned that I irritated everyone by shouting my first lesson over and over at the top of my lungs. It took the intervention of none less than my father to make me stop.

Ever since Naaba had spoken to me regarding the death of my early childhood, my self-importance grew. It became even more inflated and overblown since my mother had begun to grant me more freedom. She no longer forbade me from going alone to central Bougouni. My friends Mamadou, Issiaka, and Sirman would come to get me on Wednesday afternoons, and because the next day was a holiday, I sometimes spent the night with them. That way, we could have two full days for running through the bush and the neighboring woods. We soon formed a group of four veritable little devils, impenitent trappers of mice and lizards and incorrigible marauders of small vegetable gardens. I was careful not to bring my booty of fledglings and various other creatures back to the house, for my parents would surely have given me a thorough spanking. Neither of them liked seeing any animals being mistreated, and they would never have pardoned even the tiniest larceny!

Danfo Siné the *Dan* Player

The great Bambara chief Tiemokodian, my mother's protector from the time when she had arrived in the area, also became friends with Tidjani. Any time he went to visit the Commandant de Courcelles—which he did almost every day—he did not fail to stop by the house to say hello to the family. He was always accompanied by a group of servants, courtiers, and friends, among whom there was at times a striking man who seemed different from the others. Of average height and build, he had a rather round face and a thick nose, which certainly did not add to his appearance. But his eyes were so expressive and his gaze so piercing that it was almost frightening. A sort of mysterious power emanated from this man. As I later learned, he was a Bambara "man of knowledge," a doma, and thus a "great man of knowledge," a term often translated as "traditionalist" in the sense of being an "expert in the area of traditional knowledge."[19] There are domas in every branch or area of knowledge, but he was a full doma. He was in possession of all the knowledge of his time having to do with history, the social, religious, symbolic, and initiatory sciences, the natural sciences (botanical, pharmacological, mineralogical), not to mention myths, fables, legends, proverbs, and so on. He was also a wonderful storyteller. It was from him that I first heard the many Bambara and Fula tales and legends from the Wassoulou region, where these two ethnic groups live closely together.

Poet and grand master of the word, he was famous in all the lands that lie between Sikasso and Bamako. But above all, he was an eminent master of Komo initiation, a master of the knife (that is, a ritual performer of sacrifices, a teacher, and hence a blacksmith by profession), and one of the most famous Komo singers that had ever been known in the region.

In certain villages, the sacred mask of the Komo could appear only when he was present. When he met my father, he had just completed his *Korojuba* septenary, one of the most advanced Bambara and Senoufo initiatory schools of the savannah in Western Sudan, whose name means "great trunk of things," that is, "the great trunk of knowledge," the center of which was located in Bougouni district at the time.

He was called Danfo Siné, or, "Siné, the *dan* player" because he was never without his *dan*, a kind of five-string lute made from half of a large calabash. He played it with astonishing virtuosity, although he was no ordinary musician. When he pressed on the strings of his dan, he would recite certain incantations that had the power to plunge him into a trance. He would begin to predict the future with an exactness that stupefied all the inhabitants of the region and even of the surrounding lands, since his predictions were immediately carried very far, all the way to the banks of the Baoulé River.

For instance, he had predicted one year ahead of time that the cavalry of the kingdom of Kenedougou would invade M'Pegnasso, Bolona, and the surrounding villages. He announced that the country of Tengrela would be set on fire by four war chiefs coming from Sikasso, and he predicted the coming defeat of Samory Touré. Regarding my father, he informed him of the impending death of King Aguibou Tall of Bandiagara and my father's final release from prison, events that took place exactly as he had stated they would.

Danfo Siné traveled throughout the country with a group of neophytes, whom he was training. He sang and danced almost every evening in Bougouni. These exhibitions were not just for entertaining people, and still less were they for making money. Strictly speaking, nothing that he did was secular. His dances were ritualistic, his songs were often spiritually inspired, and his storytelling sessions were often richly educational.

As a virtuoso musician, he could make his hands and his voice do his bidding. He could make his audience shiver as he imitated the roars of an angry lion, or he could rock it softly as he imitated an entire chorus of trumpeter hornbills. He could croak like a toad or bellow like an elephant. I do not know of a single animal cry or musical instrument sound that he could not imitate. Mr. Ostrich himself, king of the bush dancers when he is courting his belle, got jealous when he danced. He was as supple as a vine, and there was no acrobatic feat that he could not perform.

This extraordinary man was drawn to the little boy that I was. Since I was at an age where my brain, as he put it, "was still a moldable piece of clay," he always placed me next to him when he spoke, and with my parents' permission, he even took me at times to see some of his away performances. These were often singing and dancing performances that symbolically retraced the different phases of the earth's creation by *Maa n'gala*, the supreme creator, God of all things.[20] Taking up his dan, Danfo Siné would begin to play with his eyes closed, without saying a word. His fingers would fly over the strings of his instrument while his face gradually became covered with shiny droplets. He would stop playing. Then, like a diver returning to the surface after lingering in the watery depths, he noisily blew the air from his lungs, took up his dan again and sang a song whose hermetic words evoked the mystery of creation from primordial unity. In this song, when he sometimes replaced the interjection *Ee Kelen* (O One!) with the divine name Maa n'gala, he would fall into a trance and begin issuing prophesies. He would sometimes also perform all sorts of impressive and prodigious feats for the public. The memory of them sometimes troubled my nights.

There were large gatherings almost every night in the courtyard of my parents' house. Here is where the best Fula and Bambara storytellers, poets, musicians, and traditionalists would meet. Koullel and Danfo Siné were their uncontested rulers. My family now spoke Bambara perfectly and it did not take the new arrivals long to assimilate. As for Danfo Siné, he had learned Fulfulde in the Wassoulou region where the Bambaras and the Fulas lived closely intermingled with one another.

As a small child, I had already heard many narratives that had to do with the history of my maternal and paternal families, and I knew the fables and little tales that were told to children. But here I discovered a marvelous world of myths and great, fantastical tales whose initiatory meaning would not be revealed to me until later. I discovered the grand, heady epics relating the exploits of our historical heroes, and the charm of the illustrious music and poetry sessions where improvisation was the challenge.

On certain festive occasions at our house, Danfo Siné would bring masked dancers from the important initiatory *Korojouba* school where he himself was a grand master. But there was also another type of dancer that I preferred above them all. These were the *Hammoulé*. Like the Korojouba, they were traditionally free of all social conventions. They jostled customs, jumbled their words, and did everything backward, performing thousands of pranks that brought joy to those in attendance. While Dano Siné could be quite frightening, the Korojouba and Hammoulé were just as entertaining. Watching them, I even sometimes forget my Koranic lessons.

Someone once asked me when I had begun to collect oral traditions. I replied that I had begun in my early youth and never stopped. I had had the luck to be born and grow up in an environment that was a permanent academy of everything concerning African history and traditions.

What I had heard during the evenings in my parents' courtyard, I would transmit the next day to my little playmates. This forged my first capacities as a storyteller. But I did not do this systematically until a few years later, when we had returned to Bandiagara, where I formed my first waaldé association, which would contain up to sixty-six boys my age.

Death of My Old Master

Worn out by prison and forced labor, my master, Tierno Kounta, was unable to recover from the exhaustion and deprivation that he had experienced. He no longer had the strength to teach me. Although I had learned the letters of the Koranic alphabet and their names in Fulfulde, I could barely read groups of letters or spell any words.

His strength was gradually draining away. His appetite weakened daily. He was wasting away before our very eyes. His memory of beings and objects was failing. Already very frail, the final blow came when he suddenly learned of the death of his only daughter, Fanta, whom he dearly loved and who had been "ravished" from him by a French soldier.

Fanta Kounta Cissé was one of the most beautiful girls of Bandiagara. Twenty sons of prominent Toucouleur families had been her suitors and had officially asked for her hand. The competition, which had cost a prodigious amount of gold and livestock, had lasted for an entire year. Finally, it was Badara Thiam, Tidjani Thiam's youngest brother, who had won out over his rivals. But his tragic death in Toïni put an end, at least temporarily, to any other wedding plans. It was at that time that Captain Alphonse, the military commander who had been assigned to the states of King Aguibou Tall, saw Fanta Kounta. I do not know exactly what the circumstances were, but in any case, he fell madly in love with the young girl, and he used the law of the survival of the fittest to make her his "colonial wife," as was the custom of high-level colonial officials.

Indignant and humiliated, the young Toucouleurs who had been Fanta's suitors hatched a plot to assassinate Captain Alphonse. King Aguibou Tall got wind of the plan. In order to avoid a tragedy, he wrote to his friend, Colonel Archinard, who was in Paris at the time. He asked him to intervene with the authorities in order to distance Captain Alphonse from Bandiagara as quickly as possible.

In those days, when they changed posts, it was the custom for colonial administrators and soldiers to abandon the women that they had taken with or without a "colonial marriage." They even often bequeathed them to their successors. King Aguibou was counting on this custom in order to bring Fanta back and to smooth ruffled feathers. Unfortunately, Captain Alphonse was the exception to this rule. He had married Fanta not just to appease a passing desire but because he truly loved her. Thus, when the order came from Paris to send him to Lobi-Gaoua, much to the great anger of all the young Toucouleurs of Bandiagara, he took her with him. On the day that Tierno Kounta learned this news, he was already in prison. He subsequently developed a lasting rancor toward all French people. And this was not without good reason. First, he had been thrown into a prison cell, and then his daughter had been taken from him.

While an insidious illness was eating away at my master in Bougouni, a pernicious fever that manifested during the birth of her first child in Lobi-Gaoua took Fanta's life within twenty-four hours of the delivery. Insane with grief, Captain Alphonse tried to kill himself. In the end, he had to be repatriated to France shortly after that for health reasons. He telegraphed the district commandant in Bougouni, along with Tierno Kounta, to announce the sad news. One afternoon, the postman walked into the courtyard holding a blue piece of paper in his hand. Tierno Kounta had just finished teaching me my lesson. I had taken refuge in the shade of his house where I was carelessly reciting in monotones the words that he had written with such difficulty on my tablet. The postman held out the missive: "Urgent blue paper from Gaoua," he said. Tierno Kounta called for my father, but because his French was still rudimentary, my father preferred to have Moustapha Dembélé, the "teaching monitor," come as quickly as possible.

As soon as Moustapha Dembélé arrived, he read the blue paper and then said in Fulfulde, "Fanta Kounta passed away yesterday morning in Gaoua. Captain Alphonse must return to France. He requests that Fanta's mother come to gather her daughter's possessions."

Suddenly, I heard an explosion of piercing cries from Tierno Kounta's two wives. I saw Gabdo Gouro, Fanta's mother, writhing and moaning on the ground. Right then and there, in the Fula women's tradition, she composed and sang a poem in which she expressed her pain, punctuating it with the long cry, "Mi héli yooyoo! Mi héli!" (I am broken, oh héli Yooyoo!), that Fula people utter when they are in distress and in memory of the original land of Héli and Yooyoo, the paradise lost, where at the dawn of time, they lived in happiness, sheltered from all the ills of existence before they were dispersed to the four corners of Africa.[21] Here are a few excerpts from that poem that I would often hear again after that, because my family members immediately memorized it.

> "Mi héli yooyoo! Mi héli!"
> O God, what have I done, what have I said against you?
> O heaven, descend to the earth
> That has just swallowed my daughter
> Take my Fanta back,
> She is my gold, my hope, my reason for living!
> Alas, the earth has just swallowed her!
> . . . .
> Mi héli yooyoo! Mi héli!
> Why had I not gone deaf,
> So that I did not have to hear the awful news,
> News that like a sharp knife
> Cuts out my seven viscera?
> Mi héli yooyoo! Mi héli!
> O Saturday of misfortune
> Lit by a dolorous sun!
> O Saturday of repetition![22]
> Your night shall cover me with a shadow
> as dense as the darkness of the earth's entrails where my Fanta lies!

Her lament, traversed by the long, despairing cries of "Mi héli yooyoo!," was heart-wrenching. Old Tierno Kounta, who had turned to stone upon hearing the news, finally fainted. My father tried to revive him, but in vain.

"Naaba, who beat my Master?" I asked.

"Nobody beat him. He is ill."

The doctor's aide, who had been summoned for the emergency, examined Tierno Kounta and declared that his heart was still beating. By performing all the necessary respiratory maneuvers, he succeeded in reviving him. But at the moment when Tierno Kounta came to and tried to sit up, he was seized with a violent contraction. An inarticulate noise escaped from his chest. He let out a mighty gasp and then a jet of vermillion blood spewed from his mouth. I was seized with a terrible fright! It was the first time that I had ever seen anyone vomit blood.

The old man was carried in to the house of his first wife, Gabdo Gouro. He was placed on his *tara*, a bed made from large sticks and covered with a mattress. A white cover was placed over him. I heard my mother say to her cowife Diaraw Aguibou, "Tierno Kounta will not outlive his daughter. He loved her too much. The news has cut his heart in two."

The entire family circled around the dying man. I had not been sent away. I felt sorry for the state that my master was in and found it quite sad. But deep inside, my *nafs*, or secret self, whispered softly to me, "From now on, you will be free to go and have fun every day with Sirman and your other friends. Tierno Kounta's illness means vacation for you."

Danfo Siné was called in. At the bedside of the sick man he spread a layer of fine sand in which he inscribed a series of symbols that he studied at length. Biting his lower lip, he shook his head pensively and looked at my father for a long while. Then he rose and drew him outside in order to speak to him. Sometime later, Batoma came to tell my mother discreetly, "Naaba said that Danfo Siné only gives Tierno Kounta two weeks, three at the most, to live. But you must hide this bad news from his wives."

My mother tried her best to soothe Tierno Kounta's wives with a few words of hope and comfort.

For a while, things went along as usual at the house, but listlessly so. In order to better assist their husband, Tierno Kounta's wives had ceased crying. Fanta had been slightly forgotten and was finally allowed to sleep peacefully in her grave. Indeed, isn't it said that tears and crying prevent the soul of the deceased from sleeping in peace and interfere with its ascent by reminding it of the attachments and emotions from which it must be able to free itself? This is why, for Muslims, it is advised to pray for the deceased not with tears, but with a heart filled with peace, love, and trust.

The care and remedies dispensed by Dano Siné had no effect. My father went to see Commandant de Courcelles in order to inform him of the state that his friend was in. "A White healer is expected to come through Bougouni tomorrow," the commandant told him. "I will ask him to examine and care for the sick man." The next day, in late morning, the White healer came to our house. In order to receive him, Tierno Kounta was helped to sit up in bed, with his back supported by cushions, and held up by his wife.

The White healer was the second toubab that I had seen up close. His movements, which were nothing like those of our traditional healers, filled me with surprise. First, he examined the hands, eyes, tongue, ears, and feet of the sick man. After that, he placed a towel on the sick man's back. He put his left hand flat on the towel, then with his index finger bent back, he gently tapped his hand, while he moved it in every direction over the sick man's back. He asked Tierno Kounta to take a few deep breaths, and then to cough. He listened closely. Next, he turned him onto his back, palpated his stomach, and then had him stretch and contract his legs a few times.

In silence, he gazed at the sick man for a long while, seemingly lost in thought. Then he rose and gave some medications to the family, explaining how they were to be taken. As he was leaving the house, he noticed me standing behind my father, from where I had watched the entire scene. He stroked my head a few times, raised my chin, and his blue eyes looked piercingly into mine. He smiled, and I could not help smiling back. Finally he left, but not before casting a final glance at Tierno Kounta, who tried without success to raise his right hand in military salute, as was the habit of the Africans in those days every time they met a White Man.

For the entire week, Tierno Kounta remained stable. When my father went into town to join in Friday prayers, he asked the faithful to pray for the man who had been chosen to recite the Koran before the door of the first king of Bandiagara, Tidjani Tall, who had served as cadi in Louta province, and finally, who, as a friend, had suffered along with him in times of hardship and misfortune.

The night of Friday into Saturday was very difficult. Tierno Kounta's wives could not sleep at all. At around nine o'clock on Saturday morning, Gabdo Goura came running to our house. Her hair was undone, her eyes were red, and her lips were dry from insomnia. With a voice made rough from crying, she called to my father, "Oh, Naaba! Quick, come see Tierno Kounta. I no longer recognize the look on his face. He is speaking a language that Koudi and I do not understand. He will not look at anything but the ceiling."

My father and mother rushed out, close behind Gabdo. I quietly followed them. My old master, who was lying on a mat in the middle of the room, was opening and closing his fingers, which seemed to be trying to grasp something. My father sat down next to him on the mat and extended his legs along the length of his body. He gently raised the old man's head and placed it on his legs. Then he pronounced the shahada for him, as it is customary to do for the dying who can no longer speak: "La ilaha ill'Allah, oua Mohammad rassoul-Allah." (There is no god but God, and Mohammed is God's envoy.) Tierno Kounta's breathing seemed to be suspended. He opened his mouth and took a deep rattling breath. His eyes seemed ready to leave their sockets. His chest swelled and then suddenly collapsed. With this final breath, the old man passed away.

My father closed the mouth that had remained agape, as though the dead man's soul had left his body through that passageway, and lowered his eyelids. Then he recited the shahada aloud, which he had been quietly reciting throughout Tierno Kounta's death throes, which had been brief and relatively painless. I saw two big tears slide down my father's cheeks. They rolled into his beard and disappeared.

As soon as Gabdo heard my father recite the shahada aloud, she ran and leaped into the air as though propelled by a spring. Then she crumpled to the ground and began to roll in the dust, crying out in grief. After a few moments she calmed down and began a soft lament. Then, as she had done on the day when she had learned of her daughter's death, half singing, half crying, she raised her voice and composed a new and heart-wrenching lament in Fulfulde.

> O Saturday of repetition, here you are, right on time!
> Fanta did not suffice, you had to take Tierno Kounta too!
> *Mi héli yooyoo! Mi héli!*
> Oh Kounta, why did you answer
> The call of the one who took your daughter away?
> . . . .
> We, your widows, have become
> Two vessels without lids
> Two bodies without breath
> Two doorways without doors
> Two gardens without water
> *Mi héli yooyoo! Mi héli!*

My mother, who was crying too, dried her tears. She took Gabdo in her arms and rocked her gently as she urged her to come to terms with her grief. "Take heart, O Inna Fanta (Mother of Fanta). Come back to your Lord, you are drifting away. To be Muslim means be able to accept God's will and to suffer courageously without committing blasphemy. Tierno Kounta and his daughter have answered the call of their Lord. When our hour has come, when it is our turn, we shall answer that same call, and we shall depart under the same circumstances as those who have gone before us. Tierno Kounta and Fanta are not the first to leave, and they will not be the last. Let your husband and daughter depart in peace. Have you forgotten that crying and tears distract the soul of the deceased as it ascends toward God and that they also trouble their accompanying angels?"

Then she added, "Tierno Kounta did not leave you alone. Tidjani's family and mine will always be with you both, for better or for worse. And even if

God only gives us one stalk of millet and ten cowrie shells, we shall share them with you."

Sometime later, visitors from town began to arrive. Each woman who arrived cried, "Mi héli yooyoo! Mi héli!" and then went to embrace Gabdo or my mother, whom Gabdo was still holding. People rivaled one another to say the most touching words in praise of the deceased. The men were welcomed by Bokari Thiam, Tidjani's half-brother, who happened to be staying with us at the time. Koullel, accompanied by two or three men from our household, took responsibility for digging the grave. My father, with the help of some servants, planted a series of poles in the courtyard upon which several mats were hung in order to create a kind of shelter. Tierno Kounta's body was carried there. In the courtyard, women began to heat water. The hot water was poured into large calabashes that were taken behind the mats, where Ibrahima Sawané, the man who washed the dead, undertook, along with my father, Tierno Kounta's mortuary ablutions.

Nobody paid any attention to me. While I pretended to be playing, I was watching everything and did not miss a single thing. I really wanted to go see what was happening behind the mats, but I feared my father too much to risk it.

Finally, the body of Tierno Kounta, dressed in funeral clothes and rolled in a mat woven from palm fronds, was carried into view. The crowd murmured a litany composed of lines from the Koran: "God is great! There is no recourse nor power but in Him! To Him we belong, and to Him we shall return! Let us exalt Him and may His will be done! Amine!"

The body was placed before the imam in the middle of the courtyard. All the men stood behind the imam and celebrated the prayer for the dead. The women, who had ceased crying, remained seated and were silent. When the prayer was over, several men took the body and carried it about five hundred meters to the grave that had been dug.

I wanted to follow the procession, but Sambourou, Tidjani's main servant, sent me away. I began to cry softly. My uncle, Bokari Thiam, who was walking by, asked me what was wrong.

"I want to accompany my Master Tierno Kounta like everyone else," I said between two sobs, "but Sambourou won't let me."

My Uncle gave Sambourou a severe look, and then leaned toward me. "Give me your hand and come with me. Sambourou is an idiot."

Then he took me with him to the edge of the grave where Tierno Kounta was to be buried. Two men were standing in the main grave, known as the "mother grave." They carefully received the body and placed it in a lateral niche that was dug directly into the east wall of the grave, and that is called the "daughter grave." Tierno Kounta was laid on his right side, turned toward Mecca. As was customary, his face was partially uncovered so as to place a few green jujuba leaves in his mouth, symbols of immortality.

While the grave was being dug, the first and last shovelfuls of earth had been set aside. Once the body was set in place, the first and then the last shovelfuls of earth were thrown on it, so that what had been on top would go underneath, and what had been underneath would go on top. Then the grave was filled in.

When the grave was finished, my father traced on top of the mound the letters in Arabic composing the name Fatima bint Assadin, the mother of Ali, cousin and son-in-law of the Prophet, who was the fourth caliph of Islam. According to tradition, the eleven letters of this name were said to have the power of making the earth weigh more lightly on the body of the deceased while also strengthening his courage as he faced the interrogating angels, Mounkari and Nakir.

Those in attendance sat at the edge of the grave and recited eleven times the one hundred and twelfth surah of the Koran, known as *Ikhlass* (purification), traditionally recited for the dead. Then, everyone returned to the courtyard. My father thanked the crowd and released everyone after first making sure to ask that the creditors or debtors of Tierno Kounta's estate make themselves known that very day or, at the very latest, within the seven days following the death.

Everyone went home. This was the end of my master Tierno Kounta Cissé's funeral, may God have mercy on him!

The two widows let down their hair, removed all their jewelry, and made themselves as unattractive as they could. For seven days, they remained completely isolated. After that they once again began to go about their business, but still dressed in mourning clothes. All told, their mourning period lasted one hundred and thirty days.

The first birth that I had witnessed was that of my little brother, Mohammed el Ghaali, and the first wedding was that of Koudi Ali. The passing of my master, Tierno Kounta, was my first encounter with death.

After Tierno Kounta's death, I no longer had a Koranic schoolteacher. I more or less kept busy by reviewing my lessons. Because there was no marabout capable of continuing my education, my father Tidjani Thiam took it upon himself to teach me. Unfortunately, since he was in the habit of being implacable with himself, he was very hard on me and, truth be told, hardly effective. The most that he accomplished was to turn me away from my studies. My mother, bound by the rules of Fula restraint, which forbade her from expressing her feelings toward her own children, could not complain to her husband. That is why her cowife Diaraw Aguibou intervened. She energetically defended my cause and got my father to stop giving me my lessons as the search continued for a competent teacher. This would not happen until our return to Bandiagara, when I would be entrusted to Tierno Bokar.

I took advantage of my freedom to go and play with my little friends, but I also spent a lot of time with Koullel, who continued my traditional Fula education, and with Danfo Siné, who often came to get me and took me with him.

It was around this time that my father put me to a test of courage quite typical of his system of education. I must have been about seven or eight years old. One evening, after dinner, when night had already fallen, he called for me. He handed me a parcel and told me to immediately go and personally deliver it to his cousin Mamadou Thiam, who lived in Bougouni city. Predicting that his cousin would want me to spend the night, he added, "You will return with his reply."

To journey in the dark the two kilometers that separated our compound from Bougouni was no small feat for a little boy my age. As was her custom, my mother said nothing, but her cowife was indignant. "Who would think of sending a child out in the dark all the way to Bougouni!"

Naaba simply replied, "He will go."

And he said a special prayer for me.

Carrying my parcel, I went out into the dark, and trotted down the road toward Bougouni. I jumped at every noise, and I had bouts of shivering. But I was filled with the certitude that my father would protect me against all danger. So on I went. In addition to the young kapok trees that Tidjani had planted along the road during the time when he was still a prisoner, there were other big trees full of bats. Well, it was that time of night when these hybrid animals, birds by their wings, dogs by their heads, and more or less reputed to be vampires, would go out to seek food for their young, incessantly flying back and forth. Their wings flapping in the dark made an impressive sound, but we were so used to living in nature that no animal, not even one with a bad reputation, was able to terrorize us to the point of paralysis. Certainly, I felt a physical fear and my body was shaking, but my mind was calm. Even so, those were two very long kilometers.

When I arrived in Bougouni, I went to take my parcel to Mamadou Thiam, who congratulated me and gave me a little bottle filled with candies of every color. When I told him that I had to return home immediately, he told me to thank my father for the parcel and he likewise blessed me for my return trip.

I returned to Kadidiabougou without incident. The lights were still on. I entered my father's house and found him in prayer. My aunt Diaraw Aguibou said, "Go to bed. You will see him tomorrow."

"That is out of the question. I have to give him a report of my mission."

And I stood there, waiting until Naaba had finished counting his prayer beads as he performed the Tijaniyyah *wird*, that is, the lengthy series of phrases and repetitions of God's name that every member of the Tijaniyyah Muslim brotherhood must recite every night. Until he had finished the main orations of this exercise, he was not to speak or move or even turn his head. I had to wait almost an hour. When he had finished I approached him. "Naaba," I said, "I gave your parcel to my father Mamadou Thiam and he thanks you."

He looked at me for some time. "Ever since the time of Louta," he said (it was the first time that I had heard him mention Louta), "nobody has behaved toward me as you have. Nobody has waited until I was not busy before giving me a report."

He sent me off to bed. I was very proud of myself.

In the Shade of Great Trees

Diaraw Aguibou, whom I called Gogo Diaraw (Aunt Diaraw), suffered periodically from very serious rheumatoid arthritis, and every time she had a serious bout of it she became impossible to live with. For my mother, with whom she did not get along at all, she was like a fishbone stuck in the throat. But strangely, while Diaraw could not stand my mother, and it had been that way since she had married my father, she sincerely cherished me and came to my defense any time that she thought I had been mistreated. Her tempestuous daily disputes with my mother never stopped her from coming to my mother's house at night and demanding imperiously, "Give me my child!" And she would snatch me away from Kadidja, who simply replied, "Go ahead, Tall! Take your child. We'll fight tomorrow!" Then Diaraw would take me back to her house, where she would shower me with goodies as she told me marvelous stories or anecdotes about the life of her father the king. I must say, she was also one of the great sources of information and education in my early childhood, especially for everything having to do with the reign of Aguibou Tall.

From among the anecdotes that she recounted, I will mention one that, I believe, allows us to better understand the complex personality of King Aguibou. Because although he was often implacable in his rancor and vengeance, he also demonstrated wisdom in his manner of governing.

One day, a stranger who was passing through, and whom the king had generously received upon his arrival in Bandiagara, wished out of gratitude to warn the king of a plot that was being hatched against him and that the stranger had discovered by chance. In secret, he gave him the names of the twenty plotters, all of them prominent citizens. In a gesture of thanks, the king offered this unexpected and benevolent informant a very beautiful boubou embroidered in the manner of the Arabs of Timbuktu.

After the man had left, one of the courtiers cried, "Fama! (King!) You certainly have a reliable friend in this foreigner!"

The king replied, "I do not deny that a foreigner can be capable of friendship, but if a friend of any sort, foreign or not, tries to push me into killing or sending any of my own away, then I will consider him to be more dangerous than my declared enemy!"

Shortly after that, a great meeting of all the prominent Toucouleurs was held. The king seized upon the moment to declare, "Oh, people of Fouta! I have been told by a friend who is not from here but who is very vigilant, that you are plotting against me. Apparently you wish my destitution or my death. This friend has advised me to eliminate the leaders and has given me their names. If I listened only to my self-interest and my desire to remain at the head of this kingdom, I would sacrifice these twelve prominent people without hesitation. Many leaders before me have done this, and many will do it when I am gone. But I was born to be a chief, and I am used to being in command. The pomp of the drums and the flattery of the praise singers have not gone to my head nor led me to be brash. The risks that face every leader in this world here below do not trouble me enough to make me knowingly commit a crime.

"I know one thing, and you, my brothers must know as well that in a land where audiences with the king are held in the shade of great trees, the king who cuts his branches will hold court under a blazing sun. It is easy to kill a defenseless being, but that is the purview of the executioner. The purview of royalty consists in cultivating life and prosperity, and it is not always an easy task."

Freedom at Last!

About four years had passed since Tidjani's exile had begun. Neither really a prisoner nor truly free, he was not allowed to leave the limits of Bougouni district. As for my mother, she had traveled several times to Bamako, from which she had brought back local African products and European merchandise that she could sell at a profit. Thanks to these various commercial activities and thanks to the efficient functioning of her lodging and accommodations business, and thanks also to my father's work as a tailor-embroiderer, the entire family or, shall I say, the entire "court"—since, God knows, there were a lot of people at our house—lived well!

Meanwhile, Commandant de Courcelles, to whom we owed so much, had had to leave Bougouni. It wasn't without sadness that we had watched him leave. As a parting gift, he had sent me a veritable treasure consisting of three illustrated catalogs from the French Arms and Cycle Factory of Saint-Etienne. My friends often came to spend the day at the house so as to leaf through the marvel-filled pages. But they weren't the only ones. A good number of adults also came to contemplate the beautiful color images that led them to dream. They found the bicycles, weapons, and mechanical tools particularly fascinating.

One morning in the year of 1908, my little brother, Mohammed el Ghaali, was sitting in the courtyard playing in the sand. All of a sudden he began to sing. "O God! Let my father be set free today! This very day. This very day," and he sang this refrain over and over. My mother repeated her son's words to her cowife.

"Little children are often messengers of God," said Diaraw Aguibou, "I've heard my father say so more than once."

That very afternoon, at about five o'clock in the evening, the new district commandant's orderly came running down from the top of the hill, where the residential palace was located, all the way to the bluff that overlooked our compound. "Tidjani Thiam! Tidjani Thiam!" he cried. Come quickly, the commandant wishes to see you. Drop everything! Don't keep him waiting!" My father, who was very respectful of authority, rushed off like a speeding bullet. This caused the entire family great anxiety. What was happening? Was Naaba going to be arrested again?

When my father arrived at the residence, the commandant received him with a smile."Tidjani Thiam," he said, "your father-in-law, Aguibou Tall, former king of Bandiagara, has just died. From this moment on, you are free to return to Bandiagara or to go and settle wherever you wish. I can now tell you that at the moment of the verdict in your case, a secret political decree was issued that placed you under house arrest in Bougouni for as long as former King Aguibou Tall was alive. That is why, even after your case had been revisited, you were still kept here under house arrest. The decision was made to keep the reason for this disciplinary action secret from you, for it was based in the fear that if you were to return to Bandiagara, you would make an attempt on the fama's life."

"I thank you for this good news, Mon Commandant, but I must tell you that I have been detained here for four years for nothing. I am Muslim. I do not have the right to kill even my enemy, and even less a close relative. Moreover, Aguibou Tall was not just my father-in-law. He was also the son of El Hadj Omar, my spiritual patron, and I would never have done him the least bit of harm. I even let myself be condemned without defending myself so that he would not be charged with anything. I am astounded at the idea that I could even harbor such intentions. But I will live with it because here below, as I have learned at my own expense, human injustice is, and will remain, insatiable. I do not approve of this state of affairs, but I accept it."

About one hour after leaving our house, my father returned home, his face rather more severe than joyful. It was his habit to smile when everything was going wrong and to frown when joy filled his heart. Was this a discipline that he had acquired in order not to be overwhelmed by events, either happy or unhappy? Upon seeing his expression, those who had stayed in the courtyard waiting for his return were overcome with worry. During this time, my mother was working in her house. Diaraw Aguibou rushed in: "Poullo! Poullo!" she cried. "Your man has returned wearing a terrible expression on his face. He went straight to his house without saying a word to anyone. Come quickly! You are the only one who can make him talk!" My mother rushed outdoors, almost bowling me over in the process. I followed close behind her.

She entered my father's house and found him seated on his prayer rug, saying his prayers by means of a thousand prayer beads. I slipped in behind her. When he saw me, Naaba took my hand, pulled me down next to him, and gently began to stroke my head with his left hand. When he had finished praying, my mother asked him what had happened. "The sun has just gone down," he said, "it is time for the *maghreb* prayer. Let us first pay God the homage that we owe Him. Then we will talk about what the commandant had to say."

His prayer rug was carried out into the courtyard. As was our custom, the entire family lined up behind him to celebrate the fourth prayer of the day, known as "the sunset prayer," and one of the must solemn in Islam. When the final salutations and blessings had been exchanged, Naaba, his brow still furrowed, took advantage of the fact that we were all quietly seated around him, and said, "Today, even more than yesterday, we must express our gratitude to God. The day that I left Bandiagara as a prisoner, I did not know where I was being taken, nor what fate had in store for Tierno Kounta and me. When my faithful companion passed away, I asked myself whether I would not one day be laid to rest at his side. Nobody knew how long I would be detained in Bougouni. Now, today, the commandant has just informed me that the sun of my confinement will set at the same time as the sun of this blessed day that we are now living. We are free to leave for Bandiagara tomorrow morning if we wish."

This was greeted with an explosion of shouts and a raft of hugs and communal tears, interspersed with the pious exclamations of "Hamdoulillah!" (Thanks be to God, praise be to the Lord!) and "Allahou akbar!" (God is greatest!) Everyone recalled the words that had been uttered by my little brother that same morning. My father remained silent for a long time, no doubt intending to allow time for these emotions to ebb from our overflowing hearts.

Thinking that he had nothing more to say, Diaraw Aguibou rushed from the compound and began to run toward Bougouni, singing at the top of her lungs, "O Happy Day, O Blessed Day!" She intended to be the first person to announce the good news to Mamadou Thiam.

My father did nothing to stop her. Then he resumed his speech. "It is written in the Holy Book that 'with hardship [will be] ease' (94: 5–6).[23] While we are happy to have recovered our freedom, we will also have to prepare ourselves for a period of deep mourning. Diaraw left like a shot, singing, unaware that our joy is cut by great sorrow. For I have learned that her father, King Aguibou, is dead."

Upon hearing the word, "dead," the great Fula lament, "Yooyoo . . . mi héli yooyoo!," rose in a single voice and floated through the air. Sometime later, when Mamadou Thiam and his entire family arrived after they had almost run to get there with Diaraw in the lead, they could not understand why people were screaming and crying when they expected to find a joyful celebration. Batoma threw herself at Diaraw's feet. Her face bathed in tears, she said to her between sobs, "O Daughter of Aguibou! Cry, tear your garments, loosen your braids, you are a fatherless orphan."

"Me a fatherless orphan?" said Diaraw. "How could that be?" When she realized that it was true, she in turn shouted the lugubrious cry "Yooyoo," and ran to her husband's arms.

At the slightest aggravation, the congenital rheumatoid arthritis that afflicted Diaraw had the particular characteristic of unleashing such violent reactions that, while she was under the effect of the intense pain, she became capable of throwing herself into the fire or down a well. She was worse than a crazed wild animal. Indeed, that is why, as much as it was possible to do so, she was never left anywhere alone.

Suddenly the pain took hold. Her braids came undone as she jerked her head about. Within minutes, she had assumed the appearance of a madwoman. She was a pitiful sight, with her disheveled hair and wild eyes. She was carried into her room and could not be controlled unless she was firmly tied to the wooden bedposts. The entire family gathered around the outside of the house and spent the night "without a hearth fire," that is, a night without any food.

When they learned that Diaraw Aguibou was in mourning and that she was ill, the Fulas and Toucouleurs of Bougouni converged on Kadidiabougou bearing pots of food for everyone. However, with the exception of me and my little brother, nobody ate anything at all.

The pain tortured Diaraw all night long. Tidjani and Kadidja remained at her bedside. By morning, she had calmed down a bit. The fit had passed, but she needed a solid week to recover.

The family prepared for departure. And one fine day in the year 1908, with no thought of ever returning, a veritable caravan set out on the road that took us home to Bandiagara, leaving behind all the Fulas, Toucouleurs, and Bambaras who had come to say goodbye.

4

Return to Bandiagara

I have no memory whatsoever of our return odyssey. Did my mind go dormant under the effects of temporary childhood amnesia? I do not know. On the other hand, I clearly remember our arrival in Doukombo, about seven kilometers from Bandiagara. Because custom dictated that one should return to a city only at sunset, we camped under the great Dogon shelter erected at the entrance to the village. An emissary was dispatched to Bandiagara to announce that we would be crossing through the city. Too impatient to wait, my older brother, Hammadoun Hampâté, took to the road at a run and joined us in Doukombo by midafternoon.

One can only imagine the joy my mother felt upon being reunited with her eldest son, who now stood before her beaming and as handsome as an angel. He was big, and about eleven or twelve years old. He greeted the entire family and then warmly embraced my little brother. I was nudged toward him. I had retained but few memories of our life together in Bandiagara and was a bit wary of him, for I thought of him as a rival who would soon capture all my mother's attention. I already had enough trouble sharing her with my little brother, Mohammed el Ghaali. But my older brother was so handsome and so cheerful that even before he had said a word, he had won me over. I rushed forward to embrace him and we broke into laughter, much to our mother's great satisfaction.

He hoisted me onto his shoulders and carried me to the banks of the Yaamé River, which flows from Bandiagara through Doukombo before emptying into the Niger. We stayed there quite a while, skipping stones. Then my brother went to pick me some jujube fruits and stuffed my pockets with them. He was very happy to see that I was now relating to him as though we had never been separated.

At sundown, Sambourou came to fetch us for the departure. Everyone in the caravan, adults and children alike, donned their most beautiful garments. At about four kilometers from the city, a large delegation of family and friends awaited us. Following the interminable series of greetings and wishes for a happy return, the cortege set off, and we finally arrived in Bandiagara just after sunset.

Tidjani and his entourage headed for his family compound, where his mother, old Yaye Diawarra, still resided. Since she did not have a room reserved for her in those lodgings, Kadidja, her three sons, and her younger brother, Hammadoun Pâté, along with Batoma and Nassouni, went to her father Pâté Poullo's compound.

Throughout the city, the only topic of conversation was the unexpected return of Tidjani Thiam, his positive demeanor, and the size of his caravan. People wondered whether he had really been put in prison.

The following day, as the rules of courtesy required, Tidjani proceeded to the district residence in order to pay his respects to the new commandant (who had replaced Charles de la Bretèche), present his traveling papers, and state his desire to remain in Bandiagara among his friends and family. The commandant refused to receive him. He had his assistant tell Tidjani to lay low in Bandiagara, and above all, for his own good, to disappear. As sensitive as a snail when its horns are touched, my father took these words very badly. He realized bitterly that the very same people who had worked diligently to provoke his destitution, condemnation, and even his death had also turned the new commandant against him.

But it was necessary to settle into our new life. Tidjani had comfortable quarters with several rooms built for my mother in his compound and asked my mother to move there. She wanted to take me with her, but Beydari Hampâté, Abidi, Niélé, and Nassouni were categorically opposed to this idea. "Amadou is no longer a small child who cannot be separated from his mother," Beydari argued. "We are here, and it is we who represent the paternal family to which he should normally return. We cannot permanently leave him to Tidjani Thiam. It is already enough that you took him to Bougouni and kept him there. But he was little, and religious law allowed you to keep him. But now he must return to his father's family. His normal place of residence is with us. But this won't keep him from coming to visit you when he wishes."

At the time, Muslim law as well as custom accorded more rights to the paternal family than to the maternal family for a child over the age of seven. In his role as head of the family, and who had been designated by my father as his successor, Beydari Hampâté had more rights over me than did my adoptive father, Tidjani. My mother formulated a new appeal to the council of elders and religious leaders, but this time she did not prevail. Due to my age, the council decided that henceforth, I belonged only to my paternal family, who took me back. Throughout the entire process, I had refrained from saying anything at all. But since I had been somewhat traumatized by my overly severe Koranic school lessons with Tidjani, deep down, I really wanted to return to Beydari, Niélé, and my old paternal household. For no matter what misdemeanor I might commit, I would always be sure to find clemency and indulgence from them. This arrangement would indeed turn out to be quite agreeable for me, since the freedom accorded to African children would allow me to go between the two households as I wished.

Upon his return, Tidjani found an empty corral and indigent relatives living in dilapidated dwellings. My mother no longer had much property left after the expense of moving such a large caravan, but she sold a part of what remained in order to restore her husband's compound so that he could live, as she had promised, in a manner befitting his name and birth. Then she resumed her business activities.

A few months later, old Yaye Diawarra gave her soul up to God with a satisfied heart. It was as though she had stayed alive only long enough to experience the joy of seeing her son again.

Before going into exile, Tidjani had offered his three wives their freedom. Only his first wife and cousin, Kadiatou Bokari Moussa, had decided to take advantage of this offer and had obtained a divorce. She then married a Fula merchant named Mamadou Bâ and had a son. Unfortunately, her husband passed away shortly after that. When Tidjani returned to Bandiagara, he found that she was alone. She was raising a daughter, Dikoré, that she had had with Tidjani, and the little boy that she had had with Mamadou Bâ. In the Africa of those days, it was unthinkable to abandon a woman to live as alone as a leaf in the wind. This was even more unthinkable if she had children, for she would be condemned to a life of poverty or be forced to live off the charity of her own family, usually one of her brothers. The usual solution consisted in integrating her, by way of marriage, into a new household where she would have the legitimate rights of a wife and her children would have a father. In those days, marriage played a role in the social protection of divorced or widowed women and their children. The family council would meet, and if nobody had asked for the widow's hand in marriage, a cousin or relative who did not yet have the four wives permitted under Islamic law was asked to marry her. (In traditional African societies, a widow generally married one of the brothers of her deceased husband.)

Since Tidjani was Kadiatou's former husband, her cousin, and the father of her little girl, he decided to take her back. After having obtained permission from Diaraw Aguibou and Kadidja, he thus remarried Kadiatou Bokari Moussa, who then rejoined his household.

A Day in the Life of a Child

As soon as our lives returned to normal, my mother, in agreement with Tidjani and Beydari, took me to Tierno Bokar so that I could continue my studies, which I had begun in Bougouni with Tierno Kounta Cissé.

Tierno Bokar had just opened a small Koranic school in Bandiagara that at the time had only two pupils: my older brother, Hammadoun, and little Dikoré, daughter of Kadiatou Bokari Moussa. I became its third pupil. We became known as the "three hearthstones of Tierno's school," an allusion to the three hearthstones that hold the cook pot in an African kitchen. Many other children joined us later.

Tierno Bokar, who had watched over the first years of my life, was as much a father to me as he was my teacher. But, truthfully, at that age, I was more interested in playing with my friends than in going to school and studying, especially since I had found Daouda Maïga again. He had been my earliest childhood friend and continued to be my friend for the rest of my life.

My daily activities did not vary much. Niélé would awaken me before sunrise. I would wash up, perform my morning prayer, and then run off to school where my wooden tablet was waiting, still covered with the Koranic text that had been written there the day before. I would settle into a corner and recite the text aloud in order to learn it by heart. Each pupil would trumpet the lesson as loudly as possible, paying no attention to the others. Strangely, this indescribable racket did not bother anyone. At around seven o'clock, if I knew my text well, I would take up my tablet and go to find Tierno. He was usually to be found in the vestibule of his dwelling or, more rarely, in his room. "Moodi!" (Master), I would say, "I have learned my lesson." I would crouch down next to him and recite my text. If he was satisfied, I could go and wash my tablet so that I could then write the new verses on it by following the model text that he had written out for me. If not, I was to keep the lesson from the previous day and review it until the next day. But in that case, I would then fall a day behind the deadline for learning the Koran. This deadline was traditionally up after seven years, seven months, and seven days. But some talented students, like my older brother, Hammadoun, were able to finish it much earlier. Every lesson that was not learned incurred a punishment from Tierno involving a few light whippings with a switch or, what was more painful, a pinch on the ear. But this seemed quite lenient compared to the treatment that I had endured in Bougouni with my father Tidjani, and when compared to the treatment meted out by a good number of Koranic school teachers in those days.

Once I had copied down the new text, I would present it to Tierno. He would correct it, then read it aloud while I followed with my index finger. Returning to my corner, I would rehash it ten or fifteen times, until about eight o'clock in the morning. Then Tierno would give me permission to go home.

As soon as I arrived at the house, Niélé would serve me my breakfast of reheated leftovers from the night before, along with rice beignets dipped in sauce, beignets with fresh milk, or millet gruel with fermented milk. I would carefully hang up the boubou that I had put on to wear to school, and then I would sit down and eat with a hearty appetite. Once I had eaten, I would remove all my clothing, and like all my friends, I would run outside completely naked. I would find Daouda Maïga and we would go and play outside of town. It was Islam that demanded that children be clothed rather than African tradition, which required clothing only once one had been circumcised.

Although younger than my older brother, Hammadoun, Daouda Maïga had become friends with him before my return to Bandiagara. My older brother was in fact the head of the largest association of young people (waaldé) in the entire city, since it included children from Bandiagara's seven neighborhoods. But ever since we had reconnected and because we were the same age, Daouda and I were always together. From that time on, we became an inseparable pair, all the more so given that our two families were joined. Daouda's mother was a childhood friend of my mother's and had been a member of her association, and our houses were on the same little street. As assiduous students of the wild bush, Daouda and I were above all incorrigible little trappers of animals. Our pilfering of vegetable gardens also sometimes earned me a few smacks on the back from Tierno Bokar's prayer beads.

Naked as jaybirds, we would run all the way to the banks of the Yaamé River. We each carried a long millet stalk with a noose on one end made of horsehair. We used these to capture geckos, those flat little lizards that use their sticky toes to run across walls and ceilings during the night, and whose guttural calls were thought to be maleficent.

This was all it took to condemn the unfortunate creatures to death, since the popular verdict even claimed that killing a gecko would bring good fortune! It is therefore with a clear conscience that we would hunt them deep in their lairs, armed with our long stalks and nooses. By the same logic, we spared neither mice, nor rats, nor margouillats, another type of lizard with nicely colored scales. Then, as if to purify ourselves, we would bathe in the river.

If other friends were there, we would organize a wrestling match, and adult passersby would cheer us on. Since like most Fula children, I was skinny, I was one of the weakest among my friends. But I was very adroit at handling a stick, and I was not afraid of getting hit. Without a stick, I was easy prey, but when I had one in hand, I commanded the respect of everyone and even became a little terror! Daouda, who was well proportioned, was stronger than I and better equipped for hand-to-hand combat. Cheerful and good-natured, he was not out for a fight, but when one did break out, he fought courageously.

We also often played *tèlè*, a game a bit like golf, where a ball is struck with a stick in order to send it into a goal rather than into a hole, and each team tries to keep the other from scoring.

At around noon, we would go home, together or separately, to eat lunch with our families. We would then meet up again after lunch in order to go behind the village and collect millet stalks, two of which would be brought to the Koranic school. They were used at night to build bonfires in the middle of Tierno's courtyard. After nightfall, the older students would study their lessons by firelight, since there were evening courses for those who wished to become *hafiz* following their studies. This meant that they would know the entire Koran by heart, an accomplishment that families would celebrate with a feast. This is how young people were able to write and recite the entire text of the holy book without a single error, even though they did not understand its meaning. Only those who would later learn Arabic could access its meaning.

For us children, classes started again at two o'clock in the afternoon. Huddled in the shade thrown by the wall of our master's house, we learned the lesson that we would have to recite the following day. At around four or five o'clock, following the midafternoon prayer, we were released. We would run home, deposit our clothing, and quickly return to our games.

In the evenings, we usually went to the riverbank to greet the herds of donkeys and goats that were returning from grazing. I was particularly fond of the donkey caravan that was led by a couple of herders and belonged to Malaw Wâki, an important Hausa merchant who had established himself in Bandiagara. Each of us would select a donkey to ride from the river to Malaw Wâki's compound. My favorite mount was a very quiet little donkey that I enjoyed pestering into a trot with my heels. One night, the little donkey, who had probably had enough of my daily treatments, decided to play a trick on me. He quietly waited for me to settle on to his back. Then, suddenly and without warning, he bucked so hard that he threw me off. I landed in the dirt about two meters away. Then he ran off at a gallop, braying loudly, as though to mock me even more. I was badly bruised when I got up. But above all, I was mortally vexed. I developed a dislike not just for donkeys, but also for their keepers, although they had done nothing against me. I stopped spending time with them.

I turned my attention to the herds of goats kept by Séga, an old, half-blind goatherd. When it was time for milking, he would hold a goat close to his body while he clamped one of its legs in his own bent leg as he milked it with his right hand. The milk flowed into a calabash that he held with his left hand. If a goat happened to suddenly get loose and upset the calabash, the children would double over in laughter and jump for joy. This provoked a tidy chain of insults, for like every self-respecting goatherd, old Séga had a bitter tongue and a copious supply of swear words. While he was busy milking, I would sometimes sneak into the middle of the herd, capture a goat, and suck on her teat. Old Séga, whose position made it impossible for him to chase me, would then aim a volley of curses peppered with all sorts of insults at me. I answered him right back, and then, satiated, I would run away as fast as I could. These little escapades went on for some time until I became interested in something else.

Like all the other children in the city, I had to be home by sunset, before the call for maghreb prayer, no exceptions. Twilight, and in particular that precise moment when the sun projects its last rays of light before sinking into the unknown, had always been considered as an ambiguous and dangerous time, when obscure forces are suddenly released. In Fula traditions of old, the sun was thought to symbolize the eye of Guéno, the Eternal One, the Supreme Being. When this eye opens, light is spread over the world, allowing humans to go about their daily tasks. Evil spirits, sorcerers, vampires, and casters of spells retreat into their respective hideaways, while sprites and hobgoblins hole up in their secret havens. But when this blessed eye closes and darkness invades the earth, the frightened chick takes shelter under its mother's feathers, the calf and the lamb press against the flanks of their mothers, women put their babes up on their backs or take them into their laps in order to protect their "doubles" from vampires and blood suckers, insects begin hammering on their anvils, and nocturnal animals deep in the bush begin sounding the innumerable calls that populate the night.

It is the hour when every mother must ward off the "evil eye" of the night. Just before sunset, without fail, Niélé would always burn some kind of special concoction on top of the hot coals. As the columns of smoke unfurled, she would sing a traditional protective litany in Fulfulde as she held me close. As soon as the smoke had dissipated, she would release me.

The White Man's Excrement and the Town Made of Trash

Wednesday afternoons, all of Thursday, and Friday mornings, no school! We were on leave. By ourselves or along with some of our other friends who had begun to join us, Daouda and I took advantage of our freedom to engage in our usual expeditions into the bush or to the banks of the Yaamé. We would pick wild fruit, trap small animals, or fish, roasting and feasting on our catch right then and there. Above all, we would go and gather earth from the termite mounds and work it at the river's edge, fashioning it into toys or little figurines. But we were soon to adventure into more dangerous territory.

At the time, out of the twenty-nine administrative precincts in the Upper Senegal and Niger colony, Bandiagara was one of the most significant, not because of the number of its inhabitants, but because of its political and economic position and the density of its European population.[1] In fact, the city was home to a battalion, which required the presence of a military administration that included ten French officers and noncommissioned officers, and a civil administration that included a district commandant, a vice-commandant, and six or seven French civil officials. In other words, this explains the significance of the French presence in the city, as compared to Bougouni, where, all told, there were just a district commandant, a few employees, and some guards.

Anything having to do with the Whites and their concerns, either directly or indirectly, was off-limits to Negroes, and that included their household refuse and their human waste. We were neither supposed to touch nor to look at them! Nevertheless, one day I heard the shoemaker Ali Gomni, who was a friend of my maternal uncle Hammadoun Pâté, declare that the White Man's excrement, unlike that of the Africans, was as black as their skin was white. I immediately related this strange information to my friends. A discussion followed that was so heated, we almost came to blows. As always, Daouda and I were of the same mind, while our friends Afo Dianou, Hammadoun Boînarou, and Mamadou Gorel vehemently disagreed.

"Okay," they shouted, "you can get away with lying sometimes but at least your lies have to stay within the proper limits! A lie that tries to climb all the way up to seventh heaven will roll right back down and land on the liar's nose!"

Daouda and I were extremely offended by the insulting criticisms proffered by our comrades. The only way to prove them wrong was to go and observe the facts for ourselves, and then to demand a reckoning with the dissenters. There promised to be a hail of blows from our sticks when all was said and done.

The Whites had their residential quarters on the left bank of the Yaamé, while the natives of Bandiagara lived on the right bank. A great stone bridge separated the two communities. The White quarter was nicknamed *Sinci*, meaning, "established." Only the Whites themselves and their principal native auxiliaries lived there. These were the district guards (security agents of the civil administration who handled policing) and the tirailleurs (indigenous military troops who handled the defense of the territory). The tirailleurs were placed under the command of a captain who was assisted by a lieutenant, two second lieutenants, and four European sergeants, in addition to two sergeant majors, four sergeants, and eight indigenous corporals. As for the native civil officials and the native domestic personnel employed by the Whites (houseboys, cooks, and others), they were required to return each evening to the native city on the right bank of the Yaamé.

Sinci was closely guarded. The residential area was under the watch of the district guards, while the military area was guarded by the tirailleurs. These were two groups of well-trained Africans who had been turned into vicious guard dogs. Natives who ventured into Sinci without having been officially invited risked landing in prison or receiving a serious lashing of the whip, at the very least. However, the only place where the White Man's excrement could be found was in Sinci, and Daouda and I were determined at all costs to verify the color with our own eyes. The decision was quickly made: we would go to Sinci and into the den of the beast, come what may! If our parents had known what we were up to, they would certainly have forbidden it by not allowing us to leave the house. But we had kept our secret quiet.

Very early one morning, Daouda and I meet up. We jog down the road leading to the Yaamé. In order to proceed undetected, we cross over to the west, a fair bit from the bridge. Once we reach the other side, we start down a path bordered on the left by the White Man's cemetery—covered in flowers like a garden!—and on the right by the race track. This comes out on the road leading to the village of Dimbolo. As soon as we reach the road, we turn and dive into the bush that borders the south side of Sinci, behind the residential neighborhood. There is a thicket about two hundred meters from the city. Hidden in the high grass, we move in and take our posts, ready to explore the area, when a serendipitous event facilitates our expedition. A line of prisoners approaches, each carrying a big bucket on his head. Under escort by an armed district guard, they are headed toward a large hole just visible in the distance. The wind, blowing in our direction, carries a revelatory odor to our nostrils that has absolutely nothing to do with the aroma of the White Man's cooking. We look at each other in amazement. "Those prisoners are carrying the White Man's excrement!" And in fact, we see the prisoners each in turn empty the contents of their buckets—as they had to do every day—into the big hole dug especially to hold the White Man's excrement, which was apparently too precious to be mixed with that of the Blacks.

Even as we observe from a distance, we are quickly convinced. The White Man drops it "soft and black." It is proof that we were right, but that is not enough. We must return with a piece of the evidence and present it to our recalcitrant comrades. As soon as the line of prisoners has moved out of the area, we carefully leave our hiding place. Hunched over, we head toward the putrid hole. Strangely, the excrements are mixed with an incredible quantity of paper, to such an extent that we begin to wonder whether the Whites also sh** paper. A rather lively discussion even ensues between Daouda and me on this topic, but this is not the moment to linger. We find an old newspaper lying nearby and roll the "main exhibit" inside as best we can in order to take it back to town.

Just as we are about to leave the area, Daouda spies several "trash towns" in the distance. These are great piles of household waste spread out behind the wall of the residential neighborhood. Driven by curiosity, we go to examine them. To our great astonishment, we discover a mine of treasures! The Whites throw out all kinds of particularly precious objects: empty matchboxes, tin cans of various sizes, bottles and flasks of every color, paper with gold and silver foil, pieces of colored cloth, broken or mismatched silverware (including knives, what a find!), pretty painted pieces of broken dishes, old pots, razors with broken handles, broken stovepipes, boards, nails, empty spools, pencil ends, glasses frames, and, above all, thick, illustrated catalogs, among them the catalog from the French Arms and Cycle Factory of St. Etienne, which had already earned me some notoriety among my friends in Bougouni. We gather what we can hold in our arms, having made up our minds to return at another time in order to complete our collection. Then, loaded with our booty, we return to Bandiagara in triumph.

Upon seeing the color of our "main exhibit" with their own eyes, our friends are duly obliged to admit that we were telling the truth. Daouda and I give them a choice: either extend an apology or receive a beating. They apologize. On that very same day, all the neighborhood children are in the know: "Amkoullel and Daouda brought back the White Man's excrement from Sinci! Go look! It's as black as coal!"

After that, Daouda and I would often return to Sinci in order to take new treasures from "trash town," thereby creating, without even realizing what we were doing, a veritable museum of the White Man's household waste. Our collection was arranged at Daouda's, where his mother, Moïré, had cleared out half a shed for our use.

Upon returning from each of our expeditions, we would happily sort through our finds. All this motley paraphernalia was organized, cleaned, and arranged according to our tastes. The pieces of cloth, for example, were used to make clothing for our little clay figurines that Daouda, who was an excellent sculptor, made with his own hands. There were little soldiers who proclaimed their truth to form, figurines of different social classes, but also goats, cows, horses, and so on.

With these clay dolls, we played at recreating real and imaginary scenes from Bandiagara: soldiers neatly lined up to celebrate the Fourteenth of July parade, horse races, the reception of native chieftains by the commandant. The deceased King Aguibou Tall and his valiant elder son Alfa Maki Tall (who had succeeded him as a traditional chieftain of the Toucouleurs of Bandiagara) held a special place. We provided the dialog, as Daouda played the role of king and I that of prince. The great imams of Bandiagara and its important marabouts—including Tierno Bokar—were not forgotten either.

Sometimes our impish and rather aggressive friend Afo Dianou would come and play with us, but we would usually end up in a fight. Since he was a lot stronger than we were, we had no hope of beating him. Our sticks were usually enough to keep him at bay, but if we happened to have forgotten them, our friend took perverse pleasure in upsetting our installation, breaking a few figurines, and especially in snatching some of them. These deeds inevitably led to furious fights where he always came out as the winner. Our only recourse was to destroy our boubous in fits of impotent rage, much to the indignation of our mothers.

During that period, Daouda and I were still the only ones who dared to venture out to Sinci. The expedition was not without risk. In fact, from time to time we would encounter groups of nasty district guards or tirailleurs who would chase us with particular zeal. And if they succeeded in grabbing us, that meant the skin off our behinds. The guards whipped Daouda and me several times and locked us up for having dared to rummage through the refuse piles of the Whites. They would set us free with a merciless barrage of blows, but nothing could make us stop playing our favorite sport. It was not until much later, as we grew older, that we would stop going to rifle through the White Man's "town of trash" like mother hens scratching through detritus looking for food for their chicks.

I Establish My First Association

Our museum, which was unlike any other, had become a destination for many of the neighborhood children. As a consequence of taking them swimming with us, going fruit picking, pilfering vegetable gardens, and holding footraces, moonlit dances, and storytelling sessions with them, Daouda and I ended up assembling a small group willing to follow us everywhere, even when it was sometimes against their parents' wishes. The time had come to establish our own age group association, or waaldé. At the outset, there were eleven founding members. Here are their names, followed by the friendly or playful nickname that we would use between us: Daouda Maïga, known as Kinel (Little Nose); Mamadou Diallo, known as Gorel (Little Guy); Seydou Sow, known as Kellel (Little Slap); Amadou Sy, known as Dioddal (Awkward); Afo Dianou, known as N'Goïré (Glans Penis); Hammel, known as Bagabouss (Beanpole); Oumar Goumal, known as Nattungal (Lazybones); Madani Maki, known as Gorbel (Little Donkey); Mouctar Kaou, known as Polongal (Big Nail); Bori Hammam, known as Tiaw Tiaw (Perturbed); and finally Amadou Hampâté, known as Amkoullel (Little Koullel).

My friends decided to choose me as the leader. This was not surprising since all the members of my family were or had been association leaders. In about 1870, after he was exonerated by King Tidjani Tall, my father Hampâté had founded the first waaldé of young Fulas in Bandiagara. My mother, Kadidja Pâté; her older brother, Amadou Pâté; her younger brother, Hammadoun Pâté; her younger sister, Sirandou Pâté; and even our tutor Beydari were all leaders of their respective associations, which gave them a good amount of power at the time.

In the meantime, we had to gain recognition for our waaldé and give it an official existence. The first step in this process was to establish a connection with an elder association. Indeed, custom required that all youth associations be sponsored by an elder association that would act as its adviser and, if necessary, its protector. Naturally we chose my older brother Hammadoun's waaldé.

We also had to choose an elder, a "father," who would be our *mawdo*, a kind of honorary president, who would always be chosen from among an adult association, which traditionally acted as an adviser, official representative, and even as a defender in case there were problems with the local population.

We chose a friend of Hammadoun Pâté's maternal uncle and a member of his association, Ali Gomni, who belonged to the shoemaker's caste. Daouda Maïga's mother, Moïré Koumba, went to make the request on our behalf. Following the customary expressions of reluctance, he accepted our invitation and set the date of our first formal meeting, when we would elect our officers and set the rules of our waaldé. Every association was organized following a hierarchy that reproduced village or community society. In addition to the mawdo elder and honorary president of our association, there had to be a chief (*amirou*), one or more vice-chiefs (*diokko*), a judge or cadi (*alkaadi*), one or more public commissioners or public prosecutors (*moutassibi*), and finally one or more griots, who would act as emissaries or spokesmen.

When the day arrived and we were all gathered in the courtyard, Ali Gomni spoke. "Before we do anything else," he said, "we must give our waaldé a leader and board of directors, as well as a name to draw it out of anonymity. Whom do you wish to designate as the chief?"

"Our chief is naturally designated," the comrades replied, "it's Amkoullel. Half of the associations in Bandiagara have a member of his family as their head. If he proves himself to be worthy, we will follow him and fight on his behalf. But if he acts like an idiot, we will whip him until he pisses red and nobody can scare us into doing otherwise!"

I was therefore elected as the chief, and the waaldé was given the name "Amkoullel's waaldé." Repeating the traditional exclamation that adults would utter in their large official assemblies, everyone shouted, "Allahou townou dina!" (May God elevate the community to the highest!)

The rest of the meeting unfolded without incident, although a certain number of comrades tried to oppose the designation of Daouda Maïga as cadi (judge). For reasons related to his birth, some recalcitrant comrades would have preferred to see a Diallo, a Cissé, a Sow, or a Dicko named instead. Our elder (mawdo), Ali Gomni, to whom Daouda was apprenticed in shoemaking, took up his defense. He pointed out that old Modibo Koumba, who had taught Daouda's mother and who was considered to be Daouda's grandfather, had himself been a cadi in the powerful association that had been founded during the early years of the Bandiagara kingdom by Amadou Ali Thiam (Tidjani

Thiam's father) before he became chieftain of Louta. In its time, this association had stood head to head with the waaldé of Noumoussa Dioubaïrou, one of the king's generals, and had gathered the most brave and noble sons of the Bandiagara Toucouleur kingdom.

Because I was the leader, my opinion prevailed. Since I did not perceive any social difference between Daouda and me, I spoke on his behalf. He was therefore accepted as cadi despite the diatribes of some of our comrades who, in fact, would really have liked to hold that position themselves, or who would have at least liked one of their own to hold it. Mamadou Diallo, known as Mamadou Gorel (Little Guy), was elected as vice-chief. Madani Maki and Mouctar Kaou, both sons of griots, were named as griots of our association. Their duty would be to call members to meetings and to collect dues, from which they themselves were exempt. They were to transmit information and would be the plenipotentiary messengers between our waaldé and the other associations in the city. In sum, they would act as spokesmen and intermediaries, exactly like the adult griots active in African society in those days. All the other child griots of the waaldé were bound to help them at some point in their duties.

It was Bori Hammam who became our moutassibi, that is, our public prosecutor or snoop. The moutassibi was the scourge of every association. As a kind of detective and moral commissioner, his job was to ensure that on every occasion the rules were respected and to publicly denounce any lack of discipline or decorum. Afo Dianou, a dîmadjo (house captive) by family status, was designated as the second moutassibi and assistant to Bori Hammam.

Once this council was instituted, we developed our own rules, which were quite similar to those of all the other associations. Infractions were first judged by the cadi. The offender could make an appeal to the chief, and then in a third stage, to the general assembly, presided over by the elder. The possible penalties were graduated.

For the most minor offenses, the sentence was to pay fines in cowries or in kola nuts, or to be thrown fully clothed into the water, or doused with calabashes full of water. For serious offenses, one could be sentenced to receive one to ten lashes with a whip, or even face temporary or final expulsion.

The chief, assisted by the vice-chief and cadi, presided over the meetings. Meetings were held once a week during the dry season and once a month during the rainy season, known as *l'hivernage*. Occasionally there would be unplanned meetings called by the chief and announced by the griots.

Once our waaldé was duly constituted, it could begin to operate. All the youngest members of my older brother Hammadoun's waaldé came to increase our ranks, since it was more suited to their age. With time, it grew in importance. Later, around 1912, once we had absorbed another rival association in our neighborhood, it would even include as many as seventy-six young boys from every ethnic group and social class in Bandiagara.

Some Western readers might be surprised to learn that boys averaging from ten to twelve years of age could hold meetings in such a regimented way while expressing themselves in such formal speech. This can be explained by the fact that everything we did was in imitation of adult behavior, and that from our most tender years on, we were witnesses to the power of speech. There was never a meeting, nor an exchange of palavers, nor a council of justice (except for war councils or meetings of secret societies) that we did not attend—on the condition that we remain quiet and well behaved. The language back then was florid, exuberant, and charged with evocative images, and children who kept their ears pricked and their eyes peeled had no trouble reproducing it. In sum, I have simplified their tirades in order not to disconcert the reader too much. The rules were also borrowed from the adult world. Indeed, life inside the children's age associations constituted a veritable apprenticeship of collective life and its responsibilities, under the discreet but watchful eye of the elders, who acted as their benefactors.

A Handful of Rice

Like all children in those days, I enjoyed a great deal of freedom, especially since I was the head of a waaldé. I took my meals just about wherever I pleased, whether in my paternal household with Beydari, my brother Hammadoun, and Niélé, or in Tidjani's house, or even in the house of Daouda's mother. But most often, especially in the evenings, I dined at my father Tidjani's house, where I could join my mother, Koullel, and all the others who enjoyed staying up late.

We took our meals in two separate groups of men and women. Special guests were served separately, unless they expressed a desire to eat with everyone else. Dishes of food were specifically set aside to be sent out to relatives, friends, and people of honor. According to tradition, a wealthy family would set a dish aside for a needy person, a married woman would send a dish to her family, and a son would send one to his parents.

At Tidjani's house, the servant who was appointed to serve meals was always gentle Yabara. She would unfold the mats in the large great room and burn incense in order to purify the air. When the dishes were ready, she would place them on the mats and go to find Tidjani, saying, "Naaba, the meal is ready!" "Call the guests!" my father would reply. Then Yabara would call the men and boys of the household. Tidjani alone had a reserved seat, a sheepskin sewn to a lambskin depicting historic scenes and accented with handsome fringe. Once he was seated, Yabara would come to present him with a large calabash of water, soap, and a towel. Once he had carefully washed his hands, the calabash was passed on to the other guests.

Tidjani was always the first served. He would always take a handful of food from the platter and then invite the others to do so as well, as he pronounced "Bissimillahi" (in the name of God). Then everyone began to eat. The head of the family was always the first to wash his hands and begin eating in order to set the example. After the meal, he would then be the last to wash his hands and the last to rise in order to give everyone the chance to eat his fill.

At meal times, children were subject to strict discipline. Those who did not comply were punished according to the gravity of their infractions with either a stern look, a swat on the head with a fan, or a slap. Some were simply sent away without any food until the next meal. We had to follow seven compulsory rules. They were: no talking; eyes must remain lowered during meals; no eating from any section of platter unless it is directly in front of one (no pilfering left or right from the common dish); no new handful of food may be taken before finishing the one chosen before that; the edge of the platter must be held with the left hand; avoid rushing, take food with the right hand. Finally, we were not to take any of the pieces of meat that had been placed in the middle of the platter. Children were supposed to be satisfied with taking handfuls of grain (millet, rice, and so on) amply covered in sauce. It was not until the end of the meal was reached that they were allowed a whole handful of meat, considered to be a gift or a reward.

This was not useless torture, for all disciplinary measures were meant to teach life skills to children. To keep one's eyes lowered in the presence of adults, especially fathers—that is, the uncles and friends of one's father—was to learn to control oneself and to tame one's curiosity. To eat what was in front of one was to learn to be content with what one had. Not to speak was to control one's tongue and to practice silence. Not to take a new handful of food without finishing the preceding one was to demonstrate moderation. To hold the edge of the platter with the left hand was a gesture of politeness, and it taught humility. To avoid rushing to eat was to learn patience. Finally, to wait to receive meat at the end of the meal and to not serve oneself led to the ability to control one's appetite and greed.

In fact, in those days, and still even today in some traditional families, the meal corresponded to an entire ritual for the adults. In Islam as well as in traditional society, food was sacred, and the great common platter, symbolizing community, was thought to hold a divine blessing at its center.

One day Tidjani noticed that most of the children were leaving the meal without having eaten enough grain while also being quick to reach for their ration of meat for fear of seeing the best morsels disappear before it was their turn. He quickly understood what we were up to. From that day forth, he decided to give each child his ration of meat in advance. We were to place it on our left and wait until the end of the meal to eat it.

In those days, millet was the main staple in Bandiagara. Since rice was not grown in our region, a plate of rice represented a great luxury that was eaten only on occasions of great rejoicing. "Rice is food for kings," said an adage from the mountains of Bandiagara. But thanks to my mother's fortune, we ate it twice a month at our house, and later we even ate it every Friday. In those days, I took care not to wash my hands at the end of the meal. I would run into the street looking for one of my friends. When I had found one, I would hide my right hand behind my back and shout, "Tell me what I had to eat today if you can!" If he hesitated, I would put my hand in his face, saying, "What's this?" And he would marvel. "It's rice! It's rice!" As swollen as a toad with pride, I would burst out laughing, "This isn't rice! It's grain for royalty!" And I would go off looking for another friend so that I could stick my hand in his face.

One day, my friend Abdallah had come over to play in the vestibule of Tidjani's compound. When it was time for lunch, he rose to leave and go home. I stopped him. "No, stay here. My mother made rice." "If I could just have a handful of it," he said, "I would be the happiest boy in Bandiagara. But I would never dare to go eat in your father's great room. His captives would beat me in order to punish me for my boldness. Maybe I could play in your father's vestibule, but I could never sit down and eat with your father!" "All right," I said. "When Yabara calls me to eat, wait here until I get back."

When Yabara called, I went to the great room. I ate as rapidly as possible. As I was standing up, I took a fistful of rice and tried to hide it in my boubou. This had not escaped my father's attention. "If you haven't had enough to eat, why are you getting up? And if you are no longer hungry, what are you going to do with that handful of rice? That is provision enough to take on the road!" Not knowing what to say, I began to tremble. I was always excessively afraid of Naaba, who did not trifle when it concerned his children. "All right," he said, "go on with your handful of rice." As happy as a prisoner on death row who has just received a pardon, I dashed out, and almost ran to find Abdallah. I gave him the handful of rice. He smelled it, and ate it slowly, savoring every bite. He had scarcely finished the last mouthful when Sambourou appeared at the vestibule entrance. My father had told him to follow me in order to discover the intended recipient of the rice. As though propelled by a spring, Abdallah jumped up and ran away, and I took off behind him without a second thought and did not return home until late at night, after dinner. My father was waiting in the vestibule. I tried to slip by without being noticed, but he caught me. At the very least, I was expecting a slap, but all he said was, "Why didn't you invite your friend to eat? And why did you both run away when you saw Sambourou?"

"Naaba," I stammered, "I invited him, but he did not dare to come and eat with you. And when he saw Sambourou, he thought that he had come to beat him, so he ran away. I followed him without thinking, and after that I was afraid to come home for dinner."

My father burst out laughing. "Starting tomorrow, there will be a special dish set aside for you. Invite any of your friends to come and share it with you."

That is when my mother prepared a very large dwelling for me and my friends. We could meet there, take our meals there, and even sleep there. It was called *walamarou*, "the association dorm." It was from that moment on that I truly began to have a following and to play my role as chief of my waaldé.

At School with the Masters of the Word

After dinner, whether we had eaten together or separately, Daouda, my friends, and I would sometimes go to the great Kérétel Square, where young men and women from several of Bandiagara's neighborhoods would gather in the evenings to sing and dance by the light of the moon. We liked to dance with the young girls of the waaldé headed by Maïrama Jeïdani, and I had already been thinking of "twinning" our waaldé with theirs, as custom allowed, in a sort of symbolic wedding of our two associations.

In the summertime, people went to Kérétel in the evenings to watch wrestling matches, to listen to the singing of griot musicians, and to listen to stories, epics, and poems. If a young man was in the grip of poetic verve, he would come to sing his improvisations. These were memorized, and if they were beautiful, they would be spread throughout the entire city by the next day. This was one aspect of that great school of oral tradition, where the education of the populace was carried out on a daily basis.

Most of the time, I stayed at my father Tidjani's house after dinner in order to attend the evening events. For the children, these events constituted a veritable living school, since a master African storyteller did not limit himself to just telling tales. He was also capable of teaching about a number of other matters, especially in the case of master traditionalists such as Koullel, his master Modibo Koumba, or Danfo Siné of Bougouni. These men were able to broach almost any field of knowledge of that time, since an expert was never just a specialist in the modern sense of the word, but rather a sort of generalist. Knowledge was not compartmentalized. The same elder (in the African sense of the word, meaning *he who knows*, even if all his hair is not white) could have deep knowledge about religion as well as about history and natural science, or a variety of human sciences. For each in their own way possessed a more or less global knowledge, a kind of vast "science of life," life being conceived here as a unity where everything is connected, interdependent, and interacting, and where the material and spiritual realms are never dissociated. Instruction was never systematic, but was delivered according to circumstances, at favorable moments, or given the attention of the audience.

The fact of never having had writing has thus never deprived Africa of having a past, a history, and a culture. As my master Tierno Bokar would say much later, "Writing is one thing and knowledge is another. Writing is the photograph of knowledge, but it is not knowledge itself. Knowledge is the light in man. It is the heritage of everything that the ancestors were able to know about and whose seeds they have transmitted, just as the baobab tree is potentially contained in its own seed."

Koullel would sometimes invite his master, Modibo Koumba, to these gatherings. A contemporary of El Hadj Omar, he shared a good deal of knowledge gleaned from his own participation in the events of that period. It was from these two men that I first heard certain explanations concerning the profound teachings hidden beneath the pleasant and amusing exteriors of the great Fula initiation tales, tales that I would later publish. Koullel was often accompanied by his fellow traditionalists, who were knowledgeable in several domains. When one of them told a tale, a guitarist would softly accompany him. Often it was Ali Dieli Kouyaté, Tidjani's personal griot. But other griots, singers, musicians, or genealogists would also come to participate in these gatherings, where music and poetry were always present.

From this apparent chaos, we learned and retained many things without difficulty and with great pleasure, because it was eminently lively and entertaining. To instruct while entertaining was always the driving principle for the

Malian masters of old. More than anything, my family environment was for me a great and perpetual school, that of the Masters of the Word.

Just as I had done in Bougouni, I would sit in a corner of the courtyard next to Koullel. I would be silent, as every child was supposed to be when in the presence of adults, but I did not miss a single iota of what I was hearing. That is where, before I had even learned how to write, I learned how to store everything in my memory, which was already very accustomed to the techniques of auditory memorization learned in Koranic school. No matter what the length of a tale or story, I recorded it in its totality, and the next day, or a few days later, I would repeat it to my association friends. Daouda Maïga, Afo Dianou, Mamadou Gorel, and a few others who also frequently attended the gatherings served as my guarantors.

It was at this time that the nickname Amkoullel took on its true sense of "Little Koullel" and began to earn me some prestige among the other youths in town. This was aided by the generosity of my parents, who lodged us and saw to all our needs, which contributed significantly to consolidating the authority that I had over my comrades.

We would return to our respective bunks at about eleven o'clock at night, worn out but happy, although this never once stopped us from waking the next day before sunrise to begin another eventful day.

Sinali's Garden

Like all children from big cities, the children of Bandiagara were famous for their rowdiness. They were true urchins: witty, mocking, and mischievous, but also generous and brave. Daouda and I liked to get them to play at seeing who could be the bravest and to take chances. Not only did we show them how to raid Sinci's "trash town," but we also got them to join our pilfering expeditions. We targeted the gardens of people reputed to be powerful or mean, like the *sofa* (former warrior in the royal armies) and retired corporal Fabere Sinali, or even the district commandant. During the rainy season we would go marauding through the fields of millet that belonged to the Dogons. Daouda was more daring than I. When we were out in the middle of a millet field ravaging the sweet stalks, he loved to howl with laughter. I was always afraid that his laughter would attract the attention of the Dogons, and indeed, we were discovered more than once, and they ran after us. But thank God we could run like gazelles and they never caught us. In those days, iniquities committed by children were tolerated. Punishment was limited to a few whippings for those who got caught, but that was where it ended.

Nevertheless, one of our adventures came close to going bad. It was when we ransacked Sinali's garden. Sinali was one of those tirailleurs who had washed up in Bandiagara after helping the French to conquer the country. Poor Sinali had not at all profited from his prolonged contact with the French soldiers, even though it was said that he had been a kind of "jack of all trades" for them. Although it may have been excessive, public opinion held that he was a dumb brute capable of drinking fresh blood.

His thirteen years of service in the colonial army had not earned him a single stripe, but they had trained him so well that he had developed the automatic reflex of standing at attention and giving a military salute (*garde-à-vous*) to anyone and everyone. He had been given the nickname *Bigardabou* (engendered by garde-à-vous) and *Hammadi gardabou* (Older son of garde-à-vous).

He had remained at the rank of tirailleur second class to the end of his career, a fact which mortified him to the extreme. After reenlisting several times, he had nonetheless managed to obtain a corporal's three stripes, which were displayed on the sleeve of an old khaki coat. He never missed an opportunity to wear that coat any time he was supposed to meet an official, especially if it was a White-White, that is, a pure Frenchman from France. He had outgrown his coat, which had become too small, but he did not care a bit.

When he found people who were ignorant of military matters, he would boast about his three stripes as though they were his glory, going as far as to claim that they were superior to those worn farther down on the sleeve! One day, when he was in the middle of recounting his exploits to a circle of gawkers, Dianou, one of the neighborhood hotheads and father of our friend Afo Dianou, came up.

"Hey Sinali!" he shouted. "Can you tell us why your so-called superior stripes are smaller than the ones worn lower down on the sleeve and why they are perched upside down on their asses? Hey, friends, believe me, Sinali is hornswoggling you! Do you want to know what he did all day as a captive of the French military for thirteen years? Well, I'll tell you!

"One: Stand at attention all day long.

"Two: Salute everybody with his butt cheeks squeezed tight together so he wouldn't fart from fear, and God knows how many times that happened!

"Three: Run, lay down on the ground, get up, and jump over a few obstacles placed on a track.

"Four: Go and get his daily ration of a handful of millet, a pinch of salt, a bunch of hot peppers, and a piece of meat. And since that is all that Sinali has ever done, when his contract was up, those sly French cleverly stuck three little upside down stripes shaped like ostrich tracks on his sleeve."

Fuming with rage, the old soldier jumped on Dianou. But Dianou was as tough as hardened steel. He opened his arms and took hold of Sinali. Lifting him into the air as if he were a wisp of straw, he began to shout at the top of his lungs, "Where can I get a good flat stone so I can smash this old fogey slave of the French?"

Some good people intervened just in time and pulled them apart. It goes without saying that the neighborhood children had seen the whole thing.

From time to time, we and a few friends enjoyed reenacting the scene that we called "Dianou-Sinali." I do not know how, but Sinali found out about it. In any case, he spied on our little group with all the patience of a wild game hunter, and one day, he succeeded in surprising us in the act, in the vestibule of a house in town. He ran at us armed with a whip of braided vines that packed quite a sting. "Offspring of shameless girls," he cried, "I'll teach you to insult and make fun of Sinali!" And with all his natural brutality, he let loose a barrage of lashings that cut into our skin. Remembering, no doubt, that kicking people in the behind was particularly popular with the tirailleurs of that time, he generously obliged us. Covered with blood, crying and moaning like the little White children of the colonials, we disbanded like a flock of frightened sparrows.

Well, contrary to what Dianou had claimed, during his thirteen years of service, Sinali had not been content with just doing physical exercise and farting with fear each time a French officer passed. No, he had, above all, learned how to garden, and once he had returned to civilian life, he had conscientiously put his new knowledge into practice. Following every rainy season, when the waters began to recede, he would plant a seasonal garden in the Yaamé riverbed that was only surpassed in beauty by the gardens of the White officials posted there, or by the garden of Chief Alfa Maki Tall (son of former King Aguibou Tall) that was maintained by Fabere, the sofa. That year, when the rains stopped and the waters of the Yaamé dried up, Sinali planted his garden just as he did every year. He planted European vegetables and many local vegetables such as tomatoes, sweet potatoes, pumpkins, okra, edible gourds, local melons, and so on.

Daouda Maïga came to propose that we take revenge on Sinali by ransacking his garden.

"I'm afraid of Sinali," I admitted.

"That means that you are not a pure descendant of the Fulas," he replied. "As for me, Daouda Maïga, I'm going to get Sinali back! Mamadou Gorel and Afo Dianou will come with me. And I'm going to tell Maïrama Jeïdani that you are a coward!"

My hesitation melted at the mention of the names Mamdou Gorel, my waaldé rival, and Maïrama Jeïdani, the head of the young women's association whom I particularly wished to impress. "In any case," I said to myself, "Afo Diano, whose father is the bane of Sinali's existence, will be on our side. Sinali will think twice before he tries to mistreat us again like he did before."

We established a plan of action. Before doing anything, we first had to get Sinali accustomed to seeing us hanging about in the vicinity of his garden. On our days off from school (that is, Wednesday afternoons, Thursdays, and Friday mornings) Daouda Maïga, Afo Dianou, and I got into the habit of going to hunt lizards and other small reptiles that lived among the rocks scattered along the bank of the Yaamé that was across from the garden. After the hunt, we would go and take a swim in the river. Sinali got used to us being there.

Soon, his vegetable garden was in full yield. It was time to take action. Our expedition would include Daouda Maïga, Afo Dianou, and myself. We were to rendezvous the following Wednesday night into Thursday. Since there was no school on Thursday, we could go and hide out all day in the bush if we had to.

That Wednesday night after dinner, Afo Dianou and Daouda came to get me. We carefully made our way to the edge of the Yaamé. Unfortunately for us, the moon shone magnificently and lit up the countryside. A few women who had been too busy during the day to leave their houses were taking advantage of the beautiful evening to fill their water jars and cool off in the river, which was lightly perfumed with the aroma of vetiver grass growing at the river's edge. They were chatting, singing, and playing tag with joyful bursts of laughter. We took a detour in order to avoid them, slipping behind the bushes as quietly as possible before finally arriving at the garden that was surrounded by a hedge of thorny branches. Afo Dianou whispered, "We have to make sure that Sinali isn't hiding somewhere. Wait here, and I'll go scout it out." He walked around the enclosure but did not see a living soul. He even took the precaution of throwing some large rocks inside. Since nothing had moved, he concluded that Sinali had returned to the village. "The old crocodile has gone home," he told us. "Let's go before the racket the women are making draws him back." We thought this a likely possibility, since the army had gotten him used to nocturnal surveillance and making nighttime rounds.

One of us was to stand guard and alert the others of approaching danger. Since everyone wanted to be in on the raid, we had to draw straws. Afo Dianou was chosen.

In order to gain access to the garden, we still had to move the bristling, thorny hedge. This took some time and earned us a few good scrapes, but finally Daouda and I penetrated the forbidden area. It was truly a magnificent garden, but we did not care. Driven by a rage fueled by the memory of the blows that we had received several months before, we ravaged it with no regrets, pulling up, smashing, and trampling everything down to the last tomato, like crazy apes let loose in a field of corn. Before taking our leave, we opened a section of the hedge with the crafty hope that a stray donkey or goat would wander in to forage at daybreak, thereby deflecting any suspicion from us.

The next day, when Sinali discovered the devastation of his garden where all his hopes had been dashed to pieces, we were not there to see it, but we could easily imagine his anger and the barrage of curses that he would let loose to the heavens! Unfortunately for us, he discovered the footprints of children on the ground. He deduced that only the children whom he had dealt with would have been capable of such devastation, and he had an idea who they were. Knowing the mentality of people from Bandiagara, he did not immediately accuse us, but instead went to visit each of our houses as though he had stopped by to say a polite hello to our parents. In fact, he was trying to catch us off guard, hoping that at the sight of him we would exhibit some sort of compromising reaction that would facilitate his accusing us. It was in vain, since Daouda, Afo Dianou, and I had not returned to our homes. We had gone to spend the rest of the night in our walamarou, our shared dorm that my mother had had built for us.

When Sinali arrived at the home of Daouda's mother, Moïré Modi Koumba, and did not find any of us there either, he could contain himself no longer and burst out, "Your son and his friends got into my garden last night. They completely upended it! That is why none of them has dared to return home tonight! But I'll make them pay when I get my hands on them, and that will be soon enough!"

Like all the other parents of the children who had been beaten by Sinali, Moïré was ready for him. "Sure, you are a master of brutality," she replied, "a man who is in the habit of whipping children. But if you are looking for an argument, we'll give you a war, a war that will make you forget your garden. You despicable old tirailleur with a heart of stone and lungs of iron! It isn't enough that you beat on children who were playing an innocent game! You show up here, wearing those rags and that smelly old fez from the days of General

Faidherbe trying to get me to swallow that nonsense! I don't know what the other parents are going to do, but I'm warning you! If you touch even a single hair on Daouda's head, I'll break your head with my pestle! You thirteen-years-of-military-service-and-no-stripes! If you don't get out of here immediately, I'll call Dianou. He knows what you weigh. But this time, if he lifts you off the ground, I will be the one to tell him where to find the rock to smash you with until your bones are driven deep into your flesh!"

Blind with rage, Sinali tried to hit Moïré. Luckily, our mawdo Ali Gomni and Kaou Daouda, both of them friends of my maternal uncle Hammdoun Pâté, were nearby in their shoemaker's shop and had been alerted by the shouting. They came running up and threatened to throw Sinali into the street if he didn't leave and to knock him unconscious if he laid a hand on Moïré.

Forced to withdraw, Sinali went straight to the sofa Fabere, chief gardener of Alfa Maki Tall. He told him his sad tale, emphasizing that all Bandiagara's gardens were at risk, and in particular, Fabere's own garden, if the marauders were not unmasked and severely punished. Convinced, Fabere took it upon himself to bend Alfa Maki Tall's ear in favor of Sinali's cause, which he had henceforth come to consider as his own.

Throughout the entire morning of this eventful Thursday, Afo Dianou, Daouda, and I had stayed in the bush, busily picking fruit and catching birds, and going as far as the "trash town" of the Whites of Sinci. Toward noon, carrying a load of wild fruit, various objects, and clay for making pots, we returned to town, laughing and covered with sweat, but in truth quite worried about the fate that awaited us. We went to Daouda's mother Moïré's house first. She told us of her encounter with Sinali in detail and, swearing to keep our secret, asked us to tell her whether yes or no we were behind the ravages committed in the old tirailleur's garden. Afo Dianou, who sometimes demonstrated a surprising naïveté cried, "Mother Moïré! We can't say a thing! All three of us have sworn on the souls of ancestors never to admit that we are the ones who ransacked Sinali's garden!"

"What you did was nasty," she said, "but Sinali merely got repaid for his viciousness. Now listen to me: even if you are whipped, you must never admit that you are the guilty ones. If you are questioned, you will say that you spent the night in your dormitory. You will say that you went to bed early because you wanted to leave early in the morning for the bush to pick your fruit and to go to Sinci to find your artifacts. Do you understand?"

We all nodded our heads to say that we did.

For his part, Fabere had informed Chief Alfa Maki Tall of the affair, who then called on Sinali to provide additional information. Sinali recited the names of all the children that he had thrashed in the vestibule: Daouda Maïga, Mamdou Gorel, Madani Maki, Abdallah, Afo Dianou, and Amkoullel. Alfa Maki Tall gave our neighborhood headman, the sofa Koniba Kondala, the job of carrying out an investigation in order to find out what we had been doing on Wednesday night. He learned that Madani Maki, grandson of Kaou Diallo, the great griot of Alfa Maki Tall, had spent the night with his grandfather in the chief's own compound and that he had not moved, and this had been verified by the wives of Alfa Maki Tall. Mamadou Gorel was away from Bandiagara. Abdallah had been sick for three days. As for us three, Koniba Kondala had heard that we had spent the night in our residence with plans to leave for the bush the next morning early, as was our habit.

When Koniba Kondala gave the chief the results of his investigation, he also made sure to tell him of the brutality of Sinali's treatment of us and the bloody blows that he had meted out for having acted out our little play at his expense. Alfa Maki Tall was benevolent by nature, and he was especially fond of chivalrous acts. Undoubtedly touched by our determination, he declared to Koniba Kondala, "Go tell Sinali to come up with an estimate of the value of the destruction in his garden. I will reimburse him. Tell him that I am happy that my boys, who still smell like mother's milk, have proven that they do not intend to suffer an affront without seeking vengeance. If they had been older, I am convinced that they would not have kept their identities hidden in getting even with Sinali. Finally, give him this advice from me: from now on, he had better watch over his garden more than he ever has, because that was just the beginning of future pillaging. This will last for two or three seasons. It is a children's custom that grew up here under Tidjani Tall, the first King of Bandiagara."

Indeed, for three seasons we never stopped invading Sinali's garden, or burying thorns in the path that led to it. But like Cerberus, he kept watch. Whether we arrived by day or by night, he was there. And as soon as he saw us, he would chase us frantically, which prompted the women carrying water to cry out mockingly, "Hey! Look at Sinali fighting with the children! Hey Sinali! Stop! Stop!"

We had nearly driven poor Sinali completely insane. It got to the point where he would have a fit at the mere sight of a boy, even in town. He couldn't help chasing after him, throwing clods of earth and shouting insults at him. He could be seen gesturing and talking to himself in the street, mumbling a jumble of words about children and their parents. One day, I do not remember how or why, we stopped harassing Sinali, the old tirailleur with three stripes.

Boy and Girl Valentines

Our waaldé grew larger every day, but it was still a "bachelor" waaldé. According to custom, in order to be complete, we need to be paired with a girls' association of the same age class as we were, so that we would become their official knight-servants and protectors, and they would become our platonic "lady loves." To use a term generated by certain French ethnologists, they would be our "girl valentines" and we would be their "boy valentines." (To my knowledge, this custom, which dates back to a remote past, existed in all sub-Saharan Africa.)

Around 1911 (I can only guarantee the exactness of the events of this period to within the space of a year), I decided to send this proposal up to my comrades for a vote, and I sent out a call for a general meeting. Our meeting was held one night after dinner, by the light of a full moon. It was one of those African nights when men and beasts, happy to bathe in so soft a light, enjoyed staying up late. Distant echoes of people singing, hands clapping to the beat of dancing feet, children crying, dogs barking, indeed an entire concert of peaceful and joyous sounds connect my memory to those beautiful evenings of my childhood in Bandiagara.

On that particular night, the moon poured such a bright and milky light onto the gray walls and winding streets that it would have been possible to see a needle lying on the ground. Defeated, darkness had sheltered in the nooks and crannies of doors and vestibules. Dark mouths and mysterious black holes projected by jutting waterspouts were the only lasting shadows.

My comrades, who had been notified two days earlier by the moutassibis and the griots, were waiting. The moutassibis were always the first to arrive in order to check the identities of the attendees and to take note of those who were tardy or absent, who would then be fined. The customary jokes swapped between friends were freely exchanged until the chief had declared the meeting to be in session, something which could take place only in the presence of the cadi.

Upon my arrival, the moutassibi Bori Hamman exclaimed in a loud voice, "Amirou wari!" (The chief has arrived!) All those in attendance cried out in unison, "Bissimillahi amirou!" (Welcome chief!), and I sat down comfortably on the ground and crossed my legs. Mamadou Gorel, the vice-chief, took his seat on my right and the cadi Daouda Maïga was on my left. My chest suddenly swollen with importance, I in turn shouted, "Waaldé joodiima!" (The waaldé is seated!), which is equivalent to the declaration, "The meeting is in now in session!," customary in Western assemblies.

The assistant moutassibi Afo Dianou proclaimed the hardly trivial interjection "Soukoumek!" which literally meant, "Shut them!" a plural which designated the two main exits of the body, the one up high and the one down low. When there was total silence, Bori Hamman, the principal moutassibi turned to me. "We are listening, chief."

I took up the subject of the meeting. "Oh, members! The goal of tonight's meeting is to propose an idea of mine to you. I wish for this idea to become your idea. Examine it closely, see if it is worthwhile, and if you agree that it is worth pursuing, say so.

"As you know, our male waaldé has no female association to act as its spouse. It is therefore still single. This cannot last long. Of all the waaldés composed of girls our age, the one created by Maïrama Jeïdani seems to me to be the most appropriate to partner with us. It has already been approached by three rival associations of boys with whom we have accounts to settle. This proposal will be yet another bone of contention, but it is not this possibility that will make us withdraw. I now give the floor to the cadi."

"I am in favor of this idea," declared Daouda Maïga, "and I ask that all those who are in favor shout, 'Allahou toownou diina!' (May God raise up the dîna!)."

"Why should we go all the way to the other side of town to find our valentines?" asked our comrade Amadou Sy. "Can't we find any in the immediate vicinity?"

"Amadou Sy," replied Gorko Mawdo, "I know you are expressing a certain resentment against . . ."

"You razor-lipped liar!" exploded Amadou Sy. "When have I ever been insulted to the point of holding a grudge? Who said anything? Where and when did it happen? Anyway, do I look like a boy that you can insult without consequences?"

I had to intervene and order the two antagonists to be quiet or pay a fine. Amadou Sy turned to me and said, "Chief, I will never allow Goro Mawdo, that son of a clumsy pigeon-toed weaver, to vilify me in the middle of a meeting!"

With that, our assistant moutassibi Afo Dianou, cried, "Cadi! I am hereby issuing a citation to Amadou Sy for being the first person to insult Gorkow Mawdo by insulting his father!"

"I have heard your citation," said Daouda Maïga.

Throughout the meeting, there were five or six more confrontations of the same type, immediately noted by the moutassibi. Finally, my proposal was accepted and I was given the task of taking the first steps toward establishing the "twinship." Amadou Sy and the other troublemakers were judged and condemned to pay fines in the form of kola nuts due to their lack of discipline and coarse behavior during the meeting.

The day after the meeting, I went to see our mawdo Ali Goni to ask him to take the customary steps in concert with Martou Nawma, the elder and honorary president of Maïrama Jeïdani's waaldé. Ali Goni presented her with our request, which he reinforced with a gift of one hundred kola nuts that he paid for himself. Martou Nawma accepted the kolas, which already implied acceptance of the proposal.

"Personally, I have nothing against Amkoullel's waaldé," she said. "I am a friend and member of Kadidja's age class, and that makes Amkoullel my son. But I will be frank. Maïrama Jeïdani's waaldé is much in demand. She has already received three requests. Yours is the fourth. As you know, custom requires that the girls choose for themselves, and I must not try to influence their decision. But if they happen to ask my opinion, in that case, I know who I will recommend. It goes without saying that it will be Amkoullel's waaldé."

In order to improve our odds, Ali Gomni advised me to take my comrades to play and dance as often as possible with the girls and to seek out all the ways in which we could please them and make ourselves useful.

That very evening, I called for a special meeting of all our comrades in order to inform them of the outcome of our efforts and to give them news of our mawdo's advice. I suggested that we immediately organize an evening of feasting and dancing, for which a so-called chivalry contribution was levied. The minimum payment was set at forty cowries. Finally, thanks to contributions from all our parents, we collected eight thousand cowries and four hundred Kola nuts. This allowed us to organize a large so-called generosity feast for the girls, where our adversaries would come to challenge us. The honors reserved for the most generous donors would be in play.

The event took place a few days later. The evening was led by singer-guitarist griots and praise-singing genealogist griots attached to various families. At the opening of the event, the griots sang the praises of Maïrama Jeïdani and her family. As was customary, the chiefs of our three rival associations gave the griots significant quantities of kola nuts and cowries in honor of the young lady. Like every good chief, I used a spokesman and had our moutassibi

Bori Hamman declare that not only would I offer a much larger sum to the griots in Maïrama's honor, but I would also add a sheep and the price of the accompanying condiments to the people of caste who were attached to the girls' families so that they could prepare themselves a good *méchoui* roast. I topped it all off by giving the griots a substantial additional amount, this time in honor of all Maïrama's comrades. As for our rivals, they had thought neither of the other girls nor of the casted people attached to their families. My announcement was greeted with enthusiastic shouts from the griots, who immediately improvised praises in my honor and in the honor of my family. They continued in this manner all evening, singing the praises of different people in their traditional way.

Popular opinion had already approved our waaldé's candidacy, but the girls' decision was not final, for we were not yet their official valentines. Every evening as we waited, my comrades went in small groups to ensure that nobody else could come to dally with our future valentines. According to tradition, we had become responsible for their virtue and we were bound to defend and assist them on every occasion. We stood guard, armed with sticks and pliant whips of vine. But it goes without saying that as much as we wished to discourage our rivals, our rivals also wished to take revenge on us, which they indeed did try to do sometime later.

As luck would have it, Maïrama Jeïdani became sincerely attached to me. She was destined to become my personal valentine according to tradition, since she was the chief of her waaldé. She was a *cherifat*, a descendant of the Prophet through her father's line. Her father belonged to a family of mixed-race Arabs from Timbuktu and was largely reputed to be righteous. And it didn't hurt that she was particularly beautiful, charming, and possessed of a strong personality. As for her second in command, Aye Abbasi, she had eyes only for Daouda Maïga, whom she liked very much. Since these two young women were the leaders of the others, our victory was certain.

Our rivals quickly understood that their place was elsewhere. Not only was our waaldé better endowed than theirs, but it included more combative and better-trained boys. A few skirmishes where our adversaries were roughed up proved that we were not the kind who would ever give up an acquired conquest.

One month after this memorable evening, Maïrama Jeïdani's comrades made their decision and chose us to be their valentines. Their honorary president Martou Nawma informed our mawdo Ali Gomni of their decision. According to custom, the boys were to send the young women a symbolic wedding dowry consisting of two baskets of millet, one basket of rice, one nicely fatted sheep, two thousand cowries, and one thousand kola nuts. My mother paid for all of it.

With these provisions, our valentines prepared a large meal of couscous and invited us to eat and dance with them. That evening, platters of food were distributed here and there throughout the city to announce the wedding of our two associations.

The following evening, a general assembly was held between the boys and the girls at the residence of Martou Nawma with Ali Gomni in attendance. Our two honorary presidents proceeded to the official twinning of the boys and the girls. According to custom, each boy leader was declared the valentine of each girl leader. I therefore became the valentine of Maïrama Jeïdani, Douada Maïga was paired with Aye Abasi, and so on. Regarding the members of the two associations who did not hold leadership positions, each girl received her valentine by drawing lots. At first, there were more girls than boys, and our presidents thought for a moment that they could be the collective valentines of our entire waaldé, but new and enthusiastic members joined and immediately reestablished our equilibrium. In fact, every boy was intent on having his own valentine, no matter how small or how homely, in order to have someone to court and protect and for whom he would be held personally responsible. However, while tradition allowed a valentine to banter gallantly with his valentine—today it would be called flirting—it was on the express condition that her chastity be respected. He was allowed to sing about the beauty of his valentine in his poems, boast of her virtues and merits, dedicate his exploits to her, consecrate an evening of poetry and music in the company of a griot to her, but the community saw him as the personal guarantor of her purity until she was married. It was a question of his own honor as well as that of his entire family.

Because marriages were finalized during childhood between cousins, it was very rare for valentines to be able to wed (doing so was said to "add honey to milk"). A Valentine's honor and glory was to be able to guard his virgin "Lady" until her wedding day. It was then said that he could "die of hunger next to a delicious dish without touching it." Master of his instincts, he was consecrated as being trustworthy and then earned the right to become the best friend of the two spouses.

To be sure, I cannot vouch for the virtue of all the male and female valentines over the centuries, but I am certain that throughout my entire youth in Bandiagara, we never heard talk of a single case where a boy valentine had not respected the honor of his girl valentine—and, given the customs, such a thing would have become public knowledge!

Our association's victory in twinning with the girls, along with our prosperity and the success of certain other exploits, had the natural effect of stirring up resentment. As we shall see, this resulted in the creation of enemies that would have to be reckoned with. In the meantime, as soon as we were released from Koranic school, we thought only of ways to entertain and dazzle our valentines. Particularly effective for this were large gatherings where we told tales and acted out certain scenes.

Kadidja and Tidjani in Crisis

Alternating between my two families and indulged equally by both, going between my older brother, Hammadoun, whom I admired, and my amiable little brother, Mohammed el Ghaali, for whom I was the protector, learning from my two teachers, Tierno Bokar and Koullel, who each drew from his respective field of knowledge to provide everything that could best enrich the mind of a child, chumming with my friends and our charming valentines, I was truly one of the happiest children in Bandiagara, the city that treated its children like little kings. But an unexpected tragedy came along and upset it all.

The Toucouleur Tall and Thiam women of Tidjani's family, who were spouses as well as relatives, had never forgiven Kadidja for being the latest wife to join the family. Neither could they forgive her for bringing her Fula offspring with her and interposing him as "first son." Most of all, they could not forgive the fact that Kadidja had become the first lady of the household, thanks to her unrelenting efforts and Tidjani's affection. Since old Yaye Diawarra was no longer there to stand up for Kadidja, they renewed hostilities, and lay in wait for the best moment to strike a decisive blow. The occasion arose when Tidjani left for Timbuktu, where he was to take up a rather lengthy sojourn on business.

Faman N'Diaye, the eldest of Tidjani's relatives, took advantage of this absence to contrive a veritable cabal against my mother. Certain of the support of all the female members of the family, she paid my mother a visit. "All of us, whether we are Tidjani's close relatives or his wives," she told her, "have seen enough of you. We have decided that if your husband will not repudiate you, we all will separate from him. All of us told him of our decision before he left, and we obtained his divorce from you. But he did not dare to tell you to your face. That is why he gave me the task of informing you of his decision. From this moment forward, you and your son Amadou Hampâté are no longer members of this household. Do what every repudiated woman must do: pack up your bags, push the child born from another bed along in front of you, and return to your father's house, or to the house of your son's father. Good-bye!"

Without a single word in reply, Kadidja assembled her things and returned to her family home. Faman N'Diaye proclaimed victory. Had she not cut down to size at the very first blow and with no trouble this Fula woman who, until then, had been immune to any misadventure?

She wrote a long letter in Arabic to Tidjani in which she announced that, following the unanimous decision taken by all the female members of the family, Kadidja had been repudiated, that she had accepted the divorce, left the conjugal compound, and returned to her father's household. Unfortunately, Tidjani, who was so courageous when faced with adversity, was very weak where his family was concerned. Instead of protesting, he remained in Timbuktu on business, thinking that it was just a small incident and that time would arrange things. Being somewhat unskilled at diplomacy, as we have seen, he committed the error of saying nothing to Kadidja, neither directly nor through the person of an intermediary.

Deeply hurt, my mother decided to leave Bandiagara forever. She sold off some of her herd and arranged her trip, taking my little brother, Mohammed el Ghaali, her faithful servant Batoma, and some other servants with her. Because my older brother, Hammadoun, and I were under the tutelage of our paternal relatives, my mother had no choice but to leave us in Bandiagara, where our maternal uncle Hammadou Pâté and our aunt Sirandou Pâté could keep an eye on us. She entrusted us to Tierno Bokar, who would continue our moral and religious education, and then she left for Mopti. Alas, she had barely just arrived there when misfortune struck. My dear, smiling, little brother who was six or seven years old at the time, caught the measles and died.

When Tidjani was notified, he rushed to Mopti in all haste. He found my mother in the midst of preparations to leave for Bamako, as far away from Bandiagara as possible, in search of peace. She needed to calm her frazzled nerves—which had indeed become even more frazzled by the silence of her husband, the death of her child, and the behavior of Tidjani's relatives. These women had never stopped trying to humiliate and cut Kadidja down since the moment she had married Tidjani, and Kadidja had been able to withstand it all. But these recent events had finally taken their toll.

"What makes you think that you, my wife, can leave for Bamako without my permission?" Tidjani asked.

"No," replied Kadidja, "your wives, all of them daughters of kings, are in Bandiagara. As for me, the daughter of the Fula herdsman Pâté Poullo, I was your servant-wife, but now I am divorced. The waiting period since my divorce is over. Now I am free. Even the tie that bound us is now broken. That tie was your son, Cheik Mohammed el Ghaali. You have just seen his grave. Tomorrow, I'll board the boat to Bamako. I wish you a long and happy life with your wives and Faman N'Diaye, the head of your family, who has the right to marry and repudiate your wives in your stead and on your behalf!"

Tidjani tried everything to convince Kadidja to rethink her decision, but she would not budge. That very day, he went to see the marabout Alfa Oumarou Hammadi Sanfouldé to ask him to intervene with my mother, but when he arrived the next day at Kadidja's lodgings, he learned that she had already set sail in the early morning hours aboard a steamboat bound for Bamako.

Tidjani returned to Bandiagara in despair. Upon his arrival, his close relatives, led by Faman N'Diaye, gathered to greet him. Counting on her authority over Tidjani through her status as the eldest, Faman N'Diaye had assumed all the moral responsibility for Kadidja's repudiation. When some of her companions worried about Tidjani's possible reaction, she replied, "That's my business!"

She greeted Tidjani and wished him welcome, but as soon as she tried to speak about Kadidja, he interrupted her. "You have all acted out of passion. Do not give me a single explanation, go give it to 'your Tidjani.' I myself am nothing to you anymore. You didn't want Kadidja around anymore because you are jealous of her. I was the tree under whose branches you rested, slept, and awoke in order to consume its fruit. But what you have deliberately decided to ignore is the fact that Kadidja was the living sap in the tree that I am. Can a tree live without its sap? I cannot live without Kadidja. Therefore, beginning next week, I will join my wife, she who has faced down soldiers and darkness, who has spent her blood and sweat so that I can eat and, in turn, feed you.

"Leave my presence! Go make yourselves a 'Tid-jani' to suit you! Isn't it said that man was fashioned from mud? Well, you will find a lot of it in Bilal Samba Lâna pond in Bandiagara. Help yourselves. You have assigned yourselves rights that even God hasn't given himself! To proclaim a divorce between a man and his wife!"

Much to the consternation of his family, Tidjani immediately began to put all his affairs in order in Bandiagara. When everything was in order and resources for his family were made available to them, he took his leave of Tierno Bokar and, in turn, left the city. He went first to Mopti and then on to Bamako, where he found Kadidja. He succeeded in gaining her forgiveness. Since their marriage had not been legally dissolved, they recommenced their life together.

From then on, far from all family problems, they lived happily together until the end of their lives.

In truth, Tidjani left Bandiagara with no regrets, for since his return from Bougouni, with the exception of a group of faithful friends and relatives who had kept him company, the other members of Toucouleur society in the city had not treated him with the respect due to his rank, and he had suffered this in silence. Therefore, he decided to go and make a new start elsewhere, which he succeeded in doing in Kati, a small city and military garrison near Bamako, where he settled with Kadidja and where their household was enriched by three more children.

In Kati, Kadidja revived her commercial activities—which brought her to Bandiagara from time to time—and Tidjani once again took up his activities as marabout and tailor-embroiderer, to which he added a small store that was well stocked due to the proximity of the military base. I would join them in 1915, after I ran away from the French school.

And this is how my adopted father Tidjani (Amadou Ali) Thiam took his feet from the silver stirrups of the Louta chiefdom and unashamedly placed them on the foot pedal of a sewing machine, facing a display of trinkets, where candy, matches, sugar cubes and cookies sat next to balls of "Guillemet bluing."[2] He sold a little of everything, the only exception being hard liquor and wine, which are forbidden by the Koran, and tobacco, which a good follower of the Tidjaniyaa would never touch under any circumstances.

Circumcision of My Brother Hammadoun

Kadidja's departure struck a painful blow to Hammadoun and me, but my older brother was perhaps even more deeply affected than I was. Deprived of our mother during the long years of her exile in Bougouni, he had become even more attached to her when she had returned. Like me, he lived in our paternal household with Beydari, Niélé, and their companions, but he saw Kadidja every day and often went to eat and sleep at her house. The void left by the departure of our mother and the death of our little brother brought him even closer to me. At Koranic school or at home, we were always together, and when I did not spend the night with my association comrades, he would always sleep with me. We had ended up with the nickname, "sons of the same blanket." The affection between us helped greatly in getting us through this difficult time.

We no longer went to Tidjani's compound since we were now banished. And anyway, the courtyard where our nights had so often been filled with the rhythm of singing, poetry, and the strumming of guitars, and where stories of the great exploits of the past had been retold, this courtyard where we had become intoxicated with the magic of the spoken word had become depressingly silent. But Koullel was still there. He would come to pick me up and take me to the sessions that he organized here and there with his friends and colleagues. My traditional education was therefore not interrupted. What's more, evening events still took place on Kérétel Square, which was the veritable nocturnal heart of the city, where there was permanent entertainment.

Sometime after that, our attention was turned to an important event that superseded all our other concerns. This was Hammadoun's circumcision.

After baptism (the naming ceremony), circumcision is the second public ceremony in a man's life, and the third is marriage. Like a baptism, it entails a number of expenses. With the help of friends and relatives, the family begins to prepare for it long in advance. After the harvest, when the granaries are full and cool winds begin to blow, the elders of the village or the neighborhood confer on the organization of the ceremony.

In general, boys are circumcised between the ages of seven and fourteen years. For the Bambaras, the ideal age for this is twenty-one, that is, at the end of the first cycle of three times seven years. But in fact, it often takes place much earlier, in particular when the child feels ready and asks for it himself, when he no longer wishes to be mockingly called *bilakoro* (uncircumcised), a term that constitutes the gravest of insults when it is addressed to an adult, for it signifies that he is not a man.

For the Fulas of the bush, the candidate for circumcision has preferably already proven his courage by going to recover a calf taken by a hyena or a panther, for example, or even a lion.

In Islam, the circumcision of a baby boy takes place on the seventh day after his birth, at the same time as his baptism ceremony. The Fulas who converted to Islam delayed this operation to the age of seven or sometimes even later.

That year in Bandiagara, the millet harvest had ended, the animals that had been taken to graze in the flood zones had returned to the region of the cliffs where there was now enough water and pasture to feed them, and my family's herds, led by our chief herdsman Allaye Boubou (who had already been my grandfather Pâté Poullo's herdsman) returned to Bandiagara. It was a time of abundance.

A family council was held with Beydari Hampâté presiding. During that meeting, it was decided to organize Hammadoun's circumcision and mine on the same occasion.[3] When this news reached the attention of Boudjedi Bâ, the elder Bâ of Bandiagara, he was opposed to the idea of me being circumcised on the same day as my older brother. "This would be a violation of custom," he explained. "Boys who are circumcised at the same time in fact become 'comrades' for the rest of their lives, with no consideration for their ages, hierarchy, or social standing, and they also benefit from the complete freedom to behave as they like with each other. This would go entirely against the duty of obedience and helpfulness owed to an older brother by a younger brother, and especially from one with the same father and mother."

My circumcision was therefore delayed, and the date was set for two years later. Very disappointed, Hammadoun asked that I at least be allowed to stay with him as his relative. "I cannot do without my little brother," he said, "and he cannot do without me either."

He argued my case so well that I was allowed to stay with him, although not during the operation itself nor during the first week of retreat, when the isolation of the circumcised is de rigueur, but during the two weeks of retreat in the bush that followed.

About fifteen neighborhood boys were selected to be circumcised at the same time. As was the custom, the ceremony would be preceded by a great feast that would last all night, from sunset to sunup. All the friends and relatives of the family were invited. Preparations for the feast lasted a good month. My mother, who was then living in Kati, was too far away to be able to join us in time. She sent orders to sell ten ten-year-old bulls from her herd in order to help Beydari Hampâté with the expenses. Her younger sister, our aunt Sirandou Pâté, provided the calabashes that would be broken to make shards for creating castanets that would be used by the future circumcised. Our maternal uncle, Hammadoun Pâté, our "male mother" by tradition, would be there to oversee it all.

The big night finally arrived. Following a veritable feast, the servants arranged the water drums (large calabashes filled with water, atop of which sat smaller, overturned calabashes, used to create a deeper sound). Male and female drummers would beat these to back the dancing and singing. The candidates for circumcision had to sleep in a common dormitory (walamarou) and not join the attendees until dawn.

Beydari had engaged five genealogist-singer griots, three men and two women. Among them was the famous griote Lenngui, one of the only ones able to sing in a voice as fluid as it was powerful in the upper and lower registers alike. Her singing style made the others sound monotonous by comparison. Since she was deeply familiar with the history of the family from which my father Hampâté descended, she was the most qualified to sing of our genealogy and the exploits of our ancestors.

The audience formed a circle around the griots, some of whom then began to play their instruments and sing praises. However, it was Lenngui who led the session. She sang all night long, alternating between herding songs, wedding songs, war songs, love songs, epics, and nostalgic songs. The drummers set the beat. The crowd clapped in syncopation, supporting the rhythm. Every so often, a genealogist griot would rise and enter the circle. Gently rocking his head and body forward and back in the Fula manner, he made a round of the circle. Following the traditional onomatopoeias, he began to sing airs to traditional melodies that he had chosen, whether slow or fast, happy or sad, and the crowd responded in unison. Then he launched into his improvised declamation.

Following each of his songs, a relative of one of the boys would go to the middle of the circle, and there, on that single occasion, contrary to usual custom, and with no reluctance or remorse, he would make pronouncements highlighting the merits of his own family in order to stir the young boy's pride. For in fact, our traditions forbid nobles from saying good things about themselves or their ancestors. Nobles are always held to a standard of extreme reserve in their movements and speech, except during circumcision celebrations and on the night before going off to war. On every other occasion, they must not speak. Griots speak for them.

"This is a solemn night for my kinsmen," sang Allaye Boubou, our principal herdsman, whose son Ali would be circumcised the next day. "This night precedes a solemn day, a day of courage, where the fearful bring shame upon their fathers and mothers. Tomorrow, my son Ali Allaye will submit to the bite of a cutting knife. If he cries, I will die of shame. If he does not flinch, I will be covered in glory!"

Then he presented the griots with gifts and returned to his place. Aunts, uncles, older brothers, and relatives took turns in the circle, singing, dancing, and covering the griots, members of various castes, and captives with gifts. The celebration lasted all night. At dawn, many fathers and mothers began to be overtaken by worry at the thought of the ordeal that their sons would soon have to face, and of the ever-possible shame that could result from it: "How will it look if our son cries?"

At the first crowing of the cock, even as dawn was nothing yet but a vague and distant promise, the candidates for circumcision were led into the courtyard. They walked in single file, led by my brother Hammadoun, who, as the chief of his waaldé, had been designated as the first to be circumcised.

Upon the arrival of the young men in the courtyard, Lenngui launched into an oration intended to excite their courage:

Oh, young men, be brave!
Do not behave like testy stallions!
Soon, your flesh will meet
The bite of sharp knives.
The steel will cause your vermillion blood to spurt
Would that it not cause your tears to spout!
. . . .
When the blacksmith cuts you, joke with him!
Lightly strike his temple
To punish him for having dared to touch
A member that he should have respected
As if it were that of his own father.
And to show that you are not afraid
Tell him to do it again!
. . . .
Tomorrow prove your virility,
And the community will recognize your adulthood!

Every parent again rose to come and encourage its candidate for circumcision and promise that if he could undergo the ordeal without flinching, he would be given one or more milk cows that would constitute the start of his own small herd.

The young men then entered the circle in turn while executing a few dance steps. The griots egged them on. "Eldest son of your father, do you fear the earth? If you are not afraid, jump, dance, hit it with your feet so that we can see your heels raise the dust!"

When the sky began to brighten, the young men, still in single file, were led to the banks of the Yaamé. They crossed the river. Each boy, accompanied by a parent witness, carried the earthen brick that would be used as his seat during the operation. Women and children were not part of the procession.

When they arrived at the foot of the two great balanza trees that had sheltered generations of circumcised boys with their shade, each boy sat upon his brick, his back to the rising sun. Bougala, the circumciser blacksmith, asked them to stretch their legs and part them as widely as possible. Because my brother Hammadoun was to go first, Bougala stood before him. He divided a kola nut in two and placed each half between the back molars in my brother's mouth, one on the left and one on the right, so that he could measure the indentions made from his teeth and thereby assess his courage. Taking hold of his member, he pulled on the foreskin such that the glans would be as far back from it as possible, then solidly anchored the base of the foreskin with a small string in order to put the flesh of the glans out of range of his blade. He then took up his knife, looked directly at my brother, and said, "Hammadoun, son of Hampâté Bâ, you shall be the first to spill your blood, which is the price of admission into the adult world. You shall be a man, and it is now up to you to prove yourself worthy. Avert your gaze so that I may now sever that which has placed you into the class of uncircumcised boys."

"Oh, old father Bougala," replied Hammadoun, "you wish me to turn my back on my first engagement with the blade? What would you say of me then? Am I not the chief who must lead his companions today? *Wallaye!* (By God!) It shall be with my eyes wide open that I will watch you cut this foreskin that holds my adulthood prisoner and detains me among the children. Cut it, O old father, and cut it well!"

Bougala smiled and then with a quick and adroit stroke of the knife he sliced my brother Hammdoun's foreskin clean off, as he pronounced the Muslim formula, "Bismillahi errahman erahimi!" (In the name of God, the Beneficent, the Merciful). Hammadoun burst into laughter, laid his right hand on the cheek of the old blacksmith as if to administer a slap, spit out his two kola nuts and cried, "*Filla fa fillo Bandiagara!* Do it again (and make it last) for as much time as it takes to travel around the city of Bandiagara! Do it again old father, I ordain it!" And he began to sing the motto of Bandiagara in a clear voice.

Old Bougala presented the foreskin and the two halves of the kola nut, where there was only a light tooth mark, to Hammadoun's relatives. "Koulou diam! Hourra!" He exclaimed. "Hampâté's son has swum across the river of ordeals despite its crocodiles!" And then he proceeded to perform the operation on the other boys, all of whom were intent upon imitating Hammadoun's attitude.

During the operation, relatives of the boys had set up a shelter between the two balanza trees. Those who had been circumcised went to sit beneath it under the watchful eye of their *bawo* (monitor), a person who was generally a member of the caste of weavers, and who, among other duties, had the responsibility of teaching them the "songs of the circumcised" during the three weeks of their retreat, a retreat which lasts for three months among the Bambaras and the Dogons.

Following the operation, all the foreskins were buried. In ancient African tradition, the foreskin is considered to be a symbol of femininity, because it covers the penis and envelops it in a kind of darkness, since everything that is feminine, maternal, and related to germination is formed and develops in the secret obscurity of enclosed places, whether it be inside a woman or inside Mother Earth. Once the boy is divested of his original mark of femininity, which he will recover later in a female partner, he is thought to become the medium for an exclusively masculine power.

During the first week, the circumcised are plied with food like pet sheep, but they are not to drink except during the main meals. They sleep on their backs, their legs spread apart. At the first cock's crow, their bawo awakens them. A large fire is built around which they turn in a circle, singing in unison the special songs that they were taught, while marking the rhythm with their castanets. Fula singers constitute a very harmonious choir, and this is even more true among the Dogons. Throughout the entire first week, the member that has undergone the operation remains wrapped in a medicinal plaster that forms a rather thick scab.

Among the Fulas, over the night from the seventh to the eighth day, the circumcised cease to be isolated and can finally be approached by women and children. It was then that I was able to join Hammadoun, never once leaving him after that, eating, sleeping, and walking with him. I owe all the preceding narrative partly to Hammadoun himself, but also to my uncle Hammadoun Pâté, who was so proud of my brother's demeanor that he never tired of retelling the details of that great day, or at least that was the case when he was in male company.

That night, after dinner, the circumcised were told to sit in a circle. The griotes who had been invited for the occasion began to sing, accompanied by a few musicians. Each boy rose and executed to the best of his ability the rhythmical dance known as *dippal* where it is de rigueur to stomp the ground with one's foot before giving way to the next in line. Before this, the bawo had already washed their wounded member with soapy water and had then slathered a layer of butter on it to begin softening the plaster. Forgetting their pain for a moment, the boys, carried away by the rhythm, danced and stomped the ground with their feet. Later on, overcome with fatigue, they returned to their dormitory, located on the outskirts of the city. They had to rest up in preparation for the important day that would follow, which would be the day of their ritual bath and the first washing of their wounds.

At dawn on the eighth day, the circumcised proceed to the river's edge. They lower themselves into the river so that the flowing current cleans the wound and gradually washes away the plaster. Later they return to the shore and lie on the sand, remaining spread out on their backs until about ten o'clock in the morning.

Elders or the blacksmith then attempt to remove what remains of the plaster. If the butter applied the night before and immersion in the water have not sufficiently softened the scab formed from powder and hardened blood, then an intervention becomes necessary. This ordeal is much more painful than the removal of the foreskin itself. Luckily, at this stage of things, boys are no longer required to display an impassiveness beyond their capacities, but the most courageous will nevertheless be honored and they will be praised in every single home. When it is all over, the bandages are reapplied, but more lightly than before. At around eleven o'clock, thoroughly washed, nice and clean, and visibly more at ease, the circumcised return to their shelter at the foot of the two balanza trees.

The lunchtime meal on the eighth day is a true feast. After having eaten their fill, the boys take a siesta, and then at about three o'clock, revived after their ordeal, they set out for a long walk in the deep bush under the supervision of a few elders and their bawo, and they will do this every day. During these walks, they receive a variety of teachings on what could be called "the natural sciences" from the elders, who possess knowledge of the local flora, minerals, and fauna.

All these teachings are based on concrete examples that are easy for children to understand. Some observed scenes provide an occasion for deeper developments. A tree spreading its branches in space offers an opportunity to explain how everything in the universe is diversified from unity. An anthill or a termite mound provides an occasion for discussing the virtues of solidarity and the rules of social life. Using each example, each lived experience, the bawo and the elders teach the boys how to behave in life, and about the rules that need to be followed toward nature, toward one's fellows, and toward oneself. They teach them how to be men.

Every evening after dinner, storytellers and griots come to enliven the evening, alternating between tales and amusing or glorious historical chronicles interspersed with stories about the exploits of our great men. And on those occasions, no matter what time it is, eyes remain wide open and nobody goes to sleep.

Early on in the second week, the circumcised dedicate their morning to carrying out a kind of quest with passersby at the side of the road leading into the city. The provisions and cowries that are collected will be used to organize a large meal commemorating the separation of those in the graduating class.

During the third week, the wound is healed, or almost. The boys acquire the right to enter the city in full daylight in order to engage in a veritable raid on the resident poultry. As soon as it is morning, the boys invade the city's neighborhoods armed with sticks and clacking their castanets, giving chase to all the chickens or other poultry pecking about in the streets, and even daring to chase them all the way into the inner courtyards, where the boys have the right to enter with impunity. As soon as the residents hear the premonitory racket announcing the arrival of the little pillagers, they try to cage their birds until the tempest has passed. But good luck trying to cage an army of poultry accustomed to free-ranging here, there, and everywhere! Soon, the streets are overwhelmed with the clucking of terrified chickens, the sharp cries of old women as they witness the capture of their best layers, the excited cries of the city's children, who are thrilled to serve as beaters for the circumcised. And every morning, the city rings anew with this joyous and good-natured cacophony.

Finally, the twenty-second day arrives! Early in the morning the group of boys goes to take its final bath in the river. Meanwhile, the shelter that accommodated them at the foot of the two balanza trees is dismantled, and the remaining detritus is divided into three separate piles onto which are thrown all the objects that were used by the circumcised boys (with the exception of their clothing, which traditionally belongs to the blacksmith who performed the operation); then the piles are set on fire. When the boys return from their baths, they must leap over the three fires, whose flames have lost some of their ferocity, but which remain challenging nevertheless. While it is their final ordeal, it is not the least perilous of them.

Once this ordeal is over, they return to their dormitory. Each boy discovers a calabash that has been placed there for him alone, containing a brand-new outfit: loose pants, an under boubou and an over boubou, a white cap known as a "crocodile's maw" (or a Phyrigian cap, the traditional head covering of adult men in all the lands of the Malinke region), an embroidered scarf, a pair of shoes or boots, a sword or a handsome cane, body ornaments, or, in a traditional milieu, protective amulets. Clothed in this beautiful finery, they enter the city and go from door to door thanking relatives and friends for everything that was provided to them during the three weeks. Those whose wound has not yet healed stay at home to continue their treatment. The rounds last for three days. If they are Fulas, the young men give verbal thanks. If they are Dogons, they accompany their rounds with singing and dancing.

For eleven more days, the graduating class remains together and continues to share the same dormitory. Then each one goes home and returns to the occupations that correspond to his age. But now, he has the status of being "a man." In losing his foreskin, the boy has lost the right to walk about naked. His male member, now consecrated as an agent of human reproduction, and therefore a receptacle of sacred power, must no longer be exposed to public view.

A powerful bond of camaraderie and even of fraternity, along with the duty to assist one another, is created between the circumcised boys of the same class, and this lasts a lifetime. They have over each other rights analogous to those permitted by the rapport known as "a joking relation," or *sanankounya* (*dendirakou*) in Fula. As the elder Boudjedi Bâ once pointed out, regardless of age or social class, they can joke with each other and even needle each other quite sharply in public without any retaliatory consequences. They can also bathe naked together in the same place, ride each other's mounts without any prior notice, sit on each other's beds (considered to be extremely discourteous for anybody else), and finally, exchange flirtatious pleasantries with each other's wives and their friends (as they do in the sanankounya relationship between brothers and sisters-in-law) without reaction from the husband—unless there is blatant proof of conjugal dishonor, which in that case would result in the banishment of the guilty party from all his comrades and even from his fellow citizens, that is, if the husband has not already dispatched his lance through the other man's body!

The Great Battle

Once we had paired with our valentines, no boy outside our association had the right to consort with them. Any transgression of this rule was automatically punished by a barrage of blows from our sticks, or lashings from our whips of vine. But between rival associations an incident could also provoke total war. Meticulously planned, the combat was formally declared and unfolded according to specific rules overseen by the elders. This is what befell us toward the end of the year 1911.

One evening, we caught a group of boys from the Gan'ngal neighborhood sitting on the mats that had been prepared for us by our legitimate valentines. They had invited the young women to join them, but this had merely earned them a series of ironic rebukes. When we arrived, they were exchanging insults. Our moutassibi Afo Dianou, who was also our grand champion wrestler, stepped up. "Who are you to come and sit on these mats and harass our valentines?"

"We are from Gan'ngal."

"Is your waaldé chief with you?"

"For what? Aren't we old enough to walk around on our own looking for beaded belts to tease and curves to fondle?[4] We just happened to come across these beautiful shapely girls whose slender beaded waists make a pleasant swishing sound like fillies walking in a fallow field. We suddenly felt like talking to them, and since these empty mats were calling our backsides to take a rest, we sat right down."

It was my turn to step up. "Did your chief give you permission to come here and violate our domain and talk to our girls using those filthy words?" Without giving them time to respond, I raised my voice even louder. "Go on! Get up! Shake out the hems of your boubous quickly and head out. We need to see the arch of your backs and the curve of your heels. Go tell your chief to send us his apologies, or else tomorrow night, as soon as the moon is up, I'll be sending you two griots. What they say will come from my mouth. It will be short but sweet. In the name of all of my comrades, I have spoken."

When a waaldé chief is within his rights to give an order to a group of delinquents, they are obliged to obey or risk an immediate beating. Our rivals groused about it but they left the premises, to the great satisfaction of our valentines, who accompanied their departure with a salvo of mocking laughter.

Extremely proud of ourselves, we settled onto our mats. The young women joined us. Our usual banter, mixed with games, laughter, and tales, went on until rather late in the evening. My friends and I had decided to meet later on after the fun, no matter what time it was, in order to discuss the contents of the message that we would send the next day to Si Tangara, the Gan'ngal waaldé chief. It was quite late when we finally returned to our bunks.

The next day, our griot Mouctar Kaou, accompanied by three of our comrades, Afo Dianou among them, paid a visit to Si Tangara. In his role as griot and spokesman, only Mouctar Kaou was to speak and deliver our message. His companions were merely there to act as witnesses. When he was before Si Tangara, Mouctar began to speak. "I, Mouctar, son of Kaou Dieli Sissoko, have come on behalf of Amkoullel, son of Hampâté Bâ, waaldé chief of our neighborhood Deendé Bôdi, to ask Si Tangara, waaldé chief of the Gan'ngal neighborhood, the following.

"One: Is Si Tangara aware of the violation committed last night by several members of his *waaldé*?

"Two: If he is not aware of it, then we have come to inform him of it, and we await a firm promise of reparations as custom requires.

"Three: If he is aware of it, we await an explanation from him and a justification of the intention that he envisions as the result of his actions.

"Four: We hereby inform Si Tangara and his associates that the youth of the Deendé Bôdi waaldé do not appreciate palavers that are as long as several day's walk, and still less, obscurely constructed palavers tinted with 'charcoal milk.' Our waaldé is commanded by Amkoullel, a pure 'red ears' Fula, descendant of the Hamsalahs of Fakala and of Alfa Samba Fouta Bâ, who was a general in Cheikou Amadou's army. I have transmitted the message. After us, Amkoullel will not send anyone else to see you, Si Tangara."

Then Si Tangara spoke. "I, Si Tangara, descendant of the Tangaras, chiefs of the land of Pemaye, declare that since my right ear has refused to obey, I have only listened with my left ear to the words that Amkoullel has instructed you, Mouctar Kaou, member of the tribe of troubadour griots, who are shameless buffoons, insolent beggars, and barefaced braggarts, to come and yowl in my ears like a mangy cat. Go home and tell your chief that I was not aware of the fine excursion undertaken by my comrades. But I am not at all unhappy about it. And this very night, before sleep places tongues at the mercy of the teeth in every mouth, I will not only advise but order them to do it again.

"Tell Amkoullel that Maïrama Jeïdani, Aye Abbassi, Mouminatou Oumarou, Aïssata Demba, Aminata Mali, and all their companions are just too beautiful a herd of young fillies for the prairie where they graze to be forbidden to us hot-blooded young stallions.

"My words are as clear as spring water, and I'm sure that they've hit the little drums inside those jackass ears of yours hard enough. Now let my words sink a little deeper into your brain and settle there like a hen sitting on the eggs in her nest."

As if this string of insults wasn't enough, Si Tangara then cried to his moutassibi, "Hey, Bila Hambarké! Bring me something to send to Amkoullel via his gangly griot."

Bila Hambarké disappeared. A minute later, he reappeared, holding a broken calabash shard containing a cowrie with one end broken off. This made it worthless, like a bank bill missing a numeral. "Here, take this!" said Si Tangara disdainfully. "This is all I owe Amkoullel in reparations. Take this to him on my behalf and tell him I give it to him willingly."

At the slanderous sight of the broken cowrie shell and the calabash shard, Afo Dianou lost complete control of his nerves, which were already so easily irritated. Forgetting that he was to remain silent and to simply play the role of a witness, he burst out, "Oh Si Tangara! For you to act as you have just done, it must be that you are the offspring of an adulterous couple, or that you are issued from a union blessed and officiated by El Waswass himself, the most shameless son of Satan the lapidated!"

And he raised his stick to the threatening position of someone who is ready to strike a blow.

Mouctar Kaou, who had not waivered, called him to order in a low voice. "Hey, Afo Dianou, there was no need for you to come and eat off my plate by speaking in my place. I have a mouth wide enough for that, and my masticating faculties are not broken. So stop stealing my speech. In the name of our chief, I order you to be as silent as the dunes in the desert. Our only duty is to sharpen our memories in order to bring back to Amkoullel all the words spoken by Si Tangara, who might boast of being a pure Bambara, but who only speaks like a carrion eater."

Turning to Si Tangara, he resumed, "In my capacity as a griot, I am ashamed on your behalf, Si Tangara, you whose name 'Si' means seven things in Bambara: 'shea,' 'hair' or 'whisker,' 'nature,' 'grind,' 'pass the night,' 'a lot,' and 'age.'

"Well, I can see that you are not a 'shea,' Si, like the tree that provides a savory butter, not any more than you are a 'nature,' Si. Rather, you are a Si in the sense of 'grind,' because Amkoullel is going to grind you up and snatch you out of his way like we pluck out a 'hair' or a superfluous 'whisker.' Does Si mean 'pass the night'? Just wait until Amkoullel makes you, Si Tangara, pass the worst night of your unlucky life. As for Si, 'a lot,' tell yourself that from today forward your path will be full of thorns and inedible fruit. Finally, Si means 'age.' Well, you will soon find out that while you and Amkoullel are of the same age, in reality, you couldn't be more different by way of birth, knowledge, and fortune!"

Following this vehement and somewhat dithyrambic rebuttal (but do not the sons of griots, like the sons of chiefs, suckle the art of speech at their mother's breasts?) Mouctar Kaou snatched the insulting gift that was intended for me from the hands of Bila Hambarké. "Does Si mean 'nature?'" he again added. "Well, Amkoullel will soon know the nature of this message, and Si Tangara will know before long and at his own expense the nature of Amkoullel!" And after having shot this last arrow, he set out on the road for home, followed by his comrade witnesses.

When they arrived at our meeting place, their features were drawn and their voices faint. In front of all my comrades, Mouctar took the calabash shard and broken cowrie from his boubou.

"We went to pay Si Tangara a visit," he said. "We found him surrounded by the members of his waaldé. He greeted us in a hostile and disdainful manner. After listening to me, as he put it, 'with his left ear,' and even replying with insults, he gave me this symbolic gift for you and instructed me to transmit his message to you."

And Mouctar Kaou faithfully repeated all Si Tangara's words back to me.

I was stunned. "A cowrie with an end broken off lying on a shard from a broken calabash!" I could not say another word. In the blink of an eye, my blood rushed to my head and then through the rest of my body. A tingling sensation spread from the soles of my feet to the top of my head. My vision became blurred. All I could see was a kind of darkness pierced with a thousand little spangles. I tried to speak but my voice caught in my throat.

While I sat petrified and unable to speak, my comrades were utterly outraged. Daouda Maïga and Mamadou Gorel cursed and swore like tirailleur infantrymen. Their exclamations brought me back to reality and I finally recovered my ability to speak. "No insult could be worse than the one that Si Tangara has just thrown at us. It calls for a clubbing, or even a few slashes from our knives."

My words, which were no doubt excessive, unleashed such violent shouts of approbation that I was a bit shocked. I had to calm my friends. I remembered my mother's advice: "A good waaldé chief should always be patient and conciliatory. He must not encourage fighting, but if there is no avoiding it, he must not back out either. During the fight, if indeed there is a fight, he must never flee, no matter the number and violence of the blows he receives. The only incurable wound for a chief," she added, "is the one received while running from an enemy." Full of these teachings, I always sought reconciliation, but when it was necessary, I met the challenges, and if I got into a fight, I saw it through to the end.

For the moment, I had to say something to calm my comrades and prevent them from going and giving themselves over to blind revenge. I signaled that I wished to speak. Everyone fell silent.

"We will fight Si Tangara's waaldé," I declared, "and for three reasons. First, to wash away his insults, by forcing him to insult himself once he has been defeated. Second, to save face before our valentines and not lose them. Third, to discourage once and for all any others who feel like confronting us for any reason whatsoever in the future."

Although still heated, the shouts of approval from my comrades were already less troubling.

I decided to schedule a confrontation that would take place following an official declaration and a set of predetermined rules. I told Mouctar Kaou and his companions to return immediately to Si Tangara and to deliver the following message: "I, Amkoullel, and all my associates, have received the gift that Si Tangara and all his associates have sent us. We are not dogs who respond to barking by barking back, since for us, Si Tangara and his gang are nothing but dogs whose tails are too long. Nevertheless, in accordance to custom, we invite them to engage in formal combat. We leave them the task of choosing their seconds as well as ours from the elders of the other waaldés, as well as the day and place of the encounter."

Si Tangara chose the following Thursday. He refused to choose our seconds but he named his own: Mouda Diourou and Nouhoun Allahadji, who were both members of my older brother Hammadoun's association. He left it to us to designate the location of the confrontation. I chose a small valley to the west of the city on the left bank of the Yaamé, near the military firing range, between two red dunes and an acacia grove, and named two seconds: Allaye Gombel and my own older brother, Hammadoun.

We had three entire days to prepare. When Thursday arrived, as soon as breakfast was over, my companions left in small groups so as not to draw the attention of the adults and our relatives who lived in town. We were armed with pliable braided lashes and fighting sticks for backup.

When we arrived at our chosen location, our respective seconds lined us up face to face. According to custom, the battle begins with a hand-to-hand bout between the two waaldé chiefs before it turns into a general melee. Nouhoun Allahadji loudly declared, "The 'appellant' camp has the floor."

I stepped forth from the ranks. "Si Tangara!" I called. "Are you indeed he who sent me foul words accompanied by a cowrie with a broken end inside some chunks from a broken calabash?"

"Yes, I am, indeed, he who did what you just said. And I am responding to your invitation in order to prove that you aren't done with me yet."

"Well then, step forward from your ranks and repeat what you said so that I can treat you like a donkey-driver treats his donkey, you stupid son of a she-ass!"

Si Tangara rushed at me, cracking his long switch. He hit me hard on my right side, but I had broken the force of the blow with my stick. The noise was louder than the pain it caused. The end of his lash had nevertheless caught my flank and marked it with a blood-filled welt. To encourage my comrades, and above all to hide the truth, I boasted, "Hey Tangara, you're a lousy shot! You tried to whip someone equal to your father and you missed! Take this blow to shred your pig flesh!"

I raised my right hand, which was armed with my whip. Thinking that I was about to strike his left side, which was within my reach, he rapidly protected it with his arms. In a flash, I took my whip into my rather deft left hand, and I lashed his right side so hard that he staggered.

He was much stronger than I was. In a hand-to-hand bout he would have floored me in a couple of minutes, and he was well aware of that fact. Overcoming his pain, he leaped toward me, obviously intending to grab me, throw me down, and beat me with his fists. Counting on the strength of his arms alone, he had imprudently dropped his stick and his whip. But I had seen him coming. As agile as a monkey thanks to my light weight, I jumped back and to the left so that just at the moment when he fell on me, I was able to strike a violent blow from my stick on his right tibia. The pain was so intense that he doubled over. I neutralized him with a volley of stick blows on his forearms as he was trying to use them to protect himself.

When his comrades saw that he was at a disadvantage, they rushed at me, but my companions had been waiting for that very moment to join the fray. An absolute blind melee ensued. The stocky and powerfully built Afo Dianou, the excellent wrestler and stick fighter Mamdou Gorel, who was also gifted with incredible agility, and the solid Daouda Maïga had been ordered to cover me and to attack any enemy who tried to grab me and engage in hand-to-hand combat.

Si Tangara had gotten up, but I was raining so many blows on him with my stick that he was unable to regain the upper hand. I beat him with everything I had, but I was not able to get him to cry out or to call for help, for such an action would have cemented my victory. Yes, I had beaten him, but I had not succeeded in crushing him or making him beg for forgiveness. Although he was wounded and covered in blood, he had remained proud. I admired his courage and drew a lesson from it for myself.

Incensed by this resistance, Afo Dianou shouted, "Hey you son of a *banmana* (Bambara), now you've got me to deal with!"

And he rushed at Si Tangara as I let go of him. Knowing the physical strength and brutality of Afo Dianou, Si Tangara deftly snatched the stick from the hands of one of my comrades. I knew that Afo Dianou was the man best suited for hand-to-hand combat rather than fighting with the stick or the whip, weapons that I handled better than he. Taking advantage of Si Tangara's move, I slipped in and hit him on his side. But he had regained his strength. As he turned on me, he was able to strike my forehead so hard with his stick that he split my scalp open. Blood poured down and blinded me, depriving me of my faculties. Si Tangara would surely have taken revenge on me at that moment if Daouda Maïga had not stepped in and launched a hail of blows, neutralizing him. Coming in from behind, Afo Dianou grasped him with his powerful arms and was able to lift him up. Si Tangara's stick dropped from his hands. Bruised by the blows from my stick, his arms no longer had the strength to loosen Afo Dianou's hold. Gripping Si Tangara's neck with his left arm, Afo Dianou butted him with his hip, felled him, and straddled him, crushing him with all his weight. He was about to pound his face to a pulp with his fists when Si Tangara finally uttered the words we were waiting to hear: "Aan jey!" (To you! meaning, Victory is yours!) This was the ritual request for peace by which one declared oneself out of combat.

The seconds for each side immediately intervened to stop the fighting. Rather badly beaten in the general melee, half of Si Tangara's comrades had fled, some running to hide behind the red dunes, others inside the acacia grove, and still others had crossed the river and returned to Bandiagara. We were victorious, but we had paid a high price. A good number of us had been seriously injured.

We dragged our prisoner Si Tangara to the entrance of the pocket of water that was home to Bandiagara's sacred crocodile which everyone called Mamma Bandiagara (ancestor of Bandiagara).[5]

"Swear by the sacred crocodile that you will never again provoke us," I said, "and that you will not join forces with another waaldé to fight against us. In return, we are ready to merge with your waaldé. All of us together can constitute a formidable force capable of standing up to all the rival waaldés of the northern neighborhoods."

Si Tangara bravely declared that he could do nothing without the consent of his comrades. He asked us to give him three days in order to consult with them. The seconds declared us the winners, but they accorded Si Tangara the waiting period that he had requested.

Three days later, at the appointed time, Si Tangara and his comrades presented themselves at the pocket of water that was home to the ancestor crocodile. My friends and I were waiting for them. Our respective seconds were there as well. They had decided that if Si Tangara's waaldé had accepted to merge with us, the required oath would not be necessary, but that our two associations would then have to swear mutual allegiance to each other, and our members would have to recognize one another as brothers with equal rights and obligations.

Since Si Tangara's companions had accepted the merger, we swore our loyalty in the following terms: "We, members of the youth associations of the neighborhoods of Deendé Bôdi and Gan'ngal, do hereby swear by the waters of the Yaamé of Bandiagara that we are joined together and that from this moment on, we will only form a single waaldé whose members will be as brothers born of the same entrails. O, ancestor crocodile of Bandiagara, be the witness of our alliance! If one of us violates his oath, O crocodile-ancestor, forbid him access to the Yaamé that he may never again bathe in it, that its waters give him diarrhea, that he may never again fish in it, and if he does, may the fish give him leprosy! And if he comes here anyway, then, O ancestor crocodile, make your fearful son Ngoudda-short-tail, whose long jaws are studded with pointed and murderous teeth, snatch his leg off. O ancestor crocodile do it in defense of the word that has been given! A mouth with no word is a queen with no crown."

And so it was that our two associations merged. Si Tangara was elected vice-chief of our new waaldé, replacing Mamadou Gorel, who became second vice-chief. From that day forward, our waaldé contained the best fighters, whips, and wielders of sticks in the entire city of Bandiagara. It reached the impressive number of seventy members. No other waaldé of our age group could hope to beat us. We soon became known throughout the city by the unflattering name of *Bonndé ounanndé*, "that which has been ground poorly," an allusion to a millet couscous to which bitter or spicy elements have been added. Truth be told, our raids on the gardens of soldiers and prominent members of the community sometimes caused as much damage as an infestation of rats or a plague of locusts. Even the superb tomatoes grown in the district commandant's garden did not escape our plundering.

5

At the White Man's School

Requisitioned by Force

My days were happily divided between Koranic school, my older brother, and my association comrades. But an unforeseen event that would mark a turning point in my existence came along and upset it all. In fact, every time I had started down a nice, straight path in my life, fate seemed to enjoy flicking its finger, sending me reeling in a completely different direction than the one I should have taken, and causing me to alternate between periods of good luck and misfortune. The process began well before my birth with my father Hampâté, who should have inherited (and his children after him) a chiefdom in Fakala, but instead ended up being the only surviving member of his family, an anonymous refugee working in an obscure butcher shop. Redeemed by the very same king who had ordered the massacre of all his family members, he then died too soon for me to really get to know him, fating me to become an orphan at the tender age of three. A rich and noble provincial chieftain comes along and marries my mother, adopts me, makes me his son and heir apparent, with the promise of the chieftain's turban of Louta hovering above my head. But flick! We are all sent into exile and I become the son of a convict. We finally return to Bandiagara, where life seems to have returned to normal when, flick! I am brutally snatched away from the traditional activities that would surely have led me to enter the time-honored career of marabout and teacher.

Instead, I'm forced to attend "the White Man's school," which the Muslim populace of the time regarded as the most direct route to hell!

In those days, the district commandants were in charge of populating three sectors by way of the schools: the public sector (consisting of teachers, subaltern officials in the colonial administration, physician's assistants, and so on), where the best students were sent; the military sector, because it was considered desirable for tirailleur infantrymen, *spahi* cavalrymen and goumier soldiers to have a basic knowledge of French; and finally the domestic sector, which received the least talented students. The governor of the territory set the annual quota for the first two sectors. The district commandants then filled the "order" by informing the canton chiefs and the traditional chiefs of the number of children they needed to requisition for school.

And so it came to pass that on one fine day in 1912, about two-thirds of the way into the school year, the Bandiagara district commandant Camille Maillet issued the order to Alfa Maki Tall, the city's traditional chieftain and the son of former king Aguibou Tall, to provide him with two boys below eighteen years of age from good families in order to fill out the ranks of the Bandiagara primary school.

Alfa Maki Tall convened the heads of Bandiagara's eighteen neighborhoods and asked them whose turn it was to provide students. Koniba Kondala, head of our neighborhood Deendé Bôdi, silently tapped his forehead with this fingertips in the traditional manner of declaring, "It's my turn, I will do it."

In order to shed a little light on the situation, I must explain who Koniba Kondala was. Born in Kondala, a village in Fakala, land of my paternal ancestors, Koniba Kondala was in fact a former dîmadjo, captive of the Alfa Samba Fouta Bâ family. Alfa Samba Fouta Bâ had been an army general and provincial chieftain in the Fula Empire of Massina during the reign of Cheikou Amadou and was one of my paternal great-uncles. When El Hadj Omar's nephew King Tidjani Tall invaded the country, took the village of Kondala, and decimated my entire paternal family, Koniba sided with the Toucouleurs and gave himself up to the king. He thereby became a sort of "voluntary captive," while at the same time serving as an agent who could provide eminently useful information during those times of war and retribution against all the once-prominent Fulas in the land.

At the time, King Tidjani Tall used the services of Koniba Kondala without ever giving him an important position in his entourage. I do not know how he later ended up at the court of King Aguibou Tall, nor do I know what role he played there. Nevertheless, during the time of King Alfa Maki Tall, Koniba Kondala was our neighborhood headman.

Our guardian, Beydari, had since become his bête noire and had been so for some time. It will be recalled that Beydari had learned butchering from my father and old Allamodio, and was deeply involved in the meat business, which allowed him to provide for the entire household. This included not just my brother, Hammadoun, and me, but also Beydari himself, his own family, and the families of his companions and former captives of my father who had married and who all lived in the family compound. Well, Koniba Kondala had gotten into the habit of coming to take from Beydari's stand without paying, and he always took the best cuts. One day, when he had had enough of seeing his best roasts and nicely fatted shoulders disappear for nothing, Beydari intercepted Koniba's hand as it was passing over the display, just at the moment when it was about to make off with the best piece of meat. "Because you lack restraint," Beydari told him, "I am forced to supply it to you. From this day forward, you will no longer have even the tiniest piece of meat without paying. Take your thievery and go somewhere else."

Koniba Kondala had no choice but to comply, but he swore to make Beydari pay a high price for the rebuke. And from that day forth he lay in wait, ready to seize the first pretext for revenge. The opportunity he had been dreaming of arose when he received the order to requisition two boys for the White Man's school. What could be worse for Beydari than to take away both of the little orphans whom he adored and send them off to the school of the "pork eaters" all on the very same day? And what ultimate vengeance against the family of his former Fakala masters! What was more, he would have the immense pleasure of placing Beydari in an impossible situation. Indeed, there was no doubt that Beydari would do anything in his power to shield at least one of us from the fate that awaited us, and in order to do that he had only two choices. He could either go and kneel before Koniba Kondala and beg for the release of at least one of Hampâté's two sons in exchange for providing him, daily and free of charge, with a selection of his best cuts of meat. Or he could go and beg the schoolteacher or the interpreter to have the name of one of the two boys removed from the list of students, a feat that would cost him a fortune beyond his means. In both cases, he thought, Beydari would be forced to lose face without ever being certain of obtaining satisfaction.

Truth be told, I had also had a hand in feeding the animosity that Koniba Kondala harbored toward us. In fact, he kept a beautiful vegetable garden in which he had scattered protective fetishes, each more fearsome than the other, and that frightened everyone. Well, one day, my waaldé comrades and I took and destroyed all his fetishes and then joyfully proceeded to trash his garden, as was our custom. He knew very well who was behind this misdeed.

This explains the jubilation with which Koniba Kondala dashed off to see Beydari as soon as the meeting of the neighborhood headmen was over, in order to inform him, his face beaming, that his two charges, Hammadoun Hampâté and Amadou Hampâté, had been designated to attend the White Man's school.

"May God's will be done, as it pleases God that it will!" Beydari calmly replied.

This was the last thing that Koniba had expected to hear! His face filled with disappointment. Deprived of the sad scene that he had hoped for, he could not help shouting,

"Well, too bad for your little masters! Everything that they will learn at the White Man's school will lead them to deny their faith. They will become good-for-nothing miscreants and social outcasts!"

Beydari did not even bother to reply. Ever more disappointed, Koniba barked, "Where are they?" quite persuaded that Beydari would not tell him, thereby giving him a chance to strike.

Without batting an eye, Beydari replied,

"Today, they are at Alfa Ali's Koranic school."

Koniba Kondala stormed out and headed straight for the old teacher Alfa Ali's house, where Tierno Bokar had placed us before leaving on a short trip. Hammadoun and I were seated under the shelter in the courtyard studying our respective lessons, guided by an assistant teacher. Alfa Ali was still inside his house.

At the sight of Koniba, everyone seemed to automatically pronounce the Koranic verse that is uttered when disaster strikes: "Indeed we belong to Allah and to Him we shall return." The sight of Koniba walking in one's direction was indeed considered to be an unavoidable announcement of coming misfortune, because he only appeared at people's houses when he needed to enlist or coercively requisition them either for forced labor or for the army. The least harmful thing that he could do was to requisition one's pack animals for the underpaid and virtually free transport of personnel or matériel destined for use by the civil or military colonial administration. In other cases, the capitations provided by the local population were destined for the large commercial French enterprises located there, and were considered as "contributions to the development of the colony."

Koniba was tall and hugely proportioned. Everything about him was harsh and tough. He had been nicknamed "the black lion with a red eye," an aptly eloquent image for those who know that black lions never fail to be man-eaters. Without the least consideration for Amoussa, the instructor who was giving us our lessons, Koniba ordered my brother and me to follow him. Someone had alerted the old teacher, Alfa Ali, who came running. He was indignant.

"This is the first time that I have ever seen two brothers from the same father and the same mother being taken away to school at the same time. What's going on here, Koniba Kondala?"

"Hey, marabout!" Koniba sneered. "Maybe it wasn't written in the Koran. But you'll learn that here below, might treads on right. If might cuts off one of your fingers and you think that unjust, it will also cut off your hand, followed by your entire arm. Nevertheless, night will continue to follow day, couples will keep coupling, the wind will keep blowing, rivers will keep flowing, and plants will keep growing. Straighten your turban and return to your books, wooden tablets, and reed pens!"

The old teacher then pronounced the phrase for warding off misfortune, and turned to us.

"Follow him, my children, and may God render justice upon you."

Koniba burst into laughter.

"When the toubab is in command, God closes his eyes and looks the other way. Don't waste your saliva."

Hammadoun and I had often seen Koniba Kondala and Beydari at each other's throats, and we were apprehensive at the idea of following him. We dragged our feet. When we reached a bend in the little street, we ran as fast as we could toward the market where Beydari kept his shop. When he saw us take to our heels, Koniba Kondala knew immediately where we were headed and caught up with us there shortly afterward, fuming with rage and spewing threats and insults. He attempted to grab us, but Beydari, who was also of considerable size, stepped between us, brandishing his double-bladed knife. Then a very bad thought entered my mind. I wanted to see Beydari slit Koniba Kondala's belly open just as he sliced into the animals he had butchered. But the idea that he would immediately be put in prison, his ankles clanking with heavy chains like the ones my father Tidjani had once had to wear chased the thought from my mind! Deep down inside of me a little voice murmured, "If Beydari goes to prison, who will take care of the family?" My fear was so great that, through a kind of unconscious nervous reaction, I cried out, "No! Beydari will not go to prison!"

"Oh, yes, Beydari certainly will go to prison!" replied Koniba Kondala maliciously, and he shoved my brother and me out the door, forbidding Beydari to follow. He took us to the street that led to Chief Alfa Maki Tall's palace.

"Walk faster!" he cried. "Do you take me for your father's slow-stepping first cousin, the chameleon? If you don't get a move on, I'll slap you so hard your ancestors will roll over in their graves when they see what is happening to their descendants."

"Where are you taking us?" my brother Hammadoun dared to ask.

"Exactly where you deserve to go, to the toubab's pigsty! You'll be turned into pigs, or better yet, into little bits of wood destined to feed the fires of hell!" And in this way, we arrived at the chief's palace, under a hail of threats and insults, our hearts heavy with the dread of those condemned to die.

The vestibule was crowded with servants and visitors waiting to be received. Koniba Kondala, who was free to come and go as he pleased, took us directly into Alfa Maki Tall's inner courtyard. There, he handed us over to a sofa who was standing guard, advising him to keep a close eye on us, as we were liable to run off. Leaving us under this surveillance, Koniba Kondala climbed the stairs to the second floor. A few moments later he came back down with chief Alfa Maki Tall preceding him. As soon as he saw us, he turned to Koniba Kondala and said, "Why, aren't these Kadidja Pâté's two sons?"

"Yes, Fama, they certainly are her two sons."

"And you expect me to choose two brothers from the same father and the same mother to send away to school and to do it on the very same day?

"Fama, these two boys are not like the others: they are the only male descendants of the Hamsalah and of Alfa Samba Fouta Bâ by Tayrou Hammadoun, Bori Hammadoun, and Houdou Hammadoun. Indeed, this is the family that Cheikou Amadou, king of the Fulas of Massina, said was the gold of Fakala. He said that if its members could be sown like millet, he himself would have planted them so that they would never be missing from any generation in the lands of the Niger Bend. These boys are the last remaining descendants of a family that is the enemy of your family."

The fama went to sit on a platform made of black earth and covered with embroidered lengths of cloth. Immediately, courtiers, sofas, servants, and visitors clothed in their best boubous surrounded the platform. He turned toward us.

"Approach, my children," he said. I felt instinctively that he meant us no harm. "Which of the two of you," he continued, "is farthest along in his Koranic studies?"

I found his question amusing. Who would think of asking which was faster, a donkey or a thoroughbred? Next to my older brother, Hammadoun, intellectually speaking, I was as a jackass is to a well-trained steed. My brother Hammadoun was a phenomenon of nature in every way. He was the best-looking boy in all Bandiagara, and although he did not possess the build of a wrestler, he had been gifted with such physical strength that never had any of our comrades succeeded in bringing him down, to the point that he had been nicknamed "the ramrod." As for his memory, it was so prodigious that by the age of eleven he had succeeded in memorizing the entire Koran by heart. When Koniba came to take us for the school, my brother had already begun his second "round" of the holy book, while I was still floundering through the first half.

After each of us had explained our respective levels of achievement to Alfa Maki Tall, the chief turned to my brother.

"Go home and return to your studies," he told him. "And this time, when you have finished your second round of the Koran, I will personally pay for your *walîma* celebration meal."

Hammadoun thanked the chief and left, his heart heavy at having to leave me behind.

Alfa Maki Tall called to one of his servants. "Go tell my wife Ta-Selli to send me my son Madani."

While awaiting the arrival of Madani, whom I expected to be an important palace dignitary, a richly appareled praise singer entered the courtyard, the lobes of her ears weighted down by a set of enormous coiled gold earrings, and the edges of her ears delicately pierced with tiny rings of precious stones. Raising her arms so as to rattle her many bracelets, she sang out a greeting to the Tall name in a high and powerful voice. She held a single long note, and then launched into a song glorifying the Toucouleur epic, then suddenly fell silent. Madani had arrived. To my great surprise I was looking at a seven-year-old boy. Dressed in a handsome boubou made from black Guinea cloth, he wore a thick braid on one side of his head. The rest of it was shaved clean, as is the custom for boys of the Tall family until they are circumcised.

He was brought before his father. Not knowing what his father wanted, nor why he had been summoned, the young boy was shaking. Alfa Maki turned to Koniba Kondala.

"Because the commandant has requested two boys from good families," he said, "here is my son Madani. He will replace Hammadoun Hampâté, whom I have sent home. Take my son along with Amadou to the commandant, and tell him that if he happened to want to release one of them, I request, for family reasons, that he not release one without the other. I want them both to experience the same fate. He will understand."

Koniba Kondala was beside himself. Losing all sense of decorum and restraint, he cried, "Oh, Fama, hold on to your son! Bring back Hammadoun Hampâté and send him to the White Man's school with his younger brother! Do not allow them to ennoble themselves through their Koranic studies. These descendants of the Hamsalahs will become great marabouts, they will become personalities, and that will be all they will need to establish their family's religious prestige!"

Alfa Maki said angrily, "Father Koniba! Know that for me the past is past. I do not intend, and Islamic morality forbids it, to place the burden of their ancestors' sins upon the shoulders of these descendants. Do not remind me ever again of what happened between us and our Muslim Fula brothers from Massina. We are all Halpoulaar, speakers of Poulaar. I have nothing against these children. They were born in Bandiagara like some of my own children and like yours too. They have the same rights and the same duties before God. They are like travelers who have embarked in the same pirogue, enjoy the same landscape, and run the same risks."

Kaou Dieli, the former grand marabout and griot of the court of King Aguibou Tall (and the grandfather of our comrade Mouctar Kaou), was present, for he had become an adviser to chief Alfa Maki Tall.

"Oh! You! Koniba Kondala!" he cried. "Cease to issue commands to the wind, for we command the water necessary for extinguishing our own blazes. Go. Take Madani Alfa Maki and Amadou Hampâté, and faithfully repeat to the commandant, without additions or subtractions, what the fama told you to say. The best servant is he who stops at the edge of the limit that has been set for him and who faithfully repeats that which he has been told to say. He who acts inappropriately is never a good auxiliary."

Visibly ashamed at having been issued such a public browbeating by the very person that he was trying to please, Koniba Kondala brutally seized my arm and shoved me along the road ahead of him while at the same time purring in the most respectful and softly spoken voice possible to Madani, "Come, *Maké*, my Lord! Follow me!"

When I think of what some of the Talls inflicted on my family, I remember how nobly a Tall like Alfa Maki behaved and I tell myself that we must close our eyes to human shortcomings and acknowledge only the good. The good is what we share. As for the shortcomings, we all have them, I have mine. Yet today I am grateful to Alfa Maki for the grandeur of his gesture, and his benevolent image remains in my memory.

Scarcely had we started down the road leading to the residence of the district commandant when the storm that had been brewing inside Koniba Kondala began to rain down on me. As I was trotting along as best I could behind him, taking care not to allow my toes to strike his heels, which were as coarse as the dried clay that remains after receding waters, the old dîmadjo delved deep into his extensive repertoire of vulgarities. He discharged a hail of the worst insults on my people, my parents, and myself, calling me a little viper hatched by a blind crocodile, an ill omen born from the coupling of a toothless lion and a tigress without fangs or claws, plus a few more nasty names that I cannot repeat. "You son of a toothless crocodile!" he fumed. "Because of you a direct descendant of El Hadj Omar will be sent to the school of the pork eaters! What misfortune!"

All along the way, he never ceased cursing me and condemning me to hell. I received all his insults without any outward reaction, as quietly as a mud-brick wall silently absorbs the torrid rays of the noonday sun. But inside, every word tore me apart and scorched my heart. More than once I almost suffocated from indignation.

The Commandant and the Five-Franc Coin

We finally reach the bridge that crosses the Yaamé River at a distance of about eight hundred meters from the commandant's residence. "O God!" Koniba continues to lament, "By the fault of this cursed son of the also cursed Hampâté, now my little Prince Tall is being sent off to attend the school of the mustachioed drinkers of wine laced with sow's milk instead of completing lengthy Koranic studies and becoming a great marabout!" And giving me a good whack on the skull, he shoves me along, then exhales what remains of his rancor in this final malediction: "May God deliver you down to the seventh level of his stinking abyss!"

As we exit the bridge, we advance along the stately road that leads to the residence staircase. Solidly laid by human hands, thanks to the obligatory "service contributions" forced upon the population, it is bordered on both sides by great flamboyant trees, so named for their beautiful red flowers and sought after for their refreshing shade. Outside the residence, groups of visitors are seated under the trees or in the shade of the walls. They are waiting for the commandant's office to open its doors and for the interpreter to signal them to approach. Everyone here speaks in hushed tones. Nobody dares voice a hearty laugh or use loud speech. The district commandant, more fearsome than a wild beast, apparently must not be disturbed as he sleeps.

Here as well, Koniba Kondala seems to be among the privileged, for he clears without difficulty or infringement the set of steps that leads up to the veranda outside the commandant's office. With Madani behind me, I follow Koniba and go to sit next to him on the floor at one end of the veranda.

A man seems to be keeping watch over the place. Incessantly pacing back-and-forth the entire length of the veranda, he is obviously proud of his comely uniform. His head is adorned with a large red fez as bright as flamboyant flowers, and he is wearing a navy blue jacket, white pants, blue puttees, and yellow sandals made from pure French leather. His waist is proudly encircled by a large yellow belt fastened with a silver buckle. This must certainly be the most important person at the residence after the commandant!

A few moments later, I see that I am mistaken. A corpulent African clothed in a sumptuous starched and embroidered white boubou, shod in decoratively stitched boots, wearing a colonial helmet in very good repair, his fingers loaded with thick silver rings, climbs the stairs to the veranda with a slow and majestic step. He has scarcely reached the veranda before the man in the red fez stops, stands at attention, executes an impeccable military salute, rushes to take his helmet, and runs to hang it on a coat rack. The man in the embroidered boubou takes his seat in a chair next to the commandant's office. At the slightest noise, as though ejected by a spring, he rises and glances furtively inside the office. I will understand later that this is the interpreter, the commandant's "responding-mouth," and that he is much more important than the preceding personage, who is known as an "orderly."

Scarcely has the man in the boubou taken his seat in the chair, when a third personage appears and climbs the stairs with a step equal in tranquility to that of the interpreter. He is clothed in the outfit worn by the White-Blacks: a jacket of white cotton drill, neatly fitted at the waist, a white shirt, trousers of Moroccan cloth the color of chocolate, polished shoes with pointed toes, and black socks, with an almost new colonial helmet to top it all off.

The orderly once again stands at attention, salutes the newcomer, takes his helmet, and runs to hang it next to that of the interpreter. Then, still at a run, he goes and opens the door to a room across a corridor facing the commandant's office. This White-Black in the white jacket (I would later learn that this was the commandant's native secretary-clerk) rapidly shakes the interpreter's hand and enters the office without paying the least mind to Koniba Kondala, much less to the two youngsters accompanying him.

I am plunged into utter perplexity upon encountering this world, which is completely new to me. What kind of house could this be where everyone speaks through mimicry and walks on tiptoe? What exactly is the role of each person? Suddenly, from inside the building, firm steps echo on the terracotta bricks. The echo comes closer. In the commandant's office somebody pulls back a chair, coughs several times, clears his throat, and noisily blows his nose. A loud voice calls out, "Orderly!"

"Oui, ma comandan!" replies the orderly as he hastily dashes toward the office, which the commandant must have entered from his private apartments by way of an inner route.

He comes to an abrupt halt in front of the door, executes a military salute, and then remains frozen in this position as though he were a statue made of bronze.

From inside, the commandant shouts something. Before the orderly can respond, the interpreter jumps up from his chair as though he had been stung by a scorpion and dashes to the door. "Voilà moi, ma coumandan!" he cries. He listens for a moment and then turns to Koniba Kondala, saying to him in Bambara, "The commandant wants you to come in and present the two new pupils."

As we pass, the orderly adds his own little jab. "Hurry up, Koniba Kondala! The Whites belong to that race known as 'Hurry up, let's go.'" Through clenched teeth Koniba Kondala replies, "Hurry up let's go leads straight to broken neck village."

He pushes us along in front of him, and all of us, including the interpreter, find ourselves in the office of the great district commandant of Bandiagara, Camille Maillet. I observe him closely: a long part divides the middle of his neatly combed and very flat black hair, his face is adorned with a full beard, marvelously accompanied by a mustache, whose two points are raised like scorpions' tails. He is wearing a jacket made of white cloth with a high collar, held together with five impressive gold buttons and trimmed with four pockets, two above and two below, also closed by two gold buttons. All told, including the trimming on his epaulets, I count eleven gold buttons. His trousers and his socks are white, but strangely, his very shiny shoes are black.

Old Koniba introduces us, repeating word for word everything Alfa Maki Tall had said, without omitting the request wherein he asked the commandant to reserve for his son the same sort reserved for me. The interpreter translates his declaration.

As he listens, the commandant softly strokes his beard and gazes thoughtfully at Madani. Troubled, Madani does not know where to place his gaze and constantly swivels his eyes in every direction.

"Are you happy to be going to school?" the commandant asks him through the intermediary of the interpreter.

"No. I would rather die than go to school," Madani replies. "I want to go back home to my mother. I don't like school and school doesn't like me either!"

"But your father and I wish you to go to school," explained the commandant. "There, you will learn to read, write, and speak French, that beautiful language that all the sons of chiefs must know, because it leads to the acquisition of power and wealth."

"My father and mother wish me to go to Koranic school and not to the White Man's school!" moans little Madani. And suddenly, he throws himself to the ground, sobbing, writhing, and tearing at his boubou, crying in a shrill voice, "Yaayaayaaye! I want my mother, I want my mother! Yaaye! I want to go back to Koranic school!"

"But you will be able to attend Koranic school every Thursday and every Sunday, and also early in the mornings," the commandant explains. To no avail. Madani continues to roll on the ground and cry.

No doubt somewhat taken aback, the commandant turns and looks at me with his big gray eyes. More curious than intimidated, I return his handsome gaze, observing his fine, straight nose, his eyebrows, his thin lips, his high forehead, and his big ears. Intrigued perhaps by my attitude, he asks, "Who are you?"

"I am myself."

He bursts into laughter.

"Very well, but what is your name and what are the names of your father and mother?"

"My name is Amadou Hampâté. My fathers, for I have two, are named Hampâté Bâ and Tidjani Amadou Ali Thiam. As for my mother, her name is Kadidja Pâté Diallo."

"And how is it that you alone have two fathers while other children only have one?"

"I don't know, but that's the way it is, and I am happy that it is so because I lost one, Hampâté, and I have one left, Tidjani. If I had only had Hampâté, I would be without a father now. And then who would I call papa?"

While listening to the interpreter's translation, the commandant laughs so hard that he leans back in his chair and beats the armrests with his hands. Well, when the commandant laughs, the interpreter also laughs, and then the orderly and all the others follow suit. The end result is that everyone in the office is laughing except for me, for I am completely serious, and Madani, who hasn't stopped crying.

Recovering his composure, the commandant again asks, "Do you want to go to school in order to learn to read, write, and speak French, which is a language spoken by chiefs, a language that allows the acquisition of wealth and power?"

Emphatically, I respond, "Yes, papa commandant! I beg you by God and his Prophet Mohammad, do not send me home, keep me here and send me to your school as quickly as possible!"

Clearly, the commandant is taken aback by such an unexpected response coming from a little Negro, especially in this deeply Islamic region. How could he not be surprised at seeing one boy rolling about on the ground, begging not to be sent to school, while the other one is pleading to be sent there?

"Why, my boy, do you wish so badly to go to school, unlike all the other children of Bandiagara?"

"Interpreter, tell the commandant that I have already missed the opportunity to become a chief twice. Once, by being the son of Hampâté, and once by being the son of Tidjani. Well, Tidjani told me that opportunity always appears three times before it turns away completely. The commandant is giving me my third opportunity to become a chief, and I do not intend to miss it as I did the first two. That is why I want to go to school."

"And why do you wish to become a chief? What will you do after that?" inquired the commandant.

"First of all, I wish to learn the language of the commandant in order to speak to him directly without going through an interpreter. Second, I would like to become a chief so that I can break Koniba Kondala's face. He is a former captive of my ancestors who, because he is the commandant's envoy, presumes to cover my entire family in insults. In my father Hampâté's household, I have nine rimaïbé captives who could, if it weren't for their fear of the commandant, make Koniba Kondala swallow his tongue along with his uvula!

"Koniba Kondala thinks that he himself is the commandant. He wanted to send my brother and me both to school on the same day. The fama opposed the idea. He gives you his own son in place of my brother. What is more, Koniba Kondala is angry with my elder brother Beydari Hampâté, because he will no longer allow him to take his best cuts of meat without paying. That is why I wish to become a chief, so that I can escape Koniba Kondala's harassment and insults and to be able to speak directly to the commandant."

I turned toward the old dîmadjo and pointed my finger at him. "Koniba Kondala! If ever I become a chief, the first thing that I will do is whip you, you mean old man! You will pay for insulting my father and mother all the way from Alfa Maki's house to the bridge, just because you think I am responsible for sending Madani to the school of the toubabs, these toubabs that you call 'mustachioed drinkers of wine laced with sow's milk,' and who, according to you are going to turn us into miscreants destined for hell!"

Having unburdened my heart, I fall silent. As the interpreter gradually translates this long speech, I see the commandant's anger mount. When the interpreter is finished, the commandant is furious, and like a demon, he pounds his hand on the table and begins to yell so loudly that I am seized with fear. Thinking that I have made a terrible blunder, I begin to look for a place to hide, but I quickly recover my wits upon seeing the interpreter, his face twisted with anger, turn not toward me but toward Koniba Kondala.

"Now you are in trouble, you old fool!" he cries. "The commandant will make you pay a high price for your attitude toward this twelve-year-old boy, who unfortunately for you is not at all shy and has the gift of gab. And you will pay for proffering insults against France."

Suddenly, armed with his whip, the orderly storms into the office uninvited, visibly ready to strike. No doubt alarmed by the loud voices, he must have sensed that slaps and blows were in the air. He is ready to strike, for this is apparently a part of his duties. It is then that I understand that this man that I had first thought to be a person of high rank is nothing but a subaltern trained to run, open doors, stand at attention at the drop of a hat, and use his whip on anyone the commandant should so chose. In sum, he is the unconditional executor of the unpleasant work commanded by the Great White Chief.

The orderly's sudden entrance has a somewhat calming effect on the commandant.

"Why," he asks Koniba Kondala, "did you insult and mistreat this defenseless boy, when all you had to do was bring him to me? You old hypocrite! You swear us love and fidelity in our presence and you call us drinkers of wine laced with sow's milk behind our backs. Just so you know what you are really talking about, I have a mind to make you drink a glass of it."

At these last words, Koniba Kondala places both hands on his head, signaling misfortune, and then bows deeply, his two arms behind his back, in the traditional posture of supplication, and begs for forgiveness.

"Oh, interpreter," he moans, "tell the commandant that I am the unhappiest of men. I have made a grave mistake. I beg the commandant's pardon a thousand times over. Let him put me in prison, let him have me whipped, but I beg of him, please do not serve me the liquid that he wants to make me drink! I swear by God, by His Prophet, by the angels who bear the divine throne, by the two interrogating angels of the deceased in their tombs, by the two guardian angels of the seven heavens and the seven hells, that I will never again mistreat anybody, and still less will I say anything bad about toubab mamas and papas!"

Disfigured by mimicking and grimacing, his wrinkled face eloquently states the extent of his dismay at the idea of being forced, perhaps under threat of a whipping from the orderly or a poke of the sentinel's bayonet, to drink a glass of wine laced with sow's milk! Fortunately for him, the commandant is not a vindictive "Negro-eater." Moved perhaps by the poor man's sheer fright, he settles with a threat, pointing the end of his pencil at the old man: "If anyone ever files another complaint against you, or even tells me that you have done something wrong, you will have to deal with me. I will make you drink not one but three glasses of that drink and then I'll send you to rot in Bougouni prison!"

The mention of Bougouni revives two kinds of memories in me: some of them are happy, because they evoke the early years of my childhood, and the others are painful, because they make me remember my father's imprisonment. In my mind's eye, I once again see Tidjani arrive in the courtyard, his feet shackled in thick chains, exhausted from breaking rocks on the roads all day long, chopping down trees with an ax, or splitting wood. While I truly wish to be able to give Koniba Kondala a whipping one day, I do not at all wish for him to go to Bougouni, no more, in fact, than I want him to drink alcohol laced with sow's milk!

The commandant turns to me. "As for you my little friend, every Sunday afternoon, you will report to my tennis court to collect the balls that get lost or roll into the underbrush."

And opening a drawer in his desk, he takes out a bright and shiny silver five-franc piece and hands it to me. "Here," he says, "go and use this to buy a smock, a pair of pants, a red fez, and a pair of baboosh slippers so that you look smart. I want you to come to the tennis court clean and well dressed."

Koniba Kondala opens his eyes wide. At the time a five-franc piece represented a fortune, the price of a comely heifer! Curious, I look at the coin up close. On it, there is a man, a woman, and a child, all of them naked. How strange! Is it a symbol? A fetish? I had once heard the Fulas say, "He who becomes attached to silver coins strips his own soul naked."

Meanwhile, the commandant has scribbled a few signs on a piece of paper. He hands it to Koniba Kondala and says dryly, "Now take these two boys to the schoolteacher."

Upon exiting the residence, we take the road that leads to the school. Like the neighborhood of Sinci, it is also located on the left bank of the Yaamé, but farther down. As we are making out way, no doubt enticed by my beautiful silver five-franc piece, Koniba says to me in a soft voice accented with a tone of amicable reproach, "I was just joking with you, as I have the right to do as a dîmadjo and a grandfather, but you misunderstood my jokes and now out of spite you have 'obstructed' me in the eyes of the commandant.[1] You are a nasty little master, and a bad Fula boy! To prove that I am still your captive and ready to serve you and your family, give me your silver coin. I will take it and give it straight away to Beydari Hampâté. I wouldn't want you to drop it or have it stolen from you by an older schoolboy."

"Hey, Koniba Kondala," I said bursting into laughter. "If you ask me again for my coin, I will immediately return to the commandant and tell him that you are trying to take my gift away from me."

"Hum!" he muttered. "The baby rodent inherits his parents' long and pointed sharp teeth. Grant me peace!"

And from that moment onward, he was silent.

And that is how I was enlisted into school and how I received my first piece of silver.

Primary School

There was no special building for the school. Classes were held under a shed that had belonged to the royal stables and that had been turned into a shelter for the school. When we arrived, the instructor was in the middle of teaching the twenty-three children in his class. He was a "native primary school monitor"; that is, he had graduated from the Bamako Professional School (only those holding diplomas from the Gorée normal school had the right to the title of "teacher"). His name was Mr. Moulaye Haïdara. He was a mixed-blooded Moor from Sokolo in Mali and belonged to a family of Sharifs.[2] When he saw us approaching, he interrupted the lesson and turned toward us. Koniba Kondala handed him the commandant's note, introduced us, and then promptly took his leave, as though he were afraid that my tongue, which wagged all too easily, might again, even in this place, cause him some further unpleasantness.

Madani and I stood before the teacher. He opened a large registry, taller than it was wide, and carefully wrote our names in it. Then, in our own language, he asked us to state the profession of our parents. Madani replied that his father was a chief. Not knowing what to say, I gave as my father's profession the one practiced by Beydari Hampâté, that is, butcher. Mr. Moulaye Haïdara turned toward the students and said loudly and in French while pointing at me, "Amadou is a butcher. Répétez!"

The students all repeated in unison, "Amadou is a butcher."

"Encore!" said the teacher.

The students all repeated this together and then each one in turn repeated, "Amadou is a butcher."

This was the first sentence that I learned and retained in the French language.

The teacher rose and led us to the back of the class. He assigned me to the second to the last seat and placed Madani in the very last one and requested that we cross our arms on the tabletop, like good children. I was lost in thought. Why had I been placed in front of Madani, son of the chief of this land, and why was one of his captives, Daye Konaré, placed in the first seat? Perhaps there was some mistake? After a few moments, I rose, gave my seat to Madani, and sat down in his.

"Who told you that you could exchange seats?" cried the teacher in Bambara.

I rose and responded in the same language, which, incidentally, was spoken by most of the children.

"Madani is my prince, sir. I cannot be placed in front of him."

"I'm the one who chooses the seats here, not you. Do you understand? Return to the seats that I have assigned you. Here there are neither princes nor subjects. You must leave all that at home, on the other side of the river."

These words made a deep impression on me. How could that be possible? In our associations, we were all comrades and equals, but our respective roles nevertheless more or less reflected the classes to which we belonged, and nobody was ashamed of that. Here, according to the teacher, this no longer existed. I tried to imagine a world where there would no longer be kings or subjects, and therefore no commanding rank, no castes of artisans or griots, in sum, no differences of any sort. I could not conceive of it.

Mr. Moulaye Haïdara returned to the lesson. On that particular day, the students were to learn and recite by heart a text that the teacher would enunciate very clearly in French, word for word, and then sentence by sentence. The students repeated each word after him, first in unison, and then each one in turn. This lasted for about half an hour. Then the teacher asked each one to repeat alone the text after him, with the class repeating it together as though the student had become the teacher. I listened carefully and repeated after all the others, making the effort to remember the words even if I did not understand their meaning. My auditory memory, like that of every good Koranic school student, had been trained for this kind of gymnastic, since we were used to learning by heart entire pages of the sacred book without understanding its meaning. This simple memory exercise did not represent the slightest difficulty for me, all the more so given that, because of my desire to learn the language of "my friend the commandant" as quickly as possible, I gave it my all.

The lesson lasted a good part of the morning. This had given me plenty of time to retain it. When the twenty-third student had finished reciting it with a few blunders here and there, and after the entire class had repeated in unison after him, I stood up to take my turn. The teacher began to laugh. "No, not you. Sit down."

"Sir, what all my comrades have just said, I can recite it too."

He stopped laughing.

"You remember all of it?"

"Yes."

"Well, then, let me hear you recite it."

All their faces turned toward me, their ears pricked and their eyes trained on me. Confident in the power of my memory, I began to recite the text of the lesson in a droning singsong, just as I had heard the students do, and that I still remember to this day.

"My notebook resembles my book . . . but it is not as thick. . . . It is thinner. . . . It is rectangular. . . . Its cover is not made of cardboard. . . . It is a thick sheet of colored paper. . . . My notebook has thirty-two pages. . . ."[3]

"Kaa koo Jeydani!" exclaimed the teacher (meaning, "Miracle of Abd el-Kader el Djilani!," a great Muslim saint of the first centuries of Islam, known for his miracles).

Extremely pleased, he came and took me by the hand and had me stand on his platform. He spoke at length to the students while pointing at me, but I never knew what he had told them. That evening, as we were leaving class, he gave me a handsome picture book, a red fez adorned with a blue pompom, and a little French flag.

The very next day, he took me to the see the district treasurer, Mr. Delestré, a former warrant officer in the colonial army, who, upon retirement, had entered the civil service as a clerk in the Office of Native Affairs. Among other duties, he was charged with placing on a list the names of good but needy students who could be nominated to receive a monthly stipend of three francs that would be paid to their family. Since I was considered to be a fatherless orphan, I was easily accepted. The treasurer placed my name on his list.

While these events were taking place, my mother was in Bandiagara. Every so often she would come to see my brother and me, as well as her own family, and would also check to make sure that her herd was being managed correctly. Since she wasn't a woman to embark on an unproductive trip, she also took the opportunity to bring Bambara products from Kati to sell in Bandiagara, and then she would take specialty items from Massina back to Kati, where they were much in demand.

She was sitting peacefully in the courtyard of the family home when suddenly she saw Beydari arrive in a sweat, propelling his two hundred-twenty-pound body forward as quickly as he possibly could while also remaining within the limits of accepted social norms, since it was unseemly, if not downright ridiculous, for an adult to run. He had come to inform her of the "abduction" to which Hammadoun and I had fallen victim by the hand of Koniba Kondala, who had seized both of us at the same time for the White Man's school. Sometime later, my brother Hammadoun also arrived on the scene. He explained to my mother that he had been sent home, thanks to the intervention of Chief Alfa Maki Tall, but that I had stayed behind. He didn't know anything more than that.

When she needed information, my mother was never at a loss. It wasn't long before she was abreast of everything that had happened: Alfa Maki Tall's generous attitude, my visit with the commandant, and my arrival at the school with little Madani.

For her the solution was simple. As was customary at the time in well-to-do families, she would pay any price to "buy me back" from the school. These types of transactions took place between the parents, on one hand, and the interpreter and headmaster, on the other, where these two would split the profits from the price of the "repurchase." There were several ways in which one could be definitively sent home from school: mental or physical illness, lack of discipline, and a few others that I no longer remember. The interpreter would present the reason for the dismissal to the commandant, and he generally approved it without difficulty since he never doubted the declarations of the school headmaster, and he certainly never doubted his interpreter. Since they were good White-Blacks, that is, half-European Negroes, they were automatically above any suspicion!

My mother chose "indiscipline" as the putative reason for my dismissal, as she found the others degrading. My reputation as the chief of an association of seventy rapscallions and the raids that I regularly undertook with my comrades amply justified this choice. Then, all that my mother had to do was to sell a sufficient number of livestock before going to propose my "repurchase" to the interpreter and the headmaster. But first, she went to see my master, Tierno Bokar, who was something of a spiritual adviser to the entire family.

She told him what had happened, vehemently expressing her indignation. "Amadou will never attend the White Man's school where he will be turned into an infidel! I will use every means at my disposal to stop it! I will buy him back, even if I have to sell half of all my livestock!"

Tierno soothed her. "Why should going to school turn Amadou into an infidel? The Prophet himself said, 'Knowledge of something, whatever it may be, is preferable to not knowing it.' And also, 'Seek knowledge from the cradle to the grave, even if it means going to China!' Sister Kadidja, do not place yourself between Amadou and his God. He who created him is the best informed concerning his destiny, therefore leave Amadou in His hands. May He place him where He wishes and do with him as He intends. If He has decided that Amadou will not study at the French school, then whatever happens, Amadou will return. If He has decided that the school is his path, Amadou will follow it. I ask you, Sister, not to buy Amadou back and not to stop him from going to the White Man's school. Keep your bulls for another occasion."

My mother had no choice but to follow this advice, for everyone in the family trusted Tierno's judgment. That is how, on that day, by the triple effect of Koniba Kondala's rancor, my master's wisdom, and, no doubt, divine will, the straight line of my destiny was diffracted. I was diverted from a set path that should have led to a career as a teacher and marabout (while also practicing the art of tailoring and embroidering as did my father Tidjani and Tierno Bokar himself), and sent off down a new path leading to destinations unknown.

From that day forth, I would set out early every morning on the road that led to the school, which was about two kilometers from my house. Over my shoulder I carried a cloth bag containing my new treasures: notebooks, books, a slate, a handsome pinewood pen-holder from France with its metal Sergent-Major brand nib, a set of pencils, a piece of chalk, two erasers, one for ink and one for pencil, a blotter, a top wound with a string, a small knife, and a sack prepared by Niélé containing some snacks of peanuts, sweet potatoes, Bambara peas, and other goodies.

I would arrive at school at around six forty-five in the morning. At five minutes to seven, when the teacher gave the signal, one of the students, Mintikono Koulibaly (whose first name means "he for whom one does not wait") would rush without waiting toward a long metal blade hung from a rail that served as a bell.

Seizing a metal rod from the ground beneath the blade, Mintikono, whom the other schoolchildren had nicknamed "little hippo" or "little hippopotamus" due to his corpulence, struck the blade with three hearty blows, as though issuing a punishment for some misdeed known only to him. He had single-handedly taken over the duty of bell-ringer and roundly castigated anyone who dared to ring or even touch his beloved bell. The other children dubbed the bell "Mintikono's lover." Even the teacher was powerless to do anything about it.

At the first tolling of the bell, the children who had been running, shouting, laughing, and playing in the courtyard like a troop of young monkeys loosed in a peanut field stopped moving and turned to face the teacher. "Fall in!" he would cry. Everyone came running and lined up in two perfect rows on either side of the large door. "Extend arms!" ordered the teacher. Everyone extended his right arm horizontally and placed it on the shoulder of the schoolmate in front of him. When the teacher cried, "Attention!" we smartly returned our right arm to our right side, palm facing forward. Then, one behind the other in a straight line, we marched into the classroom, sat down in silence, and crossed our arms on our tabletops.

Mr. Moulaye Haïdara ascended to his platform and sat down behind his desk. He opened his large registry and began to call the roll as he checked off our names. Once this little daily ceremony was over, he began the lesson. The class was divided into two sections: the first section was composed of the most advanced students, while the second section included those who were just learning to read and write. Some worked on their homework while the teacher helped the others.

Long in the habit of transcribing my Koranic school lessons onto a wooden tablet, within a month I had learned the entire alphabet and I could write it correctly. By the end of the second month, I knew my syllabary perfectly. My method of study was particularly effective. I irritated everyone in the household by reciting at the top of my lungs word pairs that shared the same sound, such as: *au loin, du foin, un coin, des liens, les miens, un chien, un point, des soins* . . . or, *qui, quoi, c'est toi, ma foi,* raising my voice and dragging out the sound of the article or the first word, as the schoolchildren did in class. So that everyone including the neighbors could take full advantage of my new knowledge, I would even go and perch on the roof where I would shout out these newfangled litanies. Even the patient Beydari himself could take only so much of this!

I am unable to describe the process by which the new students managed to learn French so quickly, since the teacher never translated any of his lessons into the local languages. Unless there was some specific reason for doing so, we were strictly forbidden to speak our mother tongues at school, and he who was caught in the act was burdened with a defamatory sign called a "symbol."

The principal teaching method was thus "language in action." Every child had to say aloud the words (first taught by the teacher) that described his gestures and actions at that moment. Although rudimentary at first, over time the sentences became more rich and more complex. For example, the teacher would tell a student to go to the blackboard. As he stood up, the child would chant in a singsong and nasal drone, "The teacher has told me to go to the blackboard.... I stand up.... I cross my arms on my chest.... I leave my bench.... I walk to the blackboard.... I approach the platform where the teacher's desk is located.... I step onto the platform.... I take the wet rag into my left hand and a piece of chalk into my right hand.... I wipe the blackboard.... I listen to the teacher.... He dictates a sentence.... I try to write it with no errors.... The teacher corrects my dictation.... He is happy.... He pats my head.... I am very happy.... The teacher tells me to return to my seat.... I proudly return to my seat,..." and so on.

Thanks to this method, it was not long before I could express myself in French. This is not surprising when one recalls that most African children, living in environments where several ethnicities generally coexist (in Bandiagara there were Fulas, Bambaras, Dogons, Haousas ...), were already, willy-nilly, linguistic polyglots accustomed to absorbing new languages as easily as a sponge soaks up liquid. Without any particular method, they had only to spend time with a different ethnic group in order to learn their language, and this is still the case today. A good number of adults, considered to be "illiterate" by Western standards, spoke four or five languages, and in any case, they rarely spoke fewer than two or three. Tierno Bokar himself spoke seven. In addition to these, there was sometimes Arabic and then French, although this last language was often spoken, it is true, in the prickly manner of the tirailleur infantrymen, known locally as forofifon naspa.

But as always, there were exceptions. Two of our comrades, one Bambara and the other Dogon, who, unlike most Fula and Toucouleur children had not undergone the intensive mnemonic training used in the Koranic schools, and who in addition were rather slow-witted, had struggled terribly to assimilate the teacher's lessons. One day, following an explicated reading, the teacher asked each student to find a verb and to conjugate it in the present indicative tense. Everyone did so, for better or for worse. When it was our Bambara comrade Moussa P.'s turn, he quickly stood.

"Have you found a verb to conjugate?" the teacher asked him.

"Yes, sir."

"And which verb have you found?"

"The verb, the verb, cabinate!"

Mr. Moulaye Haïdara's jaw dropped and his eyes opened wider.

"Really now," he said. "Well then, go ahead and conjugate that verb in the first person singular, in the present indicative, and in the future tense."

Extremely proud of himself, Moussa begins to conjugate: "I cabinate, you cabinate, he cabinates, we cabinate, you cabinate, they cabinate!"

The teacher who, to say the least, was not a patient sort and whose nerves were easily inflamed, began to chew on his lower lip, which was an obvious sign of anger, and began fingering the switch that he held in his right hand. Moussa was oblivious. Quite happy with himself, he began conjugating in the future tense: "I will cabinate, you will cabinate, . . ."

"You certainly will cabinate!" said the teacher, as he pounced on him.

And he began to whip him so violently with his switch that in the heat of the moment poor Moussa went in his pants and began to moan, "Yaa-yaa-yaaye . . . Sir! I cabinated! Wallaye (By God), I cabinated!"

On another day, our comrade, a Dogon named Sagou K., was given the task of reciting, along with every other student, a sentence pronounced by the teacher. This sentence was, "Le corps humain se compose de trois parties: la tête, le tronc, et les membres." (The human body is made of three parts: the head, the trunk, and the limbs.) When it was his turn, Sagou, who had great difficulty retaining French words, improvised and chanted in an approximate phonetic French, "Le cor himin sin kin foossi (is composed of) trois frati (parts): la tête, soreeye (ears), né . . . *foufé*!" Unable to recall the word "mouth," he had invented a sort of onomatopoeia using the verb "souffler" (to breathe, to blow), which for him evoked the mouth. Mr. Moulaye Haïdra made him do it over again several times, but the unfortunate fellow was never able to reach the end of the sentence without pronouncing the eternal foufé. The teacher was beside himself. It goes without saying that Sagou was also given a firm correction.

Luckily there were also some more lighthearted moments. One morning after the little roll-call ceremony, the teacher wrote that day's date and immediately followed it with a French adage that he slowly enunciated in a loud voice: "Ni le grenier, ni la mansarde ne se remplissent à babiller." (Neither the attic nor the granary are filled when there is useless chatter.) As soon as he uttered the words "à babiller," all the Bambara speaking students—that is, most of the class—burst into hoots of laughter.

"Hee! Hee! Monsieur, Monsieur!"

Surprised and angry, the teacher turned toward us. "What are you laughing at, you bunch of imbeciles?"

Daye Konaré, who was the teacher's pet for two reasons (he was first in the class and he was also the younger brother of the houseboy who was the "maître d'hôtel" in the household of the colony's governor) was the first to recover his composure.

"Excuse us, sir," he said, "but in Bambara the last two words that you just said are a big insult that we don't deserve."

Surprised, Mr. Moulaye Haïdara turned around and closely reread the words. Since he had been so concentrated on their meaning in French, he hadn't noticed their possible meaning in Bambara. All of a sudden, he too was overcome with uncontrollable laughter. The entire class was giddy. For if in French "babiller" means "to chatter endlessly about nothing," in Bambara the expression means, at least phonetically, "your mother's sex organs" (to put it politely). To hear such an obscenity coming from the teacher's mouth, especially when he had done it so innocently, was extremely comical. That was all it took to make everyone burst into laughter. Mr. Moulaye Haïdara laughed until tears flowed. When he had finally regained control of himself and reimposed silence in the classroom, he explained at length the grammatical aspects of the sentence along with its moral. The sentence had to be learned by heart and recited at the end of that afternoon.

At noon everyone went home for lunch except for those who were being punished and who faced in-school detention. The teacher accompanied us in our rows all the way to the main road and at a sufficient distance from the residences of the Whites. There, he would cry, "Halt!" and then, "At ease!" which immediately triggered a joyful stampede.

Classes began again at two o'clock in the afternoon. In the evening, at five o'clock, the vigorous tolling of Mintikono's bell released us from our suffering. We would line up in two rows. On one side were those who were being punished and who had to spend that night at the teacher's residence, where a special room awaited them (their parents, who had been informed of this, would bring them something to eat), and on the other side were those who were allowed to go home and have fun with their association comrades or spend a moonlit evening with their valentines.

As was the case in all the local native primary schools, most of the instruction was concentrated on teaching us how to read, write, and especially speak French correctly. Instruction in elementary mathematics was limited to four basic operations: addition, subtraction, multiplication, and division. After a year or two, when the students had earned a sufficient number of points, they were sent to a regional school where they prepared to take the *certificat d'études primaires indigène* (native primary studies certificate) exams, which were necessary for entrance into the Bamako Professional School.

I personally would not be sent to the Djenné regional school until the start of classes in 1913. As for the students who did not go beyond primary school level, they either returned to their families or, thanks to their even rudimentary knowledge of French, were employed by the Whites as domestics. They could become cooks, houseboys, or pankas, so named for the mobile screen suspended from the ceiling that was moved by pulling on a rope and which led to the circulation of a bit of fresh air.

My First Encounter with Wangrin

It was in the beginning of 1912 that I made the acquaintance of an unusual personage who was later to play a certain role in my existence, although in an indirect way, since in 1974, the publication of his life story would earn me a literary prize. I am speaking of he who, at his own request, I designated by one of his pseudonyms, "Wangrin." Wangrin was a man who, by way of his wits and gift for ruse alone, succeeded in reaching the summit of social and financial success. In those days, this was extremely rare for a native. He ended up accumulating a fortune, with capital comparable to the largest French enterprises of the time, and he did this by shamelessly tricking and cheating the rich and powerful men of the day, Africans and Europeans alike. This included the fearsome colonial administrators known as the "Gods of the Bush," along with the all-powerful members of the chamber of commerce itself. He managed to pirouette out of the worst imbroglios that he himself had created for fun, and even sometimes had the audacity to warn some of his future victims of the "dirty trick" that he was planning to play on them. Then he would redistribute a large portion of what he had made by duping the rich to all sorts of poor, infirm, and disadvantaged people.

And yet, it is not this first part of his life that is worthy of attention, but the second part, where, by way of a betrayal, he lost glory and fortune in a single day and fell into the depths of poverty and degradation. It was then that he demonstrated his greatness. Where other people would have gone insane or become filled with bitterness, he acceded to wisdom. Without rancor toward anyone, without sorrow over his lost fortune, he continued to give the little money that he earned here and there to the poor. He knew how to laugh at life, at himself, and at his own story. Having become a kind of philosopher-tramp, he held court in the city's small cafés, and people came from far and wide to hear his colorful stories full of humor and wit and his savory pronouncements concerning human nature. I was to meet him again in Upper Volta just after his ruin in 1927.[4] I was on assignment there in my capacity as a young colonial official. That was where, night after night, to the gentle accompaniment of the guitar played by his faithful griot Djeli Maadi, who had followed him into misfortune, he recounted all the incredible twists and turns of his life. It was he himself who would ask me to write down his story one day and to make it known, so that, as he put it, "it would be useful to people as both entertainment and instruction." The condition was that he be designated by one of his pseudonyms in order not to give his family, either present or future, "any ideas of superiority or inferiority."[5]

When Wangrin arrived in Bandiagara around 1911 or 1912 to exercise his profession as a teaching monitor, he was still quite young. I admit that I do not know where he taught. Perhaps there were other classes in addition to those of Mr. Moulaye Haïdara? In any case, it would not be long before he would leave this modest position in order to rise to the more honorable and lucrative one of interpreter for the district commandant. Following a memorable combat, he would later take the position away from the old interpreter and former tirailleur that I had seen at the commandant's residence, whose fingers had been covered with rings, and who could only speak forofifon naspa.

When I met him for the first time, the commandant had just temporarily assigned Wangrin to Mr. François-Victor Equilbecq, a senior civil servant from the Office of Native Affairs who was passing through Bandiagara, and who was touring the entire country in order to collect the greatest possible number of tales from the French Sudan. When Mr. Equilbecq arrived in Bandiagara in June 1912, the district commandant summoned Chief Alfa Maki Tall and asked him to send the newcomer all the men, women, and children who knew any tales. I was among the children who were chosen.

For every tale that was retained, the informant was paid ten, fifteen, or twenty centimes according to its length or importance. At first, Wangrin translated them for Mr. Equilbecq, who took notes. But soon Mr. Equilbecq assigned Wangrin the job of directly collecting most of the texts. Wangrin wrote a first translation in French and then communicated it to Mr. Equilbecq, who would eventually add his own modifications or corrections. He was to publish a good number of these collected tales in 1913, with E. Leroux, in the *Collection de contes et chants populaires*.[6] These were republished in 1972 by Maisonneuve et Larose editions with the title *Contes populaires d'Afrique occidentale*. It is not without interest to note that Wangrin was one of the main authors. His name is cited at the end of most of the tales, preceded by the note "translated by" or "interpreted by." My name is also mentioned in a few places, under the bizarre appellation of "Amadou Bâ, *rîmadio* student of Bandiagara school." It is bizarre because the word rîmadio doesn't exist. At best it can be said that it strangely mixes the two words dîmadjo and rimaïbé, the respective singular and plural forms of "house captive."

When the other child storytellers and I were introduced to Wangrin, someone told him that I was the nephew of his great friend Hammadoun Pâté (my mother's younger brother), who was the chief of the powerful adult association that he had joined upon his arrival in Bandiagara. He immediately considered me as his own nephew, according to the African tradition where the friend of one's father is a father, the friend of one's uncle is an uncle, and so on. From that point on, whether or not I had any tales to give him, I went to greet him almost every evening after school, and I frequently spent my evenings at his home.

Later, around the years 1915 and 1916, following the famous "cattle affair," where thanks to his acumen and against all odds, he had succeeded in triumphing in a trial that pitted him against a "God of the Bush," otherwise known as a colonial administrator, Wangrin would leave Bandiagara in order to go to Upper Volta to continue his dazzling ascent. However, we would never be entirely without news of him since his wife, a Dogon from Bandiagara whose family was our close neighbor, would write to her parents from time to time, keeping us informed.

The Death of My Big Brother

When the beginning of the summer of 1913 arrived, my brother Hammadoun could not resist the urge to go and see our mother, who had not come to Bandiagara for some time. He asked Beydari to authorize a trip to Kati, where she was living with Tidjani. Beydari was not much in favor of this idea, given the length and the hardships involved—it was a journey of about seven hundred fifty kilometers—especially for a fifteen-year-old young man who had never yet been away from the city of his birth.[7] But Hammadoun was so insistent, and the need to see our mother was so strong, that in the end, Beydari allowed himself to be swayed and gave his permission. However, it was out of the question to allow my brother to undertake such a trip on his own. As it happened, one of our neighbors, a griot named Madani Oumar S., had decided to go to Segou by way of the land route. Beydari gave him a certain sum of money and placed my brother in his care, convinced that he would be in good hands for his first long journey. After Segou, Hammadoun would be able to reach Bamako by taking a pirogue on the Niger River. The final twelve kilometers that separated Kati from Bamako would be an easy distance.

Since my return to Bandiagara, this was to be the first time that my brother and I would be separated. We were as close as "two sons of the same blanket." I happily completed all the errands that a little brother normally does for his big brother, and in return he gave me his protection and affection. He was my role model and I admired him. I was going to miss him very much.

But life goes on. I was quickly occupied by the thousand and one activities that filled my days: the French school, my lessons with Tierno Bokar, my evenings with Koullel and the elders, the meetings with my comrades and our charming valentines.

Summer vacation came quickly. I was on my own again and had returned to my activities as chief of the powerful youth waaldé of the neighborhoods of South Bandiagara. Daouda Maïga and I formed a duo even more inseparable than before. I did not know that I was living out my last happy summer vacation in Bandiagara.

One evening, I believe it was in the month of August, as Daouda and I were returning home after one of our bush expeditions, we found the entire family in tears. The women were wailing, punctuating their sorrowful cries with the long *Yooo . . . mi héli!* lament that announced misfortune. Beydari had hung his head and had covered his eyes with his hand. Niélé, who was slumped over, seemed completely worn out from crying. As soon as she saw me she uttered a loud shriek and ran toward me. Encircling me tightly in her arms, she informed me, between sobs, that my brother Hammadoun was dead. My mother had sent a telegram announcing that he had died shortly after his arrival in Kati. "Do not cry! Do not cry!" Niélé was saying, her own face bathed in tears. "One must not cry for the dead!" She did her best to console me.

I cannot describe my shock. It was as if my mind was unable to register the reality of the information. I remained motionless, without tears, without words. For a long time afterward, all I could say was, "Does this mean that I will never see him again? What about his association?"

Daouda was as shocked as I was. It wasn't until a few days later, when the two of us were alone, that the tears finally came. We began to sob. "Our defender is gone. So and so has a big brother, and so and so has his big brother, and we don't have ours anymore and we will never see him again."

What had happened? What could have led to the death of this handsome boy who was in the bloom of his youth? Before he died, he told our mother what had happened.

The griot Madani Oumar S., to whom Beydari had entrusted Hammadoun, had found nothing better than to use him as a foot porter while he himself traveled comfortably on horseback. He had placed all his baggage in two enormous sacks that he made my brother carry as though he were his groom. Despite the distances between stops and the risks of dangerous encounters in those times, when wild animals were everywhere, he would go ahead on his horse, leaving my brother behind to manage on his own. It was the beginning of the rainy season. Bent under the weight of the baggage, his feet sinking deep in the mud, his clothes soaking his back, Hammadoun walked alone to the next village on the road. And there, before he could eat or rest, he would have to try to find out where Madani Oumar S. had gone to spend the night. The next day, Madani would leave on horseback without looking after him. Over time, the exhaustion and worry of walking alone in the rain got the better of my brother. He developed a bad case of bronchitis, which was certainly aggravated by malaria. When he finally arrived in Segou, he was shaking with fever and his legs could barely carry him.

In Segou, Madani entrusted my brother to one of his laptots, asking him to arrange his river trip to Koulikoro. Hammadoun made the trip in an uncovered pirogue. The rain, the chilly weather, and the lack of medical care did not at all help his state. In Koulikoro he took the train for the last fifty kilometers that separated him from Bamako. There he stayed with Abdallah, an old friend of Tidjani and Kadidja's. Alarmed at his weakened state, Abdallah immediately sent word to my mother in Kati. She arrived that very day to pick up her son, but when she saw his physical state, she decided to let him rest in Bamako for a few days, where she hoped to find him medical care.

One day when he seemed less tired, she decided to take him out and show him the city. Despite his illness, my brother was still strikingly handsome—as I have already said, he was one of the best-looking boys in Bandiagara district, and God knows there were a good number of handsome young Fulas in the region! When they arrived at the market, where Kadidja was known, a swarm of curious onlookers surrounded them. The griots exclaimed, "Hey, hey! Now here is a real Fula, of the most handsome kind! Wallaye! By God! It took time to give birth to this one! He was made with care." Quite embarrassed to be the object of all these eyes, Hammadoun, who could take it no longer, asked Kadidja for permission to return home. Since his condition had not improved after several days, she decided to take him to her home in Kati. They made the short trip by train.

As soon as they arrived in Kati, my brother took to his bed. And that's where, bit by bit, he told my mother his story. In his delirium, he relived the suffering he had endured on his trip, moaning, "Hey, Madani! You were supposed to look after me and you've left me all alone in the bush, with the wild animals! Oh it's so far! I'll never make it to the next village. What am I going to eat? Madani, where are you? How will I find you? I'm so tired! I'm so tired!"

My mother lavished him with every possible treatment, but it was too late. After a few weeks, he returned to his Creator. In addition to the joy of seeing our mother again, his one great pleasure had been to embrace our little sister

Aminata, who was born in Kati. He tied a thread around her little wrist and said, "I reserve my sister for marriage to my friend Maki Tall." Later, Maki Tall did not follow through with this idea. Otherwise, neither Aminata nor anyone else in the family would have wanted her to marry anyone except the one whom my big brother, Hammadoun, had designated on his deathbed.

At the news of his death, almost all Bandiagara went into mourning. In every family, people cried for my brother. Gifted at everything, extremely clever with his hands—his little sculptures and embroidery were true works of art—he was above all an amiable boy who was respectful of everyone, and he was completely devoid of any feeling of superiority. When his friends went swimming in the river, he would often remain on shore to watch over their clothes, depriving himself of the pleasure of a swim. African children are in the habit of sharing their possessions, but he gave away everything. And he never could stand to see a stronger boy attack a weaker one and would immediately come to his defense.

As I have already said, he was very affectionate with me. But that did not stop him from being very demanding about certain things. When I got thrown in hand-to-hand fighting, where I was not very strong, he got angry and reproached me for it. But as soon as I had been thrown, I would run to get a stick and the one who had thrown me could expect to receive a volley of blows for an entire week, to the point that it was said, "If Amkoullel throws you down, then you should be ashamed. But if you throw him, then you can expect an entire week of fighting. So it is better not to fight with him at all." My brother was very proud of me for that.

When one of my comrades attacked me, he didn't come to my defense. He wanted me to manage on my own. But he never permitted any attacks from anyone older than me. Indeed, while he was alive, nobody even tried it.

The School at Djenné: My Primary Studies Certificate

Toward the end of vacation, just when we were beginning to recover a little from Hammadoun's death, Mr. Moulaye Haïdara summoned me to his home. He informed me that I had earned the number of points required to enter the regional school in Djenné, where I could prepare for a Native Primary Studies Certificate.[8] If all went well, I could take the exam in two years. I was to report to school at the beginning of classes in September. He informed my family. Beydari was so affected by the news that he fell ill. He called for a family meeting in order to announce the bad news and to devise a plan. Djenné was at a distance of about two hundred kilometers from Bandiagara, which at the time represented at least three or four days on foot to Mopti, and then the rest of the journey would be by boat.[9] We had no relatives who could look after me in Djenné. It was therefore decided that Niélé would accompany me in order to take care of me and to look after my needs.

This decision did not suit me at all. I was going to leave to begin a new life. I was a big boy and I wanted to be free. But I knew that if Niélé were to come and live with me, I would be under her constant surveillance. From the height of my thirteen years, I thus firmly refused her company. "I must go to Djenné exactly like my six other comrades are going to do," I explained. "None of them will be accompanied by a relative. Why do I have to be accompanied as though I were just learning how to walk? I'm not afraid to go abroad." They begged me. Niélé cried, but I stood my ground. Finally, to their great dismay, Beydari, Niélé, and their companions acquiesced and agreed to allow me to leave alone. They knew that they would not see me again until vacation the following summer.

The six other comrades who were also chosen were Maki Tall, Hammadoun's friend, Tégué Ouologuem, Yagama Tembély, Moussa Koulibally, Mintikono Samaké, and Badji Ouologuem.

Three days before our departure from Bandiagara, the district commandant summoned us. He congratulated us on our work and at having merited such an enviable promotion, the first step on the road that was to lead us toward wealth and power. As a token of his appreciation, he gave us each two complete outfits, a blanket, and the very hefty sum of seven francs. Koniba Kondala was given the order to recruit a porter for each schoolboy since we had to make the seventy-kilometer trip to Mopti on foot before taking the boat down the Niger River to Djenné.

Three times over, out of pure spite, I refused the porter that Koniba Kondala had located for me. I found some more or less imaginary fault in each one, only to show Koniba Kondala that I was already more of a "chief" than he. I made him spend an entire day running around looking for the ideal porter. Finally, at wits' end, he went to see Beydari in order to ask him to make me see reason. "If I only had known," he lamented, "I would never have sent that little brat Amkoullel to school! Now I'm biting my finger to the second knuckle over it!"

Beydari was overjoyed. He replied, citing the adage, "In trying to fling the frog that disgusts you too far, it will end up landing in a good pond." In other words, in trying too hard to hurt someone, it can happen that one will create the conditions of that person's happiness. "Oh, Koniba Kondala," he added, "what's happening to you with Amkoullel is what happens to an ill-intentioned man who lies on his back and pisses into the air in an effort to defile the sky. Not only does his urine never hit its target, but it ends up raining back down on his own belly."

I had taken my first revenge on Koniba Kondala. Satisfied, I deigned to accept the fourth porter. Beydari was overjoyed to see that, having just placed my left toe in the stirrup of command, I was already able to antagonize a beast like Koniba Kondala, who was the terror of the town. From then on, he stopped agonizing over my upcoming departure. "I think that we can stop worrying," he said to Niélé. "Amadou will be in good hands with his own two hands."

I dedicated the rest of the time that I had left visiting the uncles, aunts, and faithful friends of my parents who lived in town, some of whom, even to this very day, have played such an important role in my life. They loved me, taught me, educated me, and guided me. All of them had been as fathers to me: Balewel Diko, the inseparable companion of my father Hampâté; my maternal uncle, Hammadoun Pâté; my "uncle" Wangrin; Koullel, for whom I was named; and especially Tierno Bokar, who had bounced me on his shoulders when I was little, and who now was patiently waiting for me to become a man. He blessed me and entrusted me to God, and that was enough to eliminate my fears. I left him, full of confidence, keeping in my heart the memory of his good smile and his high forehead, so shiny that I could almost see my reflection in it.

As for Beydari, he had decided to go to Kati sometime after that in order to present his condolences to my mother, who was in mourning for Hammadoun. He intended to make the trip on foot all the way to Segou, taking the exact same route that my brother had, in order to experience for himself all the pain and suffering that my brother had endured.

Very early one fine morning, following the final adieus and the last tears, copiously supplied with provisions for our trip and covered with all kinds of blessings, my six comrades and I set off down the road to Mopti, accompanied by our porters and some guards. This is my fourth journey down this road. The first time, I was only a month and a half old, and was enthroned like a little king on Niélé's head, nicely tucked into a large calabash. My mother was taking me to be introduced to my grandmother. The second time, Niélé was carrying me on her back in a more typical manner. We were returning to Taykiri, where my grandmother had just died. The third time was when we had all left for Bougouni. I was four or five, and traveled attached to Nassouni's or Batoma's back. I had watched the countryside pass with the rhythm of their footsteps. Today, I am thirteen years old. I no longer have a brother, my mother is far away, I am leaving all those who watched over my childhood behind, and

I do not know what awaits me. But I walk with a firm step down this road. I am leaving to go study so that I can become a chief.

Ten kilometers outside the city, a sudden swelling of the Yaamé's waters blocks us on its banks. The torrent has carried off the small wooden bridge that once spanned the river. Two days later, an equally sudden drop in the water level allows us to wade across the river. This was a rare occurrence in that season. That year the amount of rainfall had been deficient and the population had worried about the upcoming harvest. We walk for two more days until we finally reach Mopti. Every student was to stay with a relative or a family friend. I go to stay with Tiébéssé, my mother's childhood friend. We are given a two-day break, the time required to gather the eleven students from Mopti who will join our convoy to Djenné. I take advantage of the break to explore the city in the company of some friends.

Mopti presides over the birth of the great Niger River, for it is located at the confluence between the Bani, which flows in from Ivory Coast, and the Niger as it flows in from Guinea. These two bodies of water are known, respectively, as the Black River and the White River, due to the more or less dark color of their waters. From there, the river extends into a veritable network of branches and canals that harbor a multitude of lakes and ponds. This is the beginning of the curve known as the Niger Bend, and this is the name by which the entire region is known.

It is with good reason that Mopti is nicknamed "the Venice of the Sudan," for everything is linked to the river and the rise and fall of its water levels. The marvelous long pirogues that can be seen slicing silently through the water, some carrying tons of merchandise, are handcrafted by the Bozos, the oldest occupants of the area. A people of fishermen and hunters, they are the entire region's true traditional "Masters of the Waters."

In this zone of confluence between the "black waters" and the "white waters," one can encounter a number of ethnicities of different origin, from the lightest to the darkest skinned. After the Bozos, the next most ancient inhabitants are the Songhays and the Fulas. The Bambaras and the Dogons did not arrive here until later.

The western end of the Niger Bend region once constituted a veritable reservoir containing the wealth of those lands in terms of religious and cultural traditions, agricultural and livestock production, and hunting and fishing preserves. Human beings lived there comfortably, and traditional crafts were particularly well developed. Massina, where the Fulas settled for its rich pastureland, is located at the heart of this region, and Mopti is one of its crown jewels.

On the morning of our departure, the eleven students from Mopti joined us, swelling our numbers to eighteen. The district commandant in Mopti had placed two large pirogues at our disposal, and had it stocked with all the necessary provisions. The pirogues were waiting for us at the river's edge across from the Etablissements Simon. Each pirogue carried nine boys. The students from Mopti gathered on the port side, crying and waving to their parents who had been left behind on the bank.

On cue, the punters plunged their poles into the water and imparted a vigorous forward momentum to the pirogue. I pushed a couple of my comrades aside and poked my head out in order to glimpse the crowd gathered on the bank. I was suddenly overcome with a kind of vertigo. The people on the bank seemed to be separating from us, backing away but without walking, as though they were drifting on the surface of the water. It took me a few moments to realize that it was our pirogue that was moving away from them and not the contrary. I had remembered nothing of my distant voyage on the river with my mother. I was discovering it all for the first time.

When our pirogues had reached the middle of the current, just as we were heading toward the place where the waters of the Niger and the Bani meet, the chief laptot shouted, "Open your bundles and toss a little of your food into the water!" It was the traditional tribute to Maïrama, the goddess of the waters, paid upon leaving the "black water" (the Bani) and entering the wide and majestic waters of the "white river" (the Niger). Every one of us took our little offering in hand and, at the appropriate time, threw it as far as possible into the lapping waters.

Up to that point, our pirogue had been sliding effortlessly down the Bani. Suddenly, it hit the churn that rose where the Bani met the Niger, and we had to navigate at countercurrent until we reached Kouakouru. The pirogue lurched up and over the waves. The hull shuddered and rattled the passengers and their baggage. I thought for a moment that Maïrama, princess of the waters, had become angry with us for some unknown reason and was giving our vessel a giant kick. But as soon as the laptots had maneuvered around the bend in the river and steered us out to open water, everything was calm again. The rest of the journey unfolded without incident.

At Kouakourou, we had to leave the main branch of the Niger and enter the waters of a tributary that would take us all the way to Djenné. The calm waters of this branch flowed lazily through an immense plain. This vast depression, known by several names depending on the regions it crosses, extends all the way to Timbuktu. Despite the lack of rain during that season of flooding, the plain was still largely submerged. Far in the distance, we caught glimpses of villages sitting on the surface of the waters like clay islands of ochre and gray. Almost always overhung with bouquets of slender fan palms whose spiky, crimped tufts recalled the shaggy heads of madwomen, they held dominion over an ocean of green, for the wide waters of the plain were covered with an immense carpet of grasses and aquatic plants. The patches that had been spared from this exuberant vegetation shone here and there in the sun like great clearings of plated silver.

The chief laptot shouted, "As soon as we come around the next bend of this backwater, you'll be able to see the great towers of the Djenné mosque."

Everyone rushed to the front of the boat, crying, "We're going to see Djenné! We're going to see Djenné!"

Was it not said that this city, the most beautiful of the entire Niger Bend, was located just above *Al-Djennat*, the garden of Allah (paradise), for which it was named?

As we rounded the bend, we saw this reputed beauty confirmed in the spires of the three pyramid-shaped turrets as they rose above a mass of greenery that hid the city and the body of the mosque from view. The ends of palm tree trunks embedded in the structure to ensure the stability of the building bristled artfully from the facade, and its delicate ochre spires stood out against a clear sky that seemed to have been washed and dyed blue by the very hand of God. These were the pinnacles that crowned the three great turrets of Djenné's great mosque. In those days, it was the most beautiful mosque in all sub-Saharan Africa, from Khartoum in the east to Conakry in the west.

As we approached, the curtain of greenery seemed to part and open just for us, revealing the beauties of the city. Soon the majestic east facade of the mosque emerged. It had been made famous throughout the world through photographs and illustrations. Appearing next were the city's terraced houses, framed by verdant foliage and distinguished by their exceptionally beautiful decorative motifs.

Our pirogues came ashore to the east of the city, in the bustling little port of El Gazba. Never was a port so animated. Women were bathing by the river, others were washing clothes or dishes. Animals had been brought there to drink, with the result that the braying of donkeys fused with the whinnying of horses and the bleating of sheep. Bursts of laughter exploded from all directions. Everyone was engaged in loud conversation and they paid little mind to their crying children. Like giant dozing crocodiles taking the air, great pirogues lay high and dry on shore undergoing repairs, while others were still being built.

The laptots had us disembark in an area that was not far from the house of Chékou Hassey, the city's Songhay chief, who had been charged with housing the children from the Djenné region. As for us children from Bandiagara, the commandant had asked Amadou Kisso Cissé, chief of the Fula community, to house us, and his two representatives were waiting for us. The two men led us to the compound of the Fula chief, where our lodgings had been reserved. We were divided into groups of five or six students. Maki Tall, Yagama Tembély (a Dogon whose father was a friend of Beydari), Badji Ouologuem, Mintikono Samaké, Moussa Koulibaly, and I were assigned to occupy the same room and to share the same meals.

That very afternoon, the Fula chief Amadou Kisso Cissé personally took us to the district commandant's residence. The interpreter Mamadou Sall, known as "Papa Sall," a veteran of the conquest of the country, led us into the office of the commandant, who was a colonial administrator named Max Brizeux. He lived with his concubine Fanta Bougalo, a beautiful woman of the blacksmith caste originally from Bandiagara, who also belonged to the association led by my mother. When she heard the announcement of the arrival of the children from Bandiagara, she came down from her second-floor apartment in order to see whether she might know any of us. She recognized me. Immediately she recommended me to Amadou Kisso Cissé, giving him information about my family. This recommendation would later earn me a series of favors.

The commandant summoned Mr. Baba Keïta, the native teacher and director of the regional school. Having received his diploma from the William Ponty Normal School of Gorée, he was reputed to be a very well-educated man. He took possession of his eighteen new recruits, had us line up in rows, and led us to the regional school, one of the city's largest and most beautiful monuments after the grand mosque. The entire afternoon was spent establishing our records and separating us into the school's four classes.

Mr. Baba Keïta was assisted by two teaching monitors (only those who had earned diplomas from the normal school had the right to the title of Primary School Teacher). These were Tennga Tiemtoré, a Mossi whose teeth had been filed into sharp saw-tooth points, and the picturesque Allassane Sall, son of the old interpreter Papa Sall. Physically ponderous and intellectually somewhat slow-witted, his studies had not extended beyond native primary school. His appointment had had much more to do with his father's political influence than with his personal aptitudes. He had thus become the perennial monitor of the "abécédaires" beginners, so called for their elementary ABC primers, who did nothing but endlessly repeat the rudiments of the French language.

Unfortunately, his thick tongue took up so much room in his mouth that the sounds could only come out truncated or strangely deformed. He was particularly fond of having the students recite the phrase, "I eat couscous, you eat couscous, everyone eats couscous," but in his strange voice, he pronounced it "koss-koss," which the students lost no time in joyfully repeating, and which had earned him the name "Mr. Koss-Koss."

The school's disciplinarian was named Fabarka. A tall man with very dark skin and wearing a constant frown, he was extremely severe with the children and never hesitated to hit them with a lash strung with two vines that he always carried on his right shoulder. The Fula students had nicknamed him *Baa-dorrol* (Papa whip).

As for our director, Mr. Baba Keïta, he was the very model of the great "White-Black." Always dressed in European clothes, he had married a mixed "White father–Black mother" woman with light-colored skin and long, straight hair. They did not go out much, and lived closed inside their home in the toubab manner, consuming European dishes with metal utensils while seated at a high table. Mr. Baba Keïta carried his refinement—which we found extremely comical—to the point of blowing his nose into a piece of cloth, where he carefully enfolded his excretions before stowing the cloth into the deepest part of his pocket, apparently so as not to lose them. He always carried a set of keys in his hand, and amused himself by jingling them periodically. Somewhat taciturn and nonchalant by nature, he had a nasal voice, which distracted from the pleasure of his ever-instructive conversation. The Bandiagara schoolchildren quickly nicknamed him "Mr. Stuffed-Up Nose."

Despite his qualifications, two months after our arrival, Mr. Baba Keïta was replaced by a White teacher, Mr. François Primel. Mr. Primel's primary concern was to reorganize the school by creating a fifth class. He took the first two for himself and entrusted the third to Tennga Tiemtoré and the fourth to Allassane Sall. The fifth class, composed only of "Abécédaires," was given to the students in the first and second classes, who, under the watchful eye of Tennga Tiemtoré, took turns teaching the lessons that Mr. Primel himself had prepared.

Our new director created a school fund called the "cantine." Each scholarship student had to contribute one franc, fifty centimes a month. Since our scholarship totaled seven francs a month and the pension paid to our hosts for room and board was five francs, each student was thus left with fifty centimes in pocket money to last for thirty days, which was equivalent to sixteen cowries a day and twenty-one on Sundays. By comparison, a tirailleur received fifteen francs a month and one franc was equivalent to about one thousand cowries.

Personally, I was truly privileged, a veritable "daddy's boy" or, rather, a "mama's boy," for my mother regularly sent me fifteen francs every two months. Mr. Primel kept ten francs to add to my bankroll, and I was left with five remaining francs to spend as I pleased. This raised my monthly credit to about three thousand cowries, or about one hundred cowries a day, which was more than what some entire families had. This fortune earned me friends, but some boys were jealous and generally stronger than me. They flooded me with demands for cowries, and if I refused, they would beat me up. I no longer had my stick to defend myself nor my waaldé comrades to back me up in hand-to-hand combat.

In the little barracks that I shared with my five comrades from Bandiagara, my situation was hardly much better. Maki Tall, our group leader, was the oldest and the strongest and acted like a despot with the younger boys, doing what he wished with us. We were truly his little houseboys. He forced each of us to pay him in cowries so that he could buy extra butter for himself. When the platter of rice, or any other grain arrived, he divided it in half, took the part containing the butter and sauce, and left us the remaining half without sauce. On the other hand, we were allowed to eat his leftovers, if there were any.

Well, one fine day, he decided that from then on, I alone would have to be the one to take on the cost of his extra butter. I did this for a while, but in the end, I had had enough and refused to pay. Unable to make me listen, Maki Tall handed me over to the hefty Mintikono Samaké. He beat me with all his might, and as one would expect, he floored me. Since I would still not give in, he proceeded to stuff my ears full of fine sand while he held me down, and I later had great difficulty removing it.

That very evening, boiling with indignation, I went to the courtyard where the Fula chief Amadou Kisso was holding an assembly. Because children were not allowed to enter this courtyard, especially when adults were meeting there, all eyes turned toward me. I greeted them all in a loud voice, "As-salaam aleikum! Peace be upon you, O assembly of elders!"

Surprised, the elders automatically responded, "Aleika es-salaam! Peace be upon you. Bismillah! Welcome! What do you want?"

"I want to see Chief Amadou Kisso."

"What for?"

"I have come to lodge a complaint, as I have been mistreated by some of my barrack mates." Immediately, I was led to Amadou Kisso. He suspended his meeting in order to listen to me. I showed him my ears and the traces of the blows that I had received, and explained the regime that had been established by the stronger boys in the group. "I am here to lodge a complaint," I added vehemently, "because I can't stand it anymore."

The entire assembly burst into laughter.

"Now here's someone who knows what he wants!" chuckled several of the elders.

"What city are you from?" Amadou Kisso asked me.

"From Bandiagara."

"Who are your parents?"

"My father, who is dead, was named Hampâté. He was a descendant of the Bâs and the Hamsalahs of Fakala. My mother's name is Kadidja Pâté and she is the daughter of Pâté Poullo Diallo."

As soon as I had mentioned the names Hamsalah and Pâté Poullo, a murmur spread throughout the assembly. Amadou Kisso recognized me as the boy whom Fanta Bougalo had mentioned seeing at the residence of the district commandant.

"What!" he exclaimed. "Here is a descendant of the Hamsalahs and of Pâté Poullo who has come to our city and even to our compound, and he is being mistreated? This is a dishonor for us!" He turned to me. "From now on you will stay with my wife, and you will share my meals."

And then and there he called for my trunk and bedding and sent me to lodge with his favorite wife, who prepared his food. As fortune had it, this woman, who was named Aïssata, shared this name with one of my maternal grandmothers from Fakala. In fact, she was a distant relative on my grandmother Anta N'Diobdi's side.

Of course, this unexpected promotion only increased the ranks of my enemies and fanned the animosity of Maki Tall and Mintikono Samaké toward me. This gave me the good idea of forming a kind of special body guard in the persons of two young Bobos, Koroba Minkoro and Hansi Koulibaly, whom I paid in a few select treats and twenty cowries a day. These two strong boys were bound and determined to make life difficult for anyone who dared to lay a hand on me. While at the outset they were just bodyguards, they rapidly became my friends and unconditional supporters. After each of them had personally triumphed over the big bully Mintikono, my personal peace was assured.

Once I began living in the house of Amadou Kisso, I was very happy. I took my meals with him, and every night, and sometimes on days when I did not have school, I attended all the meetings and conversations that were held in his courtyard. It was as though I had only left my father Tidjani's court in order to enter his. There as well, storytellers and traditionalists succeeded one another, evoking the history of the country, the creation of the city of Djenné, its ancient traditions, its amusing chronicles, and its conquest by the French army, all to the accompaniment of music. There I learned many things about the Bozos, the Songhays, the Bambaras of the Saro region (a principality that had always opposed the Bambara king of Segou), and the Fulas themselves. This allowed me to deepen or complete what I had already learned.

At the time, twelve ethnic groups lived together in harmony in Djenné's twelve neighborhoods. These were the Bozo, Bobo, Nono, Songhhay, Fula, Dimado (caste of Fula captives), Bambara, Malinké, Mauritanian, Arab, Mianka, and Samo groups, although these last two were the most rare. The city was administered by a Bozo-Songhay-Fula triumvirate that was seconded by two colleges: a college of elders and a college of marabouts. Policing was handled by the captive class, for the artisan class was more specialized in moral surveillance. Traditional craftspeople (smiths, weavers, shoemakers, and so on) were organized into corporations called *tennde* (workshops) and led by a committee presided over by an elder.

People sought the intercession of saints buried in the small cemeteries scattered throughout the city. But some continued to make sacrifices at ancient pagan sacred sites located inside and outside the city's walls. Among these were the wall of the virgin Tapama or the sacred forest of Toulaa-Heela, residence of the great spirit Tummelew, master of the earth and protector of that place.

One day in that year of 1913, the inspector of instruction Jean-Louis Monod (author of the primers *Livrets de lecture* from which I had learned my first lessons) came to carry out an inspection in Djenné. Flanked by our director, he entered the classroom and began to question us in order to test the level of our knowledge. At one point he asked, "What is the capital of France?"

Many hands went up. Our comrade Aladji Nyaté, who was the oldest but not the brightest in the class, raised his hand, which topped all the others, and began to shout, "Pick me, Monsieur, pick me!"

He made such a fuss that his voice and his size finally drew the attention of the inspector.

"You, over there, the tall one."

Overjoyed, Aladji Nyaté first set about extricating his large body by degrees from the little wooden school table. Once he had managed to stand up, he crossed his arms and began to croon, "The capital of France, the capital of France, is Djenné!"

He was so happy that a large smile filled half of his face. Our teacher, Mr. Primel took his head in his hands, as though he had just been overcome by a sharp pain.

"Sit down, you son of a Djenné string bean!" cried the inspector indignantly. "You had better learn that Djenné is not the capital of France. The capital of France is Paris: P-A-R-I-S, Paris!"

The Great Famine of 1914: A Vision of Horror

During the summer of 1913, the sky had not been generous with its water. The seasonal rains had been deficient in much of the entire Niger Bend, from the flood plain that stretches from Diafarabé to Gao, to the drainage basin that extends from San to Douentza. Normally, these rains begin in June, and this is when sowing and planting begin. The rains that fall during the lean, or "gap," season begin again in September, October, and sometimes even in November. It is during these months that maize and millet are harvested, and these have usually already provided a smaller, earlier harvest known as "hasty" maize and millet. But that year, the rains of the first period had been scarce and those that usually fell during the lean months did not come at all. Kammou, the guardian spirit of celestial waters, had closed his floodgates and turned a deaf ear to the incantations of the fetish priests, which hadn't been any more effective than the prayers and supplications of the Muslim marabouts. Trickling springs refused to flow from their subterranean chambers. The streams and rivers that had timidly begun to flow from their beds had quickly returned to them and sought sanctuary there. Even in the best-watered regions, the floods had not taken their usual course.

Without the long-awaited rains, the rice paddies, prairies, and fields of the wild bush watched their new shoots shrivel up and die under a torrid sun that no cloud came to temper. The grazing lands suffered the same fate as the crops. Without grass to graze on, the cows watched as their milk dried up and their calves died. Part of the entire livestock population was decimated. Even the fish were affected. For want of enough new water, the females were unable to cross the banks of the riverbeds and migrate to the flooded plains where their natural annual spawning grounds lay. In distress, they laid their eggs in the homes of their husbands, the riverbeds, so that their unprotected eggs were washed away by the current. The seasonal production of food dropped by fifty percent.

To feed themselves, the farmers had to draw on their reserves and then on their seed stocks. Soon, there was nothing left to eat.

The disastrous lack of seasonal rains in the summer of 1913 thus generated the dreadful famine of 1914 that would cause the death of nearly one-third of the inhabitants of the Niger Bend. The regions of the western part of the territory (from Sansanding and Segou all the way to Bamako, Koutiala, Sikasso, and Bougouni), which were sufficiently rich in food stores, had hardly been affected. But in those days, there were neither vehicles nor paved roads to allow for the transfer of extra food supplies to the affected regions. At the time, only the Bani and Niger Rivers connected the east and the west to the Upper Senegal and Niger region. As it happened, these two natural transportation routes had quickly fallen to their lowest water levels or were completely blocked by shifting sandbanks that caused even the smaller pirogues considerable delays.

During this time, my comrades and I had no real conception of the fearful famine that was steadily overtaking entire populations. We knew that there were shortages in other areas, but we were not affected by them. Djenné was partially spared, and our hosts were well stocked, certainly thanks to the presence in the city of the district commandant.

As the situation continued to worsen throughout the year, Beydari decided that whether I liked it or not, he would send Niélé to join me in Djenné so that she could make sure that I did not lack for anything. I was truly overjoyed to see my good Niélé. She cried and held me in her arms for a long time.

Niélé began by looking for good lodgings, which she found in the Al-Gazba neighborhood. She prepared our quarters for the two of us. When everything was ready, she went to thank the Fula chief Amadou Kisso on behalf of the entire family for welcoming me into his home and treating me like a son. Then she came for me and took me to settle into our new lodgings. Next, she found work in the household of the grand interpreter Papa Sall as a cook for his favorite wife. The favorite wife did not live with her husband but had her own beautiful two-story house a short distance away that contained a number of spacious, airy, and well-lit rooms. This house was always closed and guarded by an armed doorman. Nobody except for the servants and Papa Sall himself could go inside. However, thanks to Niélé, I was the exception and could come and go as I pleased. In addition, they lavished me with treats. I therefore did not really miss the home of my benefactor Amadou Kisso, where I continued to go from time to time to pay a visit. As far as creature comforts were concerned, I had, in fact, graduated from an average paradise to a superior one. For although Amadou Kisso was a Fula chief, the lifestyle of his favorite wife was in no way comparable to that of the favorite wife of Papa Sall, the "grand interpreter of the commandant," and thus the second most important person in the district after the commandant himself, and the person whom everyone was forced to address first in order to make a request or defend a cause. Nothing happened without the discreet offering known as the "nocturnal thing," the gift that was sent at nighttime in order to ensure that one would obtain the interpreter's "good mouth."

I was presented to Papa Sall as "Niélé's son." He tolerated my presence in his wife's home, but he never spoke to me.

Every year on June 15, all the schools in French West Africa closed their doors for three months. As this date approached, all activities doubled for teachers and students alike because of the final exams and preparations that needed to be made before departing for summer vacation. For the students who had reached the end of this stage of their studies, it was the period for preparing for the Native Primary Studies Certificate, whose laureates then either were sent to the Bamako Professional School or were directly assigned to carry out subaltern office tasks in the colonial administration.

Mr. Primel prepared our journey carefully. After calculating the amount of each of our savings, he purchased clothing and souvenirs for each student according to his means. Since my bankroll was rather large, I asked him to also buy some clothes for Niélé. I personally received a rich trousseau composed of several quality suits of clothing, which were arranged in a handsome wooden trunk fastened with a padlock. The sum of fifteen francs remained. How well my funds had been managed!

I was very proud of my new clothes, and even more proud of my mother, Kadidja, and my servant-mother, Niélé, who had both done so much to make me happy. And indeed, I was happy. Before leaving, I gave one franc to each of my bodyguards in thanks for their support and to encourage them to stay with me when I returned at the beginning of the next school year.

On the day of departure, Niélé was given authorization to ride with me in one of the two pirogues that would return the students to Mopti. This had certainly been an inspired idea, for we would join Beydari in Mopti. He was returning from his long sojourn in Kati, where he had gone to present his condolences to Kadidja after the death of my brother Hammadoun.

Fitted fore and aft with twin sun shelters, our pirogue was punted by eight Bozo fishermen under the command of former infantry sergeant Bouna Pama Dianopo, older brother to our comrade Tiebary Dianopo, who was one of the most brilliant students in our class. The riverbed was now just a long filament of water snaking around the bends of tall riverbanks and yellow shoals of sand. The water was so clear and so transparent that, except for some occasional water pockets filled with mud, the bottom of the river was clearly visible. The fish swam about as though in an aquarium.

Bouna Pama, who was marvelously deft with a harpoon, would shout to us from time to time, "My brothers, what kind of fish would you like to eat tonight with your rice?" And with masterful skill, he would harpoon as many fish as it took to feed everybody. Niélé did the cooking, which exempted both of us from having to pay for our share of the food expenses. Well stocked with provisions of rice and the fish that Bouna Pama caught, we had no need to stop until we reached Sofara. In any case, there were few villages on this section of the Bani. As a result, we were completely ignorant of the tragedy that had befallen the inhabitants of that region.

After some time, we finally glimpse the palm tree domes that crown the large town of Sofara on the distant plain. The fishermen take the pirogue ashore. Happy to stretch our legs, we stream off the boat. It is a race to see who will be the first to arrive in town, and we are in a hurry to see the famed Sofara market, so well known and well stocked that people come from Kong, and even from In-Salah, to buy supplies and run errands.

As we cross a kind of long butte that had obstructed our view of the open landscape, the road suddenly ends at the edge of a deep pit. At the sight of it, we stop dead in our tracks. It is a mass grave, ghastly beyond belief. In the pit, the dead and the dying are piled on top of one another. Some bodies are swollen to the point of bursting, others are losing their innards. Vultures squabble over scattered body parts and bits of flesh.

Overcome by the horror of it, we are unable to move or speak. Upon our approach, the carrion eaters had flown off with a heavy flapping of their wings, but they had not gone far. They watch us from their perches atop the piles of dirt that surround the cavity. They are no longer afraid of people. Are their days not spent feasting on human flesh?

Dazed and overcome with disgust, suffocated by the indescribable stench that snatches at our throats and noses, we soon witness yet another barely believable scene. Two men approach, each dragging a human body by its feet. One of the bodies seems to be dead, but the other is obviously still in the process of dying. The two grave-diggers, perhaps hardened by habit, are laughing and talking loudly as though they were not moving anything more than an ordinary pile of tree branches. Upon reaching the edge of the mass grave, they toss the two bodies in. Then they turn on their heels and head back, chatting the entire time, as though they had just completed the most banal of tasks.

What happened next, none of us would ever be able to forget. The dying man, in a final expression of his will to live, croaks out a final groan. His mouth cracks open, his eyes open wide as though he were seeing some dreadful vision. His clenched fingers try vainly to latch on to something. His body shudders, and liquid seeps from his mouth. Suddenly he stiffens like a length of dry wood, and a few seconds later, he slumps and goes slack. His immobile and almost white eyes remain fixed on the sky. The poor wretch has just expired, lying there among the already dead.

We scream and bolt away toward Sofara, crying and calling for help. As I am running, I recall the peaceful death of my master Tierno Kounta in Bougouni, and how my father Tidjani had gently closed his eyelids. Is there nobody here to close the eyes of these unfortunate people? Why are so many of them dying in such a horrible manner? Why are their bodies being abandoned and left in the hands of those two brutes who treat them like garbage collectors dumping trash?

When we reach Sofara, we discover that the streets are almost empty. Here and there, along with the random skeletal passers-by, we meet emaciated children with swollen bellies, quivering and ragged old men, and a few famished dogs. Exhausted by hunger, some no longer have the strength to keep walking. They lie down anywhere: on the ground, in their vestibules, in the shade of a wall. Then they stop moving. And everywhere, everywhere, are the cadavers that the "undertakers" come to collect, one by one.

Overwhelmed by the scale of the catastrophe, the administration is powerless to help the population. At best, it is only able to feed those in its employ. Since nobody has the strength to remove the cadavers that are strewn across vestibules and side streets, the authorities have been forced to recruit and feed teams of "cadaver collectors." From morning until night, they rid the city of its dead. The two men that we had seen working at the mass grave were among them.

Almost automatically, we head to the market square, the living heart of the city. We are possessed by the half-crazy hope that it would somehow have been spared and that we would find the noises, cries and laughter that animate every African marketplace. Alas, the square is empty. Among the deserted stalls, there are only a few vendors offering thin broths made from boiled leaves, some palm fruits, and a few varieties of wild fruit. Of course, we had heard that there was a famine in the land, but none of us had imagined what that had truly meant. It was there, in Sofara, that I was personally able to put my finger directly on the enormity of the horror.

We wander through the city, devastated, stunned, and stupefied by the deathly spectacle. We are joined by Bouna Pama Dianopo, who had been searching for us. As the one in charge of our pirogue, he orders us to flee from this place and to go get back on board as quickly as possible. As a precaution, dinner is prepared inside the cabin, but none of us is able to eat a thing. That night, many of us were haunted by frightful visions, and only a sparse few did not call out or cry for their mothers.

In Mopti, Niélé and I stayed with my mother's childhood friend, Tiébéssé. It was there that we joined Beydari, who had returned from Kati. I was overjoyed to discover that my childhood friend Daouda Maïga was with him. His mother had come to Mopti in hopes of finding food and had brought him with her. Beydari had found Daouda wandering about the city, like so many other children who had been left to fend for themselves amid the many refugees. Beydari could not bear it, for Daouda and I had been born at almost the same time. We had lived side by side as brothers, and so he felt equally responsible for both of us. He brought Daouda and his mother back with him.

Like Djenné, Mopti was both a port and the official residence of a district commandant. This meant that it held special status. Pirogues traveled there. Stocks of millet were stored there, for the administration had been unable to send them to villages of the interior for lack of transportation. What's more, the river and the wetlands surrounding the city were teeming with fish. Every day the Bozos went fishing and caught enough fish to feed a part of the population. Refugees coming from all the villages in the Niger Bend were flowing in en masse, particularly the Dogons, who knew that they could count on their unlimited ancestral solidarity with the Bozos for help. Their two ethnic groups were bound, in fact, by the sacred alliance ties known as sanankounya (which I mentioned previously), which ethnologists have called a "joking cousin" relationship because it allows them to joke with each other, mock one another, and even insult one another, without there ever being any social consequences. However, it is in fact something completely other than a joke. This relationship represents a deep and serious tie that in the past once implied an absolute duty to help and assist one another. It originated in an extremely ancient alliance that was established between the members or ancestors of two villages, two ethnicities, two clans (for example, between the Sérères and the Peuls, the Dogons and the Bozos, the Toucouleurs and the Diawambé, the Fulas and the blacksmiths, the Bâ and Diallo clans, and so on). Over time, there was often nothing left but this alliance and this tradition of mutual mockery, except between the Dogons and the Bozos, whose sanankounya relationship is, without contest, one of the most solid in the region of the African savanna, possibly along with the one that links the Fulas and the blacksmiths.

Chased down from their mountains by famine, the Dogons set out for Mopti, where the first Bozo they met did not hesitate to share his food with them. But they were so numerous that they had to spread out along the edge of the river whose banks were the exclusive territory of the Bozo fishermen. Many Dogons swarmed to Segou and Bamako, which had been spared from the famine. Some even went all the way to Kati, where they gathered around my father Tidjani, which led him to found the "Dogon quarter" around his compound.

We remained in Mopti for a few days, which gave Beydari the time to organize our return, while also returning as discreetly as possible with provisions of millet and dried fish. He brought me back to Bandiagara with Daouda and Niélé. Daouda's mother, I no longer remember why, remained in Mopti.

In Bandiagara, at least in certain neighborhoods, the situation was the same as it was in Sofara. The June rains had begun to fall, but it was necessary to wait for the month of August to gather the first early harvest. If all went well, in September the normal harvest of corn and the first early harvest of millet would be completed. The general harvest of millet would not take place until October. At least the stock animals had begun to find a bit of grass to eat and the chickens had found something to peck at thanks to the first rains.

Our neighborhood of Deendé Bôdi, largely inhabited by butchers, Fula herdsmen, and stock breeders—and where all the members of my maternal and paternal family lines were located—had suffered less than others, all the more so because every family that had food would always send platters of it to relatives and neighbors. I can affirm that it was thanks to African solidarity that the inhabitants of the Deendé Bôdi neighborhood were able to survive the great famine without too much difficulty. This was not the case in the neighborhoods inhabited by the Dogons and some tattooed ethnic groups who had come from the south. Indeed, they suffered greatly.

In our household, food was certainly not abundant, but Beydari was always able to feed us. I remember that we ate a lot of organ meats. I do not know how he managed, but he was even sometimes able to procure rice for us! All the neighboring compounds had something to eat thanks to him. He also sent food to Tierno Bokar, whose school never went lacking for anything, thanks to Beydari and some other parents. And since Tierno raised a few good hens, not to mention what the children were able to glean in the small fields, with a few sacrifices, he even succeeded in coming to the aid of the unfortunate Hausas and Dogons.

Wangrin, who was by then the commandant's grand interpreter, spared no effort in coming to the aid of people who were suffering, whether it was directly or indirectly, by ensuring that they got help from the administration. Many of them would not have been able to survive without him.

I did not suffer from hunger during my entire sojourn in Bandiagara. But I was more or less forbidden to go out of the house. Daouda and I would sometimes escape to go bathe in the river, located about three hundred meters away, but the people we saw there were so gaunt that we soon lost heart. In any case, there were no longer any waaldé activities. I had been informed that in Bandiagara only a third of my old comrades remained. Among the other missing two-thirds, many were dead, while others had fled the city with their families.

One day while the situation in the city was still critical, I was sitting in our vestibule with Niélé, Beydari's first wife, and Biga, an old tanner who lived with us. A starving man who could no longer stand entered our vestibule, crawling toward us on all fours. He was so thin that it was impossible to tell what his ethnicity was. "Give me something to eat," he said in a weak voice, "otherwise, I am going to die in your vestibule and disposing of my body will cause you problems." Already Niélé had risen and gone to find something inside. She returned with a plate of millet gruel that she had set aside for the evening meal. She handed it to the poor man, who gobbled it down in a fearsome haste. When he had finished, Niélé offered him a calabash full of fresh water. He drank a big gulp, belched, and thanked us. We were all very pleased. But suddenly, has face went deathly pale and he began to wobble. "I feel death coming on," he stammered. "I must rid you of my body." Somehow, I do not know how, he found the strength to rise to his feet. He staggered outside, crossed the narrow street and went to collapse at the base of the wall across from our house. Niélé shouted and cried for help. "It's useless, my good mother," said the dying man. "I have just consumed the last ration that was left on earth for me." And he immediately entered his death throes. He died a few moments later.

Because he had died on a public street, it was the administration's responsibility to dispose of the body. A gravedigger wearing an armband happened to pass by. He seized the foot of the cadaver and dragged it as if it were a goat's carcass. We watched it disappear around a corner. We knew that he had gone to dump the body in Bandiagara's open-air mass grave that was located next to the cemetery and that I was careful never to visit.

Declaration of War

The July 14th Bastille Day holiday was fast approaching. In other years, the *katran zoulié*, as it was known locally, gave rise to elaborate celebrations that required contributions from the entire population. Every canton was required to send to Bandiagara a significant contingent of horses, dancers, musicians, and participants. In the twenty-five days leading up to the celebration, there was a general "preparation for combat" throughout the land. Toward the 12th of July, the city's population began to increase. Kings and canton chiefs from neighboring areas began arriving clothed in their most beautiful robes, accompanied by bands of traditional musicians and troupes of dancers and followed by processions of horses adorned in superb regalia. In past years, they had reached 2,500 in number! Of course, in order to prepare for or participate in the festivities required that one's normal activities be abandoned.

On the night of the 13th and overnight into the 14th, a gigantic procession of torch-bearers made its way through the city, crossed the Yaamé, and continued until it reached the foot of the commandant's residence. Every participant, on horseback or on foot, civilian or military, man, woman, or child, carried a lit torch. It was a conflagration on the move. Some elders wondered about the reasons behind this ritual ceremony. "Every year, the Whites perform a sacrifice to fire. Surely, it is to fire that they owe the secret of their deadly weapons, since it is because of these weapons that they managed to conquer the country and turn us into their captives and private property." For the children, it was just another chance to play and have fun.

Flateni, the famous praise singer and former griote to King Aguibou Tall, generally accompanied the procession. In a powerful and moving voice that rose above the crowd, she would sing old war hymns celebrating the Toucouleur heroes of El Hadj Omar's army and their exploits in the battles of Médine, Tyayewal, or elsewhere. Her songs could draw tears from even the most hardened among them. But she could also make them laugh until they cried, because she was not easy on the toubabs, those "skins on fire" and "egg gobblers." Fortunately, the colonial dignitaries did not understand Fulfulde! The population was forced to endure colonization, but whenever it could, it would thumb its nose at the colonizers, head, beard, and all!

The next morning, there would be a military parade, with demonstrations, musicians, and dancers representing different ethnic groups, games for the youth usually involving a greasy pole, and finally a horse race, which always gave rise to great enthusiasm and inflamed passions.

That year, there was no Bastille Day celebration. The district commandant had called for all the canton chiefs to arrive in Bandiagara on July 13th, but due to the famine, no chief was to be accompanied by more than two or three dignitaries. By contrast, also summoned were all the former tirailleur infantrymen who had retired with the grade of native noncommissioned officer (a native could never attain a rank above that of chief warrant officer unless he had participated in the "first phase of the conquest" or was a citizen of one of the "four communes" of Dakar, Saint-Louis, Rufisque, and Gorée).

Certainly, the famine was still raging, but the true motive for celebrating Bastille Day without fanfare lay somewhere else entirely. Following the assassination of Archduke Francis Ferdinand of Austria and his wife in Sarajevo on June 28, 1914, the threat of war began to hover in the skies of Europe, and especially in France, Germany, and England. In Africa, all the representatives of French authority lived in worry. Military leaders were alarmed. Dignitaries in the civil administration (the district commandant and his second in command) along with the members of the military administration (the battalion captain and his second in command) met for endless palavers. This was the cause of some surprise among the native employees, because members of the military did not often work with members of the civilian administration. Most of the time, they led separate lives, as dogs do from cats.

On the morning of July 14th, there was only a modest salute to the French colors, accompanied by an extensive distribution of food supplies to all those who were still suffering from hunger. The canton chiefs, dignitaries, and retired native noncommissioned officers of the district were all in Bandiagara. The night before, when the traditional procession of torches should have taken place, the district commandant and the captain had called them all in to a meeting in order to deliver a confidential communiqué. The commandant then entrusted his audience with a "masculine secret," that is, a very important secret, the disclosure of which inevitably causes grave problems. He requested that they keep it tucked well inside their heads.

But a secret is similar in nature to smoke. For no matter how thick a hut's thatch, smoke seeps through and radiates into the air, betraying the presence of fire. The selfsame secret that the district commandant and the captain battalion commander were unable to keep, those to whom they confided it could not either. Two days later, everyone knew that a fiery tornado was poised to roar through France and that its colonies would likely not be spared.

In the family, our main informant was a Dogon, Baye Tabémba Tembély, father of my schoolmate Yagama Tembély. In his capacity as a native noncommissioned officer, he participated in the "masculine secrets" kept by the authorities and then came to pass them on to his old friend Beydari. Since I was always more or less in their vicinity, I sometimes overheard their conversations.

The morning after that first meeting, he had a long conversation with Beydari. "I'm worried," he said. "I know the Europeans and the detours of their words. What the commandant told us yesterday is not promising for peace.

I have the impression that before long, there will be gunpowder palavers in France."

Over the course of the morning of July 15, he had a talk with his son Yagama in order to prepare him for what was to come. "It might come to pass," he told him, "that I will have to undertake a lengthy journey that will not only lead me to Senegal and the shores of the 'great salted river' (the Ocean), but even beyond that great river, all the way to the land of the 'skins on fire.' They are on the verge of holding gunpowder palavers. This kind of palaver kills or maims those who engage in it. As a member of the French military reserves, I may be called up. If that happens, be courageous as the son of every tirailleur should be. But in the meantime, do not say a word of this to anyone."

Very upset, Yagama immediately came to relay his father's words to me, with the request that I not breathe a word of it to anyone. But the secret was too heavy for me to bear alone. As soon as Yagama left, I ran out to look for Daouda and told him everything. In turn, I asked him to keep it all to himself, but in vain.

A muffled uneasiness was troubling the population, and not just in Bandiagara. Everyone could sense that something was not right in the land of the Whites. They expected the worst.

During the night of August 3 and over into August 4, 1914, the clarion calls began to sound, ringing out tones of ill augur. A few moments later, the great royal Toucouleur war drum began to beat a rhythm portending great calamity. Immediately, all the compounds were echoing with the Fulfulde exclamation, *Djam! Djam!* (Peace! Peace!), which is supposed to ward off misfortune. Everyone lent an ear, awaiting a new coded message that would define the nature of the misfortune just announced. They did not have to wait long. Following the last of seven strikes of the drum at intervals of several seconds, additional strikes followed, more clipped and rapid, interspersed with the quick ringing of metal tubes. It was the traditional signal announcing the start of a war against foreigners. A clamor immediately rose from the city: "War! It's war!"

In the early morning hours, the district commandant assembled all the chiefs and dignitaries of the land and declared, "Germany has just set fire to the powder kegs of Europe. Its Emperor, Kaiser Wilhelm II, wants to dominate the world. But he will come face to face with eternal France, champion of liberty!" The French overseas territories were called upon to participate actively in the effort put forth by France to win the war by contributing manpower and raw materials. Thus began the recruitment of men and the requisitioning of millet, rice, fat, and animals for food. Fortunately, the abundant rains that fell in the month of August and the first harvests of maize and millet had held the specter of famine at bay, and this was taken into consideration in the assessment of the resources available in each region.

Old Youkoullé Diawarra had once been a military leader in the Toucouleur army. After the French conquest, he had become so impoverished that he had been reduced to begging for his daily food and kola nuts. When he learned that war was in the air, he quickly went home, overjoyed. Out of a battered strongbox, he drew his war arsenal from the days of old. He reported to Alfa Maki Tall and placed himself in his service.

Alfa Maki Tall explained to him that this was not an African war at all but a purely European war between the "skins on fire." Old Youkoullé Diawarra was extremely disappointed, for he had hoped that a new opportunity to fight and pillage had arisen to cure his poverty. In the old days, he had made a living from war alone, and had always been able to profit from it in some way. But since the French occupation, he was bereft. When he arrived at the market in Bandiagara, his hands and pockets empty, he was heard to exclaim with sadness, "Wallaye! By God! The saddest thing for me is peace, for it even deprives me of a means by which to pay for my kola nuts!"

Incensed, his hopes dashed, he began to curse all Europeans of all races and their "civilization" too. Ignoring the risk of being arrested for his seditious declarations, he would wander through the streets in a fury, bellowing, "May those accursed egg gobblers, the 'skins on fire' all get killed until there is not a single one left of them on the face of this earth!" After which everyone would exclaim sadly, "Wanaa djam! Allah doom!" (This is not peace, may God protect us!) And then Youkoullé would vociferate, "Oh God! Kill all the 'skins on fire'! Make the entrails of their women sterile so that they no longer bear any fruit!" Included in his rage was the totality of the Europeans who, for him, had been the cause of his social and material downfall, and who had now blocked another occasion for recovering a little of his old glory.

It took none less than the authority of Kaou Djeli, the king's grand griot-marabout, to silence him.

In Bandiagara, everyone had a theory. In my family there lived a retired old spahi named Mamadou Daouda, who had participated in the French military campaigns against the Almamy Samory. "Things aren't going too well between the French and the Germans anymore," he said. "There will be hell to pay! I saw how the 'skins on fire' went after the Almamy Samory. I know them. They will ruin each other's cities and villages. Believe me, it will be a mess of fire and blood! They are so smart that they've tamed the elements. They've made the elements work for them. Look at what they've done with iron. They've made it their soulless captive, but they've given it such power that it can work faster and harder than men."

"And why would such men fight against each other?" asked the old tanner, Biga.

"Ah, Biga! As the ancestor Aga Aldiou said, 'It's not for nothing that a pair of pants that was clean in the morning must be washed in the evening.' There must be a good reason, and we will know it one day. Be patient."

By two o'clock in the afternoon, news of the Franco-German conflict had spread throughout the population like smoke drifting through air. At eight o'clock in the evening, a great meeting was held between the Fulas and Toucouleurs at Kérétel, the famous square in Bandiagara where not so long ago, we had enjoyed so many pleasant evenings. The square was located near our house, and I slipped out and went to listen to what would be said.

Seated in groups, men were talking among themselves. More than anything, they were wondering why the French and the Germans had taken up arms against one another. For some, it was surely because they were fighting over land. Perhaps they were fighting over the lines separating their fields, or fighting over places to hunt or gather wild fruit, or over fishing and grazing rights, or something of that nature. Perhaps the herds of livestock belonging to the Germans had wandered uninvited onto the French prairies? For others, it couldn't be anything other than a dispute over women. The chiefs of the "skins on fire," as everyone knew, were ardent rabbits. Their male members retained their heat and got worked up as soon as a beautiful woman came swinging her fine waist and round hips past their eyes. They added that women were quite rare in France (this opinion was founded on the fact that the colonials rarely brought their wives to the colony and thus sought companions among the native women). Moreover, they said, their women had temperaments like cows rather than like cats. It was meant by this that they had few children, for cows have only one calf at a time, whereas cats give birth to plentiful litters. In addition, wasn't it also said that they gave birth to three times the number of boys than girls? In a country where there was such a shortage of women, everything related to this question could not help but detonate a war.

From the middle of another group, Diawando Guéla M'Bouré, known as "Big Talker," stood up. He called for everyone to be silent and then declared in a loud voice, "For some time now, we have been holding a discussion in order to understand why the French, our masters, and the Germans, whom we do not know, have entered into war against one another. For some, they are fighting over women. For others, they are fighting over fields. O brothers of my mother, you have missed your mark. The truth lies elsewhere! Here it is, without twists or rough spots, full and smooth as a flood plain. For the 'skins on fire,' we constitute an important resource. To some of us, they have taught their language. To others, their way of farming, and to others, their kind of warfare, and so on. Why have they done this? They are not apostles, come to carry out a charitable mission, and there is no immediate recompense. They only work for gain in this world and they expect nothing from the other world. There are even some among them who believe neither in God nor in the hereafter. It is said that their leaders have cut ties with God, their marabouts have no place in their councils, and they have separated their mosque (the Church) from their house of palavers (the State, Parliament).

"Why have the toubabs come to invade us? Why have they captured and tamed us? They have done this only to make use of us when they need us, just as every hunter makes use of his dog, every rider his horse, and every master his captive, to help them work and fight their enemies. There is nothing surprising in that. In the past, we also took war captives before we ourselves became captives.

"And why have the toubabs of Europe declared war on one another? My brothers, I will tell you. The French have gone to war to maintain possession of us and only to maintain possession of us, and the Germans want to take us away from them. There is no need to go looking for another explanation. Indeed, what is the use of wasting our time wondering about the reasons behind their dispute? We would be better off finding a way to derail this calamity, because whatever the cause of this war may be, we will have to bear the consequences of it in one way or another. Already Baye Tabéma Tembély, Sergeant Kassoum, Tiassarama Coulibaly, and Mamadou Aïssa have been called up to stand for the flag. Yesterday, they were outfitted in military uniforms, and the day after tomorrow, with their former tirailleur comrades, they will leave for the military city of Kati, and from there for *hee-hee-hedjala*, the terrible 'who knows what.'

"If this fire is not quickly extinguished, then tomorrow, the next day, or in a year from now, the 'skins on fire' will take all our sons and all our belongings in order to sustain their war, because that is what we are good for. Therefore, my brothers, early tomorrow morning, let us ask our chief Alfa Maki Tall to organize public prayers in order to beg God to reclose the sluice gates of misfortune that he has just opened. The grand marabout Tierno Sidi thinks that this war risks overtaking a good many White and Black countries and will kill innumerable victims."[10]

At this point in Guéla M'Bouré's speech, I fell asleep.

The next day, apparently at the commandant's request, Alfa Maki Tall summoned all the marabouts and dignitaries of the city. The meeting was held in front of the mosque. I accompanied Tierno Bokar and my uncle Bokari Thiam, younger brother of my father Tidjani.

When the assembly was complete, the district commandant and the battalion captain arrived, flanked by the chief brigadier of the guards Mamadou Bokary and Brahime Soumaré on one side, and Sergeant Kassoum Kaba and his second in command Bia Djerma, on the other.

The commandant began to speak. "We have been at war with Germany since yesterday. Gunfire broke out during the night and will continue every day from now on until the enemy is defeated and asks for peace. Man needs God's help in times of misfortune. That is why the French government asks that there be prayers in all our territories so that God will protect France and give her victory."

In spite of the gravity of the situation, an old "house captive," sarcastic as many rimaïbé are, leaned over and whispered into Bokari Thiam's ear, "The shameless lizard only returns to the road leading to his hole when someone tries to cut off his tail." (In other words, "Some unbelievers only return to God when they are struck by misfortune.") It was a bitter gibe.

The dignitaries chose sixty-six marabouts from among the most reputable in the district, and they in turn designated six from among them to preside over the prayers. In honor of France, they organized a Koranic vigil that was celebrated on the night of the 11th and over into the 12th of August, 1914. Beginning at eleven o'clock in the evening and throughout the night, each of the sixty-six marabouts recited the Koran in its entirety.

The administration first mobilized the reserves and then called for volunteers. Later, a draft of young men by class was instituted. In Bandiagara, this did not cause much trouble. People accepted the recruiting efforts without too much fuss. Or at least they did before recruitment became excessive, because for them, to go to war was to demonstrate their courage and disdain for death, and God knows that they demonstrated that during the last two wars! In those days, perhaps because of the former alliance between King Aguibou Tall and the French, hardly any Bandiagara Toucouleurs were drafted. This was not the case for the Dogons. In my family, there was no boy old enough to go fight under the French flag.

It was the obligatory contribution of animals and food supplies that caused the most hardship in some regions. In Bandiagara, the commandant had at first contemplated simply ordering the canton chiefs to deliver certain quantities of animals or food. The canton chiefs would then have been responsible for communicating this order to the household leaders in their canton villages. As I later learned, Wangrin had intervened. "Commandant," he had essentially said, "this is ungainly and not the way to proceed. By sending an order with no explanation for it, you will spread panic. For fear of losing everything, people will flee to the other side of the border, to the Gold Coast, taking all their possessions with them.[11] There may also be revolts. What is needed is to summon those in charge, to explain to them that France needs them, and that everyone must make an effort to feed the troops who are fighting at the front, for among these troops, there are Africans, and perhaps even their relatives."

The commandant had had the wisdom to listen to Wangrin. People accepted the requisitions because they had been mentally prepared for them. They even sometimes made their own spontaneous contributions to the war effort. Instead of "Requisition!" they were told, "We need you." This was an extremely important nuance for the older Africans. And because many of them had sons who were fighting in France, in their minds, they were contributing to feed their children. If the commandant had not gone about it in this way, there would have been an exodus to the Gold Coast that would have emptied the region of its substance and perhaps even would have led to revolts followed by terrible repressions, as had been the case in other regions.

Soon it was September again. It was the end of vacation, if it could even be called that, given that the interval had been filled with so many painful events. The famine, the horrible scenes that I had witnessed, and the declaration of war with its attendant dread and duress had conspired to make this by far the most dismal vacation of my entire life.

On the 8th of September, the commandant summoned all of the students attending the Djenné regional school in preparation for the return trip. Supplies were distributed and porters were placed at our disposal. We were expected to cover the seventy-six kilometers separating us from Mopti in two days and on foot. We would be escorted and protected against possible marauders by a district guard, for even though the first harvest was underway, there remained a good many famished people throughout the land who could be tempted by our provisions. The famine would not really be over until the general millet harvest took place in the month of October.

Once again, I left my friend Daouda Maïga and all my family members behind, not knowing that it would be several years before I would see them again. On the day of our departure we were joined by three students from Sanga, a city in the land of the Dogons. This time I was not accompanied by Niélé.

Along with a contingent of new students from the district of Niafounké and our comrades who had spent their vacations in Mopti, we boarded several pirogues. Several days later, we arrived in Djenné without any trouble, barely believing that, happy and carefree, we had left the city only three months earlier.

Clearly, the city had not suffered. Provisions were plentiful, for the flood plain offered many more possibilities for picking and planting than did the mountainous regions. This had been particularly true in the mountainous Dogon cliffs above Bandiagara, where the population had suffered from hunger longer than in any other area.

In Djenné, the colonial administration had commenced requisitioning grain and livestock in order to contribute to the "war effort," but apparently, at least as far as I could tell, this had not resulted in the placement of any restrictions on the local population. It is true, however, that we were only in the first year of the war.

I found lodgings with friends of my family. And the monotony of school life began again for us, this time with the worrisome specter of the certificate exams looming at the close of the academic year.

The only thing that was truly new was that every afternoon our director, Mr. Primel, would come to read and provide commentary on the communiqués sent by the Havas Agency that provided information about developments in the European war. We learned that over there, people were dying in the mud and cold of the trenches. But we children were barely affected, and it did not stop us from continuing with our games. On the other hand, we were very interested in the person of Kaiser Wilhelm II, whom we were told was a great sorcerer, a devil incarnated in a man, a *prince maudit* who wished to place all humanity at his mercy. We were shown illustrations of him wearing a helmet topped with a pointed horn reminiscent of a rhinoceros tusk. His chest was laden with cords: these were certainly the gris-gris and magical ornaments that the devil himself had woven expressly for him and some of his war chiefs. Kaiser Wilhelm II, we were told, wanted to command the entire world, and in order to do so, he had entered into a pact with the devil, who inspired and assisted him in everything he did.

The old Fulas of Djenné were not fooled. "The White chiefs," they said, "present their enemies to our children, and thus indirectly to ourselves, as being sorcerers and devils. But it is inconceivable that an entire race could be made up of only bad people. Human beings are like the herbs and plants in the fields. The poisonous species grow along with the healing ones and the edible ones next to the ones that are not. In all human beings, with the exception of the sages and saints, there is a common trait. Everyone tends to denigrate his enemy or adversary and to present him as a good-for-nothing. And yet, very few of them realize that in minimizing the value of their rival, they only diminish their own value."

As for the old Bozos, Bambaras, and Songhays of the city, they accorded little credit to the accusations of barbarity and sorcery against Wilhelm II and his son the *Kronprinz*. "Ha ha!" they said, nodding their heads. "Not so fast! This is all just a family disagreement like the one pitting the Toucouleurs against the Fulas."

Nevertheless, in the long run, our schoolteacher succeeded so well in making us hate the Germans that we only called them by the insulting name of *Boches*. Our hatred for them was so strong that upon seeing a snake or a scorpion we would begin to shout, "Hey, look! Here's a dirty Boche! Kill it before it gets away!" Hadn't we seen for ourselves in the portraits of Wilhelm II that the points of his mustache faced one another like two scorpions ready to strike, their evil tails in the air?

As the year drew on, Mr. M'Bodje, a native teacher who had graduated from the William Ponty Normal School in Gorée, was assigned to Djenné to replace Tennga Tiemtoré. He took kindly to me, but this was not enough to dissipate the melancholy that was slowly taking over me. I do not really know why, but I no longer liked school at all. Like my brother Hammadoun a few years earlier, I only wanted one thing: to see my mother again, and not just for a visit. I wanted to go and live with her in Kati. I easily completed my assignments, but did so mechanically and without the enthusiasm I had had in the beginning.

Flight

I obtained my Primary Studies Certificate at the end of the year. I knew that if I let things take their course, when the first days of vacation arrived I would be sent to Bandiagara and then on to the Bamako Professional School as a resident intern, or even sent off immediately to some obscure administrative post far away from Kati. I was not willing to risk it. I had to leave before that. I alerted my mother by telegram that I was intending to join her, and asked her to inform Beydari. She sent me fifteen francs to cover the cost of my trip. Ordinarily, I should have waited to find out what destiny the administration had chosen for me, or at the very least, I should have sought authorization from the school director. I did not do any of those things, which was simply the same thing as running away.

I discovered that Mr. M'Bodje was preparing to leave with his nephew to go spend his vacation in Senegal. Given that we were on good terms, I asked if he would allow me to join the convoy. Mr. M'Bodje, who knew nothing of my situation and thought that my affairs were completely in order, allowed me to join him in good faith, but under certain conditions. The first was that I alone had to be responsible for my transportation costs, whether it be by boat or by train. Concerning my food, he answered for it, knowing that we would find food as we went along. Indeed, the chiefs of the villages that we passed through fed us. In those days, it sufficed to be wearing an imported European suit or hat to be taken for an agent of the colonial administration who would then have the right to eat, drink, and sleep at will in people's homes. Well, Mr. M'Bodje wore a superb pith helmet! I showed him the fifteen francs that my mother had sent me, a sum that was largely sufficient to cover any unforeseen expenses. This convinced him.

His second condition was that I would have to travel on foot. He explained that he had only one horse that would have to carry him and his nephew, who was too young and frail to go on foot as I would have to do. "But you will only have to walk to Segou," he said in consolation. "After that, you will be able to travel by boat to Bamako." At the time, this was a journey of over three hundred kilometers, but I was not afraid.[12] At the idea of being with my mother again, my strength increased. I felt capable of walking from Djenné to Kati on foot if necessary. This was even more the case because Mr. M'Bodje had hired a team of porters. Therefore, I did not have to worry about being burdened with a heavy load, as my poor brother Hammadoun had two years earlier. I told him that I accepted his second condition and we came to an agreement. I went off to prepare my trunk.

Early one morning, in the middle of the month of June 1915, our little convoy sets off toward the west. It includes eight porters, a chief porter, a groom, Mr. M'Bodje, his nephew Cheikh M'Bodje, and myself. The sun has just come up. Mr. M'Bodje pulls his nephew up behind him and sets off atop his horse. The line of porters stretches up the road. I trot along on foot behind them. Before setting off, Mr. M'Bodje has taken care to recommend me to the head porter, who, upon payment of a few coins, has arranged to have my trunk carried by one of his men. We have calculated that it will take about ten days to cover the three hundred kilometers that separate us from Segou.

After a few days of walking, interrupted by halts in small villages, we begin to approach the large Bambara town of Say (Soka in Fulfulde), situated between the Bani and the Niger Rivers. As usual, Mr. M'Bodje has arrived before us, thanks to his horse. About two kilometers outside of Say, we find him waiting for us, sitting with his nephew in the shade of a large tree. To lend an air of solemnity to his entrance into the city, he wants us all to arrive together. Say is no ordinary city. In fact, the colossus that was the kingdom of Segou had always broken its teeth when it tried to bite into it. Not only had it never been conquered, it had also never recognized Segou as its suzerain. As the Fula proverb goes, "Segou is strong, but it knows Soka's (Say's) might. When Soka sputters, Segou shakes." It would have been quite unseemly for a White-Black of Mr. M'Bodje's quality, dressed, shod, and behatted in a manner fitting to the White-Whites themselves, to enter in quasi-anonymity the city that had defied the crown of Segou. Astride his purebred and preceded by a file of eight porters driven by a headman with a whip, he would certainly cause more of a stir than would a lone rider carrying a skinny child behind him, colonial pith helmet or not! Following a few moments' rest, our convoy sets off, winding its way through the bushes. Mr. M'Bodje brings up the rear.

Say is one of the few Bambara cities that had held on to its well-trained pack of guard dogs. Vigilant sentinels that can be surprised by neither sleep nor distraction, they are constantly on the prowl around the city walls, ready to tear limb from limb any intruder who dares to come within their reach.

As we approach the city, the dogs have caught our scent. They begin to bark in a way that I have never heard dogs do before or since. Theirs is a deafening and discordant chorus, where cavernous growls and nasal howls mingle with the most strident yelps. These abominable yowls stop us in our tracks. We hold our breath, our hearts encased in ice. Our head porter, who is apparently familiar with the customs of these canines, shouts, "Do not be afraid! Keep walking, and do not falter!" At the same time, young men clothed in traditional hunting garments come running out of the city to greet us. To the dogs they cry, "Kaba! Mah! Mah!" These three words have a magical effect! The dogs immediately fall silent, lower their ears, and flee with their tails between their hind legs as though they were apologizing for their overwrought verbosity. Then they go to sit quietly on their haunches, their long pink tongues hanging from their muzzles and drooling with saliva.

A handsome, well-built man, whose hair is plaited into tiny braids, leaves the group of young men. He walks toward Mr. M'Bodje, bows, and says in Bambara, "I am the son of the village chief. Welcome to Say, O honorable stranger. Consider yourself to be at home here. It is my father who speaks through my mouth."

Mr. M'Bodje, who only speaks Wolof (a language of Senegal), Fulfulde, and French, asks me to serve as his interpreter. Suddenly, I feel myself rise in rank, as much in the eyes of the others as in my own. Using me as his intermediary, he thanks the chief's son and asks him to lead us to his father.

Led by our escort, we enter the city. Its streets are so winding and narrow that two men cannot walk abreast without getting in each other's way. The street we have taken suddenly opens on to a rather large square bordered by great *douhalen* trees whose thick foliage provides shade all year round. The chief's house is located just across the square. The chief's son leads us into the vestibule, a well-proportioned room whose walls are hung with hunting trophies and covered almost entirely with talismans.

We are presented to the village chief. In the eyes of the administration, he is a canton chief. But he is also an elder, a master of the knife, and one of the seven grand masters of the Pondori and Djenneri talismans, which amounts to saying that he was a living idol. Beneath a crown of white hair, his forehead is shiny, high, and wide, and his eyes are at once benevolent and grave. His nose is so long and so straight that he is nicknamed, albeit reverently, *Foulalnoun*, "Fula nose." Finally, a set of very large ears, said to symbolize wisdom and knowledge, lends this Bambara patriarch a most venerable bearing.

Having lost the use of his legs in years past, he spends his days seated on a tanned cowhide in the vestibule of his dwelling. This room is at once a living room, a palaver room, the seat of the local tribunal, and the sanctuary of ancestral deities. Positioned on a kind of low earthen dais, it is from this place that he directs with an authoritative hand the affairs of his charges, solving all the problems that arise between them, or between them and the deities and ancestors, or yet again between them and those so-called gods of the bush that are the White-Whites, conquerors, and supreme leaders of the land.

This traditional Bambara chieftain is so hostile to Islam that he makes certain never to turn his face to the east, and thus to Mecca, the direction toward which all Muslims must pray. Although conquered during the time of Cheikou Amadou, founder of the Islamic Fula Empire of Massina, the chief of Say only ever feared one man: Colonel Archinard, chief of the "skins on fire." Did this great White sorcerer, wearer of "five strings," not collude with the great spirit Tummelew, who gave him the secrets of the tamarind grove that lies to the south of Djenné and that was the only place from which one could be certain to take the city?[13]

With me as the intermediary, a dialogue ensues between the chief and Mr. M'Bodje.

"What is the quality of our White-Black (*tou-baboufin*) guest, so nattily dressed as a 'White-White' from White France?" asks the chief.

"He is a great marabout from the school where people learn how to write from left to right, and not from right to left as in the Koranic schools. He was born far away in the west, in the land where the sun sets in the great salted river."

"Tell the school marabout that I am very happy that he writes from left to right and not in the other direction as the Muslims do!"

Mr. M'Bodje replies politely to the chief.

The chief says, "Ask the school marabout how the great mustachioed commandant is doing."

"He is doing well, and I thank you on his behalf," Mr. M'Bodje has me say.

"And the beardless little commandant?"

Same response.

"And the potbellied money-keeper (the treasurer)?"

"And the pen-bearer (the secretary)? The door guard (orderly)? The healer (doctor)? The master of the wire that brings news (the postman)? The pole shimmiers (the post and telegraph linemen who climb poles and maintain the wires)? And let us not forget the meal-cooker, the meal-server, the clothes-washer and the bed-maker, the pot-washer, the wind-giver (panka, or operator of the ventilator), the manure-gatherer (groom)?"

Mr. M'Bodje, accustomed to flunking repetitious and lengthy explanations with a vengeance where his students are concerned, is incensed. From time to time he mutters to me in French, "Is he ever going to stop pronouncing this litany of names!" Luckily, he is a man who knows how to control his impatience, and he responds politely to each inquiry as custom requires. He had indeed remained "Black" enough to know that, for us, the litanies of greeting are interminable and that it would be of the utmost incivility to attempt to circumvent them.

Having arrived at the end of his enumeration, the old chief pulls a snuffbox from his pocket. He takes a pinch of snuff from it and sharply aspirates it into each nostril, which makes him sneeze. Then he blesses the sky for having allowed his father and mother to beget him beneath a favorable star. Suddenly he continues, "Also ask the school marabout how are all those whom I have not mentioned, and yes, how are all those in that beautiful city of Djenné, which the Muslims say is at once paradise (*djenna*), a shield (*djouna*), and insanity (*djinna*). As for me, what I find to be the most insane, and what aggravates me the most is the shouting of the marabouts five times a day from the tops of the turrets of their mosques!"

Profiting from a moment of silence, Mr. M'Bodje says to me, "Amadou, tell the venerable and honorable great chief that everyone in Djenné is well, from the commandant on down to the lowliest of kitchen hands, and that they have all asked me to send him their greetings and to also greet his courtiers, his wives, and his children, omitting no one. Tell the chief that we are his guests for this afternoon and tonight alone. Tomorrow, as soon as the first glimmers of dawn slice through the tenebrous remains of night in the east, we will again recommence our trek toward Mounia, and from there, onward to Segou."

After listening to me, the chief exclaims, swallowing part of my name in the process, "Adou! Tell the school marabout for the 'skins on fire' that his speech is as beautiful as the tall, straight trunk of a fan palm and that I thank him. Tell him that tomorrow, at dawn, he will have everything that he needs in order to continue his journey."

Mr. M'Bodje is finally able to take leave of the old chief, who ensures that we are served an excellent lamb couscous, prepared by one of his wives.

On the Trail with the War Dogs

We spent an excellent night. At dawn, even before the cocks began to crow, a beautifully bridled horse has been led into the center of our camp by a boy scarcely older than I. A man is waiting there, surrounded by a pack of twelve dogs similar to those that we had seen the day before. Always an early riser, Mr. M'Bodje is the first to step outside and discover the spectacle. He calls to me in a loud voice. Awakened with a start, I jump up and go outside, where I in turn spy the handsome horse and the dog handler surrounded by his pack. The man is wearing the attire of a hunter. His garments are literally covered with amulets of leather and fragments of metal. This is apparently the traditional costume of the dog handlers. He is wearing an impressive headdress. Atop a wooden bowl cut to the exact size of his skull is attached the head of a lion with a full mane. Its shaggy locks encompass his head and fall to either side of his face and blend into a long, artificial beard constructed from a horse's mane. The straps of two game bags carried on either side of his body cross his chest. A bull's tail fitted with tiny bells hangs from his right wrist. Squatting, he waits patiently, surrounded by his twelve well-trained battle dogs, apparently placed at our disposal by the chief. These dogs are gigantic and thickset, with enormous heads. Tied around each of their joints are knotted cords. Their heads are covered with pieces of black cloth with holes cut for the ears and held in place with colored string tied around their muzzles and necks. A gris-gris collar fitted with sharp spikes is also placed around each of their necks. One would be hard pressed to say whether the dogs or their keeper was the more frightful.

This type of dog, known as a "war dog" and that was bred only in the land of Say, has completely disappeared today.

Like a policeman, Mr. M'Bodje is never without the whistle that he used at school and that he now uses to call the porters. He raises it to his lips: "Frr! Frr! Fitt!" chirps Mr. M'Bodje's whistle. Immediately, all the porters stand ready, each one beside his bundle.

Mr. M'Bodje goes to greet the dog handler and then, using me as his intermediary, asks him, "Why is the old chief having us escorted by a pack of dogs?"

The man replies, "Ever since Colonel Archinard made a pact with the spirit Tummelew so as to take Djenné, all the evil spirits that had once been imprisoned in the sacred grove of Toula-Heela have broken free from their prison. They have been scattered between Say and Segou where they wreak havoc by attacking unprotected travelers. They can cause illness or insanity. These rebel spirits fear only the trained dogs of Say and the powers emanating from the gris-gris that they wear. It is for this reason that the chief has decided to have them escort you until you leave this land. Tradition requires it."

The young groom then steps forward and says to Mr. M'Bodje, "The chief has placed this horse at your disposal as a mount for your two children," meaning Mr. M'Bodje's nephew and myself.

This was the only stretch of the trip that I would complete on horseback.

"Mr. Frr!-Frr!-Fitt!" as the porters have nicknamed him, gives the signal for departure with his whistle. Fourteen men, twelve dogs, and two horses strong, our convoy moves out from Say, en route to Segou. The road is narrow. Like the track of a great boa, it twists and turns between brushy tufts that riffle lightly in the pleasant early morning breeze.

Soon, the entire bush begins to quiver. It seems to be stretching up from its bed and shaking off the lingering torpors of night. To our left, a dove coos softly, as though to awaken its sleepy companion. Another dove answers from the right. Cocks crow in the distance. They have apparently sent out a signal. Informed that it is now safe to move and rustle about, the diurnal animals leave their dens. In the branches, the sparrows strive to out-sing each other, hopping from branch to branch without ceasing their chatter. Everything begins to move and come to life, and the fears born in darkness dissipate like mist under the first rays of the sun.

As long as the shadows linger in the semi-obscurity of twilight or dawn, each thicket of thorn trees seen from afar resembles a massive, ill-shapen monster, squatting on its heels, ready to leap at anyone who would dare to come within reach. The porters are so full of stories about devils and spirits that I see one in every grove of trees as soon as night falls.

Over time, I've noticed that darkness imposes silence on our porters, while the light of day makes them talkative and even a bit loud, at least until hunger, fatigue, and the extreme heat have their way with their strength. There is nothing like darkness and hunger to close a man's mouth.

As for the war dogs who precede our convoy as advance sentinels, they make no noise and attend only to what reaches their senses of hearing, sight, or smell. They are the well-trained students of the Bambara hunters of Sarro, whose motto is "Feel, hear, see, but keep quiet."

We generally walk on without lunch, not resting or stopping to eat until we arrive at the place where we will spend the night. In every village, we are received in the same manner, with the exception of a few details. Everywhere, Mr. M'Bodje, in his capacity as "Grand Marabout of the White Man's School," is received and treated as a veritable authorized representative of the "skins on fire." Couscous, platters of rice, millet gruel with milk, fresh milk, limpid honey, and seasonal fruit, all this is copiously given and, it goes without saying, free of charge.

The chief of one village even went so far as to humbly thank Mr. M'Bodje for having condescended to stop in his village and for having been willing to eat his food, which, out of modesty, he qualified as "ill prepared." And to wash away the supposedly unpleasant aftertaste that his meals must have left in our mouths, this chief offered 500,000 cowries to Mr. M'Bodje (in 1915, this was equivalent in value to 100 cents or 5 francs) so that we could buy ourselves some millet along the way!

All this generosity and respect, however equivocal, given the supposed connection between Mr. M'Bodje and the all-powerful colonial administration, are in fact based on the ancestral tradition of hospitality toward any passing traveler. In the African savanna of old—which I know well and which is the only one that I can truly speak of—any traveler arriving at an unfamiliar village had only to present himself at the threshold of the first house on his path and state, "I am the guest that God has sent you," for him to be received with joy.[14] He was given the best room, the best bed, and the best portions of food. Often even, the head of the family or the eldest son gave him his own room and went to sleep on a mat in the vestibule or in the courtyard. In exchange, the passing stranger would enrich the evenings of his hosts by recounting the historical chronicles of his country, or by relating stories of particular encounters during his peregrinations. Africans of the savanna traveled frequently, both on foot and on horseback, and this resulted in a permanent exchange of knowledge and information from region to region. This custom of "open houses" allowed people to circulate throughout the entire land, even if they were without means, as would quite often be my own experience later on.

One morning at around ten, about twelve days after our departure from Djenné and without ever experiencing any dangerous encounters, Segou comes into view. Doubtless afraid of being torn limb from limb by our pack, bad people and evil spirits have prudently preferred to keep their distance from us.

To thank the dog handler, Mr. M'Bodje offers him a worn fez and two one-franc coins. The man accepts the fez but categorically refuses the two coins. He turns and sets off through the bush again with his dogs and the handsome horse that had carried me and the little M'Bodje.

We enter Segou from its east side. This extraordinary city, which was in turn the capital of the Bambaras and the Toucouleurs and whose importance is at once mythical, political, social, and commercial, stretches along the right bank of the Niger in the shade of centenary acacia trees. Facing the city, the river spreads majestically over the plain. I do not believe that there is any other place in the region of the Niger Bend where it is this wide.

Mr. M'Bodje is hoping to take the boat known as *Le Mage* (named for the famous explorer), scheduled to depart at one o'clock in the afternoon.[15] But beforehand, he must get his documents stamped at the district residence. Pressed for time, he has us cross the city in haste. Since I am unable to visit the city, I observe the sights as best I can. The avenue that we have taken is wide, open, and bordered with magnificent trees. The red ochre houses are reminiscent of those in Djenné or Mopti. Rays of sunlight filter through the trees. The river flows lazily on our right. Everything in this city is peaceful and beautiful. One thing that strikes me is that almost every Segou woman that we encounter wears a gold ring between her nostrils. One of our porters explains that this coquettish ornament and sign of good fortune is worn only by women.

Finally, we arrive at the district residence, an elegant two-story palace whose arcades and ornamental latticework walls are pleasing to the eye.

The Three Colors of France

Once all the formalities have been completed, our little convoy heads to the port. I am dumbfounded at the sight of a gigantic metal craft rocking to and fro on the waves. It spews water and grunts loud *pch-pch-pchh* sounds through a kind of lateral anus! Plumes of smoke rise from its thick and slanting stacks. I am seeing a steamboat for the very first time. Unlike the silent, elegant

Bozo pirogues, this is a giant ironclad river monster that smokes and pisses incessantly.

A veritable miniature marketplace extends along the quays, where each vendor hopes to sell the travelers some final provisions for the road or a souvenir of Segou. The bargaining is fierce, and a few quarrels break out here and there. Mr. M'Bodje must even exercise his authority as a "marabout of the White Man's school," as indicated by his suit and "White-White" pince-nez, in order to separate a couple of stubborn combatants. Porters and laptots are transferring sacks and valises onto the boat. Mr. M'Bodje has his porters carry his baggage on board and then pays them before sending them on their way.

Suddenly, an enormous personage in official European garb comes hurtling down the embankment leading to the quay. He is so fat that his neckless head seems to have been stuck directly on to his bull-like chest. His arms, unable to fall at his flanks, extend from either side in the manner of a large bird readying for flight. It is Mr. Monnet, ship's purser of *Le Mage*, and his porters, burdened with food provisions for the white passengers. "Make way! Make way!" cry the merchants in Bambara, "Here comes Fatso following behind his belly!" Each of them steps aside as best they can in order to avoid the enormous mass of flesh that seems propelled by the force of ill-humor alone. Apparently furious to find the quay so encumbered, the purser storms ahead, upsetting all obstacles in his way and carelessly crushing with his thick shoes the displays of small wares and trinkets that the unfortunate vendors have not had time to gather from the ground. Mr. Monnet, a former aide-de-camp in the Armée d'Afrique, belongs to the group of colonials who believe that the use of brute force bolsters and sustains French authority, established in West Africa through gun and cannon fire by the likes of Borgnis-Desbordes, Archinard, and other White leaders with gold cords on their sleeves.

At that very same moment, two laptots are in the process of hoisting an enormous barrel up the inclined plank that serves as a gangway. At the sight of the purser rushing down the bank and waving his arms, the chief laptot shouts, "Hurry, or you'll end up in the water along with your barrel! Fatso is headed straight for you. If you get in his way, he'll start bugling like a bereft elephant and throw you into the water like a bunch of dead animal carcasses!" Never before had a prophecy come to pass so quickly. When Mr. Monnet reaches the base of the gangplank, the laptots still have about a meter left before the load is finally hoisted on board and they can clear the way. The purser's anger explodes with the violence of the first tropical cyclone of the year. He spews a torrent of insults. "Lazy bastards! Filthy Negroes! Sons of bitches! Dirty pigs!" just to cite some of the more moderate expressions to which he subjects the unfortunate laptots. Bellowing, he bears down on them. Knowing his strength and the violence of his character, the laptots throw themselves into the water, taking their barrel with them, preferring to take matters into their own hands rather than be expedited, *manu militari*, by the irascible purser, who clears the gangplank and disappears inside the boat.

"This is unfair, this is just so unfair!" Mr. M'Bodje complains. But who would listen? In those days the White Man, whether he was right or wrong, was always right, or at least that was the general rule. And yet, shortly after that, I would have the opportunity to observe that even deep inside a brute there can be a spark of goodness and one must never give up on humanity.

Pushing and shoving, we clamber noisily aboard. Before our departure, it had been clearly agreed with Mr. M'Bodje that I alone would be in charge of my own travel expenses. Therefore, we part ways. He and his nephew go to their third-class cabin (the boat contains first, second, and third-class cabins), while I remain on the deck, which is reserved for animals and Black-Black Negroes. People settle in as best they can, looking for a place to extend their mats. We are only to pay our fare once the boat is under way.

A preliminary harsh and nasal whistle rends the air. I hear the clank of chains banging against the sides of the boat. The laptots are busy running from one side of the boat to the other. At the second whistle, I can feel the vessel begin to move and sway. The wheels begin to turn, and the paddles churn through the river water, which falls over them in a long and creamy spray. The boat slowly pushes back from the quay and reaches deep water. Its prow seems to be cutting the river in two. It raises a powerful wake that rushes toward the banks, making the Bozo pirogues dance about like frightened colts. Some of them break loose from their moorings. Soon, the port is out of sight.

I stand and go to check the board that lists the fares. Upon reading the ticket prices, I begin to panic. The deck fare to Koulikoro—that is, the last stop before Bamako—costs seven francs. I quickly take all the money I have from my pouch. Alas! Because I had given out small sums of money in each village that we had crossed, out of the fifteen francs that my mother had sent me, I only have two francs left! I had no idea that the price of the fare would be so high, and especially not on the deck.

It was out of the question to call on Mr. M'Bodje for help since we had clearly come to an agreement. And now, I cannot even get off and finish the trip on foot.

At this very moment, the bell rings, calling all travelers to come up and pay their fares. Since in the course of the trip I had developed a bad eye infection due to overexposure to the sun, I use this as a pretext to go last. When it is my turn to pay, I blink my eyes, and almost without thinking about what I am doing, I hand my money pouch to the man who is ahead of me in line and ask him to count out the money for my ticket. As the man repeatedly roots around in my pouch, where of course, he has only been able to find two francs, my heart is beating so hard that my ears are ringing! How is this all going to end? How will the terrible purser react?

Raising his head, the man declares that the pouch does not contain more than two miserable francs. I give a shout and throw myself to the ground, crying and moaning. "I had seven francs! I had seven francs! I don't know how I lost my five-franc piece! It was a big coin! Yaye! Yaye! Mother, I've lost my money! Mother!" The more my conscience scolded me for such bald-faced lies, the more fright made me whimper and exaggerate, playing the role of a miserable victim of circumstance. Of course, Mr. M'Bodje is completely unaware of the situation, since he is now settled in his cabin.

Alerted by my cries, the purser comes out of his office. He asks me why I am bawling as though I had lost my mind. I give him a story with such a degree of composure that he never doubts its validity.

"Where are you going?" he asks.

"I am going to Kati to join my parents during my vacation."

"Who are you and why are you traveling all alone so far from your parents?"

"I am a Fula student and I go to school in Djenné."

"Ah! That's very good. And what have you learned at school?"

"I have learned to read, write, speak French, to sing, and above all I have learned to love France and to serve it even if I or the members of my family have to pay a price for it."

"Very good! Very good! Have you learned any French songs?"

"Yes, Sir."

"Which ones?"

"'La Marseillaise' and 'The Three Colors.'"

"Sing 'The Three Colors' for me."

He doesn't have to ask more than once. I begin to sing with power and conviction:

> Do you know the col-ors
> The three colors of Fra-ance!
> Those that make our hearts dre-am
> Of glory and cha-ance.
> Celestial blue, color of our days
> Red sings of blood, the color of our lo-ove

White is candor and val-or
White is candor and val-or!

The former aide-de-camp, exalted by these noble words and carried away by its rhythm, grabs both my arms and begins to dance, spinning me around as he sings with me in a powerful voice,

White is candor and val-or
White is candor and val-or!

Our two-man dance is accompanied neither by fife nor tabor, but the crowd of passengers begins to clap along, ever ready to rejoice and happy to participate in this unanticipated diversion.

When it is over, the breathless old aide-de-camp stops and says, "You truly are indeed a son of France! You are on a boat that belongs to Eternal France for whom great scholars and great soldiers have died and for whom many more heroes will die.[16] Therefore, stop crying my boy, you will travel on this boat for free, and you will dine at my table."

"Oh, thank you, my good White Man! Thank you, thank you very much!" I had not counted on profiting so well from my situation, and I am immediately sorry about the bad thoughts I had concerning the fat aide-de-camp.

The amount of noise that had overtaken the deck had resulted in attracting the attention of the travelers from the upper classes. Some of them had come down to see what was going on. All of a sudden, a beautiful Fula woman rushes up to me.

"Amkoullel! Amkoullel! Son of my uncle! Where did you come from and what are you doing on this boat?"

Wide-eyed, I see that it is Fanta Hamma, my cousin on my mother's side. She is returning to Bamako in the company of a French official. At the time, she was his "colonial wife." As luck would have it, the purser knows her well. He tells her of my misfortune and how he is planning to set things right for me. My cousin, who is far from being impressed by White people, smiles and amiably pats his fat belly.

"Have my cousin travel first class in my cabin," she says. "There are only two of us and there is room for three."

Mr. Monnet acquiesces. In one fell swoop, I am now promoted to a higher rank than Mr. M'Bodje, who is traveling in third class!

Sometime later, the purser orders that the deck tarps be gathered up in order to rinse the deck with buckets of water. All bundles and mats are removed. The tarps are taken up, and miracle of miracles, a five-franc piece suddenly appears, glinting in the sun, lodged between the deck and the side of the boat! The find is announced so that the owner can step forward. Nobody steps forward to claim the coin. Everyone thus concludes that it must be the coin that I said I had lost, and it is given to me. So as not to betray myself, and to my great inner shame, I am obliged to take it. I spend the next night regretting my lie, which is made still worse by the larceny that I have just committed, in spite of myself, by accepting a sum that I know very well does not belong to me. My head is filled with unanswerable questions. "Why has God made things turn out so well for me? Is it because over the course of my journey I gave my own five francs away to the poor? Shouldn't I instead be punished for lying?" No reason is enough to satisfy me. My conscience is unrelenting in its reprimands, and I am filled with self-contempt. I would spend the entire three-day boat trip divided between the pleasures of an extremely comfortable journey and my inner torments.

The Land-Roving Pirogue of Metal

We must catch the train for Bamako in Koulikoro. Koulikoro was once the capital of Soumangourou Kanté, the blacksmith king who conquered the Ghana Empire before he himself was defeated by Soundiata Keïta, founder of the Mandé Empire of Mali in the thirteenth century. Now, under French occupation, Koulikoro has become a simple administrative district. A squadron of spahis and a cavalry school are garrisoned there.

The pandemonium at the train station is indescribable. Unaware that tickets are not sold until the time of departure, the crowd presses against the large doors that grant access to the ticket counter. Four policemen working for the station chief repel the unfortunate masses with great blows of their whips.

"We no care! We working! Work is work! Hey, you over there! Beat it! Scram!"

Since we can do nothing for our unfortunate brethren, we calmly wait for the doors to open. There, I find Mr. M'Bodje and his nephew, who are also waiting.

Preceded by a shrill whistle, the train for Bamako finally enters the station. Somebody opens the doors to the hall, and Fanta Hamma goes to purchase our tickets.

In Segou, I had discovered my first "smoking boat." In Koulikoro, I discover my first "land-roving pirogue of metal," as people called the railroad. A smoking pirogue that could sail the waters was conceivable because water flows and carries you with it. But the idea that a long and heavy metal pirogue could manage to move on its own power over dry land, this was most certainly high magic, White devil sorcery powerful enough to astound even the greatest magicians of the wild bush!

We pile into open-air passenger cars. Stretching far away into the distance, I can see the two metal rulers over which the train will soon begin to slide more quickly than a Sahel gazelle running from a famished panther (as I learned in school reader number two, by Jean-Louis Monod, and in the booklet entitled *A Travers nos colonies*). I do not place much confidence in the idea. "What happens if the train trips and the wagons lose their balance and fall off the rails? What will happen to the travelers and their baggage?" I ask my cousin which prayer I should recite before setting off on such a formidable adventure. She laughs in my face. "The most effective prayer is to not be afraid. Be a Fula, fear not, and everything will be fine, Insha Allah (God willing)."

Once the travelers have taken their places, the stationmaster blows his whistle, signaling the departure. The conductor blows his horn, the mechanic rings his bell, and the machine utters its own long and rusty cry. The locomotive begins to disgorge plumes of smoke that rise in ragged hanks from its great stack, while every so often, ashes and live cinders fly back and hit us in the face. Puffs of steam gust from the machine's flanks. Brakes unclench, rods and the pistons slowly begin to turn, the engine rattles, the cars clang together, and there is an atrocious grating and screeching. The train finally shudders forward and slowly picks up speed as it begins to wind through the countryside. Rhythmically it chants, *apss-apss! gan-gan! apss-apss! gan-gan! apss-apss! gan-gan! apss-apss! gan-gan!* and *tchou-kou-tchou-gan-gan-gan! tchou-kou-tchou-gan-gan-gan!* in rapid succession, periodically punctuating this with a long and joyful whistle. People, trees, and animals seem to rush at us. I soon forget my fears and think only of watching the scene as it unfolds before my eyes.

It took the train about one hour and a half to cover the fifty kilometers that separated us from Bamako. Night had just fallen. Bamako had become the capital of Upper Senegal and Niger in 1908, and in this capacity, it was also the place of residence of the governor of the territory. From afar it looked otherworldly, for it was lit by electricity. A great sash of light seemed to have been thrown across the hill that rose above the city. This was the road leading from Bamako to Koulouba, the location of the governor's residence. As we drew near, its lamps made me think of large stars dangling from the tree branches.

In Bamako, my cousin and her husband took me home with them. They gave me a room with running water and electric lights. I was fascinated at being able to make water flow from a wall of rock, just by turning the faucet, and at being able to create darkness and light just by pushing a button! That night, before going to bed, I confessed everything to my cousin. She asked me whether I still had the five-franc piece. I handed it to her. She took it. The next day she had it changed into smaller amounts that she distributed, as I watched, to beggars passing in the streets. Only then did the weight that had been crushing me dissipate.

Later that morning, my cousin sent someone to Kati to inform my parents of my arrival. My father Tidjani himself came to get me. More than any outward demonstration of emotion, for that was not his custom, this gesture bore witness to his affection, and I was touched. After arriving late in the afternoon, he decided to return to Kati with me that very evening, as my mother and other relatives were impatiently waiting. At around six o'clock in the evening, at the moment when the sun was casting its final flames over the horizon, he gave the signal to depart. This meant that we would have to cover the greater part of the twelve kilometers that separated us from Kati in the dark.

The Abysmal Lair of the Great Black Hyena

In those days, the land was still heavily forested. The main part of our route passed through a thick wood overrun with hyenas and panthers. At midpoint in our journey, our route edged along a deep, dark chasm known as Dounfing and bordered a steep drop on our left. Overgrown with thick vegetation and thought to be haunted by the most evil of spirits, this chasm was the traditional abode of Diatroufing, that great mythical black hyena with four white paws and a star on her forehead and a mane that glittered in the dark with a thousand sparks of light.

The populace believed that it was preferable to look death in the eye rather than to risk meeting Diatroufing as she was taking in the cool of the evening after sundown (and they were astutely encouraged in this belief by the religious brotherhoods whose ceremonies were interrupted by their comings and goings along the road). After nightfall, the place was studded with fireflies and glowworms, all said to have fallen from the hairs of Diatroufing's coat. This amounts to saying that to journey from Bamako to Kati after nightfall was tantamount to throwing oneself straight into the jaws of the great hyena, mistress of those dark places.

Fanta Hamma was so frightened on our behalf that she wept, persuaded that we were heading straight into the arms of death or into a state of insanity that would be triggered by devils. True, we did risk being attacked by one of the wild animals that haunted the caverns in the hills, or even of being robbed by the gangs of road thieves teeming in the forest. But neither deity nor devil could stop Tidjani from doing something once he had decided to do it. His adage was, "One cannot die before one's hour, and one cannot not die once one's hour has been rung. So why be afraid?" "I promised my wife to return home tonight with our son," he told my cousin. "It is therefore out of the question for us to spend the night in Bamako. And Amadou is now fifteen years old. It is high time he learned to face darkness, devils, sorcerers, brigands, and wild animals."

He hadn't, however, come unarmed. Across his chest he wore a long, razor-sharp saber, and in his right hand he carried a halberd, or small lance with a triangular blade. Thus equipped, solid and muscular, but slender of body and face, I thought that he cut a proud figure indeed. He radiated an aura of strength and tranquility. He handed me a Moorish dagger and showed me how to use it if the need arose.

A griot from Bandiagara who had come to greet Fanta Hamma was present on that day. Taking up his guitar, he began to sing the motto of the Thiams and to praise Tidjani's courage and generosity. He improvised:

> Oh, Tidjani Amadou Thiam
> Today you have given me a new chapter
> To add to your family's glorious motto!
> Devils, sorcerers, wild animals and brigands,
> Take heed, the son of Amadou Ali comes your way,
> Leading his eldest by the hand.
> You cannot stop him.
> He will cross your domain
> Like a shooting star.

When he had finished, in honor of the motto of the Thiams that he had just sung, my cousin gave him five francs, as it is the custom to do with griots. She had engaged a porter, who took up my small trunk. We exchanged our last goodbyes and said our thanks, and we were off!

My father walked ahead of me at a good pace. The porter followed along behind us. The sun was low on the horizon. Everyone that we met on the road on their return to the city exclaimed, "Hey, Fula man! Are you setting out so late for Kati, as though Dounfing did not exist?"

"Allahou akbar!" (God is the greatest!) my father replied.

Around four kilometers outside of Bamako, he stopped under a great fig tree. He pulled a certain number of leaves from the tree, pronounced over each one of them certain Koranic verses corresponding to a particular number, and then threw them to the eight points of space, cardinal and ordinal. He kept one on his person. "Now," he said, "the mouth of the deep bush is muzzled. With God's help, we will be undisturbed until we reach Kati." And he set out again with a firm step, almost joyful, singing at the top of his lungs the great poem composed by El Hadj Omar, entitled *The Saber*, because it is said that like a saber it slices through evil spells and annihilates the workings of evil spirits.

It was almost completely dark. As we advanced, we plunged ever deeper into the obscurity made all the more dense by the trees, which were particularly thick in this region spiked with hills and low mountains, the final ramparts of the Manding Mountains. The underbrush was resonant with the rasping, clicking, and chirruping of insects, punctuated by the more worrisome, intermittent cries of nocturnal animals.

Despite the coolness of the night, I could feel the sweat dripping down my forehead. Yes, I was afraid, and every hollow seemed to be a thieves' den or a trap laid by the devil. But I was absolutely certain that nothing bad could happen to me, so great was the trust that I had in my father.

Hand-built by the squadrons of African workers requisitioned into forced labor (because it was deemed that the military garrison at Kati needed to be connected to Bamako by a road), the red earth track sliced through the shadows. Suddenly, as though confronted by danger, it reared up and then climbed carefully over a swelling in the earth. It was then that we glimpsed the dark chasm on our left peopled with giant trees clothed in an impenetrable vegetal armor of interwoven vines and thorns. This was the south entrance to Dounfing.

A blinking host of fireflies strafed the air with stripes of light like tiny stars falling from the sky. From the depths of the chasm rose a chorus of nocturnal noises to which a peculiar echo lent an uncanny scope. The croaking of frogs, mingled with the hooting of owls, was periodically interrupted by the yowling of wild cats. We could hear the cascading roar of a waterfall crashing noisily into the abyss from a height of several dozen meters. All this combined gave the place a somber and terrifying air. We were indeed on the threshold of that accursed place. A shiver shot through my entire body, but it was an involuntary nervous reaction. My mind had remained calm.

The narrow road that wound next to the chasm formed an arc that was about two kilometers in length. My father took my hand. About half an hour later, after we had crossed the final obstacle, a panther growled far behind us, irritated and no doubt disappointed at having missed out on a good dinner. My father breathed a sigh of relief and praised God. In the end, neither devil nor wild animal nor brigand had come to harass us. In the dead of the night and unharmed we had crossed the domain of Diatroufing, the terrible black hyena, sower of terror in human hearts.

After Dounfing, the road was once again wide and reassuring. Soon, the lights of Kati began to twinkle in the distance. We were finally home, where all the members of the family, surrounded by our friends, were waiting for us.

My mother stood there smiling, still just as erect, still just as beautiful as ever. A simple ribbon of black velvet tied around her neck was adornment enough for her. She embraced me, but did nothing more, for Fula decorum does not permit mothers to show their feelings toward their own children, and certainly not in public, especially where a grown fifteen-year-old boy is concerned! African tradition of old—at least in my milieu—refrained from emotional outpourings. For us, actions spoke louder than words and the long trek that I had undertaken just to come and see my mother, as well as her uninterrupted concern for me throughout our years of separation, spoke for themselves.

On the other hand, I rushed to play with my two new little sisters, Aminata (the one whom my brother Hammadoun had engaged to his friend before he died) and Fanta, the youngest. At first Aminata was afraid of me, but when I swung her into the air she quickly forgot her fears and began to laugh. Then I took little Fanta and tied her onto my back as a big sister would have done.

Following the meal, I was besieged with questions. Everyone wanted to know what I had experienced over the years that had gone by. I was asked about Bandiagara, about Djenné, about the lands that I had traveled through, the people that I had met, their customs, and so forth, as is the custom when a traveler arrives from a long journey. This was the first audience to listen to my personal adventures. I was not lacking in anecdotes, nor in words to relate them. It was a long and happy evening and it stretched far into the night.

6

In the Military Town of Kati

Surrounded on all sides by red sandstone hills, Kati is an old Bambara village that sits at the entrance to the Beledougou region north of Bamako. In days gone by, the once densely forested hills harbored tribes of vociferous monkeys and throngs of brilliantly colored birds. Today, a military camp is built atop the central hill that rises from the final sloping ramparts of the Manding Mountains. Due to these combined attributes, the Kati plateau is truly a natural fortress.

Before the French occupation of the country, Kati was but a small hamlet known for its fertile land, irrigated by a permanent river that meanders through the valley hollows before it empties into the Niger at Bamako. The French turned Kati into an army post that gradually grew in importance and became the seat of the Second Regiment of Tirailleurs Sénégalais, with the First Regiment being stationed at Saint-Louis in Senegal.[1]

During the period in question here, there were at least two thousand tirailleurs stationed in the city thanks to the war and the magnitude of the recruitment effort. Either they were leaving for the front or they were in military training. Most of the soldiers deploying to France left their wives behind in Kati. The wives lived off of their husbands' small pensions, but in order to add to their incomes, they often became merchants, open-air cooks, caterers, cloth dyers, seamstresses, and more. African women are courageous and very resourceful, and it is quite rare for them not to exercise some small trade in order to survive, particularly when times are hard.

Because of the size of the population, the city had become a rendezvous for artisans and tradesmen of every ethnicity. But the place was also a haven for a variety of unsavory characters. Swindlers, card sharks, prostitutes, con artists, and thieves of all sorts, in addition to a good number of charlatans, fetish priests, fortune-tellers, and false marabouts, all vied to outdo one another selling charms and protective gris-gris, which sold like hotcakes to the unfortunate souls who were leaving for the front.

In the crowded streets of the city, where ambling soldiers rubbed elbows with people dressed in a wide-ranging array of clothing styles, one could hear all the Sudanese languages being spoken, with a sprinkling here and there of French words and expressions accented with "local flavor." In those days, this was not called "petit nègre" but, rather, "moi ya dit toi ya dit," or "me say you say." By day, the cramped population worked and milled about in close quarters. By night they drank, sang, and danced until the wee hours of the morning.

Compared to life in Bandiagara and Djenné, this colorfully frenetic and overcrowded city constituted a surprising spectacle for me. As I was free to roam on my own, I suddenly found myself immersed in a world where good role models were not exactly present on every street corner. Luckily for me, my parents kept me firmly in hand and provided a good example that kept me from losing myself.

When I arrived in Kati in 1915, the city was divided into three large sectors: the military camp located at the top of the hill, the residential zone known as Sananfara located at the edge of the river, and Katidougou-koro, or "old Kati." My parents lived in Sananfara, where my father had created a new neighborhood. When he had arrived in Kati with my mother, in order to house the family, he had commissioned the construction of several mud-brick houses on unoccupied land near the military camp. Later, at the time of the great famine of 1914, the Dogons had fled the region of Bandiagara and come to take refuge in Kati, where they offered their labor to anyone who would hire them. Because they knew Tidjani Thiam and his status as a former provincial chieftain, they naturally gathered around him and were soon joined by others. It was then that my father created and organized for them the neighborhood known as Kadobougou ("village of the Dogons"). Today this neighborhood is known as Kadokoulouni (*Kado* being another name for the Dogons). In that land of exile, Tidjani became a kind of adviser and natural defender for them.

The size of the neighborhood eventually attracted the attention of the military authorities, and notably that of Colonel Bouery and Colonel Molard, commander of the garrison in Kati. They suggested that my father be named neighborhood headman. By a curious reversal of fortune, he acquired this position with the support of an Upper Senegal and Niger inspector of administrative affairs who was none other than Charles de la Bretèche, the former commandant of Bandiagara district, and the very same man who, following the sad events that took place in Toïni, had had no choice but to condemn Tidjani to prison and exile.

As she had done in every other place where she had lived, my mother had succeeded in developing a sizable trade in cloth and various regional goods. And thanks to an entirely new activity for her, that of fashion designer, she had even become famous. One day, the director of the CFAO (Compagnie française de l'Afrique occidentale, the French West Africa Company), had asked her who had created the design of her wrap, the beauty of which he had found striking. She replied that she had created the design herself and that she had had it made by her own weavers. The director asked her to supply him with small samples of all her designs. If he liked them, he would send them to France to have them produced in large quantities. From that day forward, my mother created a number of designs that were all accepted by the CFAO and that she named after the most beautiful or famous women in the city. These designs remained fashionable for nearly fifteen years.

Not only did the CFAO pay her five francs for every new design that she created, but in addition—and this was extremely rare at the time for natives and especially for a woman—it extended her a line of credit. At the beginning of every month, without having to pay up front, my mother took out a certain quantity of merchandise that she would then resell in the city. At the end of the month, she would reimburse the sum due and take out more stock. To say that she lived well is an understatement.

With the influx of military wives in Kati, buyers were not lacking. A number of them acquired the habit of coming to chat with my mother, discussing their problems, asking for advice, and, in times of need, borrowing money from her. For all these women who were alone, cut off from their families, and often burdened with children, Kadidja had become a kind of mother figure. When one of them had problems, her companions told her, "Go to see *Flamousso*" (Fula woman, in Bambara). If it was a man, he was told, "Go to see Tidjani."

Little by little, without any sort of proselytizing and solely by virtue of his qualities and his example, my father ended up converting a number of Bambaras to Islam. He was, I believe, one of the first in the region to do so.

The small shop that he had opened was located across from the military camp, and this led to friendships with a number of French and African soldiers. He continued to work as a tailor-embroiderer and always created extremely beautiful embroidered boubous. But above all, what attracted people to him was his moral and religious reputation. As in Bougouni, people considered him to be a kind of marabout and came to ask him for his advice and even for his prayers.

He had a strange ability, either innate or transmitted, I do not know which, that consisted of healing the mentally ill. When a deranged person was brought to him, he kept the patient at the house until the unfortunate had an attack, began shouting, and threw himself to the ground. Then Tidjani would remove his sandal, recite several verses from the Koran over it, and then use it to administer a substantial blow to the ear of the unfortunate person. By means of a curious phenomenon, the person would immediately fall into a deep sleep that could last half a day. Sometimes, the person would drool abundantly and mucus would run from his nostrils. When he awoke, my father would have him take a bath and that was that. The person went home cured.

One day, a marabout friend of his said, "Be careful Tidjani! Your manner of caring for the mentally ill will turn against your family. Evil spirits always get their revenge when they have been violently dislodged. And that is what you are doing."

"Too bad!" replied my father. "I prefer to care for the greatest number of mentally ill people possible at the risk of seeing my own children become mentally ill themselves, rather than leave these unfortunates in their current state."

Alas, to a large extent, the marabout's prediction came true. One of the daughters born to Tidjani and Kadidja in Kati became mentally ill, and Tidjani was unable to heal her. Their younger son, my half-brother, also went insane. My father did everything in his power to heal him, but in vain. The children born from the marriage of my half-sister also experienced problems of this sort at various times in their lives, but fortunately these were intermittent.

Of course, my father never received payment for his services or for his religious aid. Not only would such a thing have been against his nature, but it would also have been against the divine categorical injunction that figures in the Koran and enjoins, "Do not exchange My signs for a small price" (2:41).[2] Unfortunately, too many marabouts, or so they are called these days—for a simple veneer of Islamic knowledge seems sufficient for some to assume this title—accept money to "do something" in someone's favor or, even worse, to harm others. Very often they set a price for their services, thereby making the entire practice into a veritable profession. This kind of behavior, unfortunately now commonplace in Muslim African societies today, is formally contrary to Islam, and the great marabouts from Bandiagara such as Alfa Ali, Tierno Bokar, and Tierno Sidi, who were famous for their knowledge and spiritual elevation, never did anything of the sort.

My New Waaldé Association

In the days following my arrival in Kati, I began to feel lonely and somewhat adrift. Luckily, there was a young Dogon from Bandiagara at the house who was two years older than I. Oumarou Tembély had come to Kati in Captain Minary's "baggage," so to speak. He had served as the captain's houseboy back in Bandiagara and had been brought along to Kati in 1914. Oumarou led me around the city and even took me to see the captain's house. But because since childhood I had been used to being surrounded by boys of my age, it wasn't long before I began to miss being in an association with other young people. I decided to start looking for some friends.

It was then that I learned of a Bambara youth association in the Sananfara neighborhood that was led by someone named Bamoussa. Bamoussa was also a master of the knife (performer of ritual sacrifices) of the Bambara N'Tomo initiation society for uncircumcised boys. He therefore held a powerful position. I went to see him to request admission into his association (called a *ton* in Bambara, the equivalent of a *waaldé*). It was announced that at that moment he was in the N'Tomo sacred grove. I asked for directions to that place and went to seek him out. Bad idea!

I found him in the process of immolating a chicken that he was offering as a sacrifice to N'Tomo. As I approached, he raised his eyes and recognized by my Fula skin and my manner of approach that I was not an initiate of his ton. To ensure that he was not mistaken, he rose and walked toward me. "Halt!" he cried. He asked me several questions while executing a series of ritual gestures. I understood nothing, and for good reason! I could not answer a single question or identify a single gesture. At that point he called out, "*Boussan-tigi!* Carriers of the whips! Here you have someone who is deaf, dumb, and blind. Heal him!" Immediately, two young men armed with switches rushed at me. Without further ado, they began to strike me with so many blows that I had to cut and run, but not without first vehemently insulting them for their unjustified aggression. I had just learned at my own expense that in the land of the Bambaras, not just anybody can go just anywhere.

I returned home, extremely mortified. For an entire week I thought of nothing else except seeking revenge and finding a way to gain support among the youth of Bamoussa's ton. Meanwhile, I made the acquaintance of a Bambara boy my age who lived in our neighborhood in Kadobougou. His name was Famory Keïta. Physically stronger than Bamoussa, he also performed ritual sacrifices for N'Tomo. After I told him of my misadventure, he not only offered me his friendship, but also offered to create an alliance against the boys of the Sananfara neighborhood led by Bamoussa. Conditions were ripe for founding our own association. With the young people of our neighborhood, along with the sons of the tirailleur families who knew my parents, our recruitment effort would be easy, as long as my parents would grant me their permission.

I knew that as a former provincial chief, Tidjani would always be happy to host people at his home and that he would not have any objections. But my mother had yet to be convinced. And the least that can be said is that she was not malleable and moldable like potter's clay. I decided to wait for a favorable occasion. One day she asked me what might make me happy. Seizing the moment, I replied, "Mother—may God lengthen the weave of your days!—what I would really like would be that you allow me to create a waaldé here."

"Ask your father's permission first," she said. "If he agrees, I will also agree. I will give you the money you need to cover your expenses."

I immediately went to see my father. As I expected, he was very favorable to the idea. He even gave me some advice.

"Organize a big feast in order to gather as many of the neighborhood youths as possible," he said, "and use the occasion to announce your plan. I will give you one or two lambs for a good méchoui roast."

My mother gave me ten francs. I then sent out a general invitation to all the boys and girls in the neighborhood, as well as to the children of the tirailleurs. On the big day, my family prepared a great feast. Twenty boys and ten girls from different backgrounds gathered in our courtyard. After everyone had eaten well and performed a variety of different African dances, I took the floor amid a general euphoria. "O sons of my mother! An idea has come to me. It is inspired by the joy that we have all felt this evening at being together. I propose that we join into an official association so that we can meet regularly, organize our activities, and be strong enough to stand up to the boys in the other neighborhoods." This declaration was greeted with a cheer. "And because it is wartime and we live in a military city, I propose that our ton be organized in a manner similar to the army. I, Amadou Hampâté Bâ, also called Thiam, will enroll first. Who else wants to sign up?"

"I will!" cried Oumarou Tembély, who was immediately followed by Famory Keïta and all the others. Then it was Famory Keïta's turn to speak. He was the oldest and also the strongest of us. "Because he knows paper and pen, and because the idea was born in his head, I propose that Amadou Bâ-Thiam serve as our Colonel Molard. May each of the enlistees go to him and raise his right hand and state, 'You are my Colonel Molard, and I am a soldier in your regiment!'"

Each of the boys who were my friends came to raise his right hand while pronouncing this new kind of pledge of allegiance. In turn, I climbed atop an overturned mortar and swore to help my friends and brothers in every circumstance and to never betray them. The first youth association in the neighborhood of Kadobougou was born.

To lead our little ton, I chose seven boys whose duties corresponded to a series of military ranks. Since I myself was the colonel, my second in command, who could be none other than Famory Keïta, received the rank of battalion commander. After him came Oumarou Tembély, captain of the supply corps, and then a captain chief of staff, a lieutenant commander of the section known as "native recruitment," a second lieutenant, sergeant majors, sergeants, corporals, and so on.

In the month of August 1915, our ton already included nearly fifty boys and thirty girls from a variety of ethnic groups and was spread over several neighborhoods. Each neighborhood constituted a "regiment" with its officers and troops. For military cords, our officers wore braids that we made ourselves and that were dyed yellow with kola nut juice and sewn onto a black background. They looked just like the "threads" on the uniforms of French officers! As for our medals and other decorations, they came from Petit-Beurre cookie boxes, where we found all the necessary honor insignia of the French Republic in rather thick cardboard and true to size.

We organized "military parades" through the bush, our wooden guns on our shoulders, and sometimes marched as far as the Dounfing chasm in order to go and defy the vicious Diatroufing at the far edge of her lair. We also held pitched battles that we pompously called "military exercises." The real soldiers of Kati found our military parodies quite amusing. As for the army cooks, they enjoyed offering me as many empty boxes of Petit-Beurre cookies that we needed in order to decorate our valiant soldiers.

When our troops were finally tough enough, I officially declared war on Bamoussa and his association. Organized according to the customary rules, the confrontation took place one night under a beautiful full moon on Lingué-Koro square in Kati. Bamoussa and his young men were defeated, and we ran to take over his sacred wood. It took the intervention of the elders to force us to return the sacred objects, since these could not be removed by anyone, not even a conqueror!

Our association would continue to exist until February 1918, the date of the arrival in Sudan of Blaise Diagne, whom Georges Clemenceau had sent on a tour of French West Africa as part of a massive recruitment effort that specifically targeted young people. The entire associative and traditional way of life of the youth was disrupted. I will have the occasion to discuss this further a bit later.

Sometime after these events, I was admitted into the Bambara N'Tomo society for uncircumcised youth. In Bougouni, I had become acquainted with the Tiebleni society, which was reserved for very small children. As I mentioned earlier, it was the custom at the time for minority Muslims living in a majority Bambara or Malinké society to accept for their children a purely formal affiliation in the children's initiation societies, which in this milieu, blended with age associations. Otherwise, no social life would have been possible. Of course, we did not participate in ceremonies or in sacrifices, but at least we were not obligated to hide when the great masks made their ritual appearance. Knowledge of the ritual gestures also allowed us to approach the sacred groves without risk of being chased away at the end of a whip.

In those days there were three sanctuaries in Kati: the Christian church, with its school and nursery; the mosque, with its madrasa (school) and its *zaouïa* (meeting and prayer room for the members of Sufi brotherhoods); and finally the *djetou*, the sacred grove of the Bambaras, where they generally celebrated their ceremonies.

Although my father Tidjani was an extremely rigorous Muslim where he and his family were concerned, he was also very tolerant. He had taken this verse from the Koran as his motto: "There shall be no compulsion in [acceptance of] religion. The right course has become clear from the wrong" (2:256).[3] I had a Christian friend named Marcel who regularly attended mass every Sunday. Compelled by my endless curiosity, I went with him one day in order to see what was happening inside. As soon as I returned home, I told my father about this experience and described to him in detail the ceremony, the songs, the words, and the movements of the priest, whom I had observed very carefully. I knew that he would not blame me for doing this because, like Tierno Bokar, he was not opposed to what could contribute to gaining knowledge, and especially to what could allow someone to judge something for himself and not from hearsay. He listened to me calmly and when I asked him if I could go back he said, "Accompany your friend if you wish. Listen to everything that the priest says and accept it, except if he says that there are three Gods and that God has a son. God is unique and he has no son. Other than that, take and retain what is good from his words and leave the rest aside."

A Hasty Circumcision

When classes began again in September 1915, it was out of the question for me to return to Djenné, given that I had slipped away without telling anyone that I was leaving. In truth, this did not worry me in the least, and it certainly did not displease my mother, who had never viewed my studies at the White Man's school with a favorable eye. As for my father, he did not seem to have any particular opinion on the subject.

There was another problem that worried me much more: that of my circumcision. According to Fula as well as Toucouleur custom, I should have been circumcised at the age of twelve at the latest, while I was still living in Bandiagara. But because I had been requisitioned for school, this had not happened. The date for circumcisions always fell during the cold season, when school was in session. Later in Djenné, it had also been impossible, so that when I arrived in Kati in 1915, despite my age, I was still uncircumcised and a bilakoro (literally a "let it ripen"). Traditionally, I belonged to the class of "boys with dirty hands": those with no rights, only duties. Any circumcised boy, even if he were only eight years old, had the right to send me on errands, to insult me, even to beat me, without my being permitted to protest. And if I had protested, the circumcised boys would have taken me by force into a thicket and pummeled me for having dared to stand up to one of them.

I badgered my parents constantly to have me circumcised, but my father avoided the subject. When the cold season arrived toward the end of 1915, I knew that all my friends were preparing to be circumcised. I would then be the last older bilakoro of all. I would be forced to defer to them in everything. Not only would I no longer be able to be their chief, but I wouldn't even be able to belong to their association. I begged my parents to have me circumcised at the same time as Bamissa, Youba Sidibé, and others. My father replied that the family was not prepared for such an event. As I was to understand later, the circumcision of a boy in my family would have in fact rallied all the Toucouleurs, Fulas, and even Dogons living in Kati, Bamako, and Bandiagara, not to mention all sorts of griots and courtiers. And all the people who would arrive to participate in the great feast that precedes the event would no doubt have stayed at my parents' house during the entire length of my seclusion in order to also participate in the "emergence feast." It would have cost a fortune.

My father asked me to wait until the following year. Disheartened and completely dejected, I asked my mother—without telling her what my intentions were—for permission to go to Bamako to visit my cousin Fanta Hamma. My mother gave me the money for a Bamako-Kati round-trip ticket, which cost sixty centimes. I bought a one-way ticket for the price of thirty-five centimes.

When I arrived at my cousin's house, I explained my problem to her and asked whether she could have me circumcised at the Bamako dispensary. We would then send someone to inform my parents that I had gotten circumcised and that I had renounced all the customary ceremonies.

My cousin, who was very fond of me, was moved by the thought that if I were to remain a bilakoro for another year I would lose the status that I held with all my comrades, and that I would be at the mercy of their mockery, jokes, and even their brutality.

She went to see a friend of hers who had once been a doctor's concubine and who had later become a nurse. She was called Fatouma Dogotoro (Doctor Fatouma). My cousin told her my story and assured her that there would be no negative reaction from my parents. Fatouma Dogotoro spoke to Doctor Griewand. He instructed the male head nurse to circumcise me the next day at eleven o'clock in the morning.

The next day, I arrived at my appointment exactly on time. My cousin had had a special boubou sewn for me along with a hat shaped like crocodile jaws, which was the traditional costume worn by circumcised boys. The operation was successful, at least at first. A friend of the family named Abdallah (and thus my "father," according to tradition) took it upon himself to go to Kati to inform my parents that I had quietly gotten circumcised. Apparently, when he gave Tidjani the news, Tidjani stared at him, nodding.

"Amadou is truly your son," he said, "for he is just as stubborn as you are!" And then he burst into laughter. My mother had a fit, as she was extremely disappointed that she would not be able to host a grand feast. I had not really understood that the reason my parents had wanted to delay the circumcision by a year was that they needed time to garner the means to host a great celebration feast worthy of the Bâs, Diallos (my mother's clan), and Thiams.

Following the operation at the dispensary, I should have been healed within four or five days. Unfortunately, when he applied the bandage, the nurse had not left an opening for passing urine, and the site got infected as a result. I was cared for competently, but I had to stay in Bamako for about two weeks. This was of little importance to me. What was important was that

I had been circumcised ahead of my comrades, who would still have to face a three-month period of seclusion as Bambara custom required. I would be the first to return to Kati wearing the traditional hat, and invested with the quality of *kamalenkoro* ("adult" in the traditional sense of the word). I was thus able to retain preeminence over my comrades and remain their chief.

When I arrived home, my parents did not rebuke me. They had also finally understood the reason for my indiscipline and they forgave me for it. They showered me with gifts in celebration of the circumcision. My father bought two beautiful horses and not only began to teach me everything he know about horses (their anatomy, their illnesses, the names and symbolic meanings of their colors and markings, and so on), but also the art of equitation in all its fine points. Like every young Fula born in Bandiagara, I knew how to ride a horse, but I had not considered myself a true horseman worthy of that name. It was in Kati that I acquired my equestrian knowledge, at the painful price, it is true, of several serious falls and numerous fractures that left my left leg somewhat deformed.

My father also taught me to sew and embroider so that one day I could exercise the profession of tailor-embroiderer as he and Tierno Bokar did. And he also found the time to teach me his religious knowledge.

I therefore was not lacking in activities, all the more so given that our association, as it grew older, had more and more to face the traditional duties reserved for the youth to contribute to the community. These duties included such tasks as mortaring houses, helping the elderly and the isolated, and so on.

None of these activities interfered with me spending a good amount of time with my young Dogon compatriot Oumarou Tembély, who served as a houseboy for Lieutenant Cottelier, Captain Minary's successor. When Captain Minary had gone to fight at the front at his own request, he had, in the good old colonial tradition that predated 1936, left to his successor his dishes, his camping gear, and his cookware, along with his entire domestic staff. This included a tirailleur who served as an errand boy, a ventilator operator (panka), a sweeper, and us, his two little unpaid helpers. I sometimes went to work with Oumarou. I helped him make the bed and set the table, I operated the ventilator, and occasionally I did the dishes. Of course, my parents were completely unaware that I was carrying out these domestic tasks without any other pay than the satisfaction of my curiosity toward the ways in which White people lived, and the possibility of sampling the leftovers and crusts of white bread. What punishment my father, and especially my mother, who did not take honor lightly, would have inflicted on me if they had known that I had gone to scrape the bottoms of the pots of White people! My mother would have been capable of cutting off the end of my tongue!

Although not as brilliant as they had been in Bandiagara, the evening gatherings at the house were not lacking, and the traditional tales I heard continued to sustain me.

To these various activities I soon added that of public scribe for the wives of the tirailleurs who wished to correspond with their husbands. I read their letters, and composed and wrote their responses in exchange for a few small coins. With these women, who could become widows from one day to the next, I discovered the nature of worry and misfortune. But I also learned about joy, courage, frivolity, chastity, and debauchery, for the weakest of them were easy prey for the numerous seducers operating in the city.

Return to School

Time was passing. One day, I believe it was in the year 1917, I had gone to the station in Kati to wait for the arrival of the travelers coming from the west by the daily express train that connected Kayes to Bamako (this was known as the "K-B train"). To my great surprise, in one of the train cars, I saw my former classmate and school rival from Bandiagara and Djenné dressed in the superb uniform of the Gorée normal school students. It was Yagama Tembély, whose father, Baye Tabéma Tembély, had alerted us to the forthcoming declaration of war during the summer of 1914.

He wore a suit of navy blue cloth decorated with gold crests and gold buttons, and proudly sported a cap adorned with an insignia in the shape of a golden bee. His shoes, a rare luxury, were made of real leather and were laced at the ankles. "What!" I said to myself. "Your former schoolmate from Bandiagara is studying at the normal school, he is almost as well dressed as a noncommissioned officer, and here you are, wasting your time as a little houseboy for soldiers and women?" It was a shock. I was suddenly filled with the desire to return to school.

As soon as I reached the house, I spoke to my father about it. Instead of making a fuss, he took me to see the native school monitor who was the director of the Kati primary school at that time, Mr. Fatoma Traoré. Very shortly afterward, there I was, seated on one of the school benches. Of course, it was a step backward to return to primary school after I had already attended the regional school and obtained my Primary Studies Certificate. But since I did not have the papers to prove it, I had to start all over again from the beginning. That was the price to be paid for running away.

Taking my level into account, Mr. Traoré admitted me into the first and most advanced class. Although the school year was almost over, I earned the ranking of first in the class with no trouble. Yagama's image haunted me. I wanted to be admitted to the normal school like him and not be a tailor-embroiderer-horseman, and still less a volunteer houseboy and dishwasher, or public scribe for tirailleurs and women. I had decided to study arduously and to cram doubly hard to make up for lost time. Unfortunately, I didn't learn much of anything new since our teaching monitor barely knew more than I did. It was not until the following year, with the arrival of Mr. Molo Coulibaly, who was a real schoolteacher with a diploma from the normal school (Mr. Traoré had been deployed), that the school in Kati began to improve and benefit from serious instruction.

I had scarcely returned to my studies when Warrant Officer Fadiala Keïta, the Second Regiment's mail officer, requested that a literate schoolboy be assigned to him to help him with his work. The volume of mail exchanged between the tirailleurs at the front and their wives who had remained behind in Kati was ever more voluminous, and he was not able to sort through and distribute all the letters by himself. I was assigned to do that job, and that is how I became "vaguemestre auxiliaire de l'armée à titre civil" (civilian auxiliary army mail officer). Once a week, I went to help Warrant Officer Fadiala Keïta sort and distribute letters. I sometimes also served as a second witness in the payment of money orders to the wives of the tirailleurs. At the same time, I continued my activity as a public scribe, which became even more substantial thanks to my new job, and I earned an income that was far from minimal. I was sometimes able to earn up to five or six francs a week at a time when an African soldier was only paid fifteen francs a month! I used part of what I earned to buy clothing (people said that I was "dressed up like an ear of corn"), and the rest went to helping to support the members of my association.

In those days, I ended up getting to know all the native and noncommissioned officers (as they were called to distinguish their corps from that of the French officers) of the Second Regiment in Kati. It goes without saying that I became—and I have remained—an expert on the subject of military bugle calls.

The Warrant Officer and the King's Son

Thanks to my unlimited free entry into the camp and to my connection to Warrant Officer Fadiala Keïta in particular, I ended up playing a special role as eyewitness to an incident whose consequences could have been tragic. Warrant Officer Fadiala Keïta and Abdelkader Mademba Sy, son of Mademba Sy, king of Sansanding (a city-state located on the Niger to the northeast of Segou) were the actors. The details of this incident are apparently still recounted in Kati today.

In truth, Mademba Sy was not an ordinary king. Born in Senegal, he had grown up in Saint-Louis where he had completed secondary school. Like all those born in the four privileged communes of Saint-Louis, Rufisque, Dakar, and Gorée, he enjoyed the status of "French citizen." This was a royal title that was much coveted at the time, because it granted its holders equal rights with the metropolitan French. It also sheltered them from the arbitrary and humiliating treatment that could befall all other Africans, who were nothing but "French subjects."

An official with the postal service by profession, he had launched into politics. Thanks to his status as a French citizen, he had even served as the head of the Sudan Political Bureau. Very close to Colonel Archinard, he had worked with the colonel in establishing the French presence in the country through the gradual installation of telegraph lines as the conquest progressed. In particular, it was he who had installed the telegraph line linking Kayes to Bamako. This he had done at gunpoint under particularly difficult and dangerous conditions, for the line was the target of frequent attacks at the time.

In compensation for his good and loyal service, Colonel Archinard had gifted him the city-state of Sansanding, and "in the name of the French Republic," he had named him king of this state, just as he had done in Bandiagara for his friend Aguibou Tall. This is how Mademba Sy went from exercising the profession of simple postman to finding himself king of the city-state of Sansanding. Backed by unconditional support from the French, he exercised such absolute power over his subjects that he was nicknamed the "Pharaoh of the Niger Bend."

When the war broke out, Mademba Sy sent his own sons to fight under the French colors as a sign of his gratitude to France, as did other important Sudanese families who were on more or less good terms with France.

One of his sons, Abdelkader, had, like all his brothers, studied in Algeria at the Maison-Carrée. He had returned with a *Licence* and had entered into a series of very profitable business activities.[4] He owned four trading posts: one in Sansanding, and three others in Segou, Barmandougou, and Djenné. As soon as he was able, he put his affairs in order and enlisted under the French flag for the duration of the war. He enlisted in Segou and was then sent to the Second Regiment in Kati in order to complete his military training.

Although his father was a French citizen, he and all his other brothers were nothing but "French subjects," because they had not been born in one of the four privileged communes of Senegal.[5] He thus arrived in Kati as a simple Tirailleur Sénégalais, on a date that I am not able to identify. He was issued two regulation uniforms, which duly came with that obligatory emblem of the native soldier, the classic red fez topped with a pompom.

He was housed in a round hut with a thatched roof along with three other comrades in the tirailleurs camp. In those days, the daily ration was two hundred fifty grams of rice, five hundred grams of whole millet or corn, a handful of salt and hot peppers, and a piece of beef. Being a prince and wealthy merchant, Abdelkader was used to eating fine food and sleeping in a nice, big bed. From one day to the next, he found himself deprived of all comfort, sleeping on a thin mat on the ground, which was very humid during the rainy season, and eating for the most part millet gruel seasoned with salt and hot peppers. He was so unsettled by the experience that he almost went insane. He could be seen pacing up and down like an automaton. He talked to himself as though he were questioning the void. He, who had hoped to be sent off to the front in glory to fight and even to sacrifice his life if it came to that, confided these words to some of his friends: "How could I have willingly signed up for such misery?"

One day, Warrant Officer Fadiala Keïta was resting on a chaise longue under the shelter where, just across from the camp entrance, my father Tidjani had laid out his wares for potential buyers. Abdelkader happened to come out. Lost in thought, he walked right by the warrant officer without noticing him and thus without saluting him. Offended by this dereliction of duty, Fadiala Keïta ordered Sergeant Mari Diarra, who was in the vicinity, to call the tirailleur back and to have him do it on the double.

The sergeant ran after Abdelkader, who was already about one hundred meters away. Not remembering his name, the sergeant called out, "Hey! Tirailleur!"

All the tirailleurs who were walking on the road turned their heads except for Abdelkader, who kept walking, lost in his inner thoughts. Catching up with him, Sergeant Mari Diarra gave him a vigorous tap on the shoulder and cried, "Halt!"

Abruptly wrenched from his daydream, Abdelkader jumped. He turned, saw the sergeant and executed a military salute.

"Are you, or are you not a tirailleur?" exclaimed the breathless Mari Diarra in Bambara.

"Yes, Sergeant, I am."

"Then why do you not respond when you are called 'tirailleur'?"

"I did not realize that you were talking to me, Sergeant."

"Oh, I see," sneered the sergeant. "The title of tirailleur does not suit you. Turn around! March! On the double! Warrant Officer Fadiala Keïta is waiting for you."

Abdelkader took off so fast that the sergeant had to run to keep up with him. Warrant Officer Fadiala Kaeïta was still reclining on the chaise longue under my father's shelter, and my father was watching the scene. When Abdelkader arrived, he looked him over with a stern eye, and without getting up he said, "Tirailleur! Do we walk past a warrant officer without saluting him, and then not respond when we are called? This is because the warrant officer is beneath you, and even contemptible, correct?"

"No, sir," replied Abdelkader. "I did not see you. I am sorry and I beg your pardon."

"Of course," replied the warrant officer. "The Prince of Sansanding, with a *Licence* diploma in who knows what, cannot even see a minuscule warrant officer of the colonial infantry, especially when this warrant officer is nothing but a Malinké peanut eater![6] Well, Abdelkader Mademba! Now hear this! In this place, there are no sons of Haïdara, no sons of Tall, nor of Ouane, nor of Sy. There are only the sons of *this*." With his right index finger he pointed at the warrant officer's stripe on his left sleeve and then traced a circle around his wrist with his finger. To teach you to be more attentive in the future," he added, "you will spend three days in the brig!"

The warrant officer ordered Sergeant Marri Diarra to lead the tirailleur Abdelkader Mademba Sy to the brig, where every day he would have to walk several times around a six-meter circle carrying all his equipment on his back. This included his gun, his bayonet, his cartridges, and his other military gear, all of it topped with a brick.

So poor Abdelkader was led away like a guilty criminal to the brig where he stoically completed his three-day punishment. As soon as he was released, he wrote to his father the king to tell him of his misfortunes. He reminded him that he had enlisted of his own accord, not to collect wood and pick up garbage, but to go and fight at the front in the service of France. He added that, because he could not rescind his enlistment before the war was over and since it was out of the question for him to desert, he had decided that if he was not sent to the front within three months, he would kill himself.

Certainly, as a simple "French subject," Abdelkader had no right to any special treatment. But the king of the city-state of Sansanding had a long arm. He wrote to his former leader and benefactor Colonel Archinard, who had since become a general and military governor in the city of Paris, and described the predicament in which his son Abdelkader, whose birth Archinard had witnessed, now found himself. Immediately, Archinard intervened with all the power at his disposal, which was significant. He presented the affair and situation of the tirailleur Abdelkader Mademba Sy to the council president and war minister. The case was given priority status and was settled within two weeks. "Monsieur" Abdelkader Mademba Sy (and not the "so-called," or *nommé*, as simple French subjects were designated) was henceforth a naturalized French citizen, which gave him the right to transmit this status to his future descendants.

A cablegram, addressed to the governor general in Dakar and to the general superior commander of the outfit troops, stipulated that ex-tirailleur second class Abdelkader Mademba Sy, garrisoned with the Second Regiment of Tirailleurs Sénégalais in Kati, was to be transferred to the French army as a French citizen, with all the rights and privileges pertaining to this quality.

On that very same day, Abdelkader traded his simple tirailleur's garb for a handsome French uniform. He was placed in a comfortable barracks, and his name was added to the list of French soldiers with whom he would henceforth work, recreate, eat, and sleep. He was through with having to do the bidding of the native noncommissioned officers, and he was through with their punishments.

But material comforts were not Abdelkader's main concern. What he wanted was to go to the front, preferably on the battle lines. His honor and lineage were at stake. He did not have to wait long. A battalion was preparing for departure. The week after he was promoted to the French ranks, he was deployed for combat.

For as much as Warrant Officer Fadiala Keïta had taken issue with not being saluted, he seemed to find Abdelkader's change in status normal. In any case, he did not react to it. Everyone knew of King Mademba's power, not to mention his son's intellectual capacities. No doubt, such a reaction had been expected. Time passed and the warrant officer seemed to have forgotten about the incident.

One day, it was in the summer of 1917, I believe, Warrant Officer Fadiala Keïta attended a debriefing. I went with him. Captain Gastinelle read the report, and this was how we learned of the pending arrival of Second Lieutenant Abdelkader Mademba Sy. Having been issued a pass for a leave in Sansanding, he was to be housed and fed by the Second Regiment of tirailleurs. No bigger calamity could have befallen the warrant officer! Now, the recruit that he had punished so brutally and mistreated on a whim had become a second lieutenant and belonged to the French ranks on top of that, while he, Fadiala Keïta, was still distributing letters and packages to women. And he was still just a warrant officer in the tirailleur corps, and therefore doubly inferior to Abdelkader, in rank and by corps.

Extremely upset, he left before the debriefing was over and went to the post office to get the mail. I was walking behind him. He was so irritated that the postmaster asked me under his breath whether the warrant officer had "suddenly gone insane." From there he went straight to the square in town where we usually distributed the mail from behind a table set up for that purpose. With a surly gesture, the warrant officer tossed the packages and letters at me. "Hop to it!" I began to call out the names that were written on the envelopes. Aminata Traoré! Kadia Boré! Naa Diarra! Koumba So!" Ever more wrathful, he pounded the table and bellowed, "You're a real pain in the ***, with that shrill little voice of yours drilling into my eardrums!" I lowered my voice, trying to make it as deep as possible. "Denin Koné! Aïssata Diallo! Koumba Coulibaly!"

"And now you're mocking me with that cavernous tone! Go on, get out of here! To hell with you! I don't want to see you here again before next week!" And to the great surprise of the women, he took back all the letters, including those that had already been distributed to their addressees. "I'm suspending distribution of the mail until next week," he cried. "I'm the warrant officer, and I do as I please!"

The women looked at each other in astonishment. What bad news could possibly have piqued the ire of the warrant officer to make him so furious? It must have been something quite disagreeable to have changed the temperament of this man who was normally so patient and jovial with them!

A week before the arrival in Kati of Second Lieutenant Abdelkader Mademba, the warrant officer came to speak to my father of his worries, for he considered him to be a friend and good adviser. He was worried that Second Lieutenant Abdelkader would seek revenge for the treatment to which he had been subjected. And if that were to happen, he, Fadiala Keïta, would be forced to react, and the outcome would be tragic.

My father took him to see Chief Warrant Officer Mara Diallo, who was in charge of the camp and to whom he explained the problem. When he had finished, Fadiala spoke. "Chief Warrant Officer, Sir, as a Malinké and a descendant of Sundiata Keïta, I give my word to the Fula man that you are, that if Abdelkader Mademba tries to make me pay for the punishment that I inflicted on him, I will kill him first, and then I will kill myself. I swear I will, by the spirits of my ancestors, beginning with the spirit of Emperor Sundiata himself."

Chief Warrant Officer Mara Diallo assured Fadiala that he would reflect on the question, and then he sent him home. After that, he spoke with my father at length. Finally, my father advised him to go and speak to his superiors in favor of the warrant officer and to explain the dangers involved in a possible confrontation between the two men. The chief warrant officer explained the situation to Captain Lavalée, who decided to inform Colonel Molard himself. In order to avoid a confrontation, the colonel decided that at the moment of the arrival of Second Lieutenant Abdelkader Mademba, Warrant Officer Fadiala Keïta would be sent on a mission to recruit and train young men in Ouagadougou (Burkina Faso).[7]

As soon as the warrant officer heard the news, he recovered his good humor and begged forgiveness from all of those whom he had treated unfairly during his crisis. "I went a little crazy," he said by way of excuse. He left for Ouagadougou via Bamako on the very same train that Second Lieutenant Abdelkader Mademba had taken from Dakar and from which he had alighted just moments before. Abdelkader Mademba stayed in Kati for one week, traveled to Segou to take care of some business, and then went on to Sansanding where he was to spend the rest of his leave with his family. Warrant Officer Fadiala Keïta returned to Kati with his recruits, who would be trained on the premises.

The end of the training period coincided with the return of Abdelkader from his leave. This time, the warrant officer was sent to Dori (Burkina Faso) on another recruiting mission. Abdelkader thus returned to Kati in his absence. Three days later, he left to join his regiment at the front, where the war raged on. France was in dire straits. An inveterate warrior, Abdelkader volunteered for all the missions that involved the risk of no return.

Once again, Warrant Officer Fadiala Keïta returned with his contingent of new recruits to Kati and once again calmly took up his double duty as instructor and mail officer, with Yours Truly as his assistant. Everyone was relieved. The little game of tag had worked perfectly and it seemed that nothing would bring the two men together for a long time. We carried on with our little routine.

We could not have foreseen the turn of events that would arise with the arrival in Africa in February 1918 of the only Black deputy in the French Parliament, Blaise Diagne (a native of Gorée with full French citizenship). The French government had given him the task of promoting a vast recruitment effort in West Africa, for France was in desperate need of troops.

The French government had first asked the governor general of French West Africa, Joost Van Vollenhoven, to undertake a new and intensive effort to recruit at least 75,000 to 100,000 men. Van Vollenhoven, who had arrived at his post in 1917, had been heavily involved in the organization and increased production of certain products as part of the war effort. For several reasons he had expressed his reluctance to carry out such a vast recruitment effort, and in a report dated September 25, 1917, he pointed out the shortcomings of the plan. Unlike the British colonies, French Black Africa had already been painfully drained by previous recruitment efforts, which had in fact provoked violent revolts in certain regions in 1916.

At the beginning of January 1918, Van Vollenhoven traveled to France in order to explain his position to government officials. On the very day of his arrival, January 11, 1918, the President of the Republic signed a decree "regarding the organization of a mission charged with intensifying recruitment efforts in French West Africa and French Equatorial Africa," stipulating that "Mr. Diagne, Deputy of Senegal, is placed in charge of this mission with the title High Commissioner of the Republic (Haut-commissaire de la République) in West Africa with the rank of Governor General."

Von Vollenhoven immediately informed the Minister of Colonies that this was totally incompatible with the terms of the 1904 decree establishing the general government of French West Africa and making the governor general the sole depositary of the powers of the Republic. "The powers of the Republic cannot be divided up like a piece of cake," he declared, "and no governor general would accept such a division."[8] Consequently, he asked to be relieved of his duties and to be placed at the disposal of the army and sent immediately to the front.

An interview with President of the Council and Minister of War Georges Clemenceau changed nothing. True to his nature, Clemenceau "The Tiger" decided that the two decrees could coexist, because such was his desire. "I'm at war, do you understand? I need the tirailleurs, and I need a lot of them to beat the f——ing Huns, and I want to beat the f——ing Huns, do you hear?"[9] He asked Van Vollenhoven to rethink his decision to step down, but Van Vollenhoven refused. He returned to the army on January 26, 1918, with the rank of captain. Van Vollenhoven left shortly after that for the front, where he would die a heroic death on the 20th of July, 1918. Africans remember Governor General Van Vollenhoven as a man of integrity. He had dared to oppose an excessive new recruitment effort because, it was said, he could not accept that men would go and get themselves killed without even having the same rights as everyone else. Native soldiers were in fact considered to be "demi-soldiers." They were paid half of what French soldiers earned, and such was the case for the pensions attached to military medals and other distinctions.

Blaise Diagne thus arrived in Dakar surrounded by a brilliant all-Black military staff composed of young officers wearing gold stripes and white gloves and covered with medals and braided cords. They all came from good backgrounds and they could all boast that each of their families had its own traditional motto, the equivalent to the coats of arms and crests of the old noble families of Europe. The High Commissioner was received with unprecedented pomp. More cannons were fired in his honor than on a day in battle. Administrators of all ranks, superior officers, officers of the armies of land and sea were all at the port of Dakar, accompanied by European, Asian, and Middle Eastern merchants of various degrees of wealth, along with a crowd of penurious Negroes. Presiding over the entire ceremony was the new Governor General of French West Africa [Gabriel Louis] Angoulvant, successor to Van Vollenhoven.

Blaise Diagne appeared, his face enigmatic and solemn. Clothed in his great parade uniform, he was as troubling and anachronistic as a cross in a mosque. In Dakar as elsewhere, the great Negro tenor spoke French. People listened in rapt attention. His vibrant voice awoke people's hearts and inflamed their courage. He knew how to appeal to the African sense of honor by showing them that France, besieged at its very heart by barbarians, needed them. This was the magic word and it had been uttered by one of their own, someone who was honored even by the Whites! The granting of French citizenship was also mentioned. That was all it took. Masses of young people dropped everything in order to go and fight under the French flag. The mission of the Senegalese deputy was on the road to fulfillment. A massive recruitment effort was under way, while the troubles and revolts of previous recruiting efforts had been avoided.

Blaise Diagne decided that after Dakar, French Sudan (today's Mali) would be the first territory of the interior that he would visit. Instructions were given so that nothing would be lacking and so that his reception would be grandiose. All European officers and noncommissioned native officers were to meet in Kati.

At the debriefing in Kati, Commander Bouery personally came to read the instructions and to explain the goal of the mission. It was only then that the news broke: Lieutenant Abdelkader Mademba Sy, Chevalier of the Legion of Honor, recipient of the *Croix de Guerre avec palme* medal and other military decorations, recipient of several military citations to the Order of the Army and consequently possessing a military braid, was part of the mission, and bore the title Officer and Interpreter of the High Commissioner of the Republic in Black Africa to Mr. Blaise Diagne himself!

For Warrant Officer Fadiala Keïta, this was a crushing blow. He staggered under the effect, to the point that he had to lean against the wall of a building. He went home, devastated.

Chief Warrant Officer Mara Diallo went to assure him that he would not suffer any vindictive acts from Abdelkader Mademba. "Chief Warrant Officer," replied Fadiala Keïta, "I'm tired of running away like a rabbit. I'll wait here for Abdelkader, come what may!" In any case, this time it would have been difficult to send him elsewhere, because all the French and Native sergeants and warrant officers of the regiment were required to be present in Kati and in Bamako at the reception of the high commissioner of the Republic.

One day in February 1918, the high commissioner's train, decked out as no official train in Black Africa had ever been before, made a quick stop at the station in Kati, where it was greeted with a twenty-one-gun salute. From there, it continued on to Bamako, where every door, every window, every tree branch was decorated with the tricolor flag and a garland of flowers.

At the station in Bamako, the governor of the territory, assisted by all the administrators of the colonies, officials for Native Affairs, and superior officers of the Second Regiment of Tirailleurs Sénégalais, awaited the illustrious guest. All were wearing their stripes, their military decorations, and the insignia of their rank. The entire city was celebrating. People were singing and dancing in the streets as they had never done even for a traditional feast. When the train stopped, the high commissioner, saluted as was right and proper, went immediately to Koulouba, a hill near Bamako where the governor's palace was located. The official visit to Kati was set for the next day at two o'clock in the afternoon.

A new road, known as the "high road," had been quickly constructed in order to establish a direct route between the governor's palace and the residence of Colonel Molard in Kati. An armed tirailleur had been posted at ten-meter intervals and loaded cannons had been placed at fifty-meter intervals on both sides of the road. The next day, as soon as the high commissioner's car set off down this road, the tirailleurs presented arms and 480 cannons boomed in succession as his car advanced! This unprecedented spectacle demonstrated what an intense bombardment could be like. The circuit took thirty minutes to complete.

In Kati, Captain Lavalée delivered the welcome speech on behalf of all the officers, noncommissioned officers, and soldiers of the Second Regiment of Tirailleurs Sénégalais. In my capacity as auxiliary mail officer of the army, I watched the entire ceremony from a corner of the camp.

The high commissioner responded with an improvised speech that impressed even the Europeans. We were all very moved. It was the first time that we had ever seen a Black man give a speech addressed to White people, who listened quietly. Lieutenant Abdelkader Mademba Sy, in his parade uniform, his chest covered with medals, then translated the high commissioner's speech into Bambara.

When the official ceremony had ended, Chief Warrant Officer Mara Diallo spoke. He announced that the officers and Native officers of the Second Regiment of Kati were offering a welcome dinner that very evening to the officers and African noncommissioned officers in the high commissioner's entourage. The dinner would be served on the public square of the Kadobougou neighborhood since it was the closest to the camp. With this dinner, the meeting between Warrant Officer Fadiala Keïta and Lieutenant Abdelkader was inevitable.

The meal was prepared by the best cooks in Kati, who had all been recruited for the grand occasion. I was among the youth who had been chosen to help serve the food. A table fifty meters in length had been set up. The guests were to mingle. A member of the Second Regiment was seated next to each member of the delegation without attention to rank. As chance would have it, Lieutenant Mademba Sy was placed almost directly across from Warrant Officer Fadiala Keïta. For Fadiala Keïta, this was extremely uncomfortable. Throughout the entire dinner, he kept his head down or looked to one side so as to avoid the lieutenant's gaze.

At the end of the meal, Chief Warrant Officer Mara Diallo rose and gave a great speech in Bambara to welcome the members of the delegation. In particular, he mentioned Lieutenants Galandou Diouf, Amadou Diguey Clédor, Dosso Ouologuem, and Abdelkader Mademba Sy. Abdelkader Mademba Sy stood and replied, "African brothers in arms from this land, my comrades from the Diagne delegation have given me the floor so that I can speak on their behalf. I owe this consideration to the sole fact that I am Sudanese and I speak the local language, for I have no superiority of any kind over those who have designated me. All of them were great military heroes well before me and have preceded me in the acquisition of military glory. I am obligated to thank them for having chosen me as their spokesman, and I also thank you for lending me your attention. But before them and before you all, who are my relatives, there is an elder toward whom I must pay a debt of recognition. For today, in the solemn circumstance that unites us around this table, the occasion has arisen that allows me to pay a great debt.

"When I was a young recruit and voluntary enlistee, I was enrolled in the Second Regiment of Tirailleurs. I thus arrived with a great sense of superiority that I had inherited from my birth, my education, and my good fortune. I expected to be received here by the colonel himself. Was I not one of the sons of King Mademba Sy, and a descendant through my mother's line of the great El Hadj Omar himself? Who in the Second Regiment could boast of so many titles? Thus, I was utterly disappointed when, upon alighting from the train,

I was received, at the same time as fifty other recruits, by an ill-humored warrant officer, who spoke a colorful language that was utterly *tirailleuresque*! He began by telling us, 'Hurry up you pigs! Out of that train car on the double! The last one out will get his ass kicked! Faster! Faster! Move it!'

"We rushed to jump out at the risk of breaking our necks. The warrant officer led us on double march to the tirailleur camp. It was a collection of round huts with mud walls and conical thatched roofs. Inside, the huts were damp and the tirailleurs slept on the ground or on mats woven from palm fronds. Our food rations consisted of the most miserable foodstuffs. All this made me regret my enlistment and even took away my will to live. I could see nothing else. I walked without paying attention to what was happening or what was being said, and thought only of myself.

"That is how one day, I walked past this superior and did not salute him. He called me to order and ordered a reprimand of three days in the brig. I was treated harshly. I lost my illusions of being a rich and cultivated prince and found the trooper in me, that is to say, the slave of duty, forced to submit to an iron discipline. Those three days changed me from top to bottom and allowed me to later become the soldier that I am today in every sense of the term. Well, this superior to whom I owe my education is right here in front of me. It is Warrant Officer Fadiala Keïta, hero of the wars of Morocco and Madagascar, holder of the Military Medal of Tonkin."

The silence was deafening. Lieutenant Abdelkader stood at attention and then cried, "Warrant Officer! My two gold stripes and my medals are the sons of your honorable silver braid. Raise your head with pride. You are not in a place here where you will lose face, but in one where your work bears its fruit. Accept this warm thanks from your recruit, which I will be proud to remain until the end of my days."

Abdelkader Mademba then slowly removed his officer's sword from his belt and presented it with both hands to the warrant officer.

"Warrant Officer Fadiala Keïta," he said, "I would be honored if you would return this sword to me in the tradition of our warriors of old."

The warrant officer, whose head had been bowed the entire time (we later learned that his pocket held a loaded revolver ready for use) stood up. His face was bathed in tears.

Looking directly into Abdelkader's eyes, he received the sword. He took it from its scabbard and slowly touched each of Abdelkader's shoulders with the blade before resheathing it.[10] He then returned the scabbard to the lieutenant and said, "With this sword, may you pursue an ever more brilliant career!"

And to the other guests he said, "My brothers! Lieutenant Abdelkader Mademba Sy has just proven his nobility. He has shown himself to be worthy of his ancestry, on the paternal and on the maternal sides. And neither am I of low lineage! I descend from the Emperor Sundiata Keïta, conqueror of the Sosso Empire. To return the honor that Abdelkader has just paid me, tomorrow I will volunteer to fight at the front, and I swear here and now that I will return to him wearing the stripes of a lieutenant, in honor of those that he has just presented to me before you this evening. I have spoken as a Keïta, and so it will be done as a Keïta. I salute you all. I have finished."

Everyone embraced and tears of joy mingled with the good wine that had been served.

Ten days later, Warrant Officer Fadiala Keïta, who was the first volunteer, left for the front. As he had promised, he duly returned at the end of the war with the rank of lieutenant, chevalier of the Legion of Honor, was decorated with the military medal, and held several citations to the Order of the Army.

When they each reached the end of their lives, Abdelkader Mademba Sy died a batallion commander, and the other, Fadiala Keïta, died a captain. The two heroes had conducted themselves like our African warrior knights of old. They were relentless fighters but they never dishonored themselves. For them, the dignity of their enemy was as precious as their own.

Blaise Diagne's efforts resulted in massive enlistment. Almost all the youth who were at least eighteen years of age signed up. As a result, the pursuits of the youth and adult associations were deeply disrupted. Indeed, our own association was no longer able to function, and most of the initiation societies witnessed the departure of their successor groups. Although this is not a well-known fact, one major effect of the war of 1914 was that it precipitated the first great rupture in the oral transmission of traditional knowledge not only within the initiation societies but also in the trade brotherhoods and corporations of craftsmen, whose workshops had once served as veritable centers of traditional instruction. The hemorrhage of young people sent to the front—from which many would never return—the intensive recruitment of forced laborers on behalf of the war effort, and the mass exodus of people to the Gold Coast deprived the old masters of their all-important successor groups. In a more or less distinct manner, depending on the region, this caused the first great eclipse in the oral transmission of a vast cultural heritage. Over the decades that followed, this process would gradually become more acute under the effects of new social factors.

As for me, I had been exempted from being enlisted because of "insufficient physical development" and retained in my position as auxiliary in the army at Kati. In their youth, Fulas often exhibit a thinness that some mistake for constitutional weakness. The Bambaras, who call us "Skinny Fulas," have this customary saying: "When you see a Fula, you will think that he is ill. But do not believe your eyes. This is his usual state." As for the tirailleurs, they add in their salty tongue, "Ah, de Fula! Alway sick, nevah die!"

Fadiala Keïta was replaced by Warrant Officer Mamadou Bâ, and I continued to work at his side in my weekly duties as assistant mail officer.

At the end of the 1918 school year, our new teacher, Mr. Molo Coulibaly, had the satisfaction of being able to name his five best students to the Bamako Regional School, for they had easily garnered the required number of points. I was part of the group. I knew that I would again have to get through the obligatory step of attending regional school before being allowed access to the professional school, where I would finally begin to prepare for the entrance examination to the normal school at Gorée. But I wanted to become a normal school student so badly that this did not faze me.

7

Final Studies in Bamako

My Second Primary Studies Certificate

Located on the Place de la République, the Bamako Regional School was under the leadership of Mr. Séga Diallo, who had obtained his teaching degree from the normal school. The only match for his severity was his boundless pedagogical expertise. He had therefore earned the admiration of all the European teachers, and particularly that of Mr. Frédéric Assomption, who was the inspector of teaching for the entire territory. I will have the occasion to speak of him again later.

There were two classes at the school. In the autumn of September 1918, I was placed in the second class, which was taught by Mr. Séga Diallo himself. In order to get to school, my four comrades and I had to travel the twelve kilometers separating Kati from Bamako on foot, in the morning and at night. Everyone left separately. Sometimes we ended up walking together, but this was not the rule.

I would leave my parents' house at about four thirty in the morning, without having eaten a thing. The household was still asleep. The night before, my mother would give me the sum of sixty-five centimes to spend on food for the day. Halfway there, I had to walk along the Dounfing chasm, but it had lost some of its mystery since my first encounter with it. The few hyenas that still cackled here and there in its depths had no chance of being mistaken for the terrible Diatroufing.

With a bag full of books and notebooks anchored firmly to my back, I walked along at a good pace, singing at the top of my lungs the refrains or military calls to arms that I knew by heart. Dounfing's walls echoed,

We are marching in the aaa-rmy!
We are marching little soo-ldiers!

Five kilometers outside of Bamako, at the place known as the "abreuvoir des ânes," or the donkey's water trough, I would buy a millet cake from a street vendor for five centimes and eat it on the way. I would arrive at school at seven in the morning, fifteen minutes before it was time to go inside.

Between eleven in the morning and two in the afternoon, we were free. I would go to the market or to Maurer's store to buy a piece of bread for ten centimes and a can of sardines for fifty centimes. That was my lunch. Even now, I still have a certain penchant for canned sardines. Since we had no other place to go, my comrades and I would return to the schoolyard. There we would devour our provisions in the shade of a wall or a tree, not far from the public faucet. Once we had eaten our fill, we would learn our lessons or go to the river's edge to bathe.

As soon as the bell rang at five o'clock in the evening, our little group would scatter and set off down the road to Kati, singing and running the entire twelve kilometers. Depending on my pace, I would arrive home between seven or eight in the evening. It goes without saying that a good meal awaited me.

During that year, my parents left Kati and settled in Bamako. My father had been hired as a tailor at the Point G Hospital. It sat atop a hill of the same name in Bamako. The entire family moved. I no longer had to travel twelve kilometers morning and night, but I still had to climb up and down the hill four times a day, which was located at a distance of four kilometers from the school. I learned all my lessons while walking back and forth between the Place de la République and the summit of Point G. Fortunately, my parents subsequently acquired a vast compound in Bamako itself. To me, this was living in the lap of luxury!

My mother continued to work at the Bamako CFAO (Compagnie française de l'Afrique occidentale, the French West Africa Company), as a buyer of local products and pattern designer of cloth wraps for native women.

It was not without a certain feeling of nostalgia that I left Kati. I left many memories behind and especially a great group of friends: Oumarou Tembély, Famory Keïta, Alassane Djité, Bamoussa, and so many others, as well as the "little brothers" of the age groups below ours but with whom we were close. These included Tiékoura Diawarra, who would later become the father of

Mohammed Diawarra, minister of planning in Ivory Coast; Sounkalo Djibo, who would become the deputy mayor of Bouaké in Ivory Coast; my friend Samba Diallo, who would also dedicate himself to collecting oral traditions, especially folktales; Paul Leblond, who would become a doctor; Paul Taxile; and others.

In November 1918, Africa and France celebrated the end of the great war and the victory of France and its allies over the Kaiser's armies. We were proud of the role that the African soldiers who had been sent to the front had played in this victory. In spite of the difficult conditions that they had had to endure, particularly because of the cold, we knew that they had distinguished themselves by their courage and their disdain for death.

When the survivors returned home in 1918–19, they incited a new social phenomenon that had a significant impact on the evolution of certain ways of thinking. I am speaking of the *demise of the myth of the White Man* as an invincible and flawless being. For up to that point, in fact, the White Man was thought to be a special creature. His power was crushing and unstoppable, his wealth was inexhaustible, and, moreover, he seemed to have been preserved from any mental or physical flaws. Nobody had ever seen an infirm or misshapen colonial administrator. They were always well dressed, rich, strong, certain of their authority, and spoke in the name of the Mother Country where, according to them, everything was just and good. What we did not know at the time was that a preliminary selection eliminated anyone who was infirm, deformed, ill, or unstable, and that when a colonial fell ill, he was very quickly repatriated to France.

But since then, Black soldiers had fought in the trenches next to their White comrades. They had seen heroes and courageous men, but they had also seen men crying and afraid. They had discovered the misshapen and the deformed, and what was even more unthinkable and barely believable, they had seen thieves, poor Whites, and even White beggars in the cities of the Whites!

When the tirailleurs returned home, they spent many an evening telling stories about everything that they had seen. No, the White Man was not a superhuman endowed with some unknown divine or diabolical protection. He was a man as they were, with the same mixture of qualities and faults, strengths and weaknesses. And when they found out that their medals and their titles as combat veterans would earn them less than half the pensions that their White comrades were earning, even though they had shared the same battles and the same suffering, some of them dared to speak out and demand equal treatment. It was then, in 1919, that for the first time, a spirit of emancipation and a demand for action arose and gradually spread to other sections of the population.

In the meantime, for the regional school students, the school year progressed, with the prospect of the Primary Studies Certificate looming at the end. Throughout the entire year, our teacher, Mr. Séga Diallo, so dedicated himself to his students that by June he had lost his voice. But the success of all thirty of his Native Primary Studies Certificate candidates for the academic year 1918–19 was his reward. I thus took the exam for the second time, since I had already done so in Djenné in 1915.

I do not know why, but during the exam, I was gripped with such intense fear that I was paralyzed. I no longer knew anything. It was as though my brain had been emptied of its contents. What a terrible day! I passed, but I was ranked fortieth out of ninety candidates! Mr. Séga Diallo, who had counted on seeing my name listed among the top five students, was floored. As for me, I never quite recovered from finding myself placed at this ranking, for I considered it a disgrace.

All the students who had passed the certificate exam were automatically transferred to the Bamako Professional School as boarders. There, over a period of one or two years, they could prepare for the entrance examination for the upper-level governmental *grandes écoles* located on Gorée Island in Senegal.

But for now, we were on vacation, and the administration had arranged to send students back to their home regions. I obtained transportation to Bandiagara. After spending a few days with my parents, I joined my comrades and took the train with them to Koulikoro, where we were to take the boat for Mopti. I did not know that on this boat a chance encounter would have an unforeseen but enduring effect on my view of worldly honors.

In Vain Pursuit of the Wind

All told, we were a group of sixty students hailing from different regions in the Niger Bend. My comrades from Bandiagara and I formed a group of seven students, for whom I was responsible since I was the oldest.

After obtaining the requisition orders at the Koulikoro subdivision office that were necessary in order to board the boat, we were led to the port by an ill-tempered district guard. We were to board *Le Mage*, the very same steamboat on which I had sailed without a ticket a few years before. Mr. Monnet was still the purser, but I was careful not to recall myself to his memory.

After waiting for several hours in the torrid sun, we were finally allowed to embark at about four o'clock in the afternoon. Like a flock of sheep being sold at auction, we were herded on to the deck reserved for native travelers. Toward four thirty, a beautiful carriage drawn by two well-fed horses and driven by a district guard drew up at a trot. The team belonged to Commandant Courtille, who was in fact a mere clerk in the Office of Native Affairs and director of the Koulikoro subdivision, but who went by the customary title of "commandant." To our great surprise, a richly dressed young Black man was seated next to him. The team stopped next to the embarkation ramp. A crowd gathered to watch, fascinated. The district guard and driver jumped down from his seat. He rushed to open the door and then stood at attention and executed a military salute. Commandant Courtille was the first to alight, holding his ever-present whip in his left hand. Next, the district guard helped the young Black man out of the carriage while pushing the overly curious crowd out of the way.

The rather corpulent young man was a few years older than I. His ebony black face shone like polished wood. Dressed in a fine Moroccan robe of pure linen, he smoked with a detached air, and deliberately allowed the ashes from his cigarette to drop onto his embroidered *djellaba*, which did not burn. As dictated by the latest fashion, his expensive Robéro Jaune London shoes, crafted from fine leather, squeaked obligingly. A thin gold arrow threaded through his black silk socks. Crowning this glory was a superb fez adorned with silk fringe, and his well-cut hair had been carefully straightened and flattened with the assistance of a shiny pomade.

The native travelers who were either already aboard or still waiting on the quay were speechless. This was indeed the first time that anyone had seen Commandant Courtille act in such an amiable and considerate manner with a native, for the commandant was more often seen using his whip than exchanging courtesies. He even stepped aside and allowed the native to go first! Who was this young man? The mystery was solved when we heard Commandant Courtille declare to the purser, "This is *Mister* Ben Daoud Mademba Sy, son of the king of Sansanding. He has just arrived from Algeria, where he is studying, and will spend his vacation with his father in Sansanding. The highest authorities have ordered me to receive him and to recommend him to your warmest attentions. He will travel in first class. Watch over him with the greatest of care."

This explained everything. Natty as an "ear of corn," this boy was the young son of King Mademba Sy, the darling of the French authorities in those days. He was thus the younger brother of Lieutenant Abdelkader Mademba Sy, whose story I told earlier.

Mr. Monnet took leave of Commandant Courtille and led Ben Daoud toward the stairway leading to the first floor, where the first- and second-class cabins were located. This level was normally strictly forbidden to natives, with the exception of the houseboys who worked there. The travelers, who had gathered en masse to watch this rare Black specimen climb the forbidden staircase, returned to their places. Toward six o'clock, boarding was complete and in a booming voice Mr. Monnet gave the order to depart. The laptots swung into action. The boat's two great wheels slowly began to turn. The hull throbbed, and then the ship's prow gently came around toward the middle of the river. With a light shudder, the stern broke loose from the bank, and the boat headed toward deep water, where it soon gained speed and settled into a regular rhythm.

Sometime later, the young prince began his evening toilette. In spite of the wind, a wonderful scent wafted down to the stern of the boat and lingered for several minutes. "Ah! What a wonderful aroma!" the travelers exclaimed. "Now that is real perfume!"

At about eight o'clock the bell rang, inviting the travelers in the first, second, and third classes to come and take their dinners in the rooms corresponding to their respective categories. As for the passengers camped on the deck, they were served badly cooked rice from enameled pails. It wasn't quite as bad as the *chacabati* served to convicts (which was a kind of slop), but it wasn't far from it. The only ones who ate it were those who had no other choice. Fortunately, my comrades and I had a supply of dried millet couscous with peanuts, a dish that is usually mixed with milk.

Following the dinner that he had taken with the first-class passengers on the upper deck, Mademba's son had a houseboy collect all the leftovers in a big bucket and take them down to the young students on the deck. He personally followed the houseboy and stopped just above him on the second to last step of the staircase. "Hey, you!" he cried. "Come and get it!" The students swarmed up. The houseboy plunged his hand into the bucket and tossed out pieces of meat, bits of potato, pieces of bread, and other European foodstuffs. My six comrades from Bandiagara rose to join them. I held them back. "Return to your places and sit down!" I told them. "If your parents in Bandiagara ever find out that we ran up to eat the White people's leftovers, leftovers that Ben Daoud Mademba, son of Mademba Sy, a former postman turned king, is handing out like grain scattered to chickens, we run the risk of being severely beaten with ropes on the square in front of the mosque. Stay here and eat our dried couscous. If we have to, we will water it down with river water, but we will never go and pick up Ben Daoud's leftovers!"

These words carried weight, all the more so because my comrades and I were well aware of the rivalry and latent hostility that divided the two French creations, the kingdom of Sansanding, given to Mademba Sy, and the Toucouleur kingdom of Bandiagara, given to Aguibou Tall, son of El Hadj Omar.

A certain animosity reigned between the people of Sansanding and those of Bandiagara, and we kept our distance from one another.

Ben Daoud continued to hand out the food, but he only had eyes for our group, which had remained seated and aloof. After the food had been distributed, he came over to us.

"What region are you from?" he asked.

"From Bandiagara," I replied.

"Why didn't you come to get some food?"

"We are not going far, just to Bandiagara, and we have enough couscous to last for the rest of the trip. We did not want to keep the other students, especially those going all the way to Gao, from benefiting from the food."

He smiled. "That's not why. It's because you are from Bandiagara."

He had understood. He returned to the first floor and one hour later he returned, carrying a platter that he had asked the boat's cook to prepare especially for us, filled with an excellent rice in sauce and garnished with lamb. He came and set the platter before us.

"Sons of my father from Bandiagara," he said, "here is a good dinner that Sansanding offers to you by my hand!"

He moved off. I invited my companions to eat.

Surprised, they cried, "What? You want us to eat food from Mademba's son? Have you forgotten what you just told us?"

"I haven't forgotten anything," I replied. "But the situation has changed. The manner in which this meal was presented to us obligates us to accept it. Whether we like it or not, no matter what the origins of his family are, Ben Daoud is the son of a king, which is not the case for all of us here. And rather than having the leftovers thrown to us by a houseboy, as he was doing earlier, he took the trouble to bring it to us himself. Now he has treated us with honor. If we refuse this honor and our parents hear about it, there again, they we will have the right to beat us with ropes for having conducted ourselves like spoiled children." Reassured, my comrades ate heartily, sharing the platter with some of the travelers seated nearby.

Ben Daoud, who had remained at the top of the stairs, had heard everything. He came back down and spoke to me. "Do you want to be my friend?" he asked, and took me with him up to his cabin. This is how I entered into Prince Ben Daoud Mademba Sy's inner circle and how, after him, I became the second Negro to climb to the boat's upper deck.

Mr. Monnet gave me permission to visit Ben Daouad in his cabin whenever we wished. We greatly enjoyed our conversations. The few days that our trip lasted were wonderful.

On the afternoon of the third day, Segou had come into view. Before docking in the commercial port, the boat stopped over in the official port that was located across from the district commandant's residence. The commandant, a Corsican named Battesti, came aboard with his assistant and went up to the first level to salute Mister Ben Daoud Mademba Sy, to whom he had also brought some good things to eat. Then he went back down to the deck. I heard him tell the purser, "If you arrive at Sansanding before daylight, cut the power and have the boat pushed by punt pole, and be sure to make absolutely no noise until King Mademba himself has awakened. Your job is at stake."

"Yes, Commandant. Sir, your orders will be followed."

This shows the reach of King Mademba's power and prestige. The commandant shook Mr. Monnet's hand and then went back down to the quay. Leaving the official port behind, we then headed for the commercial port where travelers and cargo were unloaded and others were taken on board. That evening after dinner, Mr. Monnet gave the signal for departure. The boat left Segou behind and plunged into darkness.

It was early dawn when Sansanding came into view. Mr. Monnet ordered all lights extinguished and the engines stopped. The laptots, who were now steering the enormous craft with punt poles, succeeded in coming ashore in silence. The port was just across from the royal palace. Between the palace and the river's edge stretched an esplanade seven hundred to eight hundred meters in length. It was neat and clean. The square was carpeted with fine sand that had been hauled from the river and carefully sifted so that every morning and every evening the king could come and take the air. In order to avoid raising dust, the square was never swept. The dozens of workmen engaged in the upkeep of the palace had to pick up by hand every blade of grass blown in on the wind. For who, if not the wind, would dare to commit such an offense?

That morning, as if by chance, His Majesty did not rise early. The entire city held its breath. Even the dogs did not bark. Those known as vociferous barkers had surely been shut inside the granaries the previous evening, for inopportune barking came at a high price. If a dog was heard barking during the night, the king's policemen went searching for the source of the noise, and the next day, before the noonday meal, the dog's owner was summoned to the king's vestibule and given a beating of thirty lashes with a rope. Only a few muffled rooster crows (could it be that even they were closed deep inside people's houses?) succeeded in piercing the silence. For anyone familiar with the joyful noises that animate African villages at daybreak, this was very strange indeed.

A file of women bearing empty water jars advanced in a meandering line toward the river. Draped in white robes, they glided silently like ghostly shades, without making a sound. They did not even nod their heads to each other in greeting and seemed lost in some secret dream. Upon reaching the river's edge, they slowly entered the water up to their knees and carefully lowered their jars, holding them under water until they were quite full. When they returned to shore, they gracefully lifted the jars, placed them atop their heads, and retraced their steps, their naked feet skimming the white sand.

Even our boat seemed to have fallen under some magical, languorous spell. On the bridge, everyone waited, immobilized. Some dared to engage in conversation but only with their mouths pressed to each other's ears. For who would have dared to make the slightest sound when even the Whites themselves were hiding in fear deep inside their cabins?

The sun had finally risen, but only the sparrows celebrated its appearance. Life itself seemed to have been suspended as it awaited the first flutterings of the king's eyelids. At around seven in the morning, three great salvos shattered the silence. All at once, a clamor arose from every quarter: "Fama kounouna! Fama kounouna!" (The king has awakened! The king has awakened!) In a single stroke, people began to speak, dogs began to bark, children began to cry, and pestles began to pound in their mortars. It was as though sound itself had been stuffed into a tightly sealed jar. When the salvos shattered its lid, sound escaped and exploded in the air. The city had just resuscitated from a temporary death imposed by the caprices of a king who had been created by the very secular and democratic French Republic. And this Republic had cut off the head of its own last king! Try to make sense of that!

The palace occupied a one-hundred-square-meter parcel of land and was surrounded by a wall (or *tata*) that rose so high that the topmost tuft of a palm tree growing on the other side was just barely visible. The palace environs were so well guarded that after five o'clock in the afternoon, any man passing in the vicinity was dragged into the vestibule by a guard and cruelly beaten, sometimes to death, for having committed the crime of coming to inhale the odor of the incense that the women of the royal harem were accustomed to burning at that hour of the evening.

About three-quarters of an hour after the salvos had been fired, the heavy doors of the vestibule swung open. Around thirty soldiers known as Mademba's spahis appeared, dressed in their grand parade uniforms. Each wore a red fez, a blue jacket, loose white pants, blue puttees, and shoes. Each of them carried an embossed native long rifle called a *long'ngan*. After deftly executing the maneuvers proper to soldiers with stripes, they separated into two rows to form an honor guard.

A quarter of an hour later, Mademba appeared, accompanied by his usual entourage. Following directly behind him was his griote, loudly singing his praises. This griote, named Diéli Yagaré, was bewitchingly beautiful. Endowed with a remarkable voice that was at once powerful and sweet, she sang of Mademba's war exploits during the French conquest of the Sudan. If one were to believe her version of events, it was Mademba and not Colonel Archinard who had done the conquering. She almost seemed to be crediting him with the founding of Saint-Louis of Senegal! Truly, she said whatever she wished, but her voice was so captivating and she was so beautiful and marvelously attired that she herself was an entire spectacle unto herself and an enchanting vision for the young men that we were.

Lulled by the voice of his griote, the king slowly crossed the square, lifting first one foot and then the other, like a duck. His spahis presented arms. As he passed, everyone crouched to the ground in salutation and shouted one of his honorific surnames. "Sy Savané! Sy Savané!" And he invariably replied with the traditional phrase, "Marhaba! Marhaba!" I was able to observe him more closely as he approached the quay where a carpet had been unfurled so that his shoes would not get wet.

Marred by a nose that seemed to wish to occupy the entire width of his face, he was not the most handsome of men. But his face was illuminated by large eyes whose commanding look imposed upon those who happened to meet his gaze. The king's ugliness was overshadowed by the majesty of his attire and the brilliance of his ornaments. He wore an Arab chieftain's burnous cloak, embroidered in gold. Its left side was raised at the shoulder, displaying his boubou of shiny Bazin cloth and his chest, studded with French medals and military decorations. Among these was the Officer's Cross of the Legion of Honor, even though French superior officers generally did not rise above the rank of chevalier!

With a majestic stride, he crossed the gangway and stepped onto the boat. In unison, the travelers on the bridge cried out, "Sy Savané! Sy Savané!" Turning his open palms toward them, the king replied, "Marhaba! Marhaba!" Mr. Monnet, who had been buzzing about like a fly in a panic, rushed up to greet the king. The king shook his hand. Mr. Monnet responded with a deep bow that was undoubtedly intended to express his gratitude for such an honor, and then he stepped in front of him so that he could show him the boat.

Ben Daoud had come down from the upper deck dressed in his most beautiful garments. Eyes lowered in respect, he stood on the deck next to his baggage.

Preceded by the purser and followed by his chamberlain, the king walked past his son without even glancing at him. This did not surprise anyone. Feelings for one's children are not displayed in public. In fact, this is one of the African customs that Europeans have difficulty understanding. For us, it is the uncles and aunts who must outwardly manifest their affection for their nieces and nephews, whom they consider to be their own children. This traditional reserve is even more pronounced among the ranks of important people when they appear in public.

When he had finished touring the boat, the king signed the ship's log, where he wrote a few lines, and then crossed the gangway, without ever looking at his son. Then I saw six big muscular fellows run up to Ben Daoud. Two of them took his bags, while the other four formed a kind of chair with their interlaced fingers, where Ben Daoud took his seat. They lifted him with ease and carried him to the palace on this improvised sedan chair. As he was leaving, Ben Daoud turned and gave me a little wave. I dolefully waved back, convinced that I would never see him again.

The royal procession moved off, and the boat blew its whistle. Whether it was in honor of the king or to announce its departure, I do not know. Then it slowly pulled away from the bank. I took one last look at Sansanding. This was the famous Marka city that had been under the command of the Cissés during the Fula Empire of Massina, then under the command of the Koumas during the time of the Toucouleur Empire of El Hadj Omar, before it became the personal paradise of "King" Mademba Sy, pharaoh of the Niger Bend.

Twenty-eight years later, in 1947, I was to return to those banks under circumstances that I will tell of now, for they lend this story its meaning.

During the course of that year, Professor Théodore Monod, founder and director of the Institut français d'Afrique noire (IFAN), where I had been placed at his request and assigned to the Ethnology Department, went to Lake Debo to study its fish. Located near Niafounké in the Niger Delta, this large lake was famous not just for its fish, but also for the innumerable birds of different species that flocked there every year from all over the world, to convene and cackle together to their heart's content in a kind of great avian UNESCO meeting. The professor chose me to accompany him. I was to use the trip to continue collecting oral traditions from that region.

Once work was completed, Professor Monod headed back toward Segou by car, while I was assigned to gather our workers and laptots in the city of Ké-Macina so that they could be paid. I decided to travel to Segou by pirogue and to stop off in Sansanding along the way, in the secret hope of perhaps meeting my old friend Ben Daoud again, for I had not forgotten him.

One evening at about five o'clock in the afternoon, the pirogue drew up at Sansanding. I climbed out from under the shelter where I had been resting. The sight that met my eyes made me doubt the laptots. "Are you sure this is Sansanding?" "Yes," they replied. "Sansanding, the city of King Mademba?" "There is no mistake, this is Sansanding." I could not believe my eyes. The entire bank had fallen into disrepair. The palace, now in ruins, seemed to have been swallowed up by the earth. The beautiful square that had been covered with fine sand and cleaned by hand was nothing but an abandoned lot where a miserable little market had been set up. Many of its rickety and unmaintained stalls had been blown over by the north wind.

In my mind's eye I saw the imposing mass of the palace, the women coming to draw water in the muffled silence of the morning, the spahis, the courtiers, and the griote Diéli Yagaré, whose voice had soothed people's hearts and charmed their ears. I once again saw Mademba draped in silk, in fine cloth and rich Bazin, his chest shiny with medals, and his son, Ben Daoud, carried in the arms of his servants. And then this beautiful image disappeared like a mirage in the dry season, and I returned to the view of a crumbling square where all Sansanding came to empty its garbage and where scrawny donkeys roamed with dogs, goats, and pigs.

I disembarked, ordered my laptots to wait, and headed in to the city. Halfway there, I met a boy about twelve years of age, and asked him, "Do you know Ben Daoud Mademba, son of former King Mademba?"

"Yes."

"Is he in Sansanding at the moment?"

"Yes."

"Can you take me to him?"

"Of course."

He turned and beckoned me to follow. When we reached the city, I saw a handsome building several stories tall, similar in style to the commandant of Segou's residence. I stopped to gaze at it, certain that this must be Ben Daoud's abode. The boy turned around.

"Stranger," he said, "this is not the son of Mademba's house. This belongs to Madiansa."

I had no idea who Madiansa was. My little guide began walking again. I followed in silence.

He soon stopped at the end of a small street in front of a miserable compound whose entire surface area was no greater than a few dozen square meters. The low wall enclosing the little courtyard was so run-down that its naked, unmortared bricks were visible, like the ribs of an old mare during the dry season. The entrance was barred by nothing more than two thick branches placed at diagonals, probably to keep the animals from escaping. At the back of the courtyard sat the dwelling, a single, tiny hut that was almost like a cell. The decrepit walls had been gnawed by rough weather. Through the gaps between the badly matched planks in the wobbly door, a man could be seen sitting inside. The boy pointed at him.

I stepped over the branches into the courtyard and greeted him loudly, "Sy! Sy! Ben Daoud Mademba Sy! I wish you a good evening. I am your old friend from the boat *Le Mage*, Amadou Hampâté Bâ of Bandiagara. I did not want to pass by Sansanding without coming to visit you."

After a brief moment of silence, the voice of a malnourished man rose from inside the hut. "Oh my friend! Welcome! Welcome!"

Ben Daoud—for it was indeed he—opened his rickety door and stepped outside. For the second time since arriving there, I could not believe my eyes. He was wearing an old *forkiya*, a kind of long, full shirt that must once have been white but which now seemed to have been dipped in a dye of red mud. I could see his emaciated chest through the large opening of the forkiya. His pants were sewn from mismatched pieces of cloth. Sandals cut from old tires trailed from his feet. I could not stop my mind's eye from recalling his beautiful Robéro Jaune London shoes, which had *squeak, squeak, squeaked* with every step.

His skin, which had been black as ebony, had now taken on a grayish tint. His hair and the whiskers in his beard had gone prematurely gray. In his hand he held a pipe filled with native tobacco that gave off the most unpleasant odor that I have ever had the occasion to smell. Again, a memory returned and I thought of the delicious scent of his eau de cologne and how it had wafted over the entire stern of the boat.

"What happened to him?" I wondered. "What is the meaning of this? What lesson can a reasonable man learn here?"

Once we had completed the customary litanies of greeting, I mustered the nerve to ask him the question, "Ben Daoud, my friend, after everything that you were, how is it that you have been reduced to such a state?"

He answered me in a calm voice, without acrimony, as though speaking of someone other than himself. "A few years ago, during World War II, I was a teacher in Timbuktu, but I was accused of being a Gaullist. For this, I was led before a tribunal of colonial officials faithful to the Vichy Regime. I was dismissed from my position and condemned to house arrest in Sansanding. All my belongings were confiscated. With no work and no fortune, I had nothing left to live on.[1] But, thank God, I am only poor in material wealth. My state of mind, my dignity, and my pride have not been affected. I even smile sometimes at the thought that it was a Frenchman who made my father a king, and it was also a Frenchman who changed me from an idolized prince and wealthy official into a social outcast and ill-housed wretch, surviving on one meal a day and sleeping on a mat on the ground. Yes, I look destitute, but I am not as unhappy as my appearance could lead one to believe. I am in harmony with myself, and I have nothing to reproach myself for. The proof of this is that I sleep peacefully. When I find food, I eat it with gusto, and when I don't, I endure hunger. I do not beg. I read a lot, I meditate, and I reflect."

Not once did Ben Daoud utter a bitter word about his situation nor a criticism toward his father's former vassals who had become rich and powerful men. He had accepted his fate with serenity. In this destitute state, he seemed to me to be infinitely more grand than the prince had once been.

I dared to ask, "What happened to your father's palace?"

He burst into laughter. "My father's palace? It collapsed. It became a great mound under which my family's glory and fortune are buried."

"My dear friend," he added, "life makes and unmakes things. Life had once made my family all there was in Sansanding. Then it unraveled its handiwork, and now my family is nothing in Sansanding. And yet, the river keeps flowing and the sun keeps rising and setting."

"May I visit the ruins of the palace?"

"Of course! Let us go now, while it is still light."

He led me to the site of the old royal compound. Everything had collapsed. There was nothing left but a pile of dirt and some weeds. The women's quarters, whose walls it had once been forbidden to approach at a distance of less than five meters without incurring a whipping, had now become a public toilet, where people from nearby neighborhoods came to deposit their waste. A great termite mound had risen in the middle of the first wife's bedroom. On the parcel where the immense guardroom had stood, there was now a livestock market. In the very spot where Mademba's own personal lodgings had stood, there was nothing to see but a pile of rubble.

As I was silently contemplating this sight, an old billy goat (I would later learn that he was the village's mascot) approached and placidly entered the compound. Every night at the same time he would climb to the top of the mound and lie down to spend the night, his head turned toward the east. With his bearded face and his jaw in constant rumination, he looked like an old marabout muttering his prayers. Efforts had apparently been made to chase him away, but he invariably returned. In the end, he was left alone.

At the end of the tour, Ben Daoud took me to see a corner of the compound that was apparently the only well-maintained area amid all the neglect. It was here that the remains of King Mademba Sy and his son Battalion Commander Abdelkader Mademba were buried. The administration had taken charge of the upkeep of their graves. Following a moment of silence, Ben Daoud took his leave and went home. I remained alone with my thoughts.

I watched the old billy goat chew his cud atop the very spot where Mademba had once reigned in all his glory. I saw creeping nocturnal creatures crawl from the cracks and crevices of what had once been a reception room filled with courtiers, resonant with the praise songs of the griots. And here at my feet were a pair of modest, almost forgotten graves that held the remains of an absolute monarch and a war hero. I was forty-seven years old. My master Tierno Bokar, the sage with a heart full of tolerance and love—"the man of God" as Théodore Monod had called him—had already been dead for seven years. He had died in isolation and reclusion under cruel conditions provoked by the malice, or as he had put it, the ignorance of men. So this was life?

I leaned over the king's grave: "Mademba Sy? *Sinsani Fama* (King of Sansanding)? *Fa demba* (father)?" Silence.

I turned to his son's grave. "Abdelkader Mademba? Commander Abdelkader Mademba, man of the Dardanelles and Verdun and so many great battles?" Nothing but my own voice echoed through this mournful waste. "So here you are, both lying in your graves, while all of Sansanding cuts through your compound to get to the market? This compound that everyone once had to tiptoe around in fear and respect! All your splendor, all your glory, all of it has disappeared and faded away like a fleeting mirage? Well if this is life in this world, then as the Koran says, it is truly, 'only temporary enjoyment.' And the Bible is indeed correct when in Ecclesiastes it says, 'All is vanity and pursuit of the wind!'"

On that day, at that moment, I broke with the world and made the firm resolution to follow my master's directives for the rest of my life. To serve, and to serve always. But never to seek acclaim, nor power, nor to rule.

I took the road back into town. Along the way, I encountered a griot and asked him who Madiansa was, as he was the owner of the handsome two-story building that I had at first thought belonged to Ben Daoud. He informed me that Madiansa's father had been the captive of one of King Mademba's captives, and that he had been so destitute that he had twice indentured his son

Madiansa as a servant. As a result of having carried bricks, firewood, and heavy loads, the top of poor Madiansa's head had peeled away, and so it had remained for the rest of his life. On the day when a group of one hundred boys was circumcised, Madiansa, who was one of the group, had been forgotten in a corner. This is how inconsequential he was in Sansanding! And yet, it was this very same Madiansa who later became an important merchant and who had acquired such a great fortune that he did not know what to do with it all. Meanwhile, the son of the former king was clothed in rags, starving, and languishing in a miserable hovel.

"Oh Fula man!" added the griot, "have you gone to see the ruins of Mademba's palace?"

"Yes."

"Did you see the path that cuts across the ruins of the palace that nobody could approach at a distance of less than five meters after five o'clock in the afternoon and that leads to the marketplace?"

"Yes, I did."

"Do you know what the inhabitants of Sansanding call this path?"

"No."

"They call it, *Allah yé sé*. God can do anything!"

Before returning to my pirogue, I went back to bid farewell to my friend Ben Daoud. We parted with tears in our eyes. We never saw one another again.

Ben Daoud Mademba Sy, whom I had first met during my school vacation in 1919 and then again in 1947, is among the men who have touched my life most deeply.

Boarding School in Bamako

At the start of the new school year, I moved into the Bamako Professional School as a boarder. This school has a history. It had originally been created in 1854 by Faidherbe in Kayes, Mali, which at the time was the headquarters of the Upper Senegal and Middle Niger colony. Very officially called the School for Hostages, its ranks were filled by forcefully requisitioning the sons of chiefs and other dignitaries from recently conquered regions, with the aim of ensuring their submission. However, when they could, some of these chiefs sent captives in place of their sons, a decision that they perhaps came to regret later on. In 1908, when Governor Clozel transferred the colony's headquarters from Kayes to Bamako, the school was reopened in that city and given the more discreet but nevertheless explicit name School for Sons of Chiefs. With the development of the administration and the increased need for native subaltern personnel, it then became the Bamako Professional School. Later, it was renamed Upper Primary School, then Terrasson de Fougères School, before becoming known today as the Lycée Askia Mohammed.

Colonization is never philanthropic, except in words. One goal of every colonial enterprise, wherever and whenever it may be, is always to clear the conquered territory, for one can sow neither in fallow nor in already cultivated land. Like so many weeds, the thought, values, customs, and local cultures must be torn up so that the values, customs, and culture of the colonizer can be sown in their place, for they alone are considered to be superior and of value. And what better way to accomplish this than through the schools?

But as it is said in the tale *Kaïdara*, everything necessarily has a diurnal and a nocturnal side. Nothing in this world here below is ever bad from A to Z, and colonization also had its positive sides, which may not have been intended for our benefit at the outset, but which we have inherited, and which now belong to us to use to our advantage. I would choose the colonizer's language as the most important of these inherited benefits. It is a precious communication tool for ethnic groups who do not speak the same language, and a means of opening up to the outside world. There is a condition, however. Local languages must not be allowed to die, for they carry our culture and our identity.

The Bamako Professional School (where, as in all the other schools, the use of one's mother tongue was banished and punished) prepared students within a period of one or two years for the entrance examination to one of French West Africa's general governmental grandes écoles in Gorée. Native teachers, native assistants in the colonial administration, and physician's assistants graduated from these schools. Thus, through one of those ironic twists of fate, Gorée Island, which had been the port where ill-fated millions had been loaded onto ships bound for the other shore of the great "salted lake" during the slave trade, became the crucible where Black elites would be trained to better serve French colonial interests, the majority of whom would later fight for the liberation and independence of their countries.

In the meantime, it was a matter of training an entire army of competent, loyal, and disciplined assistants, who would aid in the development and management of the conquered colonies by working the vital cogs that made the formidable colonial machine function. Those who did not walk through Gorée's royal doors after their studies at the professional school could still aspire to holding similar positions, but at lower ranks. These were "teaching monitors" rather than "teachers," "secretaries" rather than "clerks," and so on. Some "secretaries" were even forcibly recruited as soon as they had obtained a Primary Studies Certificate.

The professional school included four classes into which students were divided according to the results of the Primary Studies Certificate examination. The first class prepared to be "teaching monitors," the second and fourth prepared as future assistants to the administration, and the third was for laborers and technicians. Because of my ranking after the certificate exam, I was almost placed with the laborers. I was finally admitted to the fourth class, which trained future administrative assistants. We all prepared concurrently for our entrance examinations.

Upon arriving at the professional school, I had once again found my peer group, composed of students from Bandiagara. Because of my age, I automatically became their leader. I was extremely happy to find my old friend Daouda Maïga among their ranks. He had cycled through the school system without difficulty (he was in his second year) and would later become a schoolteacher. Also present were Madani Tall, who had been sent to attend school in my brother's place and who would become a printer; Oumar Bâ, who became the writer, ethnographer, and researcher that we know; and so many others.

During my first year, my teacher was Mamadou Konaté, who would later become the second deputy from Sudan and one of the great leaders of the RDA (Rassemblement démocratique africain) party before political rivalries brought about his tragic end under circumstances that I prefer not to discuss here. Mamadou Konaté was only two or three years older than I was, but I respected him very much. We became friends and stayed friends until his death.

Generally, I was on good terms with my teachers and my classmates. Because of my Islamic knowledge, I was nicknamed "the marabout student," for my more mundane occupations hadn't earned me any other nicknames. I can no longer remember for what reason I had been exempted from the heavy domestic chores, but I was made the guardian of the straw brooms. I was to ensure that every work crew returned them all undamaged. Otherwise the supervisors could apply various sanctions. Students from the Diallo clan, the sanankoun (joking relation) of the Bâs, dubbed me "Amadou Broom."

The supervisors—there were three of them—played an important role in our lives as boarders. It was their job to take turns waking us every morning at six, and each of them had a particular way of doing it. With Fama, the general supervisor, we were awakened gently. With his assistant, One-Armed Bala, an old tirailleur with fire in his eyes, it was brutal. But the most picturesque method was without contest the one used by the assistant supervisor Mamadou Sissoko, who was also a former tirailleur. We had nicknamed him "Don Quixote," because he was as tall and thin as Fama was short and stocky, a quality that had automatically earned the latter the nickname "Sancho Panza."

When General Supervisor Fama, alias Sancho Panza, entered the dormitory in the morning, he slowly called to us in a sweet, low voice. "Get up, Get up! Out of bed, out of bed! It's morning! It's morning! Let all good students get up and stand on their two feet! Let them go to the washroom and bathe while they reflect upon their unfinished homework and their unfinished lessons!

"Let's go Bagaro Dagana! What's stopping you from getting up, making your bed, and folding your blanket? And you Bokari Nibié, if you want to keep your ranking as first in the class, you must not linger in bed at the hour of the day when the brain is best prepared to learn and work.

"Hey! Mamadou Traoré, no taller than a mushroom, you did not know your lesson yesterday. And you, Dantoumé Kamissoko, you miscalculated your math problem because you are not studying your lessons correctly. And both of you are lying there spread out on your beds like coconspirators? Get going! Get up, get up! It's morning, it's morning!"

For each one of us one hundred thirty students, the general supervisor had a comment, an epithet, some praise, or a specific jab. By the end of the week, everyone had earned a comment. Fama, who had been a supervisor in the School for Hostages since its creation and who spent the entire day seated under the veranda, kept abreast of everything that went on in every class. And because he had listened to the students conjugating their verbs and reciting their lessons aloud, he had learned to speak French as correctly as any of the students.

As for One-Armed Bala (he had lost his right arm in combat), like any self-respecting tirailleur, he would come bursting into the dormitory bellowing, "Everybody up! If you not happy, I kick you in the ass!" With his still powerful good left hand, he would raise the head of one bed and the foot of another, not caring whether he dumped its occupant on to the floor. "Come on! Get up! Get up one time, get up two times, no be three times! Stragglers watch out, you band of good-for-nothings, you bunch of useless imbeciles, you sick pigs! Everyone up!" From the twisted mouth of this great wounded World War I combat veteran, nothing but threats and insults ever came out. And yet, One-Armed Bala was not as mean as he seemed! If a student was punished and made to go without a meal, he always made sure to set something aside for him to eat, unlike the soft-spoken General Supervisor Fama, who never did.

As for the assistant supervisor Mamadou Sissoko, otherwise known as Don Quixote, he was the most colorful. He spoke only forofifon naspa, or "Tirailleur French," a colorful and piquant language, where the word for "thigh" is "drumstick," and the one for "mouth" is "big hole in the head." Whenever he entered the dormitory, he would begin by introducing himself. "Here is I, Don Quixote! Come on! Get up, get up! Itsh mo'nin-Itsh mo'nin! Gev up! Gev up! Sun he gonna open he zeye! Gev up! Gev up! Make bed! Make bed! Math problem waiting, Dictée waiting, Don Quixote also waiting. Last one up, gonna be last in he class. Gev up! Gev up! I no say insult, I no hitting, but army trumpet say, Gev up pig, gev up pig, pig ge-ev up! You same thing pigs. So gev up gev up quick so director no get mad and break you face!"

One night, at about two in the morning, Don Quixote had a nightmare. Softly he began to moan, "*Hin . . . hin . . . hin . . .*," and then more and more loudly he began to shout, "*Ouïmba . . . Ouïmba . . . ouiïïmbaaa!*"

Inspector Assomption, who had been sleeping on the terrace because of the heat, awoke with a start. "Would you pipe down over there!"

Suddenly pulled from his dream, Don Quixote shouted, "Otéméné sir" (It's not about that), "cé quéquechose qui m'a pris mon guiorje" (Something grabbed me by the throat).

The phrase spread through the school. After that, all we had to do was look up and say, "quéquechose," for someone else to say, "qui m'a pris mon guiorje!" and everyone would burst into laughter.

I completed my first year at the professional school with no trouble. My teachers judged that I had worked hard. It was during that year that a fire destroyed my parents' compound in Bamako. Fortunately, nobody was hurt, but they lost everything: their house, their furniture, money, jewelry, and their stock of merchandise. They were ruined. All that my mother had left was a single piece of jewelry, a large gold ring that she had continued to wear ever since the holy woman she had consulted fifteen years earlier in Bandiagara had told her that "following a day of great distress" there would be nothing left but that ring. My mother sold it for a good price, and that is how she was able to start over. The most important thing was that everyone had come through the ordeal unscathed. As for their fortune, as the adage goes, "It is not worth much more than a nosebleed. In the same manner, it appears for no reason and also disappears for no reason."

And then I was into my second and final year. Of that year, I can remember nothing but a furious work pace. The exams were waiting for us at the end, and the results would determine our future. My most fervent wish was to pass my entrance examination. But my ideas about the future that awaited me were still vague. I had thought about becoming a doctor, but for some unknown reason my father Tidjani was opposed to the idea. In any case, I had no inkling whatsoever of the unexpected destiny that once again, through its usual reversals, fate had in store for me.

Mr. Bouyagui Fadiga, who would later become famous in Sudan (Mali), was my second-year teacher. Gifted with a sharp intellect, his intellectual baggage was thought remarkable by the Europeans of the time, who liked to read his writings. The school was still under the supervision of Mr. Frédéric Assomption, a former teacher who became primary school inspector and the person who, it can be said, was the cultural father of all the old native colonial officials from Sudan. He is certainly the one French teacher who left the deepest impression on our country.

Mr. Assomption was particularly proud of Bouyagui Fadiga, whom he termed "a pure intellectual product of French culture." And indeed, this is exactly what they wanted to do with us, albeit with the best of intentions. Empty us of ourselves and fill us with the colonizer's way of being, acting, and thinking.

In our case, it cannot be said that this policy failed. There was a time when the depersonalization of the "French subject," duly educated and instructed, was such that, in fact, he wanted only one thing: to become the exact copy of the colonizer to the point of adopting his clothing, his cuisine, often his religion, and sometimes even his tics!

Shortly before summer vacation, before we had been informed of our entrance examination results, the excise man at the Bamako office of Enregistrement et des Domaines (Official Registry and Tax Records), a Guadeloupean named Mr. Bourgeois, requested that Mr. Assomption send a detail of six or seven good students who could help to sort through packages containing the effects and personal belongings of tirailleurs who had died on the front during World War I. Mr. Assomption chose a group of six or seven students, and I was among them.

Sometime earlier, the territory of Upper Senegal and Niger had been divided in two: the part known as "the land of the Mossis" had been set up as an autonomous colony and been given the name of Upper Volta, and the rest retained the old name of French Sudan. Mr. Jean Sylvandre, of West Indian descent (and who would later become a deputy in the Constituent Assembly in Paris), had been named to the post of excise man at the office of Enregistrement et des Domaines in the new colony of Upper Volta. He had come to Bamako to organize with Mr. Bourgeois the transfer of archive documents concerning the administrative districts of Upper Volta. The sorting and shipping of packages containing the effects of tirailleurs who were originally from Upper Volta was part of this work.

My comrades and I were assigned the task of sorting through several tons of packages. Most of them had sat piled for years in a damp, dark warehouse in trusteeship to the public curator. They were extremely mildewed. We had to open them, identify the name of the deceased and his heirs with the help of an enclosed identification slip, and then carefully rewrap the package with its new address.

The property left behind by these heroes who had "died for France" was generally quite scant. A few personal effects, some small objects, photographs of family members, fellow soldiers, or a couple of White benefactors dubbed "White Papas and Mamas," and at times the photo of a White girlfriend, sometimes named "Madame, My Crush." But occasionally, along with this modest and touching legacy, there were also rings, watches, and wallets containing money, and this made our work more sensitive.

We did our sorting in a large room under the direct supervision of Madani Bamantia Tall, a clerk who hailed from Bandiagara. Mr. Bourgeois eventually ordered Madani B. Tall to train me to do the work that was assigned to this position, so as to be able to make up for the absence of one of his agents, who had taken a lengthy leave. Since I was a compatriot and younger than he, according to the rights bestowed by tradition, not to mention the entire administrative hierarchy, Madani B. Tall could have treated me as he pleased. But he was a good friend. He cheerfully taught me the job, down to its smallest details, and explained the function of each unit of the bureau. These included Records, Estates, Land Registry, Property Guardianship, Stamps, guardianship of the wealth of deceased officials with no near living relatives, and so on. In particular, I was given the job of recording private deeds and selling tax stamps, which placed me in frequent contact with the French Tribunal and the Treasury.

While awaiting the results of my exams, I worked at these tasks as an unpaid student during the entire vacation period. Mr. Sylvandre, who had not yet returned to Ouagadougou, often came to the office to watch us work. I was introduced to him along with all my other comrades. I had no inkling of the role that he would soon play in my life.

The Consequences of a Refusal: Exile in Ouagadougou

As my vacation was drawing to a close, the examination results were announced. I had passed and was admitted! The entire class of admitted students was to leave together for Gorée Island, via Kayes and Dakar.

"What? Leave for Senegal and several more years of study?" My mother was categorically opposed to the idea. "You have studied enough French now," she said. "It is time for you to learn how to become a true Fula." Since my master Tierno Bokar was no longer around to soften her resolve, I had no choice but to submit to her wishes. This was not too much to bear. In those days, it was absolutely unthinkable to disobey the orders of one's mother. In a pinch, one could disobey one's father, but never one's mother. Everything that came from the mother was considered sacred and a source of blessings. It would thus never have occurred to me to oppose my mother's wishes. Since she had decided that it would be so, it was thus God's will, and therefore such would be my fate.

The most difficult part of this was that I had to go and explain to Mr. Assomption that I would not be joining the group of my classmates bound for Gorée because my mother did not wish it. Upset at seeing me take this stance, he tried everything to make me change my mind. But he also knew that he would not succeed, as he was also familiar with my character. He therefore decided to take me in to the governor's office, in the hope that intimidation would sway me.

Upon arrival at the residence, he introduced me to the chief of staff, who was named Mr. Mandagoux. "Here's a very good student who is refusing to go to Gorée," he said.

While the two were discussing my case, the governor walked in. He was on very good terms with Mr. Assomption. "Well, Frédéric," he said, "what's new?"

"Here's a good student who has passed the exams but who is refusing to leave for Gorée because he says that his mother is against it."

"It is out of the question to refuse," the governor said sternly. "You must join your classmates. If your parents try to stop you, I'll put your mother and father in prison."

Without thinking, I shot back, "My mother, maybe, Mr. Governor, but not my father!"

"What?" he exclaimed. "I can't put your father in prison?"

"No, Mr. Governor."

"And why not?"

"Because he is dead."

The governor quickly suppressed a smile, and then turned to the chief of staff. "Mandagoux, don't send this boy to Gorée. Send him off to the devil with all the others who are starting to get bad ideas."

In those days, "the devil" referred to the administrative outposts that were as far away from Bamako as possible. In other words, this meant Ouagadougou or Fada-N'Gourma, which were in Mossi country, the newly named Upper Volta.

Devastated by this turn of events, Mr. Assomption returned to his school and I headed for the office of Enregistrement et des Domaines to tell Mr. Bourgeois what had happened.

As soon as he had learned that I no longer intended to go to Gorée, Mr. Bourgeois sent an official letter to the governor requesting that I be allowed to join the ranks of *écrivains auxiliaires* (assistant secretaries) and be appointed to a position in his bureau, where I had already been working. The governor categorically refused. He announced that because of my attitude, I would be sent outside of Sudan to work in the new colony of Upper Volta. He personally did not have the power to send me there, since that territory was not under his direct jurisdiction but fell under the authority of a new governor named Mr. Fousset. He therefore ordered Mr. Mandagoux to have me sign an application for the position of *écrivain temporaire à titre essentiellement précaire et révocable* (temporary secretary classified as essentially revocable and subject to repeal), for there was truly nothing lower that could be found in ranks of the administrative hierarchy. This application would then be addressed to the new governor of Upper Volta. I was forced to comply.

At a time when simply failing to salute the commandant or the flag was cause for administrative internment, it was out of the question for a French subject to disobey an order emanating from even the lowliest bearer of a parcel of colonial authority, and here was an order from the governor himself. If I had refused, I would have automatically been sent to prison for noncompliance, without any other justification or trial. I therefore signed the letter and informed Mr. Bourgeois of the fact.

Quite angry that I was to be sent off to "the bush" when he needed my help, Mr. Bourgeois said, "Because I can't have you, at least I will try to have you placed in good hands." He immediately wrote to his friend Jean Sylvandre, who had returned to Ouagadougu, to alert him about my "application," reminding him who I was and advising him to place me in his office.

In the meantime, I went to bid farewell to my old teachers, to thank them for their help, and to explain the reasons behind my decision. I still remember the words of Mr. Bouyagui Fadiga: "Do not regret anything. You must still continue to learn and perfect yourself, and you will not be able to do that by going to school. Schools hand out diplomas, but we learn by living."

This was wise advice that I did indeed put into practice, especially where French culture was concerned, for I became a pure autodidact and voracious reader. The books I read were not particularly literary, however, for I remained faithful to the great classics that we had studied at school. I especially read anything related to history, religious thought, and the disciplines related to anthropology. Even now I still consider myself to be an eternal student, always eager to learn and to be enriched through contact with others.

For the moment, the single fact of having passed the entrance exams was enough for me. My normal school friends could no longer mock me and boast to our valentines at my expense. Concerning my mother's decision, it was in line with those taken by every good Muslim family in those days. All in all, I regret nothing.

Time passed, and we reached the month of November 1921. While I waited for what would follow, I continued to work regularly at the bureau of Enregistrement et Domaines. I held the position of a native civil servant, but with no title, and I was not paid. Since the governor had refused to appoint me to a position, it was out of the question for me to be paid. I was like the imbecile in the old Fula fable where an excellent cook once lived in the mythical village of Héli. Her services were requested on the occasion of every grand banquet. Every time she had finished making all the food perfectly, the mistress of the household would dip her hand in the sauce, walk up to the cook, and wipe the sauce on her lips. "Ah!" she would say. "You truly are the queen of cooks! Goodbye until next time!" And the poor woman would be sent away with sauce on her lips and no food in her stomach. Everyone who met her in the street thought that she had eaten her fill, when in fact, she had simply forgotten to rinse her mouth.

My situation was similar. Over the course of all those months of work, I was fed good words and congratulations. Troubled by my situation, Mr. Bourgeois sometimes slipped me a small gratuity, but fortunately I did not really need it. I lived with my parents and lacked for nothing.

Over time, I had gotten used to the idea that perhaps I would be able to remain in Bamako, where I had in fact received several good employment offers in the private sector. But the conjoined efforts of Mr. Bourgeois and Mr. Sylvandre had borne their fruit. On November 25, 1921, I was summoned to the office of a man named Sinibaldi, the representative of Upper Volta in Bamako. He was a Native Affairs clerk from Corsica. The night before, he had received a telegram from Upper Volta and read it to me as following:

> PLEASE INFORM AMADOU BA, PREVIOUSLY OF THE OFFICE OF DOMAINES BAMAKO THAT HE SHALL BE NAMED TEMPORARY SECRETARY MONTHLY SALARY 125 FRANCS. STOP. IN CASE OF ACCEPTANCE PLEASE UNDERTAKE TRAVEL OUAGADOUGOU WITH VOLTA FUNDS. SIGNED FOUSSET.

Certainly the words "à titre essentiellement précaire et révocable" (classified as essentially revocable and subject to repeal) did not appear in the telegram, but they were implied since I was still nothing but a simple "temporary" local secretary, although with my education level and success on the exams, I should have been hired into the upper ranks and given a permanent position. Strangely, however, I was to be paid an exceptionally high salary. Everything was ambiguous, and I secretly feared the worst concerning what my fate in Upper Volta would be, where I would be far from my family, if by misfortune I did not happen to please my bosses.

"Well, well, young man," said Mr. Sinibaldi, "you must be happy, for you've been given a good job, hmm?"

It was too much. I once again replied too quickly, frankly expressing my thoughts, which was the last thing that was expected of me! I explained that my position seemed to be rather unstable. That Ouagadougou was too far for me to go under what had been qualified as "temporary" conditions, and that, all things considered, I preferred to remain in Bamako, where a large trading company, the Compagnie française d'Afrique occidentale (French West Africa Company), had offered me a job. Mr. Sinibaldi gave me a sardonic look.

"My boy, you are more impertinent than a Negro king! Do you think the French Administration gave you an education so that you could go and work somewhere else? I'm going to report your case to the Governor of Sudan. Once he makes a ruling, I'll tell you the flavor of the sauce that you'll be eaten with."

I returned home with my heart full of worry. My mind was filled with the blackest of thoughts concerning that Corsican, Mr. Sinibaldi. His head was bald and his rabbit-like buckteeth stuck out so far they almost completely covered his lower lip. Fearsome and feared even by his superiors, he did not fool around. It did not matter whether people were White or Black. For the latter group, he even kept a whip hanging in his office and he did not hesitate to use it when he was angry. Alas, his fits of anger were so frequent that the Africans in his entourage said that they could not differentiate between it and his breathing and would say, "Is he breathing, or is he just angry?"

A few days later, a policeman came to get me. He took me to Koulouba, to the governor's office. First, I was made to wait in the office of Mr. Daba Keïta, the future father of Modibo Keïta, who was to become the first president of the Republic of Mali. Mr. Keïta, who knew me, advised me not to refuse to go to Ouagadougou. Otherwise, I would run the risk of being taken there by force and under very disagreeable conditions.

An orderly came to get me and led me in to see Mr. Mandagoux, the chief of staff. I remained standing before him with my arms crossed over my chest.

This was an old habit I had learned in school that I had not yet abandoned. Mr. Mandagoux casually took out the letter that Mr. Sinibaldi had written about me and sent to him. "Well young man! First you refuse to continue your studies and now you refuse to go to serve France in Ouagadougou because you don't think your job is secure?"

Just then the governor walked in to the office to discuss an urgent matter with his chief of staff. As he was about to leave and since he hadn't noticed me, Mr. Mandagoux reminded him, "Sir, you have before you here the young and insolent Amadou Bâ, who has been making trouble about reporting to his post in Ouagadougou."

Holding the door ajar, the governor turned around and looked at me. I felt all my blood rise to my head. He could do anything he wanted with me. "Enough of your whims," he said severely. Mandagoux, send this young man to Ouagadougou. He is to go on foot. Dispatch a district guard to watch him." And then he left the room.

Mr. Mandagoux threw up his two big arms. "See what you get for arguing! Now you'll be going to Ouagadougou under the escort of a district guard, who will be on horseback. You little troublemaker, go on, get the hell out of here!"

I slowly walked back down the hill, completely devastated. Mr. Sinibaldi's parting words echoed in my head: "I'll tell you the flavor of the sauce that you'll be eaten with."

What was waiting for me in Ouagadougou?

At the sight of my dragging feet and long face, my mother asked me what the governor had said. I reported the scene. She was all the more upset, for she no doubt felt partly responsible for the situation. When she had forbidden me to leave for Gorée, she had not at all foreseen that the consequences of that interdict would be that I would be sent to a country much farther away, with no hope of any kind of vacation for a period of several years and under deplorable working conditions. "God is greatest!" she said with a sigh. "He will protect you." She cited the Koranic verse, "Happiness is next to sadness" (or, "With hardship will be ease"). "Who knows," she added, "maybe your luck is out there?" She tried to make me feel better, but I knew that she felt bad.

That night, before going to bed, I don't know what crazy idea took hold of me. I had heard that for chronic malaria sufferers, as we all were, a sudden change in temperature could provoke a high fever. So I took a very hot bath followed by a very cold bath. The reaction came quickly. That very night, my temperature shot up, and I fell into such an alarming state that my mother took me to the dispensary. I was placed in the emergency ward in the Point G hospital. I fell into a kind of coma and came out of it two days later, but I couldn't speak, and I didn't recognize anyone. My mother, who never left my side, fed me, but I know not how. After ten or twelve days, I recovered my wits. I had returned from far, far away! Along with the extremely grave case of malarial fever, I had contracted a pulmonary pleurisy, which in fact left me with respiratory problems for the rest of my life. My mother was so happy to see my recovery that on that very day, in order to thank God, she distributed a great quantity of food, clothing, and money to the poor.

I was still very weak, however. Worried, my mother went to consult a marabout who was famous for his surprising clairvoyance and who had been nicknamed *Mawdo molebo gotel*, "the old man with only one hair," which meant "the old man (or, the Master), who only has one word," and also, "who is one of a kind." After casting a chart that was most likely numeric or geomantic, he declared, "Oh, Kadidja, rejoice, for your son will leave the city, and his failing health will be completely restored. His sojourn in a foreign land is inevitable and he will remain there for a rather long time before returning, but he will not be unhappy there. He will make a name for himself there and will start a family. He will live there in ease, but without amassing a fortune. He will have many Black and White friends. You must allow him to leave." In conclusion, he added, "Throughout his life, your son will enjoy the good graces of important people. One day, he will even build a house several stories in height. When that day comes, if I am still alive, I will come and ask him to build me a little hut at the foot of his house." In this friendly quip, there was, in the indirect manner of our old wise men, an indirect lesson urging gratitude and humility. The house of "several stories" exists today in Abidjan, and one of my great regrets is that the old man was not able to come and join me there. I would have been overjoyed to have been able to build his lodgings in my compound.

All my mother's fears were alleviated. With a light heart she quickly distributed to the poor the sacrifices that the marabout had prescribed.

Meanwhile, Mr. Sylvandre was getting impatient, wondering why I had not yet arrived. He had sent three telegrams to the governor of Upper Volta inquiring why I was late and emphasizing the urgency with which I should embark. A message, emanating from Mr. Madagoux, I believe, although I am not certain of it, was sent to Dr. Lairac, the chief physician at the hospital, telling him to discharge me as quickly as possible, and above all not to authorize me any time to convalesce, implying that I was just a "slouch." Dr. Lairac, who was a colonel and who sported five gold cords on his arm, took offense at this behavior. He decided that I would not leave his care until I was completely well. As for Mr. Sinibaldi, who was completely exasperated by the situation, he had apparently decided that I would leave Bamako for Ouagadougou on

December 31, at the very latest, dead or alive. Luckily, on the 20th of December, I felt myself coming back to life and began to recover my strength. On the 25th I was still under the effects of my illness, but I felt well enough to travel. I returned home on the 28th or the 29th, just in time to prepare for my departure as scheduled.

As soon as I left the hospital, Mr. Sinibaldi had telegraphed Ouagadougou with the news that I would be sent off on December 31st without fail. District guard first class Mamadou Koné was assigned to escort me to Mopti, where another guard would take over. I was to travel down to Ouagadougou via Bandiagara. The entire journey from Bamako to Ouagadougou covered a little over a thousand kilometers. In the end, thanks to the kindly intervention of the guard or a last-minute authorization due to my health, I no longer recall which, I traveled the fifty kilometers from Bamako to Koulikoro by train, and completed the Koulikoro–Mopti leg by pirogue. Between Mopti and Ouagadougou, that left just about 150 kilometers to cover on foot. Still, this was much better than the thousand kilometers that I had anticipated!

Before my departure, my mother gave me a complete "colonial outfit," as befitted any young "White-Black" administrative employee. This was comprised of a three-piece gabardine suit, a three-piece suit of white cotton drill, three shirts, a pair of black shoes, three pairs of socks, a pith helmet—vital for my prestige!—and, to top it all off, the essential symbols of my status, a European cane, a pair of dark glasses, and a pince-nez! She had also added a complete set of African clothes, which included a superb boubou embroidered by my father Tidjani. To ensure my comfort along the way, she also included a chaise longue, a folding table and chairs, a cook pot, a frying pan, some silverware, a two-liter jerry can, a hurricane lamp, and a very handsome carved dagger from my father, which reminded me of our first nocturnal crossing of the Dounfing chasm.

I also wore pinned to my chest a very beautiful silver pocketwatch given to me by Mr. Bourgeois. It had come from a package belonging to a tirailleur whose heirs could not be determined. Each of my coworkers had also received a watch commemorating his service in the bureau. Mine was German and my unknown tirailleur had probably found it on a dead German officer. In any case, Mr. Bourgeois was of this opinion. Before I left, he also gave me a spyglass that I was very proud of.

My mother had decided to stay with me until we reached Koulikoro. On December 31, 1921, after bidding my final farewells to the friends and relatives who had come to the train station with us, covered with blessings and full of good advice, I boarded the train and settled in between my mother and the district guard. A porter loaded our baggage.

During the entire trip, nobody said a word. As I watched the scenery slip by, I recalled the happy moments of my childhood. In my mind's eye, I also recalled the schoolteachers who had influenced me the most. These included my first teacher, the tough but effective Mr. Moulaye Haïdara, who taught us French at the point of his ever active switch, and Mr. Primel, our French teacher in Djenné, who had worked so arduously to make us into good and loyal French subjects and whose love for the "Mother Country" was unmatched by anything other than his hatred of Wilhelm II and his pointy mustache. This very good teacher, so entirely devoted to his craft, had provided us with a rich and solid base of instruction that would later be extremely valuable to me. I also remembered the very good African teachers that I had had in Bamako: Séga Diallo, who was so devoted to his teaching that he lost his voice; Mamadou Koné, who had had to leave and was missed; and Namoussa Doumbia, Namakan Coulibaly, and Bouyagui Fadiga, all of them remarkable as much for their devotion as for their erudition and competence. And let us not forget the "father" of them all, Mr. Frédéric Assomption, who had thought it a good idea to take me into the governor's office and who had succeeded only in getting me sent to "the devil."

While the district guard who was in charge of security in Koulikoro worked with my guard and warden to arrange our pirogue trip to Mopti, my mother went to visit a chief laptot whose wife was one of her association comrades from Bandiagara. We spent several days with them. As it happened, our host held great storytelling sessions every evening at his home, as was the custom among the laptots when they were between trips. His friends joined with griots, who had come to perform to the music of their guitars. It was there that, for the first time, I took down in writing everything that I had heard, either word for word when it was possible, or in a general overview. I had brought a stock of large ledger books along with me. One of them became my first "journal." In Koulikoro, and for the entire rest of my trip, I would write about the principal events of each day, and especially anything that I saw or heard that was of interest and that had to do with our oral traditions. Once I had gotten into the habit of doing this, I never stopped, and I have continued to do this all my life.

Three days before our arrival, my health was so much better that I felt strong enough to lift stones. My mother was so happy that she once again distributed money, food, and clothing to the poor.

For my trip, the Commandant of Koulikoro requisitioned a large and comfortably outfitted pirogue that was powered by six punters. Our departure was set for January 5th at ten o'clock in the morning. The night before, the laptots had loaded the pirogue with all the necessary provisions. As for Mamadou Koné, the district guard whom the authorities in Bamako had charged with keeping an eye on me for fear that I would escape, he had quickly traded his role as warden for that of devoted assistant and amiable traveling companion. Administrative directives were powerless to overrule African customs when we were among ourselves and once the customary small gifts had been exchanged.

I Bid Farewell on the Riverbank

On the morning of our departure, my mother accompanied me to the edge of the river. Just before reaching the water's edge, we had to cross a small sand dune. We held hands as we walked. As we descended the dune facing south, a north wind pressed our clothes to our backs. My mother insisted on climbing aboard the pirogue and looking under the canopies to see with her own eyes that nothing was missing. Reassured, she distributed a few final gifts and returned to shore. Taking my hand, she drew me away from the group. There she gave me fifty francs to cover my travel expenses, and then, taking both of my hands in hers, she said, "Look me in the eyes."

I looked deep into her eyes, and for a moment, as we say in Fulfulde, "our two eyes became four." All the energy from this indomitable woman seemed to be flowing into me through her gaze. Then, as African mothers will do, she turned my hands over, and in a grand maternal blessing, she passed the tip of her tongue over my palms.[2] Then she said, "My son, I am going to give you some advice that you will be able to use throughout your adult life. Remember it well." And she punctuated each piece of advice by touching the tip of one of her fingers.

"Never open your trunk in the presence of others. A man's strength comes from his reserve. One must neither display poverty nor wealth. A display of wealth attracts jealous people, beggars, and thieves.

"Never be envious of anyone or anything. Accept your fate with resolve. Be patient in adversity and restrained in your happiness. Do not judge yourself in relation to those who are above you, but in relation to those who are less fortunate than you.

"Do not be miserly. Give alms as often as possible, but give to the unfortunate and not to itinerant little marabouts.

"Be as helpful as you can and ask the least possible recompense for your help. Do this without being prideful, and never be ungrateful to God nor to people.

"Be faithful to your friends and do everything you can not to hurt them.

"Never fight with a man who is younger or weaker than you.

"If you share a dish with friends or people you do not know, never take a large portion. Do not overfill your mouth with food and, above all, do not look at people while you are eating, for nothing is more repellent than mastication. And never be the last to rise. Lingering around a meal is for gluttons, and gluttony is shameful.

"Respect the elderly. Every time that you meet an elder, approach him with respect and give him a gift, however minimal. Ask for advice and ask questions discreetly.

"Beware of flatterers, loose women, games of chance, and alcohol.

"Respect your leaders, but do not put them in the place of God.

"Say your prayers regularly. Entrust your destiny to God every morning when you rise, and thank Him every night before you go to bed.

"Do you understand?"

"Yes, Dadda."

"Finally, do not forget to go and greet our relatives in Diafarabé, Moura, Saredina, and Mopti. And as soon as you arrive in Bandiagara, reserve your first visit for Tierno Bokar. When you see him, you will say, 'My mother, your little sister, has ordered me to come and place myself in God's hands through your intervention.' Can you remember all that?"

"Yes, Dadda, don't worry. I will keep every one of your words before me for the rest of my life."

As we returned to the pirogue, our feet sank into the fine sand. Before I boarded, my mother recited the Fatiha and blessed me. "May the Peace of God accompany you! Go in Peace, may your sojourn be peaceful, and may you return to us with peace!" As I was saying "Amine!" she turned away and walked back toward the dune. She marched straight ahead without ever once turning back. I think she was crying. No doubt this extremely proud woman did not want me to see her tears. She whom no one had ever seen cry was unused to grand displays of emotion, especially in front of her grown son.

I boarded the pirogue where the guard Mamadou Koné had already taken his seat, his musket strapped across his chest. The six punters, three in the prow and three in the stern, stood waiting for the order to depart. "Mister Boss," cried the guard, "laptots all be ready, wait word you mouth only." It was the first time that I had ever heard myself called "Boss." It had a strange effect on me. Instead of immediately replying, I instinctively turned to look at my mother one last time. I saw her reach the top of the dune. The wind was billowing through the hems of her boubou and lifting her delicate head veil.

She looked like a damselfly preparing for flight. Slowly, her elegant silhouette disappeared behind the dune as though swallowed by the sand. As she disappeared, so too did Amkoullel, along with all my childhood.

The voice of the guard reiterating his request pulled me from my daydream. I was no longer a little boy, protected and fussed over by his mother, but a "Mister Boss," about to give orders to a district guard armed with a musket and bayonet and six strapping laptots. I do not know how, but the command that I had heard many times coming from the mouths of officers in Kati automatically reached my lips. In all seriousness, I issued the command, emphasizing it with an energetic gesture.

"Well, if everyone is ready, then forward march!" What was worse, I suddenly felt very proud of myself. With my colonial pith helmet on my head, I forgot for a moment that I was only a *temporary secretary classified as essentially revocable and subject to repeal* and took myself for a great chief.

"*Aïwa!*" cried Mamadou Koné. "Let's go!"

In admirable unison, the laptots raised their poles, and in single broad stroke, plunged them into the water. By leaning on them with all their weight, they were able to push us free from the muddy banks. The pirogue reared like a horse spurred by a rider before it slowly drew away from the banks, trailing yellowish eddies in its wake.

Once we had reached a part of the river where the descending current worked in our favor, the pirogue picked up speed, rocking gently from side to side with the rhythmical strokes of the punters. Little by little, Koulikoro's sandy dune faded into the distance.

I turned and faced forward. The prow of the boat was slicing through the limpid and silky waters of the old river. Its current bore us along, drawing us ever more quickly toward the unknown world that was waiting for me, toward the great adventure of my adult life.

TRANSLATOR'S ACKNOWLEDGMENTS

I would like to express my deepest appreciation to Ralph Austen for his early encouragement and unflagging support of this project and for agreeing to write the foreword to this translation. I am also extremely grateful to him for having generously read drafts of the entire manuscript and for providing valuable feedback.

I would also like to extend sincere thanks to my dear friend and colleague Dianne Johnson for having read an early version of the introduction, and for offering publishing advice and general moral support. I also thank my friend and colleague Ashley Williard for her generous and tactful feedback, and I am extremely grateful to Mamadou Diouf and Louis Brenner for their support and encouragement.

I also extend my sincere thanks to the Camargo Foundation for a Core Fellowship Residency Grant in Cassis, France, in 2019. Camargo's capable director, Julie Chénot, and all of the members of the Camargo staff ensured that the residency provided precious time, material support, and rich intellectual exchange. I would also like to thank my fellow Camargo core residents for sharing their artistry and scholarly acumen during our time together. In particular, I had the great pleasure of meeting and working with the gifted translator Sika Fakambi, whose French translations of such writers as Zora Neale Hurston and Sonia Sanchez are an inspiration. I would also like to thank Béatrice and Georges Benchetrit of Cassis for their support, and for introducing me via e mail to the actor and comedian Saïdou Abatcha, who draws a great deal of inspiration from the works of Amadou Hampâté Bâ. I thank Mr. Abatcha for introducing me (via WhatsApp) to Rokiatou Hampâté Bâ, daughter of Amadou Hampâté Bâ and director of the Fondation Amadou Hampâté Bâ, who kindly gave me her blessings for this and future translations of her father's work.

I am deeply indebted to my husband, Garane; my children, Shakhlan and Gashan; and my parents, Don and Mary, for their constant love and support and for "holding down the fort" during my residency in Cassis. Finally, I must thank the sage Kana Garane Ahmed, who first began to teach me about Africa in 1982 and who passed away much too soon.

This translation was also supported by a series of grants from the University of South Carolina. Two Provost's Arts and Humanities Grants and additional research grants from the Walker Institute and the Department of Languages, Literatures, and Cultures have helped this translation come into being. For these, I am extremely grateful.

NOTES

Foreword to the Translation

1 See Monod's preface to this volume and also Triaud, "D'un maître à l'autre."
2 Amadou Hampâté Bâ, "Pourquoi j'écris," interview with Isaïe Biton Koulibaly, Abidjan, ca. 1975. Fonds Amadou Hampâté Bâ, L'Institut Mémoires de l'édition contemporaine, l'abbeye d'Ardenne (hereafter IMEC), 4FHB 6GE8-4/359 (this archive is now held by the Fondation Amadou Hampâté Bâ, in Abidjan, Côte d'Ivoire).
3 For more on this point, see chapter 5, note 5, in this volume.
4 For Hampâté Bâ's fullest statement on this role, see his "The Living Tradition," in Ki-Zerbo, UNESCO General History of Africa, 166–203.
5 Hobsbawm, and Ranger, Invention of Tradition.
6 This theme of local initiation disrupted by European education also plays a major role in perhaps the most widely read of all francophone West African coming-of-age memoirs/novels, L'Enfant noir, by Camara Laye.
7 I am still pursuing some inquiries into the ethnography of Fula youth associations but have thus far found very little material, suggesting that they became more prominent in the twentieth-century urban situations experienced by Hampâté Bâ.
8 The term comes from the Arabic *muhtasib* (market inspector).
9 In the file titled Carrière: Notes by Hélène Heckmann, IMEC 6GE9-2/416; see also note 12, pages 332–33, in this volume.

Introduction. Between Memory and Memorial

1 My translation of volume 2 is in progress under the proposed title *At Your Service, Commandant!*
2 See Izzo, *Experiments with Empire*, for a reading of *Oui Mon Commandant!* as ethnographic fiction.
3 The colony of French West Africa (1895–1958) was a federation that joined Mauritania, Senegal, French Sudan (now Mali), French Guinea (now Guinea), Côte d'Ivoire, Upper Volta (Haute Volta—now Burkina Faso), Dahomey (now Benin), and Niger. The administrative capital was located in Dakar, Senegal. French Sudan is not to be confused with the Republic of Sudan, whose capital is

Khartoum. A. H. Bâ explains Fula and Toucouleur (also spelled Tukulor) ethnic identities in chapter 1.

4   A. H. Bâ provides a similar explanation in *L'Etrange destin de Wangrin* (*The Fortunes of Wangrin*), which tells the story of an African interpreter who undermines colonial authorities in the French Sudan. He writes that the sons of chiefs "were given the kind of education that enabled them to become servants, houseboys, cooks, or low-ranking civil servants [such] as copy clerks, telegraphists, or male nurses." Bâ, *Fortunes of Wangrin*, 262n9; Bâ, *L'Etrange destin de Wangrin*, 367n10.

5   The colonial administrator known as the "commandant" is ubiquitous in both volumes of A. H. Bâ's memoirs. As historian Ralph Austen explains in a personal communication, "The title [of commandant] derives from the French marine infantry, which played an important role in the French conquest of West Africa. But unlike its American equivalent, the marine infantry was considered a low prestige branch of the national military order" (Austen to Garane, October 2019).

6   As Mamadou Diouf points out in "L'Universalisme (europeén?) à l'épreuve des histoires indigènes," the contradiction between the "universalisme de la mission civilisatrice et les pratiques coloniales a été mise en évidence et largement exploitée par le sujet colonial" (universalism of the civilizing mission has been underscored and largely developed by colonial subjects). Although Diouf cites the work of Bernard Dadié as an example of an ironic gaze cast on colonial practices that had the effect of keeping the colonized "hors du territoire de l'universel, malgré les proclamations civilisatrices" (outside the territory of the universal despite its civilizing proclamations), attentive readers of *Amkoullel* will discover a similar ironic gaze, particularly where the descriptions of various colonial authorities and their "acolytes," as Bâ calls them, are concerned. Diouf, "L'Universalisme (européen?)," 35.

7   Literally, *The Black Boy* or *The Black Child*, which Kirkup chose to translate as *The Dark Child: The Autobiography of an African Boy*.

8   See chapter 4, "Return to Bandiagara," under the heading "The White Man's Excrement and the Town Made of Trash."

9   Lebdai, *Autobiography as a Writing Strategy*, 1–2.

10 A. H. Bâ explains the intricacies of this plot in chapter 2, "Khadidja, My Mother."

11 While the "native" Primary Studies Certificate, or Certificat d'etudes primaires (CEP), was modeled on that of France, it was not legally equivalent before World War II. See also chapter 5, note 6.

12 See Hélène Heckmann, "Petite histoire éditoriale du conte Kaïdara," in Bâ, *Contes initiatiques peuls*, 343–45. Hélène Heckmann was also an important figure in Amadou Hampâté Bâ's professional and private life. According to Bintou Sanankoua, who grew up in A. H. Bâ's household, it was after A. H. Bâ met and married Hélène Heckmann in 1966 that he began to sign his works with his signature alone. Sanankoua writes, "C'est elle qui l'encourage à publier ses livres sans co-auteur alors que, jusqu'ici, il avait signé tous ses ouvrages avec quelqu'un d'autre" (It was she who encouraged him to publish his books without a co-author, for until then, he had always signed all of his other works with someone else)" (409–10). Sankankoua

explains that it was also Heckmann who urged A. H. Bâ to write *L'Etrange destin de Wangrin* and then the *Memoirs*. He later appointed her his literary executor. See also Austen and Soares, "Amadou Hampâté Bâ's Life and Work" (141–42), for more information on Heckmann and A. H. Bâ's archived works.

13 For further information on this subject, see Brenner, *West African Sufi*.

14 On the sometimes paternalistic role of paratextual materials such as forewords and introductions, see Watts, *Packaging Post/coloniality*.

15 Kusum Aggarwal notes that Bâ named the ichthyologist Jacques Daget as coauthor of *L'Empire peul du Macina* in recognition of the logistical support that Bâ had obtained from this director of the Hydrobiology Lab in Diafarabé, Mali, who had helped him to reach his numerous oral sources and to organize his notes (201). By contrast, the 1957 edition of *Tierno Bokar, sage de Bandiagara*, named as "coauthor" Marcel Cardaire, a colonial official who held the title of "Officer of Muslim Affairs," who had been assigned to investigate Bâ's Tidjani Muslim beliefs, for the French colonial officials considered them at the time as potentially subversive. In *Vie et enseignement de Tierno Bokar*, Bâ explains that Cardaire had been sent by the French government to "manage Muslim affairs and to carry out an investigation on me" (31). A. H. Bâ later revised this work and published it under his own name in 1980 with the title *Vie et enseignement de Tierno Bokar: Le sage de Bandiagara*. For more information on the relationship between Cardaire and Bâ, see Louis Brenner, "Becoming Muslim in Soudan Français."

16 Irele, *African Imagination*, 83.

17 When one enters the statement in its French version on an internet search engine, it is still attributed to A. H. Bâ, while in its English versions, the statement is vaguely known as an "old African proverb." Although there has been some confusion surrounding the exact time and place in which A. H. Bâ made his so-called burning library statement, he did in fact address the Africa Commission at the 1960 UNESCO General Conference in Paris where he was representing Mali, newly independent from France. In that speech he declared, "Je considère la mort de chacun de ces traditionnalistes comme l'incendie d'un fonds culturel non exploité" (I consider the death of each of these traditionalists to be like the incineration of an untapped archive). He was arguing for the urgent need to collect and record Africa's endangered oral traditions from a dying generation of elder "traditionalists," the guardians of memory as transmitted through the spoken word.

According to Yacouba Konaté, in "Le Syndrome Amadou Hampâté Bâ," the now famous aphorism about "the burning library" was in fact pronounced in an interview between A. H. Bâ and Baba Kaké, in which Bâ was explaining a traditional West African view of the difference between writing and knowledge:

> L'écriture est une chose et le savoir en est une autre. L'écriture est la photographie du savoir, mais elle n'est pas le savoir lui-même. Le savoir est une lumière qui est en l'homme; héritage de ce qui lui a été transmis. La parole EST l'homme. Le verbe est créateur. Il maintient l'homme dans sa nature propre. Apprenez que dans mon pays, quand un vieillard meurt, c'est une bibliothèque qui brûle.

[Writing is one thing and knowledge is another. Writing is the photograph of knowledge, but it is not knowledge itself. Knowledge is a light that is in man; the heritage of what has been transmitted to him. The word IS man. The verb is creative. It maintains humanity in his own nature. Know that in my country, when an elder dies, it is a library that burns]. (58)

In chapter 4 of *Amkoullel*, A. H. Bâ attributes a similar citation to Tierno Bokar. He writes:

The fact of never having had writing has thus never deprived Africa of having a past, a history, and a culture. As my master Tierno Bokar would say much later, "Writing is one thing and knowledge is another. Writing is the photograph of knowledge, but it is not knowledge itself. Knowledge is the light in man. It is the heritage of everything that the ancestors were able to know about and whose seeds they have transmitted, just as the Baobab tree is potentially contained in its own seed." (page 160)

18 Kisukidi, "*Laetitia Africana*," 60.
19 Kisukidi, "*Laetitia Africana*," 61.
20 Kisukidi, "*Laetitia Africana*," 61.
21 Watts, *Packaging Post/coloniality*, 17.
22 Moudileno, "Qu'est-ce qu'un auteur postcolonial?," 161.
23 Mbembe and Sarr, *Ecrire l'Afrique-monde*, 162.
24 Bancel and Blanchard, "La colonisation," 137 (my translaton). "L'histoire colonial a fait l'objet d'un processus de refoulement qui a maintenu en parallèle le mythe de 'la mission civilisatrice de la France.' Ce mythe a eu pour fonction d'éviter d'ouvrir une 'page douloureuse de notre passé' dont les conséquences sur notre contemporanéité ont été jugées potentiellement dangereuses, du fait notamment de la présence sur le territoire français ... de 'descendants' d'immigrés issus des anciennes colonies. Jusqu'au début des années 1990, la marginalisation de l'histoire coloniale répondait à la double exigence d'oublier un traumatisme historique heurtant la représentation de la nation et de prévenir tout ressac des affrontements coloniaux."
25 As if to confirm this, both volumes were reissued by their original publisher, Actes Sud, in 2012 in its prestigious Thesaurus collection under the title *Mémoires*. The volume also includes a book of photographs by Philippe Dupuich and aphorisms and excerpts from works by Bâ entitled *Sur les traces d'Amkoullel l'enfant peul*. This led critic Tirthankar Chanda to conclude, "In Africa as elsewhere, every time an elder dies, it is not a library that burns!" See Chanda, "Les 'Mémoires' réédités." See also Mbembe's *Sortir de la grande nuit* for a detailed study of the ways in which this past is being remembered. See in particular his chapter 3, for an in-depth study of why, although France "decolonized" its empire, it never "decolonized itself" (12).
26 See Garane, "What Is New about Amadou Hampâté Bâ?," for a contextual analysis of Mabankou and Waberi's satirical citations of A. H. Bâ's so-called burning library aphorism. On the relationship between Yambo Oulouguem and A. H. Bâ, see Christopher Wise's introduction to his collection of essays entitled *Yambo*

Ouloguem. This collection also contains an interview with El Hadji Sékou Tall, the direct descendant of the Toucouleur conqueror El Hadji Omar, who appears in chapter 1 of *Amkoullel*. In the interview Tall recalls that his father was responsible for sending A. H. Bâ to the French School for Hostages ("Interview with Al-Hajj Sékou Tall," in Wise, *Yambo Ouloguem*, 238). This event is vividly recounted in chapter 5 of *Amkoullel*. In a different interview, Jean Ouédraogo and Ivoirian writer Ahmadou Kourouma mention A. H. Bâ's *Wangrin* and the possible connections between that work and Kourouma's 1990 novel *Monnè, outrages, et défis*. To cite another example, A. H. Bâ is one of three authors to whom Tierno Monénembo dedicates his 2008 novel, *Peuls*.

27 See chapter 3 of Mbembe's *Sortir de la grande nuit* for an analysis of the ways in which French republican "laïcité" is invoked to "police" (110) French Muslims.
28 Diagne, "Penser de langue à langue," 80.
29 Appiah, *Cosmopolitanism*, 85. (The following two quotes are also from this work.)
30 Mbembe, *Sortir de la grande nuit*, 229.
31 Scholars such as historian Ralph Austen, whose contributions to the study of A. H. Bâ have long been a mainstay for researchers.
32 Eggan, "Strange Fate of Amadou Hampâté Bâ."
33 Ndiaye, "Les mémoires," 13 (my translation). "Parmi les volumes qui portent sa signature, figurent des récits historiques qui se lisent comme des contes [*L'Empire peul du Macina*], des hagiographies et récits épiques qui se lisent comme des romans [*Vie et enseignement de Tierno Bokar*], une biographie que bien des lecteurs ont pris pour un roman autobiographique [*L'Etrange destin de Wangrin*], etc. Tous ces écrits se situent délicatement entre l'oral et l'écrit, entre réalité vécue (ou histoire) et fiction, entre l'individuel et le collectif, et entre les langues. Que cette production prolifique se termine par une autobiographie, genre ambigue entre tous, ne devrait alors pas tant nous étonner."
34 Camargo Foundation Fellowship, Spring 2019; Provost's Humanities Grant, Fall, 2019; African Studies Research Grant, 2012; Provost's Humanities Grant, 2012.
35 Benjamin, "Task of the Translator," 76.
36 Cited in Bâ, *Sur les traces d'Amkoullel, l'enfant peul*, 839.
37 Bâ, "Lettre d'Amadou Hampâté Bâ à la jeunesse africaine" (my translation). "Jeunes gens d'Afrique et du monde, le destin a voulu qu'en cette fin du vingtième siècle, à l'aube d'une ère nouvelle, vous soyez comme un pont jeté entre deux mondes: celui du passé, où de vieilles civilisations n'aspirent qu'à vous léguer leurs trésors avant de disparaître, et celui de l'avenir, plein d'incertitudes et de difficultés, certes, mais riche aussi d'aventures nouvelles et d'expériences passionnantes. Il vous appartient de relever le défi et de faire en sorte qu'il y ait, non-rupture mutilante, mais continuation sereine et fécondation d'une époque par l'autre." This letter is now widely available on the internet. Christian Ndiaye provides the original citation as "Préface," *Notre Librairie* 75–76 (1984): 10–11. See also https://www.youtube.com/watch?v=tHDbYMwbiJQ.
38 See https://www.youtube.com/watch?v=EDP7U8rx5sI. "Personne n'est plus chez lui. Nous sommes tous citoyens du monde. . . . Nous avons un lieu de naissance,

nous devons être citoyens de partout. C'est pourquoi il serait plutôt bon que nous soyons à l'entendement, à l'écoute les uns des autres pour essayer de trouver ce que nous avons de commun pour bâtir le bonheur de demain."

39 "Au moment où l'Européen écoute l'Africain, il faut qu'il cesse d'être européen pour être un élève ne connaissant absolument rien." "Bâ Amadou Hampâté-Savoir qu'on ne sait pas," https://www.youtube.com/watch?v=sAsjD5C073Q, ina.fr.

40 "Si tu veux que je t'enseigne il faut cesser d'être toi, pour être moi. Oublie-toi, pour être moi. Sinon, si tu restes à être toi, nous serons, tout en étant face à face . . . aussi éloignés que le ciel et la terre. Ça veut dire qu'il ne faudrait pas que tu ramènes ce que je vais te dire en le comparant à ce que tu sais . . . il faut te vider de ce que tu sais pour apprendre. Alors c'est là qu'on vous dit qu'il faut savoir qu'on ne sait pas. *Anda a anda*. L'expression peul dit: '*Sa andi a anda a andat.*' Si tu sais que tu ne sais pas, tu sauras. '*Sa anda a anda a andata.*' Si tu ne sais pas que tu ne sais pas, tu ne sauras pas." See "Bâ Amadou Hampâté-Savoir qu'on ne sait pas." https://www.youtube.com/watch?v=sAsjD5C073Q, ina.fr. Readers may recall that Socrates also said, "I know that I know nothing."

41 This tale is reprinted in Bâ, *Sur les traces d'Amkoullel* (126–29) and is also widely available on the internet. See, for example, http://www.trilogies.org/blog-notes/hampate-ba-lecole-cameleon and https://www.youtube.com/watch?v=aedTErSmqME. See also Sika Fakambi, "Parler caméléon," France Culture, June 20, 2016, https://www.franceculture.fr/emissions/au-singulier/sika-fakambi.

42 For an interview with Roukiatou Hampâté Bâ recorded on RTI (Radio Télévision Ivoirienne), May 16, 2018, about the current role that the works of A. H. Bâ play in the preservation of African cultures, see https://www.youtube.com/watch?v=hlEsy36jru4. See also the Fondation Amadou Hampâté Bâ Facebook page, https://www.facebook.com/Fondation-Amadou-Hampâté-BA-273258896173922.

43 These readings can be found at "Dîners lectures de paroles Indigo," in Arles, France, May 10, June 18, and June 24, 2019. See Festival Paroles Indigo, at https://www.facebook.com/FestivalParolesIndigo. I have also read some of his work at the 2016 and 2017 meetings of the American Literary Translator's Association.

44 "Amadou Hampâté Bâ," African Studies Centre Leiden, September 15, 2007, https://www.ascleiden.nl/content/webdossiers/amadou-hampate-ba.

45 For more detail on this performance, see Tierno Bokar, 2005, http://www.tiernobokar.columbia.edu.

46 "Bâ, Amadou Hampâté," WorldCat Identities, accessed June 21, 2020, http://www.worldcat.org/identities/lccn-n84149759/.

47 Austen and Soares, "Amadou Hampâté Bâ's Life," 135.

48 Mbembe, "L'Afrique qui vient," 26.

Preface to the Original Edition

1 [*Trans. note*: On the relationship between Bâ and Monod, see Austen and Soares, "Amadou Hampâté Bâ's Life," 133–42, and Triaud and Robinson, *La Tijâniyya*.]

Author's Foreword by Amadou Hampâté Bâ

1 Amadou Hampâté Bâ made these remarks to Hélène Heckmann, his literary executor, in 1986.

Chapter 1. Roots

1 [*Trans. note*: See Bâ and Dieterlen, *Koumen*, 94-95, and *A la découverte des fresques du Tassili* by Henri Lhote. For a contemporary approach to the history of the Fulas, see Monénembo's *Peuls*.]
2 [*Trans. note*: In Bâ and Daget, *L'Empire peul du Macina*.]
3 [*Trans. note*: For a more elaborate portrayal of Fula history, including the history of the Bâ clan, see Monénembo's *Peuls*, which is in part dedicated to A. H. Bâ.]
4 The old hypothesis taken up by Maurice Delafosse, according to which the Fulas, upon their arrival in the Fouta Tooro, were thought to have adopted a local language that is supposed to have developed into Pulaar, or Fulfulde, does not stand up to analysis for anyone who knows the Fula world and traditions from the inside.
5 *Silatigui*: Not to be confused with *saltigui* or *saltiki* (chief).
6 "Tidjaniya brotherhood": One of the principal Muslim brotherhoods of sub-Saharan and North Africa. The brotherhoods (literally, *tourouq*, "ways"; sing., *tarika*) are not sects since they are not exterior to Islam; rather, they are a kind of internal spiritual family, somewhat akin to the different orders within Catholicism (Franciscans, Dominicans, and so on). Sub-Saharan Africa was essentially islamicized through brotherhoods, which have played a very important role in religion as in society and even in politics. [*Trans note*: See the appendix to Bâ, *Vie et enseignement de Tierno Bokar*, or its translation, *A Spirit of Tolerance*.]
7 In African tradition, the paternal uncle is considered to be like a father and is directly responsible for the child.
8 The servant-mother, often a very young girl, helps the mother and takes care of the child from birth or a very young age.
9 Diawando (pl., Diawambé): member of a Fula-speaking ethnic group living alongside the Fulas since distant antiquity.
10 [*Trans. note*: Bâ also mentions Gueladio in chapter 2 of *L'Empire peul du Macina*, but no explanation is given for the term *peredio*.]
11 "Captives": At first, captives were people who had been captured in raids or taken as prisoners of war. They were bought and sold and could be exploited at will. Their descendants reacted by forming a special class within the African societies of the savanna called *rimaïbé* (sing., *dîmadjo* in Fulfulde, or *wolosso* in Bambara, meaning "born in the house"). Generally, they are servant families, free or not, who for generations had remained attached to a "noble" household whose fate they would share and whose name they would often bear. One became a dîmadjo once a first or second generation was born in the household. The rimaïbé could not be sold, and their patrons owed them and their families shelter, sustenance, and protection. The wealthy patrons often placed the management of their wealth, and almost always the education of their children, in their care. There

were also villages of rimaïbé farmers. The captives purchased and rescued by my father (page 33) were not yet rimaïbé because they could still be sold. They became rimaïbe in his household.
12. Cowries: Small seashells that were used as money.
13. [*Trans. note*: A *marabout* is a religious guide.]
14. Nobles: The Fula word *dîmo* (*horon* in Mandinka) is more or less translated as "noble" and means, in fact, "a free man." A noble is someone who is neither a "captive" (see above, note 11) nor a member of an artisan class (see chapter 3, note 8). For example, every Fula considers himself to be noble by the very fact of being Fula. Over time, positions of authority generated a kind of power aristocracy, but a simple Fula herdsman considered himself to be as noble as a king, all questions of power aside.
15. Red Ears: An expression referring to full-blooded Fulas who are often still connected to traditional pastoral life.
16. [*Trans. note*: Griot(s): A caste comprised of musicians, singers, and knowledgeable genealogists, either itinerant or attached to certain families who are the subjects of their songs and whose history they celebrate. They can also be simple courtiers. See chapter 3, note 8. In French, *griote* with an "e" is the feminine form.]
17. *Je te divorce* [*Trans. note*: rather than the standard French *Je me divorce d'avec toi*] is the literal translation of an African expression that has passed directly into "African French."
18. Instituted in Bandiagara for executed prisoners of war, the drag of degradation consisted in handing the corpse over to children, who would tie its feet together and drag it through the streets before dumping it into a mass grave.
19. I obtained this story from Beydari himself (who would be better known later on under his new name, Zeydi).

Chapter 2. Kadidja, My Mother

1. [*Trans. note*: See Bâ, *Vie et enseignement de Tierno Bokar*, or its translation, *A Spirit of Tolerance*.]
2. To "give birth to a corpse" is a threat that announces a person's death.
3. [*Trans. note*: The "captives" in question are members of Tidjani's household.]
4. A magical-religious practice in which a newborn (or an adult) is bathed in a decoction made from certain plants, sometimes accompanied by the inhalation of smoke and sacred words.
5. "Your 'star'": Literally, your *tiinde*, meaning "the fate attached to your forehead." It is said that someone has a good or bad tiinde.
6. The number thirty-three is an important symbol both in Islamic and in African traditions, just as it is in Western and Eastern ones.
7. *Naaba*: "King" in Mossi, the language spoken in Louta province. It was a familiar nickname given to Tidjani by his family and friends.
8. Colonial marriages: Many colonial officers and administrators lived with young native women who were either commandeered by force or married in a sham "traditional colonial marriage," which automatically expired at the departure of the

"husband." The children who were born from these unions were rarely recognized (there were nevertheless a few exceptions that were all the more meritorious for that). Once the father had returned to France, the children were forcibly placed by the administration in "orphanages for mixed children" in order to carry out their education.

9   *Djandji*, Kadidja's nickname, meaning "she who is joyously equipped."
10 *Poullo*, or *peul* (Fula), in the sense of "noble." This was another familiar nickname for Kadidja used by Tidjani.
11 *Akbar* is the superlative of *kabir* (great). The exact translation is "Allah is the greatest," in the sense of "beyond everything." Whatever Man can conceive of or imagine, God is always beyond that. The verse also expresses the idea of all-powerfulness.
12 *Bismillahi*: The African form of the phrase Bismillah (in the name of God), which appears at the beginning of each verse in the Koran. In Africa this phrase is used as a salutation of welcome.
13 *Toubab*: In Arabic, "doctor" (sing. *toubib*). The word is used in Africa to designate Europeans, in the singular and the plural.

Chapter 3. Exile

1 [*Trans. note*: 25 kilometers is about 15 miles.]
2 [*Trans. note*: The original French reads, "un instrument à vent appelé piston." I believe that this is a typographical error and that it should have been written, "un instrument à vent et à piston," which would be a cornet.]
3 [*Trans. note*: 2 hectares is about 5 acres; 2 kilometers is 1.24 miles.]
4 [*Trans. note*: The Dioula ethnic group was known for its itinerant commerce. Also spelled Dyula, or Juula.]
5 [*Trans. note*: About 65 by 16 feet.]
6 [*Trans. note*: 15 kilometers is about 9 miles.]
7 [*Trans. note*: 66 to 77 pounds.]
8 Castes: hereditary artisan corporations that have always played a very important social and even religious role in the traditional society of the savanna. A distinction is made between the artisans (blacksmiths, weavers, shoemakers, and so on) and the public entertainers (*dieli* in Bambara; known as *griots and griotes* in French). Members of castes (an inappropriate word because of its connotation in the West) are known as *nyamakala* in Bambara, which means "antidotes to *nyama*," that hidden force found in everything. Thought to be the holders of occult power, they were once much more feared and deferred to than looked down upon. Under no circumstances may they be taken into captivity, and the nobles must give them gifts, deferential treatment, and subsistence.

In the past, every artisanal role corresponded to a specific initiatory path. In order to conserve secret knowledge within the lineage and to not mix different and even incompatible "occult forces," the different branches of nyamakala practiced endogamy through sexual taboos and formed closed hereditary groups. There is no notion here of being "untouchable" or inferior as there is in India. The feeling of superiority demonstrated by some toward the nyamakala classes rests on ignorance of the ancient sociological realities, where "not mixing" did not mean contempt.

9 [*Trans. note*: 76 kilometers equals 47 miles.]
10 [*Trans. note*: Two rivers: the Bani and the Niger.]
11 [*Trans. note*: Almost 1 mile.]
12 [*Trans. note*: Like the infantrymen known as tirailleurs, *laptots* were African troops in the service of France during the colonial period.]
13 [*Trans note*: 50 kilometers is about 30 miles; 160 kilometers is about 100 miles.]
14 [*Trans. note*: A formula partially composed of onomatopoeias representing a kind of invocation to the ancestors. My anonymous outside reader provides the translation: *N'fani'mba* means "My father and my mother."]
15 [*Trans. note*: The French text reads "six jours," but this must be a typographical error since the author has just explained that they could not leave before seven days had passed. Therefore, they must have stayed for ten (dix) days, as the text also states below that they departed from Donngorna on the tenth day.]
16 This was, in fact, the first form of relationship between the Blacks of the forests bordering the coast and the first European navigators.
17 Komo: One of the most important Bambara initiation societies in Mali, open only to circumcised adults. Before circumcision, the child starts out by belonging to the children's societies of Tiebleni, and then N'Tomo. Once initiated into the Komo, he receives a basic education from his teachers that will then be broadened throughout his entire life.

The word *Komo* at once designates the brotherhood itself, the knowledge associated with it, its god (or, rather, one of the sacred forces at work in the universe), and the sacred mask that supports it. Among the Komo initiates are the main ethnic groups of Old Mali: Bambaras, Malinkés, Sénoufos, and so on. (Among the Sénoufos of Ivory Coast, the Komo became the *Poro*).
18 In the phrase "la ilaha ill'Allah" (There is no god but God), the two Arabic words *ilaha* (god, divinity) and *Allah* (literally "The God") are from the same root, but evoke different dimensions. The most concise and most exact translation would be, "There is no God but *the* God (and not, as it is sometimes said, "There is no God but Allah," for the introduction of two words from different languages opposed to one another only leaves room for a very exclusive and limiting interpretation).
19 Traditionalist: Since this word has taken on a particular pejorative connotation these days, in order to avoid any confusion, when it concerns experts in traditional knowledge, some prefer to use the word "traditionist."
20 All the African religions that I am familiar with refer to a single and unique god who is the source of existence. For the Bambaras, it is *Maa n'gala*, "Master of all," "Master uncreated and infinite," "That which can do anything," "The great unfathomable depth," "The single unknowable thing" (to mention just a few of its 266 names). For the Fulas, it is *Guéno*, "the Eternal," without beginning or end. It is the *Amma* of the Dogons, the *Wounnam* of the Mossis, the *Olorun* of the Yorubas, and so on. But human beings consider that this Supreme Being is too distant to be

addressed with requests. Instead, they prefer to go though its intermediaries: the gods (who are only aspects or specific manifestations of the great divine primeval force), the *Sé* for the Bambaras, and especially the ancestors, considered to be very effective. On these subjects, see my article, "The Living Tradition," in Ki-Zerbo, ed., UNESCO *General History of Africa*, 1:166-203. See also Bâ, *Les Religions africaines, aspects de la civilisation africaine*, and the beginning of *Njeddo dewal* in Bâ, *Contes initiatiques*.

21 Today, this incantation is no longer really heard in the Niger Bend, and the great, improvised poetic lamentations of old have almost disappeared.
22 According to tradition, an event that takes place on a Saturday will generally take place again.
23 [*Trans. note*: Qur'an, Sahih international translation.]

Chapter 4. Return to Bandiagara

1 [*Trans. note*: The Upper Senegal and Niger colony (colony of Haut-Sénégal et Niger) later became known as Soudan Français (French Sudan) and then as Mali.]
2 [*Trans. note*: The correct name for "le bleu de Guillemet" is, in fact, "le bleu Guimet."]
3 [*Trans. note*: "And mine on the same occasion": This phrase is in fact missing from the text, but it is implied by what follows.]
4 "Beaded belts": A belt made of beads (*galli*) worn by women around their waists.
5 Guardian animal (*dassiri* in Bambara): Bears witness to a distant sacred alliance formed between the founding ancestor of a village and the first animal inhabitant of the place, or the spirit of the place incarnated in that animal. Here, the sacred crocodile is called an ancestor, not in the sense of its filiation (it is not a "totem") but because it is the oldest inhabitant of the place.

Chapter 5. At the White Man's School

1 The class of "house captives" (pl. *rimaibé*; sing. *dimadjo*) traditionally enjoy complete liberty in their speech, gestures, and behavior. In addition, because of his age, Koniba Kondala is assimilating himself with the class of "grandfathers" who have the right to joke freely with their grandchildren..
2 [*Trans. note*: Sharifs are descended from the Prophet Mohammad through his daughter Fatima.]
3 This text can be found in the first *Livret de lecture du français pour des écoliers noirs* (First French reader for Black schoolchildren), by Jean-Louis Monod.
4 [*Trans. note*: Upper Volta is today's Burkina Faso.]
5 *Note from Hélène Heckmann, literary executor of Amadou Hampâté Bâ*: Despite an explanation from the author in his introduction to *L'Etrange destin de Wangrin* (*The Fortunes of Wangrin*), some literary specialists have read the work as being founded in part on an imaginary fiction (and some have even called it an "autobiographical narrative"). Amadou Hampâté Bâ contradicted this reading in an afterword that should have been included in the 1989 printing of the book but was not, due to

negligence on the part of the editor. We have been assured that it will be included in the 1992 printing of the book. Whatever the case may be, the text of this afterword, which also adds new information about the personality of Wangrin, appears at the end of a book printed by Nathan Editions (Paris) in the collection, "Une oeuvre, un auteur," entitled, *L'Etrange destin de Wangrin d'Amadou Hampâté Bâ. Etude critique*, by Antoine Makonda. [*Trans note*: The explanatory note was indeed added in the 1992 edition as promised. See also Austen, *Africans Speak*, and "Who Was Wangrin?"]
6 [*Trans. note*: The title of Equilbecq's contribution to this multivolume collection is *Essai sur la littérature merveilleuse des noirs: suivi de contes indigènes de l'ouest-Africain français*.]
7 [*Trans. note*: 750 kilometers is a distance of about 466 miles.]
8 [*Trans. note*: The Primary Studies Certificate, or *Certificat d'études primaires* (CEP) was created in 1866, made mandatory in 1882, and discontinued in 1989. However, while the "native" CEP was modeled on that of France, it was not legally equivalent before World War II.]
9 [*Trans. note*: 200 kilometers is about 125 miles.]
10 See Bâ, *L'Etrange destin de Wangrin*, 71–73, and Bâ, *The Fortunes of Wangrin*, 36–39.
11 [*Trans. note*: The Gold Coast is today's Ghana.]
12 [*Trans note*: 300 kilometers is about 186 miles.]
13 [*Trans. note*: The five cords on a colonel's uniform under the Third Republic.] Before taking Djenné, Colonel Archinard had hidden his troops and cannons in the Tamarind grove south of the city, which is consecrated to the Spirit Tummelew. This gave rise to the legend according to which Archinard had made a pact with the protector spirit of that place.
14 This was on the condition, however, of knowing and respecting the annual periods when taboos were enforced in some animist villages.
15 [*Trans. note*: See Mage, *Voyage dans le Soudan occidental*.]
16 At the time, words such as these were not considered excessive. Upon the slightest occasion, "Eternal France" was invoked, and people would shout, "Vive la France!"

Chapter 6. In the Military Town of Kati

1 Tirailleurs Sénégalais: This was the original name of the corps that, in fact, included soldiers from all the territories in the colony: Senegalese, Sudanese (Malians), Upper Voltans, and so on.
2 [*Trans. note*: Qur'an, Sahih international translation.]
3 [*Trans. note*: Qur'an, Sahih international translation.]
4 [*Trans. note*: A *Licence* is the equivalent of an associate's degree.]
5 It was not until after World War II, on June 1, 1946, that, on the initiative of Lamine Gueye, deputy of Senegal, a law put an end to "French subject" status and endowed the inhabitants of all the overseas territories with French citizenship.
6 Malinké (or Manika, or Mandingue, that is, from the Mandé of Mali), one of the principal peoples of the Mandinka ethnic group and heir to the empire founded in the thirteenth century by Soundiata Keïta. The Malinkés were nicknamed "peanut eaters" because of their unflagging love for the nut.

7 [*Trans. note*: Ouagadougou, the capital of Burkina Faso, is also spelled Wagadugu.]
8 Préveaudeau, *Joost Van Vollenhoven*, 51, 53–54.
9 Mangeot, *La Vie ardente*.
10 The sword ritual: The ritual gestures executed by Fadiala Keïta, which are curiously reminiscent of the dubbing ceremonies of medieval knights, in fact belonged to an old Mandinka ritual (according to Youssouf Tata Cissé). When a young *sofa* (literally, Father of the Horse) became a cavalry warrior following a lengthy apprenticeship, his sword was ritually returned to him after it had touched each of his shoulders, because in the shoulder resides the strength of the arm.

Chapter 7. Final Studies in Bamako

1 According to a member of the family of King Mademba Sy, the king's first wife, born in Saint-Louis of Senegal and thus a French citizen, was the only one whose marriage had been legitimately recorded. Upon the king's death, the oldest son born from that union, considered to be the only legitimate son, was said to have inherited all the wealth. All of the other children who had been born from unions with different wives were said to have been dispossessed. This would explain Ben Daoud's extreme destitution.
2 In traditional Africa, as in Islam, saliva is thought to carry the spiritual power of words. It often accompanies blessings and healing rites.

BIBLIOGRAPHY

Aggarwal, Kusum. *Amadou Hampâté Bâ et l'africanisme*. Paris: L'Harmattan, 1999.
Appiah, Kwame Anthony. *Cosmopolitanism: Ethics in a World of Strangers*. New York: W. W. Norton, 2006.
Austen, Ralph A. *Africans Speak, Colonialism Writes: The Transcription and Translation of Oral Literature before World War II*. Discussion Papers in the African Humanities, no. 8. Boston: African Studies Center, Boston University, 1990.
Austen, Ralph A. "From a Colonial to a Postcolonial Voice: *Amkoullel, l'enfant peul*." *Research in African Literatures* 31, no. 3 (2000): 1-17.
Austen, Ralph A. "Interpreters Self-Interpreted. The Autobiographies of Two Colonial Clerks." In *Intermediaries, Interpreters, and Clerks: African Employees in the Making of Colonial Africa*, edited by Benjamin N. Lawrence, Emily Lynn Osborn, and Richard L. Roberts, 159-79. Madison: University of Wisconsin Press, 2008.
Austen, Ralph A. "Who Was Wangrin and Why Does It Matter? Colonial History 'from the Middle' and Its Self-Representation." *Mande Studies* 9 (2007): 149-64.
Austen, Ralph A., and Benjamin F. Soares. "Amadou Hampâté Bâ's Life and Work Reconsidered: Critical and Historical Perspectives." *Islamic Africa* 1, no. 2 (June 2010): 133-42. https://www.islamicafricajournal.org.
Bâ, Amadou Hampâté. *Amkoullel, l'enfant peul: mémoires*. Paris: Actes Sud, 1992.
Bâ, Amadou Hampâté. *Aspects de la civilization africaine*. Paris: Présence Africaine, 1972.
Bâ, Amadou Hampâté. *Contes des sages d'Afrique*. Paris: Seuil, 2004.
Bâ, Amadou Hampâté. *Contes initiatiques peuls: Njeddo Dewal, mere de la calamité suivi de Kaïdara*. Paris: Stock, 1994.
Bâ, Amadou Hampâté. "Discours d'Amadou Hampâté Bâ á la commission Afrique de l'UNESCO." Ina.fr, accessed November 21, 2011. http://www.ina.fr/economie-et-societe/vie-sociale/audio/PHD8607.
Bâ, Amadou Hampâté. *L'Eclat de la grande étoile suivi du bain rituel*. Paris: Les Belles Lettres, 1974. Bilingual edition.
Bâ, Amadou Hampâté. *L'Etrange destin de Wangrin: ou, Les roueries d'un interprète africain*. Paris: UGE, 1973.
Bâ, Amadou Hampâté. *The Fortunes of Wangrin: The Life and Times of an African Confidence Man*. Translated by Aina Pavolini Taylor. Bloomington: Indiana University Press, 1999.

Bâ, Amadou Hampâté. *Il n'y a pas de petite querelle*. Paris: Stock, 1999.
Bâ, Amadou Hampâté. *Jésus vu par un musulman*. Abidjan: Nouvelles Editions Ivoiriennes, 1976.
Bâ, Amadou Hampâté. *Kaïdara*. Translated by Daniel Whitman. Washington, DC: Three Continents Press, 1988.
Bâ, Amadou Hampâté. *Kaidara: Récit initiatique peul*. Paris: Association des Classiques Africains: UNESCO, 1968. Bilingual edition.
Bâ, Amadou Hampâté. "Lettre d'Amadou Hampâté Bâ à la jeunesse africaine: 'Soyez au service de la vie sous tous ses aspects.'" Mali-Web, April 27, 2015. https://mali-web.org/societe/culture/lettre-damadou-hampate-ba-a-la-jeunesse-africaine-soyez-au-service-de-la-vie-sous-tous-ses-aspects.
Bâ, Amadou Hampâté. "The Living Tradition." In *UNESCO General History of Africa*, vol. 1: *Methodology and African Prehistory*, edited by Joseph Ki-Zerbo, 166–203. London: Heinemann, 1981.
Bâ, Amadou Hampâté. *Mémoires*. Arles: Actes Sud, 2012.
Bâ, Amadou Hampâté. *Oui, mon commandant!: mémoires II* Arles: Actes Sud, 1994.
Bâ, Amadou Hampâté. *Petit Bodiel et autres contes de la savane*. Paris: Stock, 1994.
Bâ, Amadou Hampâté. *La Poignée de poussière: contes et récits du Mali Abidjan*. Abidjan: Nouvelles Editions Ivoiriennes, 1987.
Bâ, Amadou Hampâté. *Les Religions africaines comme source de valeur de civilisation*. Paris: Présence Africaine, 1972.
Bâ, Amadou Hampâté. *A Spirit of Tolerance: The Inspiring Life of Tierno Bokar*. Translated by Jane Casewit. Bloomington, IN: World Wisdom, 2008.
Bâ, Amadou Hampâté. *Sur les traces d'Amkoullel, l'enfant peul*. Arles: Actes Sud, 1998.
Bâ, Amadou Hampaté. *Vie et enseignement de Tierno Bokar: Le sage de Bandiagara*. 1957; Paris: Seuil, 1980.
Bâ, Amadou Hampâté, and Marcel Cardaire. *Tierno Bokar, le sage de Bandiagara*. Paris: Présence Africaine, 1957.
Bâ, Amadou Hampâté, and Jacques Daget. *L'Empire peul du Macina*. Paris: Mouton, 1962.
Bâ, Amadou Hampâté, with Germaine Dieterlen. *Koumen: texte initiatique des pasteurs peul*. Paris: Mouton, 1961.
Bâ, Amadou Hampâté, with Lilyan Kesteloot. *Kaïdara: récit initiatique peul*. Paris: Armand Colin, 1968. Bilingual edition.
Bancel, Nicolas, and Pascal Blanchard. "La colonisation: du débat sur la guerre d'Algérie au discours de Dakar." In *Les Guerres de mémoires. La France et son histoire. Enjeux politiques, controverses historiques, stratégies médiatiques*, edited by Pascal Blanchard and Isabelle Veyrat-Masson, 137–54. Paris: La Découverte, 2008.
Bandia, Paul F. *Translation as Reparation: Writing and Translation in Postcolonial Africa*. Manchester, UK: St. Jerome Publishing, 2008.
Barry, Kesso. *Kesso, princesse peuhle*. Paris: Segers, 2015.
Benjamin, Walter. "The Task of the Translator: An Introduction to the Translation of Baudelaire's *Tableaux parisiens*." Translated by Harry Zohn. In *The Translation Studies Reader*, 2nd ed., edited by Lawrence Venuti, 75–85. New York: Routledge, 2004.

Brenner, Louis. "Amadou Hampâté Bâ, Tijâni Francophone." In *La Tijâniyya: une confrérie musulmane à la conquête de l'Afrique*, edited by Jean-Louis Triaud and David Robinson, 289–326. Paris: Kartha, 2000.

Brenner, Louis. "Becoming Muslim in Soudan français." In *Le temps des marabouts: itinéraires et stratégies islamiques en Afrique occidentale français v. 1880–1960*, edited by David Robinson and Jean-Louis Triaud, 467–92. Paris: Karthala, 1997.

Brenner, Louis. *West African Sufi: The Religious Heritage and Spiritual Search of Cerno Bokar Saalif Taal*. Berkeley: University of California Press, 1984.

Chanda, Tirthankar. "Les 'Mémoires' réedités d'Amadou Hampâté Bâ." Rfi.fr, October 19, 2019. http://www.rfi.fr/afrique/20120413-memoires-reedites-amadou-hampate-ba.

Chemain, Roger. "*L'Enfant peul*: l'interprète, et le commis des affaires indigenes." In *Lecture de l'oeuvre d'Hampâté Bâ*, edited by Robert Jouanny, 85–91. Paris: L'Harmattan, 1992.

Devey, Muriel. *Hampâté Bâ, l'homme de la tradition*. Paris: Livre Sud, 1993.

Diagne, Souleymane Bachir. "Penser de langue à langue. " In Mabanckou, *Penser et écrire l'Afrique aujourd'hui*, 72–80.

Diouf, Mamadou. "L'Universalisme (européen?) à l'épreuve des histoires indigènes." In Mbembe and Sarr, *Ecrire l'Afrique-monde*, 17–50.

Eggan, Taylor. "The Strange Fate of Amadou Hampâté Bâ in the Anglophone World." Taylor Eggan, August 13, 2017. https://www.tayloreggan.com/exploded-view/2017/8/13/the-strange-fate-of-amadou-hampate-ba.

Equilbecq, François-Victor. *Aux lueurs des feux de la veillée*. Vol. 43: *Essai sur la littérature merveilleuse des noirs: suivi de contes indigènes de l'ouest-Africain français*. Collection des contes et chansons populaires. Paris: E. Leroux, 1913–16.

Equilbecq, François-Victor. *Contes populaires d'Afrique occidentale*. 1913; reprint, Paris: Maisonneuve et Larose, 1972.

Garane, Jeanne. "How Postcolonial Translation Theory Transforms Francophone African Studies." *The Comparatist* 38 (October 2014): 188–205.

Garane, Jeanne. "The Invisibility of the African Interpreter." *translation: A Transdisciplinary Journal* (Fall 2015). Accessed August 22, 2020, at https://sc.edu/study/colleges_schools/artsandsciences/dllc/documents/faculty_pubs/garane/invisibility_of_the_african_interpreter.pdf.

Garane, Jeanne. "What Is New about Amadou Hampâté Bâ? Translation, Interpretation, and Literary History." In *Francophone Cultures and Geographies of Identity*, edited by H. Adlai Murdoch and Zsuszanna Faygal, 164–89. Cambridge: Cambridge Scholars Press, 2013.

Heckmann, Hélène, ed. "Petite histoire éditoriale du conte Kaïdara." In *Contes initiatiques peuls*, by Amadou Hampâté Bâ, 343–45. Paris: Pocket, 2001.

Hobsbawm, E. J., and T. O. Ranger, eds. *The Invention of Tradition*. Cambridge: Cambridge University Press, 1992.

Irele, F. Abiola. *The African Imagination: Literature in Africa and the Black Diaspora*. Oxford: Oxford University Press, 2001.

Irele, F. Abiola. "Introduction." In Bâ, *The Fortunes of Wangrin*, vi–xvi.

Izzo, Justin. *Experiments with Empire: Anthropology and Fiction in the French Atlantic*. Durham, NC: Duke University Press, 2019.
Julien, Eileen. *African Novels and the Question of Orality*. Bloomington: Indiana University Press, 1992.
Kisukidi, Nadia Yada. "*Laetitia Africana*: philosophie, décolonisation, et mélancholie." In Mbembe and Sarr, *Ecrire l'Afrique-monde*, 53–69.
Konaté, Yacouba. "Le Syndrome Amadou Hampâté Bâ ou comment naissent les proverbes." In Tour and Mariko, *Amadou Hampâté Bâ, homme de science et de sagesse*, 49–67.
Lawrance, Benjamin N., Emily Lynn Osborn, and Richard L. Roberts, eds. *Intermediaries, Interpreters, and Clerks: African Employees in the Making of Colonial Africa*. Madison: University of Wisconsin Press, 2006.
Laye, Camara. *The Dark Child: The Autobiography of an African Boy*. Translated by James Kirkup. New York: Noonday Press, 1954.
Laye, Camara. *L'Enfant noir, roman*. Paris: Plon, 1953.
Lebdai, Benaouda, ed. *Autobiography as a Writing Strategy in Postcolonial Literature*. Cambridge: Cambridge Scholars Publishing, 2015.
Lhote, Henri. *A la découverte des fresques du Tassili*. Paris: Arthaud, 2006.
Mabanckou, Alain, ed. *Penser et écrire l'Afrique aujourd'hui*. Paris: Seuil, 2017.
Mage, Eugène Abdon. *Voyage dans le Soudan occidental (Sénégambie-Niger)*. Paris: Hachette, 1868.
Makonda, Antoine. *L'Etrange destin de Wangrin d'Amadou Hampâté Bâ: étude critique*. Paris: Editions Nathan, 1988.
Mangeot, Pol-Victor. *La Vie ardente de Van Vollenhoven: gouverneur général de l'A.O.F*. Paris: Bibliothèque de l'institut maritime et colonial, Editions Sorlot, 1943.
Mbembe, Achille. "L'Afrique qui vient." In Mabanckou, *Penser et écrire l'Afrique aujourd'hui*, 17–31.
Mbembe, Achille. *Out of the Dark Night: Essays on Decolonization*. Translated by Daniela Ginsburg. New York: Columbia University Press, 2020.
Mbembe, Achille. "Penser le monde à partir de l'Afrique: questions pour aujourd'hui et demain." In Mbembe and Sarr, *Ecrire l'Afrique-monde*, 379–93.
Mbembe, Achille. *Sortir de la grande nuit: Essai sur l'Afrique décolonisée*. Paris: La Découverte, 2013.
Mbembe, Achille, and Felwine Sarr, eds. *Ecrire l'Afrique-monde*. Dakar: Jimsaan, 2017.
Monénembo, Tierno. *Peuls*. Paris: Seuil, 2004.
Moudileno, Lydie. "Penser l'Afrique à partir de sa littérature." In Mabanckou, *Penser et écrire l'Afrique aujourd'hui*, 137–49.
Moudileno, Lydie. "Qu'est-ce qu'un auteur postcolonial?" In Mbembe and Sarr, *Penser et écrire l'Afrique-monde*, 159–73.
Ndiaye, Christiane. "Les mémoires d'Amadou Hampaté Bâ: récit d'un parcours identitaire exemplaire." In *Récits de vie de l'Afrique et des Antilles*, edited by Suzanne Crosta, 13–36. Sainte-Foy, Québec: GRELCA, 1998.
Niranjana, Tejaswini. *Siting Translation: History, Post-Structuralism, and the Colonial Context*. Berkeley: University of California Press, 1992.

Ouédraogo, Jean. "Entretien avec Ahmadou Kourouma." *French Review* 74, no. 4. (2001): 772-85.
Préveaudeau, A. *Joost Van Vollenhoven*. Paris: Editions Larose, 1953.
Robinson, David, and Jean-Louis Triaud, eds. *Le Temps des marabouts: itinéraires et stratégies islamiques en Afrique occidentale française v. 1880-1960*. Paris: Karthala, 2012.
Sanankoua, Bintou. "Amadou Hampâté Bâ: A Testimony." *Islamic Africa* 1, no. 2 (June 2010): 144-67.
Sanankoua, Bintou. "Amadou Hampâté Bâ (v. 1900-1991)." In Robinson and Triaud, *Le Temps des marabouts*, 395-411.
Sankara, Edgard. *Postcolonial Francophone Autobiographies from Africa to the Antilles*. Charlottesville: University of Virginia Press, 2011.
Sow, Alpha Ibrahim. *Inventaire du fonds Amadou Hampâté Bâ*. Paris: Klinsieck, 1970.
Touré, Amadou, and Ntji Idriss Mariko, eds. *Amadou Hampâté Bâ, homme de science et de sagesse: mélanges pour le centième anniversaire de la naissance d'Hampâté Bâ*. Paris: Karthala, 2005.
Triaud, Jean-Louis. "D'un maître à l'autre: L'Histoire d'un transfert: Amadou Hampâté Bâ entre Tierno Bokar et Theodore Monod (1938-1954)." *Sociétés politiques comparées* 20, December 2009. http://www.fasopo.org/sites/default/files/article_n20.pdf.
Triaud, Jean-Louis, and David Robinson, eds. *La Tijâniyya: une confrérie musulmane à la conquête de l'Afrique*. Paris: Karthala, 2005.
Venuti, Lawrence. *The Scandals of Translation*. London: Routledge, 1998.
Venuti, Lawrence. *The Translator's Invisibility: A History of Translation*. London: Routledge, 1995.
Watts, Richard. *Packaging Post/coloniality: The Manufacture of Literary Identity in the Francophone World*. Lanham, MD: Lexington Books, 2005.
Wise, Christopher, ed. *Yambo Ouloguem: Postcolonial Writer, Islamic Militant*. Boulder, CO: Lynne Rienner Publishers, 1999.

BIOGRAPHIES

Jeanne Garane is professor of French and Comparative Literature at the University of South Carolina, Columbia, where she teaches courses in French and Francophone literature and film, Postcolonial Theory, and Translation Studies. She has published a number of essays, introductions, and interviews in her field and is the editor of *Discursive Geographies: Writing Space and Place in French/Géographies discursives: L'écriture de l'espace et du lieu en français* (2005); *French Literature Series* Volume 41, *Odysseys: Travel Narratives in French/Odyssées: récits de voyage en langue française* (2017), and *French Literature Series*, Vol. 42, *Hybrid Genres/L'Hybridité des genres* (2018). She organized the republication of Ken Bugul's *Abandoned Baobab* (translated by Marjolijn de Jager, 2006) and is the translator of Abdourahman A. Waberi's *Le Pays sans ombre* (*The Land without Shadows*; 2005), and Daniel Picouly's *L'Enfant léopard* (*The Leopard Boy*; 2016).

Ralph A. Austen is professor emeritus of African History at the University of Chicago. His publications include *African Economic History: Internal Development and External Dependency* (1987), *Middlemen of the Cameroons Rivers: The Duala and Their Hinterland, c. 1600–c. 1960* (with Jonathan Derrick; 1998), *In Search of Sunjata: The Mande Oral Epic as History, Literature, and Performance* (edited volume; 1999), and *Trans-Saharan Africa in World History* (2010; under revision), as well as numerous articles and book chapters dealing with Amadou Hampâté Bâ. He is presently working on a comparative study of protocolonial, colonial, and postcolonial history in tropical Africa, the Caribbean, and South Asia.

INDEX

Abatcha, Saïdou, xxxi
Abbasi, Aye (girls' *waaldé* member), 171
Abdallah (friend of Tidjani Thiam), 80
Abd el-Kader el Djilani (Muslim saint), 211
Abdou, Wourma, 39
Actes Sud, 6, 334n25
African traditions: adoption, 33, 45–48; adoption of captives, 30, 39, 69, 99; bachelors not respected, 38; child remains with mother, 99; children imitate adult activities, 110, 156–58; dreams and predictions, 8, 35, 39–41, 67–68, 80, 323; ease of language learning, 88, 215; friend as oneself, 36–37; Fula double allegiance, 4–5; lineages, xvi, 11–15, 27, 286, 294; "master of the earth," 89–90; meals, 36, 156–58; mental illness, healing of, 273; mother, respect for, 4, 29, 36; mothering, African, 65, 107, 326; naming practices, 11; nicknames, 24, 41, 67, 89, 115, 176, 213, 313, 339n10, 339n11; nobles, extreme reserve expected of, 179; "open houses," 258–59; parents, reserve expected of, 306; poetry composed in grief, 128–29, 132; religious tolerance, 121, 233, 277–78; solidarity, 183, 239–40; sunset, meanings of, 142, 148; zone of reference, 8. *See also* marriage; oral traditions
Afropolitanism, xxv–xxvi

Aguibou, Diaraw (wife of Tidjiani Thiam), 47, 51, 63, 98, 114, 130; A. H. Bâ, relationship with, 135–37; rheumatoid arthritis, 136, 140–41; Tidjiani's freedom and, 138, 140
Aïssata (wife of Amadou Kisso), 232
Aïssata, Diafara, 119
Ali, Alfa (Koranic teacher), 197–98
Ali, Gabdo Hammadi, 67
Ali, Koudi, 99, 101, 103, 105–7, 112, 114
Allahadji, Nouhoun (friend of Hammadoun Bâ), 190
Allamodio (captive, butcher), 22–23, 31–33, 35, 196
Alphonse, Captain, 127–28
Amadou, Amadou (grandson of Amadou Cheikou), 14
Amadou, Cheikou (founder of Fula Empire of Massina), 4, 13–14, 17, 24, 85, 187, 195
Amadou, Cheikou (son of El Hadj Omar), 24, 49–50, 72, 85
Amadou Hampâté Bâ, le sage du fleuve Niger (film), xxviii
Amfarba (griot), 33–34
Amkoullel, the Fula Boy (*Amkoullel, l'enfant peul: mémoires*) (Bâ): awarded Grand prix littéraire d'Afrique noire, xi; as both autobiography and memoir, xv; "dialogicity" of, xxv; English translation, reasons for, xxvi–xxx; French title, *Amkoullel, l'enfant peul: mémoires*,

Amkoullel, the Fula Boy (continued)
xviii; initiation theme in, xi; "In the Military Town of Kati" (chapter 6), xxii–xxiii; publication of, xxiv
ancestors, 89, 160, 192–93, 254, 334n17, 341n5, 341n20
Angoulvant, Gabriel Louis, 290
Appiah, Kwame Anthony, xxv
Arabs of Timbuktu, 96
Archinard, Louis, xvii, 49–50, 97, 283, 342n13; Abdelkader Sy and, 285–86; spirit Tummelew associated with, 254, 257, 342n13
Armée d'Afrique, 260
artisan castes, 96, 233, 339–40n8
Assomption, Frédéric (teaching inspector), 296, 315, 316, 318–19, 325
Austen, Ralph A., xxiii, xxxi, 332n5
autobiography, xv, xxv, xxvii, 341–42n5
Autobiography as a Writing Strategy in Postcolonial Literature (Benaouda), xviii

Bâ, Alfa Samba Fouta (A. H. Bâ's paternal great-uncle), 195
Bâ, Amadou Hampâté (A. H.): adoption of by Tidjani Thiam, xvii, 47–48, 99; as ambassador to Mali, xxx; Amkoullel as nickname of, 63, 161, 163, 328; as autodidact, 319–20; at Bureau of Enregistrement et Domaines, 316–17, 320; "burning library" aphorism, xxii, 333–34n17; circumcision of, 277–80; as civilian auxiliary army mail officer, 282, 287–88, 291, 295; embroidery skills, 96, 280; end of early childhood, 121–24; equestrian training of, 280; at French primary school, xi–xii, xvii, 209–18, 223; as interpreter, 253–54, 286; as life-long traveler, 42; lineage of, xvi–xvii, 12–14; malarial fever and, 322–23; memory of, xix, 107, 117, 208–10; oral traditions collected by, xix–xxii, 127, 306, 325; Ouagadougou assignment, xv, xvi, 318–28; Primary Studies Certificate earned by, 251, 281; school, leaves without notice, 251–66; school, return to, 281–82; school attendance, 194–264; as storyteller, x, xix, xxi, xxv, 4–6; travels to Bougouni, 99–100; UNESCO address, xxii, 333n17; *waaldé* associations formed by, 127, 152–56; Works: "The Calamitous Coccyx," 4; *Kaïdara: récit initiatique peul*, xxii, xxvi, 312; *Koumen: texte initiatique des pasteurs peul*, xxii; "A l'école du caméléon," xxix, xxxi; *L'Empire peul du Macina*, xxi–xxiii; *L'Etrange destin de Wangrin: ou, les roueries d'un interprète africain*, ix–x, xix, xxii, 341–42n5; "Open Letter to the Youth," xxviii; *Oui, Mon Commandant!: mémoires II*, xxiv–xv; *Tierno Bokar: le Sage de Bandiagara*, xxii; *Vie et enseignement de Tierno Bokar, le sage de Bandiagara* (*A Spirit of Tolerance: The Inspiring Life of Tierno Bokar*), xxvi, xxxi
Bâ, Boudjedi (elder Bâ of Bandiagara), 177–78, 185
Bâ, Gabdo, 42–43
Bâ, Galo, 88, 120–21
Bâ, Hammadoun, xi, 33, 42, 44, 99, 109; *waaldé* association and, 154, 155–56, 190
Bâ, Hampâté, 20–37, 194, 225; Beydari as heir and head of family, 33, 44, 66, 84, 98–99; captives, freeing of, 33; death of, 44; divorce from Kadidja, 43–44; gaze of, 21, 44–45; generosity of, 45; as heir to the Hamsalah, 23, 27–28, 30, 33; hidden from Tidjani Tall, 21–23, 28–32; livestock business, 32–33; marriage to Baya, 35–36, 38–39; marriage to Kadidja, xx, 41–45; *waaldé* (youth associations) founded by, 32, 153
Bâ, Mamadou, 144, 295
Bâ, Oumar (writer, ethnographer, and researcher), 313
Bâ, Tierno Amadou Tapsîrou, 114
Bâ, Tierno Haymoutou, 24, 26, 31
Bâba, Diêli (public crier), 79

Bâbilâli, Koorka (captive), 68–69, 71, 73, 85
Bâ clan, 20
Bafour region (Mali), 8, 96
Bamako (Mali), 2, 175–76; famine and, 240; Point G Hospital, 297
Bamako Professional School, 209, 217, 236, 251, 295, 296–97, 299, 311–17; history of, 311–12; as School for Hostages, xvii–xviii, xx, 311, 314. *See also* education
Bamako Regional School, 295, 296
Bambara military fortress, 72
Bambara people, xii–xiii, 13, 177, 226; chiefs, 254; circumcision retreat, 181; Komo society of Donngorna, 107, 121, 340n17; N'Tomo initiation society, 274–75, 277, 340n17; of Saro region, 233; Tiebleni initiation society, 120–21. *See also* Wangrin
Bambara region (Mali), 83–87
Bamoussa (son of Donngorna village chief), 110–11, 297
Bamoussa (*ton* leader), 274–75, 276–77
Bancel, Nicolas, xxiv, 334n24
Bandia, Paul, xxv
Bandiagara (Mali), xii, xv–xvi, 4, 17; as Bannyagara, 18–19; Deendé Bôdi district, 65, 77, 186–87, 193, 195, 240; European population of, 149–52; famine and, 240; Gan'ngal district, 185–87; growth of, 23–24; Kérétel Square, 159, 177, 246; kingdom of (1864–93), 4, 35, 301–2; motto of (*bi-iribaara bantineeje*), 77, 78; Sansanding, rivalry with, 301–2; *Sinci* (White quarter), 150–52; Yaamé River sacred crocodiles, 192–93
Bani River, 13, 226–27, 252
"Bark of the Blessed, The" (Omar), 46
Bastille Day holiday (*katran zoulié*, July 14), 241–43
Battesti, Commandant, 303
bawo (monitor), 181, 182, 183

Baya (captive). *See* Hampâté, Nassouni (adopted child of Hampâté Bâ)
Baya (first wife of Hampâté Bâ), 35–36
Baya (wife of A. H. Bâ), 39
Ben Daoud (son of King Mademba of Sansanding), 5
Benjamin, Walter, xxvii
Beydari, Kalando (healer), 70
Biga (tanner), 246
Black-Blacks, 261
blacksmiths, 125, 229, 239, 264, 339n8; circumcision and, 180–81, 183–84
Blanchard, Pascal, xxiv, 334n24
Bo, Morobara (friend of Koorka), 69
Bobos (Mande ethnic group), 232
Bocoum, Hassane, 22–23
Bokar, Tierno: on spoken word as true knowledge, 160, 333–34n17
Bokar, Tierno (Tall), 51, 66, 114, 197, 225, 327, 334n17; adopted by El Hadj Omar, 45–46; death of, 310; as embroiderer, 96; famine and, 240; influence on A. H. Bâ, xxi–xxii, xxvii, 3; languages spoken by, 215; as teacher, 45, 99, 121, 135, 145–46, 160, 173–74; "White Man's school" and, 212–13; World War I and, 248
Bokary, Mamsou (chief brigadier of the guards), 248
Boubou, Aïssata (griote), 64, 74, 75
Boubou, Allaye (herdsman), 177, 179
Bouery, Commander, 290
Bougalo, Fanta (blacksmith caste), 229
Bougouni (village, Mali), x, xiii, 2, 87–98, 149, 208
Bourgeois, Mr. (excise man), 316–17, 318
Bozos (Mande ethnic group), 226, 233, 239–40
Bretèche, Charles de la, 53, 56–62, 71, 75, 80, 81, 143; names Tidjani Thiam as headman, 272
Brizeux, Max (district commandant), 229
Brook, Peter, xxxi

Burkina-Faso, 33. *See also* Louta province (Mali, now Burkina Faso)
"burning libraries" aphorism, xxii, 333–34n17
el-Bushiri, Cheikh Mohammed, 92

cadi (judge), 154–55
canton leaders, 48, 53, 56, 88, 195, 242–43, 254; World War I and, 248–49
captives (*dimadjo, rimaïbé*), 5, 22, 68, 95, 195, 208–9, 219, 337–38n11; adoption of, 30, 39, 44; as police, 233; sarcasm of, 248
castes, 171, 233, 339–40n8; hereditary artisan corporations (*nyamakala*), 339–40n8. *See also* griots
Chanda, Tirthankar, 334n25
Chateaubriand, 4
childhood games, 146–48; gardens, plundering of, xii, 124, 146, 153, 161–68, 193, 196
circumcision, xi–xii, 176–85, 277–80
Cissé, Amadou Kisso (chief of Fula community), 228, 231–33, 235
Cissé, Fanta Kounta (daughter of Tierno Kounta), 127–30, 263–67, 279
Cissé, Ousmane, 96–97
Cissé, Tierno Kounta, 52, 53, 60–62, 79, 112; in Bougouni prison, 85, 91, 93, 97–98; death of, 127–36; freed from prison, 114; marriage to Koudi Ali, 99, 114; as teacher, 121–22
civilizing mission (*mission civilisatrice*) xviii, xix, xxiii, xxiv, 332n6, 334n24
civil wars between Fula and Toucouleur, 15–20; execution of Fulas of Fakala, 20, 21, 28, 35, 194; Toïni revolt, 49–64, 80
Clemenceau, Georges, 277, 289
Clozel, Governor, 311
colonialism. *See* French colonial empire
commandants, district, 49, 52–53, 56–58, 88–89, 202, 332n5; education, role in, 224, 229; guards, relationship with, 69; schools and, 195; World War I and, 244

Conférence internationale des africanistes de l'ouest, xxi
Contes populaires d'Afrique occidentale (Equilbecq, Leroux, and Wangrin), 219
Cottelier, Lieutenant, 280
Coulibaly, Molo (teacher), 282, 295
Coulibaly, Tiessaraman, 86
de Courcelles, Commandant, 89-98, 113, 130, 138; A. H. Bâ's first meeting with, 115–20
Courtille, Commandant (clerk), 300
crocodiles, sacred, 192–93

Daget, Jacques, 333n15
Dakar (French Sudan), 243, 283, 286, 289–90
Daouda, Mamadou *(spahi)*, 245–46
Dark Child: The Autobiography of an African Boy, The (Laye, trans. Kirkup), xviii
Daw, Tidjani (friend of Tidjani Thiam), 114
decolonization, epistemological, xxiii
Deendé Bôdi district, 65, 77
Déguembéré (Dogon country), 19
Delafosse, Maurice, 14
Dembélé, Moustapha, 114, 128
Dembélé, Niélé (captive), 44, 48, 66, 99, 145, 221; A. H. Bâ's school attendance and, 224, 235, 326–237; famine and, 241; Hampâté Bâ, story of, 20–32; as servant-mother, 20, 33, 42, 236
Deves-et-Chaumet Company, 100, 104–5
Dewel Asi (marabout), 67–68
Diaba, Eliyassa Hafiz, 40, 42, 43, 98
Diafara, Binta (friend of Kadidja), 119
Diafarabé (Mopti region, Mali), 24
Diagne, Blaise, 277, 288–90, 294
Diagne, Souleymane Bachir, xxv
Diaguité, Fambougouri, 95
Diallo, Mamadou (friend of A. H. Bâ), 155
Diallo, Mara (Chief Warrant Officer), 287–88, 292
Diallo, Pâté Poullo, 15–20, 62, 143, 232; Anta N'Diobdi, marriage to, 24–26;

death of, 44; Kadidja and, 41; takes Hampâté Bâ to Tidjani, 28–31
Diallo, Samba (friend of A. H. Bâ, collector of oral traditions), 298
Diallo, Séga (teacher), 296, 299, 325
Diallo clan, 15, 25–26, 313
Dianopo, Bouna Pama (former infantry sergeant), 236–39
Dianou, Afo (friend of A. H. Bâ), 149, 152, 155, 164, 169; rival *waaldé* and, 185–86, 187–88, 190–91
Diarra, Mari (Sergeant), 283–84
Diarra, Sado, 13
Diatroufing (mythical black hyena), 266–69, 276, 296
Diawarra, Mohammed, 297–98
Diawarra, Tiékoura (friend of A. H. Bâ), 297–98
Diawarra, Yaye, 63, 64–65, 76–78, 143, 144, 173
Diawarra, Youkoullé, 245
Dieli, Kaou (griot, marabout), 201, 245
Diko, Balewel, 22, 23, 29, 31–32, 36–37, 44, 225
dîmadjo (captives). *See* captives (*dimadjo, rimaïbé*)
Dinguiraye (Fouta Djallon, Guinea), 50
Dioubaïrou, Noumoussa, 155
Dioula merchant caravans, 90
Diourou, Mouda (friend of Hammadoun Bâ), 190
dippal (dance), 182
Diterlen, Germaine, xxii
Al-*Djennat* (garden of Allah), 228
Djenné (city, Mali), 2, 85–86, 223–24, 227–28; Al-Gazba neighborhood, 235; Bozo-Songhay-Fula triumvirate, 233; history of, 232–33
Djennonké, Ousmane, 33
Djerma, Bia (guard), 248
Djibo, Sounkalo (friend of A. H. Bâ), 298
djinns (genies), 117
Djité, Alassane (friend of A. H. Bâ), 297

djonngoloni (warrior song), 72
dog handlers and war dogs, 256–58, 259
Dogon people, 17–19, 67, 142, 226; Bozos, sanankounya relationship with, 239–40; circumcision retreat, 181; drafted, World War I, 248; famine and, 239–40; in Kati, 271; millet fields, 161–62; singing of, 182
doma (man of knowledge), 19
Dommo (Dogon hunter), 18
Domoni (Louta region), 58–60
Donngorna (Bambara village), 105–10
Donngorna River, 109
Dori (Burkina Faso), 288
Doukombo (Dogon country), 17–18, 142
Dounfing chasm, 266–69, 276, 296–97
dreams and predictions, 8; Kadidja's, 39–41; of marabouts, 35, 39, 40, 67–68, 80, 323
drought, 234–41
drum signals, 244
Dupuich, Philippe, 334n25

Ecclesiastes (Bible), 310
Ecrire l'Afrique-monde (Mbembe and Sarr), xxiv
education: A. H. Bâ recruited for "White Man's school," 194–202; at French primary school, xi–xii, xvii, 209–18, 223; general governmental *grandes écoles*, 312; Koranic, 121–24, 134–35, 144, 146, 161; oral traditions and, 159–61; Primary Studies Certificate, 217, 223, 236, 251, 299, 342n8; regional school in Djenné, 223, 229–36; school routine, 213–17; William Ponty Normal School of Gorée, xx, 209, 229, 251, 281–82, 295, 296. *See also* Bamako Professional School
Eggan, Taylor, xxvi–xxvii
elder associations, 153–54
El Waswass (son of Satan), 188
emancipation, spirit of, 298–99
Equilbecq, François-Victor, xix, 219

Fabere (chief gardener of Alfa Maki Tall), 166–67
Fadiga, Bouyagui, 316, 319
Faidherbe, Louis, xvii, 166, 311
Fakala, Fulas of, 20, 24
Fakala region (Massina, Mali), 13–14
Fakambi, Sika, xxix
Fama (General Supervisor), 313–15
famine, 5, 234–41, 244–45, 249; refugees from, 239–40
Fanta (sister of A. H. Bâ), 269
fate, fickleness of, xvi–xvii, xxviii, 5, 20, 194–95, 213, 264, 310, 315–16
Ferlo region (Senegal), 13
Flateni (praise singer, griote), 242
flè (wooden flute), 111
Fodio, Ousmane Dan, 13
Fondation Amadou Hampâté Bâ, xxx–xxxii
Fortunes of Wangrin, The (Bâ). See *L'Etrange destin de Wangrin: ou, Les roueries d'un interprète africain* (Bâ)
Fouta Djallon (Guinea), 50
Fouta Tooro region (Senegal), 12–14, 50
France, 120, 303; French Republic, 50, 52; French Revolution, 119; Vichy Regime, 308–9. See also French colonial empire
Francis Ferdinand. Archduke, 243
French Arms and Cycle Factory Company of Saint-Etienne, 138, 151
French colonial empire, 20, 120; Africans as "French subjects," xxi, 283–86, 316, 319, 325, 342n5; canton leaders, 48, 53, 88, 254; civil administration, 243; civilizing mission (*mission civilisatrice*), xviii, xix, xxiii, xxiv, 332n6, 334n24; communes, privileged, 283; French citizens, Africans as, 283, 286, 288, 290; fun poked at, 242; goals of, 312, 316; "Gods of the Bush," administrators as, 218, 220, 254; interpreters for, 58–60, 80, 83–85; ironies of, xxi, 52, 304, 308–12; military administration, 149, 243; tribunals, 80. See also

Bretèche, Charles de la; de Courcelles, Commandant
French Equatorial Africa, 289
"French subjects," Africans as, xxi, 283–86, 316, 319, 325, 342n5
French Sudan, xvi, 290, 316, 331–32n3, 341n1
French West Africa, xvi, 288, 331–32n3
French West Africa Company (CFAO, Compagnie française de l'Afrique occidentale), 272, 297, 321
Fula Empire of Massina (1818–62), xvi–xvii, xxii, 4, 11–15, 21, 306; Hamdallaye (capital), 14, 17, 19, 67
Fula people, xii, 4–5, 226, 233; blacksmiths, *sanankounya* relationship with, 239; of Fakala, 13, 20–24, 26, 28, 30, 33, 35, 41, 48; grief and mourning traditions, 128–29; as nomadic, 12–14; "old Futa" (*Foutakindi*) and "new Futa" (*Foutakeiri*), 15; origins, 12–13; "Red Ears," 25, 187, 338n15; singing of, 182

gecko (*geddel Allah*), 117, 119, 146–47
generosity, 5, 22, 258, 323
Germany, 244
Ghana Empire, 264
gifts, 5, 51, 68, 73, 110–11, 114, 138, 326; acceptance of, 170; to elders, 327; French gifts of cities, 283; as insults, 188–90; for newborns, 107–8, 111; "nocturnal thing," 235–36
Gombel, Allaye (friend of Hammadoun Bâ), 190
Gomni, Ali (shoemaker), 149, 154, 166, 170, 171
Gondougou region, 58
Gonfin (guard), 92–95, 97
Gorée Island, 5, 312
Gorée Normal School. See William Ponty Normal School of Gorée
Gorel, Mamadou (friend of A. H. Bâ), 149, 168, 189, 193

Gouro, Gabdo (first wife of Tierno Kounta), 98, 114, 128–33
"grandfathers," 208–9, 341n1
Grand prix littéraire d'Afrique noire, xxii
Great Famine of 1914, 234–41
Griaule School of French anthropology, xi
griots, 155, 170–71, 188, 242, 267, 325, 338n16; genealogist-singers, 160, 170, 178–79, 338n16; Kouyaté, 79, 114, 115, 160
gris-gris (amulet), 250, 256–57, 271
Gueladio (*peredio* king of Kounari), 22
Guéno (Fula Supreme Being), 148–49
Guinea worm (parasite), 33

Haïdara, Moulaye (primary school monitor), 209–11, 213–16, 219, 325
Hambarké, Bila (moutassibi, Gan'ngal waaldé), 186–87
Hamdallaye (capital of Fula Empire of Massina), 14, 17, 19, 67
Hamman, Bori (friend of A. H. Bâ), 155, 168, 169, 170–71
Hampâté, Abidi (captive), 44, 66
Hampâté, Beydari (former captive), 33–35, 143–44, 196, 209; A. H. Bâ's primary schooling and, 223–24; famine and, 239; Hammadoun's circumcision and, 177–78; Hammadoun's death and, 225, 236; as heir and head of Hampâté Bâ's family, 33, 44, 66, 84, 98–99; Kadidja's quest for Tidjani and, 73–74, 77
Hampâté, Hammadoun (older brother of A. H. Bâ), xi, xii, 33, 41–42, 44, 99, 110, 142–43, 146, 251, 269; circumcision of, 176–85; death of, 42, 220–23, 225, 236, 252; "White Man's school" and, 199–200
Hampâté, Nassouni (adopted child of Hampâté Bâ), 39, 44, 99, 101, 106
Hamsalah clan, 13–14, 20–23, 27–28, 30, 33, 232
Hassey, Chékou (Djenné city chief), 228

Haut-Sénégal-and-Niger penal colony, 83, 91
Havas Agency, 250
Heckmann, Hélène, x, 332–33n12
Héli and Yooyoo, land of, 129
honor, 4–5, 11, 28–32, 51, 64, 293–94, 302; valentines and, 171–72; war service and, 286, 290
"house captives." See captives (*dimadjo, rimaïbé*)
"Hymn to Love" (Apostle Paul), 3

informants, 95–97, 137, 195, 219, 243. See also interpreters
initiation societies, xi–xii; Bambara, 120–21; minority groups affiliated with, 120–21, 277; World War I disrupts, 277, 294. See also waaldé (youth associations)
Institut français (fondamental) d'Afrique noire, ix, xv, xxi–xxi, 306
interpreters, 58–60, 80, 83–85, 202; of African languages, 88; A. H. Bâ as, 253–54, 286; power of, 219, 235. See also informants
Irele, Abiola, xxii
Islam, ix, xi–xii, xxv, 4; circumcision, 177; conversion to, 123; *dina* (Islamic state), 13, 14; Fula converts to, 177; funeral preparations, 132–34; Islamic Law, 99; Koranic education, 121–24, 134–35, 144, 146, 161; Koranic vigil for France, 248; *maghreb* prayer, 139, 148; money not accepted for religious aid, 273–74; paternal family's rights, 143–44; prohibition against killing, 138–39; *shahada*, 123, 131–32; Tidjaniya (Tijaniyyah) brotherhoods, 15, 97, 136, 176, 337n6. See also Koran

Jeïdani, Maïrama, 159, 164, 169–71
"joking relation" (*dendirakou, sanankounya*), 185, 239, 313
jourou kelen (instrument), 72

K., Sagou (Dogon student), 216
Kaba, Kassoum (sergeant), 248
Kadidiabougou ("Kadidja's village"), 87–91, 97–98, 111
Kamara, Toumani (Brigadier), 94, 96
Kammou (guardian spirit of celestial waters), 234
Kanté, Soumangourou (blacksmith king), 264
Kaou, Mouctar (griot, friend of A. H. Bâ), 155, 185–88
Kati (town, Mali), xii–xiii, 2, 176, 236; Dounfing chasm, 266–69, 276, 296–97; Kadobougou (village of the Dogons), 271–72, 276; as military town, 270–71, 290–91; N'Tomo sacred grove, 274–75, 277; religious sanctuaries, 277; Sananfara zone, 271; *waaldé* association in, 274–78
Kayes (Mali), 311
Keïta, Baba (native teacher), 229–30
Keïta, Daba (father of Modibo Keïta), 321
Keïta, Fadiala (Warrant Officer), 282–88, 290–94, 343n10
Keïta, Famory (friend of A. H. Bâ), 276, 297
Keïta, Modibo (first president of Republic of Mali), 321
Keïta, Sundiata (Emperor), 121, 287, 294
Kenyouma (friend of Koorka), 69–70, 72–73
Khalil, Amadou (cadi), 99
Kirkup, James, xviii
Kisukidi, Nadia Yada, xxii, xxiii
knowledge, 160, 213, 333–34n17
Kolâdo, Abdallah (friend of Tidjani Thiam), 114
Komo society of Donngorna, 107, 121, 340n17
"Komseer," Kadiatou (friend of Koorka), 70–71
Konaré, Daye (student), 216–17
Konaté, Mamadou (teacher, RDA leader), 313

Konaté, Yacouba, 333–34n17
Kondala, Koniba (neighborhood headman), 167, 195–209, 212, 224–25, 341n1
Koné, Mamadou (district guard), 324–27
Konyouman (magician of good fortune), 72
Koran, 67, 277; *Al-Fatiha*, 123, 327; *Ikhlass* surah, 134. *See also* Islam
Kossodio, Ellé, 17, 19
Kouakourou (town, Mali), 227
Koulibally, Moussa (schoolmate of A. H. Bâ), 224, 229
Koulibaly, Hansi (student), 232
Koulibaly, Mintikono (student), 213–14, 217
Koulikoro (town, Mali), 264, 299
Koullel (friend of Tidjani Thiam), xviii, 63–64, 114, 115, 160, 177, 225; Fula education taught by, 135; Tierno Kounta's death and, 133
Koumba, Modibo, 154–55, 160
Koumba, Moïré Modi, 154, 165–66
Koumba joubbel (hammerhead stork), 117
koumbareewel (trumpeter hornbill), 74
Kountas of Timbuktu, 20
Kouyaté, Ali Diêli (griot guitarist), 79, 114, 115, 160

"L'Afrique qui vient" (Mbembe), xxxii
Lairac, Dr., 323
Lake Debo (near Niafounké in the Niger Delta), 306
languages: African children as linguistic polyglots, 215; African words, transcription of, 8–9; Bambara, xxx, 109, 209, 216–17; of colonizer, 312; *forofifon naspa (le français des tirailleurs)*, xxx, 215, 219, 314–15; French, 214–15; Fulfulde, ix, xviii, 3, 242, 337n4; Halpoulaar (speakers of Poulaar), 201; "language in action" method of teaching French, 214–15; "moi ya dit toi ya dit," 271; Pulaar, 14, 201, 337n4; Sudanese, 271; Wolof, xviii, 14, 253

laptots (punters and boatmen), 100–105, 113, 227, 325
Lavalée, Captain, 288
Laye, Camara, xviii
Lebdai, Benaouda, xviii
Leblond, Paul (friend of A. H. Bâ), 298
Le Mage (steamboat), 259–64, 299–301, 305–6
L'Empire peul du Macina (Bâ), xxi–xxiii
L'Enfant noir (Laye), xviii
Lenngui (griote), 178–80
Leroux, E., 219
"Le Syndrome Amadou Hampâté Bâ" (Konaté), 333–34n17
L'Etrange destin de Wangrin: ou, Les roueries d'un interprète africain (Bâ), ix–x, xxvi
Lhote, Henri, 12
lineage: of A. H. Bâ, xvi–xvii, 12–14; marabouts in, 40, 42, 45, 273–74
lineages, xvi, 11–15, 27, 286, 294
Livrets de lecture (Monod), 233
Louta province (Mali, now Burkina Faso), 2, 45, 47–49; Amadou Ali Thiam as head of, 45, 47, 51; Domoni, 58–60; Ousmane Oumarou Thiam as head of, 49, 50–51; Toïni revolt, 49–64, 80
Lycée Askia Mohammed. *See* Bamako Professional School

Maadi, Djeli (griot), 218–19
Madiansa, 307, 310–11
Magnier, Bernard, xxxi
Maïga, Daouda (friend of A. H. Bâ), 244, 249; at Bamako Professional School, 313; childhood games with A. H. Bâ, 145–46, 149–52, 163–64; famine and, 239, 241; Hammadoun's death and, 220, 221; rival *waaldé* incident and, 189, 192; valentines and, 168, 171
Maillet, Camille (district commandant), 195, 204–7, 224
Maïrama (goddess of waters), 227
Maison-Carrée (Algeria), 283
Maisonneuve et Larose editions, 219

malaria, 322–23
Mali: as French Sudan, xvi, 290, 316, 331–32n3, 341n1; independence, 96–97; Mandé Empire, 121, 264; map of, 2. *See also* Fula Empire of Massina (1818–62); Toucouleur kingdom of Massina; specific locations
Malinké people, 184, 187, 277, 285, 342n6
Mandagoux, Mr. (chief of staff), 318–19, 321–22, 323
Mandé Empire, 121, 264
Mandé ethnic group, xi–xiii, 342n6. *See also* Bambara people; Fula people
Manding Mountains, 270
Mannawel (captive), 70, 71
marabouts, 25, 338n13; in family lineages, 40, 42, 45, 273–74; political advice given by, 24, 52; predictions made by, 35, 39, 40, 67–68, 80, 323; Tidjani Thiam as, 115, 176, 273–74; World War I and, 247–48. *See also* Cissé, Tierno Kounta (marabout)
marriage, 14, 24–25; "colonial," 70, 127–28, 338–39n8; divorce by friends and family, 36–37; parties need not be present, 47; social protection of divorced or widowed women, 144–45; valentines and, 172
"masculine secret," 243
Massina (Mali), xvi, 11–14. *See also* Fula Empire of Massina (1818–1862)
Massina Empire (Mali). *See* Fula Empire of Massina (1818–1862)
"master of the earth," 89–90
master of the knife, 107–8
Mbembe, Achille, xxv–xxvi, xxxii
M'Bodje, Cheikh (nephew of teacher), 252
M'Bodje, Mr. (teacher), 251–64
M'Bouré, Diawando Guéla, 246
Mecca, 254
memoir, xv, xviii, 4
memory, ix, x, xix, 7, 107, 117, 161, 208–10
Minary, Captain, 274, 280

INDEX   361

Minkoro, Koroba (student), 232
Mohammad, Prophet, 9, 33, 39, 81; *cherifat* (descendant of), 171; *hadiths*, 67, 75; on seeking knowledge, 213
Molard, Colonel, 276, 288, 291
Monnet, Mr. (purser, *Le Mage*), 260–64, 301, 302, 305–6
Monod, Jean-Louis, 233, 265
Monod, Théodore, ix, xxi–xxii, xxiii, 306, 310
Mopti (town, Mali), 2, 225–26, 236, 239, 299; Etablissements Simon and quay, 100, 227
Mossi country (Upper Volta), 316, 318
mottoes, 181, 267, 277, 290; of Bandiagara, 77, 78; of Thiam clan, 267
Moudileno, Lydie, xxiii–xxiv
Moussa, Kadiatou Bokari (first wife of Tidjani Thiam), 47, 98, 144–45
moutassibi (public prosecutor or snoop), 155, 168

Nawma, Martou (president of girls' *waaldé*), 170, 171
Nawna, Maartou (friend of Koorka), 69
Ndiaye, Christiane, xxvii, 335n33
N'Diaye, Faman (relative of Tidjani Thiam), 173–75
n'dimaakou duties, 59–60
Ngoudda-short-tail (Yaamé River crocodile), 193
Niafounké (village, Mali), 249, 306
Niapandogoro (captive), 39
Niger Bend, 13, 19, 33, 35, 226, 259
Niger River, 4, 13, 100, 226
"Njî Donngorna" (younger brother of A. H. Bâ), 105–10
N'Tomo initiation society (Bambara), 274–75, 277, 340n17
Nyaté, Aladji (student), 233–34

Office of Native Affairs, xix, 211, 219, 300
Omar, El Hadj, xvi, xxix, 11–12, 139, 160, 335n26; death of, 19, 24, 49; as General Caliph of the Tijaniyaah of Black Africa, 114; Pâté Poullo and, 15–18; poetry composed by, 46, 92, 268
oral traditions, xviii–xxii, xxviii, 4; A. H. Bâ as collector of, xix–xxii, 127, 306, 325; "burning library" aphorism, xxii, 333–34n17; child storytellers, 219–20; education of populace through, 159–61; memory and, ix, x, xix, 7; spoken word as true knowledge, 160, 333–34n17; World War I disruption of, xxii–xxiii, 294. *See also* African traditions
Ouagadougou (Haute-Volta), xv, xxi, 2, 288; A. H. Bâ assigned to, xv, xvi, 318–28
Ouane clan, 49
Oui, Mon Commandant!: mémoires II (Bâ), xxiv–xv
Ouologuem, Badji (schoolmate of A. H. Bâ), 224, 229
Ouologuem, Tégué (schoolmate of A. H. Bâ), 224, 229

Packaging Post/coloniality (Watts), xxiii
Pâté, Amadou (brother of Kadidja Pâté), 44, 49, 66, 74, 153
Pâté, Barkérou (captive), 68
Pâté, Bokari (brother of Kadidja Pâté), 45, 46, 48, 51, 65–66, 98
Pâté, Hammadoun (uncle of A. H. Bâ), 48, 65–66, 98, 143, 149, 153, 178, 182, 219–20, 225
Pâté, Kadidja (mother of A. H. Bâ; wife of Tidjani Thiam), xvii, xx, 5, 26, 38–83; advice given by, 189, 326–27; birth of "Njî Donngorna" and, 105–10; cabal against, 173–76; dream and prediction of, 39–41; exile of, 49; as fashion designer, 272, 297; gold ring of, 67–68, 315; Kadidiabougou (welcome station) set up by, 87–91, 97–98, 111; *laptot* boss incident, 100–105, 113; marriage to Hampâté Bâ, xx, 41–45; marriage to

Tidjani Thiam, 45–48; misfortunes of, 48–49, 67–68; nicknames, xx, 41, 44; opposition to A. H. Bâ's continued study, 317–18, 320; quest to find Thiam, 64–79; "White Man's school" and, 211–13
Pâté, Sirandou (aunt of A. H. Bâ), 98, 178
Pennda, Moro (friend of Koorka), 70
P. Moussa (Bambara student), 215–16
Ponty, William, 97
Postcolonial Francophone Autobiographies from Africa to the Antilles (Sankara), xxv
Présence Africaine (journal), xxi
Primel, François (teacher), 230–31, 233, 236, 250, 325

"Qu'est-ce qu'un auteur postcolonial?" (Moudileno), xxiii–xxiv

Rassemblement démocratique africain (RDA), 313
religion: God, concepts of, 240–41n20, 240n18; tolerance, 121, 233, 277–78. *See also* Islam; marabouts

S., Madani Oumar (griot), 220–21
Saber, The (Omar), 268
Safinatu Saada (Omar), 92
Saint-Louis (Senegal), 270, 283, 305
Sall, Allassane (teaching monitor), 229, 230
Sall, Mamadou (Papa) (interpreter), 229, 235
Salmon, Prophet, 117
Samaké, Mintikono, 224, 229, 231, 232
Sambourou (servant), 65, 133, 143, 159
Sammodi family, 24
Samo people, 53–61, 85–87
sanankounya ("joking cousin") relationship, 185, 239, 313
Sanfouldé, Alfa Oumarou Hammadi (marabout), 175
Sanga (city, Mali), 249
Sankara, Edgard, xxv

Sansanding (city-state), 2, 282–83, 301–2, 307–10
Saro (Bambara town), 85
Sawané, Ibrahima, 133
Say (Soka) (town, Mali), 252–57
School for Hostages (School for Sons of Chiefs, Upper Primary School, Lycée Askia Mohammed). *See* Bamako Professional School
Sebara, battle of, 20
Segou (Mali), 2, 24, 87, 259–60; famine and, 240; French capture of, 50; kingdom of, 253
Senegal: Fouta Tooro region, 12–14, 50; Upper, xvii, 149, 235, 241n1, 265, 272, 311, 316
"service contributions," forced, 202
Sharifs, 209
Sidi, Tierno (grand marabout), 247
silatigui (grand master of initiation), xxix, 15, 16, 19
Sinali, Fabere (retired corporal), 161–68
Siné, Danfo, xiii, 124–27, 130, 135, 160
Sinibaldi, Mr. (civil servant), 320–24, 323–24
Sissoko, Mamadou (assistant supervisor), 313–14
Si Tangara (Gan'ngal *waaldé* chief), 186–93
slavery, 33, 312
Soares, Benjamin F., xxxi
Sofara (town, Mali), 237–38, 237–40; executions at, 20, 21, 28, 30, 35, 194
Sokoto Empire (Nigeria region), 13
Sokoto region (Mali, now Burkina Faso), 50
Songhay ethnic group, 226, 233
Sonngo (Dogon sacred mountain), 67
Soumaré, Bouraïma (guard), 73–77, 79, 85–87
Soumaré, Brahime (guard), 248
Sow, Anta N'Diobdi, 24–30, 32, 78–79, 100, 232; death of, 48–49; first visit with A. H. Bâ, 42; Kadidja's dream and, 39–40; as "Queen of the Milk," 25

Sow, Batoma (captive), 48, 78–79, 84, 85, 90, 98, 103, 140
"Strange Fate of Amadou Hampâté Bâ in the Anglophone World, The" (Eggan), xxvi–xxvii
Sudan Political Bureau, 283
sword ritual, 293, 343n10
Sy, Abdelkader Mademba (son of Mademba Sy), 283–94, 310; as Diagne's interpreter, 290, 291
Sy, Ben Daoud Mademba (son of Mademba Sy), 300–303, 305–11, 343n1
Sy, Mademba (king of Sansanding), 282–83, 303–6, 310–11, 343n1
Sylvandre, Jean (excise man), 316, 319

talismans, 43, 68, 84, 254
Tall, Aguibou (King of Bandiagara), 42, 45, 47, 49, 71, 80, 195, 301; clay doll of, 152; "colonial marriage" incident and, 127–28; death of, 138–39; deposed by French Republic, 52–53, 56–57; disrespectful poem about, 50–51, 52; installed as king by French, 50, 283; Ponty and, 97–98; selects A. H. as storyteller, 219; as traditional chief of Toucouleurs, 52, 56–57; trap laid for Tidjani Thiam by, 57–60, 63; wisdom of, 136–37
Tall, Alfa Maki (Toucouleur chieftain), 152, 163, 166–67, 195, 198–201; World War I and, 245, 247–48
Tall, Amadou Seydou, 17, 24
Tall, El Hadji Sékou, 335n26
Tall, Koreïchi, 35
Tall, Madani Bamantia (clerk), 317
Tall, Maki (son of Alfa Maki Tall), 223, 224, 229, 231–32, 313; at Bamako Professional School, 313
Tall, Tidjani Aguibou (son of Aguibou Tall), 57–60, 57–61, 63, 80, 131, 195
Tall, Tidjani Amadou Seydou (first king of Bandiagara), 17–24, 63; death of, 35, 49; execution of Fulas of Fakala,

20, 21, 28, 35, 194; as *Hela hemmba*, "breaker-bonesetter," 24, 35; reparation and reconciliation policy, 24–25
Tall, Tierno Bokar, 45–46
Tall clan, 45; rivalry with Thiams, 46–47, 49–53, 49–64, 173
Tané, Mamadou, 25
"Task of the Translator, The" (Benjamin), xxvii
Tassili n'Ajjer caves, 12
taxes, capitation, 53–54, 80, 197
Taxile, Paul (friend of A. H. Bâ), 298
Taykiri region (Mali), 42, 48, 225
Tekrour (Fouta Tooro region of Senegal), 14
telegraph lines, 283
Tembély, Baye Tabémba, 243, 281
Tembély, Oumarou (friend of A. H. Bâ), 274, 276, 280, 297
Tembély, Yagama (schoolmate of A. H. Bâ), 224, 229, 243–44, 281–82
Tenengou (Mali), 24, 26
tennde (workshops), 233
Thiam, Abdoul (brother of Tidjani Thiam), 81, 98
Thiam, Amadou Ali (chief of Louta), 45, 47, 51, 80
Thiam, Aminata (sister of A. H. Bâ), 221–22, 269
Thiam, Badara Amadou Ali, 51, 53–56, 64, 127
Thiam, Bokari (brother of Tidjani Thiam), 98, 133, 248
Thiam, Cheik Mohammed el Ghaali, 114, 115, 138, 173–74
Thiam, Débé (brother of Tidjani Thiam), 98
Thiam, Dikoré (daughter of Tidjani Thiam), 144
Thiam, Mamadou, 88, 112, 120–21, 135–36, 140
Thiam, Ousmane Oumarou, 49–52
Thiam, Tidjani Amadou Ali, xi, xiii, xvii, xxx, 45; A. H. Bâ's first meeting with, 111–14; character traits of, 52, 113–14,

139; as chief of Louta province, 47, 49, 51, 56; deposed, xi, xvii, xx, 49; Dogon refugees and, 271–72; embroidery skills, 96, 115, 176, 273; exile, march to, 84–87; fearlessness of, 266–69; freed from exile, 137–41; freed from prison, 113–14; as healer, 273; under house arrest, 113, 137–38; imprisonment of, xx, 49, 64–79; Islamic converts due to, 273; Kadidja, marriage to, 45–48; Kadidja's quest to find, 64–79; Kati, move to, 175–76, 240; Koranic teaching attempted by, 134–35, 144, 146; leaves Bandiagara, 175–76; as marabout, 115, 176, 273–74; misinformation given to, 57–58; physical strength of, 86, 91–92; Toïni revolt and, 49–64, 80; trial and sentencing of, 79–82, 91; truth-telling and, 80–81

Thiam clan, 45; motto of, 267; rivalry with Talls, 46–47, 49–64, 173

Tidjaniya (Tijaniyyah) brotherhood, 15, 97, 136, 176, 337n6

Tiébéssé (friend of Kadidja Pâté), 100, 226, 239

Tiebleni (Bambara initiation society), 120–21, 120–21, 340n17

Tiebleni society, 277

Tieman, Garba (bodyguard), 72

Tiemokodian (Bambara canton chief), 88, 89–90, 114

Tiemtoré, Tennga (teaching monitor), 229, 230, 251

tirailleurs (indigenous military troops), 53, 57–59, 150, 152–53, 162; *forofifon naspa* spoken by, xxx, 215, 219; at Kati, 270–71; World War I service, 247

Tirailleurs Sénégalais, First Regiment, 270

Tirailleurs Sénégalais, Second Regiment, 270, 282–83, 286, 291–92

Toïni (town, Mali), 53–54

Toïni revolt, 49–64, 80

ton (Bambara initiation group), xiii, 274–76

Toucouleur, origin of term, 14

Toucouleur kingdom of Massina, xv–xvi, 11–12, 17, 23–24, 45, 49–50, 155, 301

Toucouleurs, xii, 14–15; Ly clan, 91; opposition to marriage between Kadidja and Tidjani Thiam, 45–48; repatriation of, 50; rivalry between Talls and Thiams, 46–47, 49–64, 173; World War I and, 245

Tougan district (Burkina-Faso), 33

Tougouri, Tombo, 54–55, 60, 79, 81, 85–87

Touré, Bâbilen, 58–60, 80, 83–84

traditionists, x, x–xi, xviii, 63, 124, 126, 159–61, 232–33, 333–34n17, 340n19

train (metal pirogue), 264–65

Translation as Reparation (Bandia), xxv

Traoré, Fatoma (teaching monitor), 281–82

Traoré, Ousmane Ouaga, 89

Tummelew (great spirit), 233, 254, 257, 342n13

Ture, Almamy Samory, 245

"undecolonisable," xxiii

UNESCO, 333n17

Upper Senegal and Niger colony, 149, 341n1

Upper Volta (Haute-Volta), xx–xxi, 316, 318. *See also* Ouagadougou (Haute-Volta)

uprisings, French fears of, 56

valentines, 168–73, 185

Van Vollenhoven, Joost, 288–89

Vie et enseignement de Tierno Bokar, le sage de Bandiagara (*A Spirit of Tolerance: The Inspiring Life of Tierno Bokar*), xxvi, xxxi

waaldé (youth associations), xii, xiii, 146; diverse backgrounds in, 5, 32; elder associations and, 153–54; famine and, 241; founded by A. H. Bâ, 127, 152–56; founded by Hampâté Bâ, 32,

waaldé (continued)
153; "generosity" feast, 170; in Kati, 274–78; organization of, 154; rival associations, 185–93; *ton* (Bambara), xiii, 274–76; traditional duties of, 280; "twinning" of boys' and girls', 159, 168–73; *walamarou* (association dorm), 159, 165; World War I disrupts, 277, 294; for young women, 41, 68–69, 159, 168–73. *See also* initiation societies

Wangrin, ix–x, xix, xxii, 218–20, 225, 249, 332n4, 341–42n5; as grand interpreter, 240

Watts, Richard, xxiii

West African savanna, 4, 8, 12–13, 258

White-Blacks, 115, 116, 202, 212, 230, 254–55; "colonial outfits" worn by, 324

"White Man's school." *See* education

White-Whites, 115–20; demise of myth of, 298; effect on African kinship ties, 65; excrement episode, 149–53; as "Gods of the Bush," 218, 220, 254; healers, 130–31; neighborhoods of, 73; as "skins on fire," 115, 242, 244–47, 245, 254, 256, 258

Wilhelm II, 244, 250–51, 298, 324

William Ponty Normal School of Gorée, xx, 209, 229, 251, 281–82, 295, 296

women: amazon warriors, 63, 65; courage of, 270–71; mother, respect for, 4, 29, 36, 38, 318; mothering, African, 65, 107, 326; servant-mothers, 20, 33, 42, 236, 337n8

World War I, xxii–xxiii, 243–47, 270; communiqués, 250; "demi-soldiers," native soldiers as, 289; effects of tirailleurs from, 316–17; end of, 298; enlistment of African youths in, xxii–xxiii; food and animals requisitioned, 248–49; revolts against recruitment and requisitions, 249, 289; sons of kings sent to fight, 283; Wilhelm II, Fula views of, 250–51

World War II, 308

Yaamé River, 143, 146, 226
Yabara (captive), 114, 156–57
Yagaré, Diéli (griote), 305, 307
Yérémadio (village, Mali), 13
Youssoufi (prophet Joseph), 106
"Youthful Memories" genre, 4

Zan, Koro, 95